Happiest days

For
BRIAN BARFIELD
ROSEMARY HART
JOHN POWELL
with thanks for
a kaleidoscope of memories

Happiest days

The public schools in English fiction

JEFFREY RICHARDS

Manchester University Press

Distributed exclusively in the USA and Canada by
St. Martin's Press, New York

Copyright © Jeffrey Richards 1988

Published by Manchester University Press
Oxford Road, Manchester M13 9PL, UK

*Distributed exclusively in the USA and Canada
by* St. Martin's Press, Inc.,
Room 400, 175 Fifth Avenue, New York, NY 10010, USA

British Library cataloguing in publication data

Richards, Jeffrey
        Happiest days: the public schools in
        English fiction.
        1. English fiction—History and criticism
        2. Public schools, Endowed (Great Britain)
        I. Title
        823',009'355 PR830.P/

Library of Congress cataloging in publication data
Richards, Jeffrey.
        Happiest days : the public schools in English fiction/Jeffrey Richards.
                p.   cm.
        Bibliography: p. 302.
        Includes index.
        ISBN 0-7190-1879-X : $35.00 (U.S. : est.)
        1. English fiction—History and criticism.   2. Education in
        literature.   3. Public schools, Endowed (Great Britain), in
        literature.   4. Schools in literature.   5. Teachers in literature.
        I. Title.
        PR830.E38R53 1988
        823'.009'355—dc19

ISBN 0-7190-1879-X *hardback*

Printed in Great Britain by The Alden Press, Oxford

Typesetting by Heather Hems, Tower House, Queen St., Gillingham, Dorset

Contents

Acknowledgements

As far as the public schools are concerned, I have no interest to declare. I was educated at a small boys' grammar school, where I was profoundly happy, and have no experience either as pupil or teacher of public school life. I have, however, found it an endlessly fascinating object of study, and hope that I may have shed some light on its formative role in British culture. I have confined myself to boys' public schools and boys' fiction. Girls' fiction is a universe of its own and has already received perceptive analysis in Mary Cadogan and Patricia Craig, *You're a Brick, Angela* (London, 1976). I am indebted to the following friends and colleagues for help and advice of various kinds: W. O. G. Lofts, James Cornford, Patrick Dunae, John MacKenzie, Steve Jones, Dorothy Sheridan, John Springhall, Owen Dudley Edwards, C. M. Deering, George Webb, Mrs. L. Lewis. I would like to thank the staffs of Lancaster University Library (particularly Thelma Goodman and her colleagues in Inter-library Loans), the British Museum Reading Room, the London Library, the Royal Commonwealth Society Library and the Kipling Society Archive for their unfailing courtesy and helpfulness. Lancaster University generously allowed me two terms of sabbatical leave to complete the writing of the book.

THE BEST SCHOOL OF ALL

It's good to see the School we knew,
The land of youth and dream,
To greet again the rule we knew
Before we took the stream;
Though long we've missed the sight of her,
Our hearts may not forget;
We've lost the old delight of her,
We keep her honour yet.

The stars and sounding vanities
That half the crowd bewitch,
What are they but inanities
To him that treads the pitch?
And where's the wealth, I'm wondering,
Could buy the cheers that roll
When the last charge goes thundering
Beneath the twilight goal?

The men that tanned the hide of us,
Our daily foes and friends,
They shall not lose their pride of us
Howe'er the journey ends.
Their voice, to us who sing of it,
No more its message bears,
But the round world shall ring of it
And all we are be theirs.

To speak of Fame a venture is,
There's little here can bide,
But we may face the centuries,
And dare the deepening tide;
For though the dust that's part of us
To dust again be gone,
Yet here shall beat the heart of us—
the School we handed on!

We'll honour yet the School we knew,
The best School of all:
We'll honour yet the rule we knew,
Till the last bell call.
For, working days or holidays,
And glad or melancholy days,
They were great days and jolly days
At the best School of all.

Henry Newbolt, 1899

1

'The land of youth and dream': context and contours

It is generally acknowledged that popular culture holds up a mirror to the mind set of the nation. It does more. It distils, generates and confirms sets of values, attitudes and ideals which for good or ill cohere to form the national identity. Alfred North Whitehead declared, 'If we hope to discover the inward thoughts of a generation, it is to literature that we must look.'[1] It is there 'that the concrete outlook of humanity received its expression'. Hugh Kingsmill noted, 'Popular literature reveals the desires of a nation.'[2]

In particular reading in childhood when the mind is at its most impressionable has a lasting effect. Sir Charles Grant Robertson said in the 1930s of films that they leave a kind of sediment in the mind.[3] As it was with films, so it was also with books. George Orwell expressed it best when he said that:

> most people are influenced far more than they would care to admit by novels, serial stories, films and so forth, and that from this point of view the worst books are often the most important because they are usually the ones that are read earliest in life. It is probable that many people who would consider themselves extremely sophisticated and 'advanced' are actually carrying through life an imaginative background which they acquired in childhood from (for instance) Sapper and Ian Hay.[4]

Orwell himself comes into this category. He created the rather defensive concept of the 'good bad book', which was his way of signifying intellectual disapproval but emotional commitment to writers like Haggard, Kipling, Doyle or Hornung, who dominated his childhood reading. But, since most people are governed by their emotions rather than their intellect, this critical dichotomy would not exist for them.

Diehard opponents of the study of popular culture claim that it is valueless because its influence cannot be proved absolutely. By that argument, all history is valueless, because in the last resort nothing can be proved absolutely. Historians deal in the balance of probabilities, in the sympathetic interpretation of such hard evidence as there is, in the evaluation of the testimony of participant observers, who are by their very nature self-selecting.[5] It is pointless to ask for the first-hand accounts of ordinary people about how their reading or leisure has affected them. For such evidence cannot exist. The nature of popular culture and of its consumers provides no means of articulating such a conscious verbal response. But the pattern of consumption of popular culture contains unconscious evidence, arguably more valuable because it is unconscious. 'Tell me what you like,' said John Ruskin, 'and I'll tell you what you are.'[6]

Joan Rockwell has written:

> My basic premise is that literature neither 'reflects' nor 'arises from' society, but rather is an integral part of it and should be recognized as being as much so as any institution . . . Fiction is a social product, but it also 'produces' society . . . Fiction is not only a representation of social reality, but also paradoxically an important element in social change. It plays a large part in the socialization of infants, in the conduct of politics, and in general gives symbols and modes of life to the population, particularly in those less-easily defined areas such as norms, values and personal and inter-personal behaviour.[7]

The paradox she talks about suggests a model for the study of the collective unconscious and the impact upon it of popular culture. First, it is necessary to establish the dominant ideology, then to probe alternative and oppositional ideologies, next to identify significant breakpoints of change and development, and lastly to chart convergences, if any, between the viewpoints.[8] All this must be set in a general historical context of the social, political and cultural ideas, structures and values of the age.

In a recent survey of British social attitudes, 67 per cent of those questioned—and they covered all ages, sexes and classes—favoured the retention of the public schools and only 19 per cent favoured their elimination or reduction. Even among Labour voters, only one in three favoured a reduction in the number of public schools and only one in five favoured abolition.[9] This of course comes after twenty years of comprehensivisation, with the Labour Party committed to the abolition of the public schools and with the public schools often being depicted as symbols of a class-divided society.

Why, when only 3 per cent of the population attend them, is there this high proportion of support for the continued existence of the public schools? The elite would obviously favour them, for they are seen to constitute a passport into the establishment. But why the rest, when the bulk of respondents can themselves have no hope of going there? I suggest it is because of 100 years of exposure to a favourable cultural image of the public schools, largely through popular fiction. The volume of public school fiction is immense. By comparison, other forms of schooling have had a much smaller degree of fictional exposure. It was not until the 1950s in the work of writers like Geoffrey Trease, E. W. Hildick and Lawrence Meynell that day schools as opposed to boarding schools gained any substantive fictional dramatization. But none of these writers has attained the kind of celebrity and mythic stature of the great public school story writers such as Thomas Hughes, Talbot Baines Reed or Frank Richards, whose work has remained continuously in print for between fifty and a hundred years. The most significant contribution to school fiction since the heyday of the public school story has surely been Phil Redmond's long-running television series about life in a London comprehensive school, *Grange Hill*, which since the mid-1970s has provided role models, social comment and mythification for the newest form of British schooling. Its long-term effects have yet to be seen.

The school story has been the subject of two excellent in-depth surveys, one by an English literature expert (Isabel Quigly) and the other by an educational sociologist (P. W. Musgrave).[10] There remains room perhaps for an historian to examine the genre. E. C. Mack pointed the way in his magisterial and still unsurpassed two-volume study, *Public Schools and British Opinion, 1750–1940* (1940). He pioneered the contextual approach, using fiction along with non-fiction as evidence on attitudes towards public schools. It is on his book that I wish to build. But in view of the work of Quigly, Musgrave and Mack in providing comprehensive surveys, I want to adopt a somewhat different approach, one that I have already employed in two books on cinema, written in collaboration with Anthony Aldgate (*Best of British* and *Britain Can Take It*).[11] In those volumes we took a series of key films and examined them in depth and in context to illuminate various aspects of British life. The importance of novels to historians is nowhere here better exemplified than in the public school story. For it appeals directly to the emotions as well as or often instead of to the intellect. It repeats and ritualises the messages, providing social and cultural sanction for a set of attitudes. It furnishes role models and conduct validators.

The mass media—and this includes popular literature, theatre and cinema—operate in five basic ways, all of them overlapping and mutually supportive, to transmit the dominant ideology and to create for it a consensus of support. First, they provide images of the lives, attitudes and values of various groups in society, created out of selected recognisable facets. Second, they provide images of society as a whole, again selecting acceptable elements and aspects from everyday life, organising them into a coherent pattern governed by a set of presuppositions and making sense of them. The process of selection confers status or acceptability on those issues, institutions and individuals which regularly appear in a favourable light. What J. S. R. Goodlad says of the popular drama applies equally to popular literature. 'It may serve as a vehicle by which a community expresses its belief about what is right and wrong; indeed it may function instrumentally as a medium through which a community repeatedly instructs its members in correct behaviour.'[12] Fifthly, there is a tendency in mass culture to promote uniformity and standardisation which affects not only dress and vocabulary but also and more subtly attitude and world view.

All this applies to the school story genre in its dominant form. The school story selects aspects of school life and creates an attractive, acceptable image from them. It excludes unacceptable or dissident elements. It confers automatic status on the public schools. It instructs the wider community in the educational values and virtues embodied in the image. It tends towards conformity. It is the nature of most children to conform to the prevailing norm. It makes life easier. That is as true now as it has always been, in music, fashion, attitudes, even accents. The adoption of cockney accents by children in many different parts of the country testifies to the combined power of *Grange Hill*, *Minder* and *East Enders*. The children deem this accent *de rigueur* for 'street credibility'.

There are two alternative interpretations of the creation of the cultural image of the dominant ideology—the hegemonic and the commercial. Gramsci argued that popular culture acts as one of the agencies by which the ruling class exerts its authority over the other classes. Its view of reality becomes their view. The dominated classes maintain their own distinctive forms of social life and class practice, but they are incorporated into the structure and assigned a place within the dominant ideology. Consent to hegemony is provided by the promotion of consensus around a set of agreed values and beliefs, and the mass media play a crucial role in the creation and preservation of consensus.[13] The hegemonic view, however, has been rejected by Richard Maltby, who has brilliantly articulated an alternative, commercial view.[14] Taking Hollywood as his example, he claims that there was no desire in popular culture to impose the dominant ideology but rather to maximise profit by projecting the most acceptable and least demanding world view. But since this will almost certainly be the one perceived as the dominant world view, the effect is likely to be hegemonic anyway.

Over the years, through the recurrence of themes and variations, a composite picture emerged. It was summed up by George Macdonald Fraser:

Consider again the pictures that 'public school' conjures up. A series of images occurs—small boys in Eton collars—stately buildings amidst immemorial elms—straw boaters—Bunter yelling 'Yarroo! Leggo, you beastly cads!'—Freddie Bartholomew getting his lumps from a gloating Flashman—stern, granite-faced Doctor so-and-so, in cap and gown, cane in hand, glowering at the trembling infant on the study carpet—fags burning toast—sex-starved adolescents indulging in unnatural vice—wastrel fifth-formers in the toils of unscrupulous bookies—singing of 'Forty Years On'—Twits of the Year sneering loftily at oicks—speech day with sunlight through stained glass—fist fights behind the fives court—tuck-boxes and exeats—blotted letters home—footballs in the October dusk and the smell of cricket pitches and linseed oil . . . take your choice.[15]

He adds that all these images are straight from public school fiction, but they are also straight from public school fact. The process by which the fact is transmuted into fiction is part of my subject there. Popular literature sanctions and spreads social norms and dominant value systems. But the changes in popular culture have not left public school fiction behind. The coming of the cinema has seen such major works of public school fiction as *Tom Brown's Schooldays*, *The Fifth Form at St Dominic's*, *Tell England*, *Mr Perrin and Mr Traill*, *Goodbye, Mr Chips* and *The Guinea Pig* brought to the screen. Television similarly provided a new outlet for Frank Richards's Greyfriars stories and has in recent years permitted the serialisation of *Tom Brown's Schooldays*, *Stalky and Co.*, *Vice Versa*, *To Serve them all my Days* and *Goodbye Mr Chips*.

For the historian, the public school story individually or as a *genre* provides four kinds of evidence. Firstly, it offers straightforward factual evidence about the customs, practices, conditions and methods of public schools at various stages. A large proportion of the great public school stories are autobiographical, often very thinly disguised autobiography. Alec Waugh's *The Loom of Youth* and Thomas Hughes's *Tom Brown's Schooldays* were based directly on their own school careers, for instance. Arnold Lunn's *The Harrovians* was based on a diary he kept at Harrow. Kipling reworked characters and incidents from his schooldays in *Stalky and Co.* These books tell us a good deal about life at Sherborne, Rugby, Harrow and Westward Ho! during their authors' boyhoods there. The authenticity of these accounts is testified to in the subsequent fates of the authors of public school fiction and of their characters. Alec Waugh and his father were expelled from the Old Shirburnians after the publication of *The Loom of Youth*. Hugh Walpole was boycotted by Epsom College after the publication of *Mr Perrin and Mr Traill*. Major General Lionel Dunsterville and George C. Beresford earned considerable celebrity in later life as the originals of Stalky and McTurk and both wrote accounts of their schooldays with Kipling. A minor industry has grown up in identifying the originals of the characters in *Tom Brown's Schooldays*. W. H. Balgarnie of the Leys was invited as guest of honour to the premiere of the stage version of *Goodbye, Mr Chips* in recognition of the fact that he was widely believed to be the model on which the character was based.

Secondly, the books tell us something about the boy mind and the experience of boyhood. For it is a remarkable fact that the best school stories have been more often than not written by boys; that is to say, the authors have been either literally or metaphorically boys. Alec Waugh was seventeen when he wrote *The Loom of Youth*. Ernest Raymond was eighteen when he wrote the first half of *Tell England*. P. G. Wodehouse was in his early twenties when he penned his serial stories, but was still emotionally bound up with Dulwich. Even more interesting is the phenomenon of the boy–man, the permanent adolescent, whose emotional clock stops and remains fixed at a certain age. He is therefore able more easily to empathise with and understand and interpret the feelings, interests and preoccupations of real boys. Kipling believed that everyone remained in essence what they were at seventeen. It was certainly true of him and many others. But it is not universally true. Some men have never really been boys at all. They were in essence born old and passed rapidly and with some distaste through boyhood to blossom gratefully into adulthood. Alec Waugh noted, perhaps more accurately, 'Age is an arbitrary definition of development. Many boys reach the age of seventeen and stay there for the rest of their lives: others are twenty-five years old before they have done with their teens.'[16] It is at the very least a working hypothesis that everyone's emotional and imaginative development stops at a certain point in life and that whatever happens thereafter to widen their experience and learning does not alter this fundamental fact.

Certainly one of the common characteristics of successful boys' writers is their essential and permanent boyishness. His friends described Charles Turley, one of the most highly regarded school story writers of his day, as a 'boy eternal'.[17] The same is true of Kipling, Wodehouse, Hughes, Reed and Richards. Whatever age they attained, they remained seventeen. This will be explored in the book.

The third area of interest for the historian is the promotion of particular ideas, attitudes, educational and social policies. It remains true that it is perhaps fictional representations such as *Tom Brown's Schooldays*, *Eric* and *The Loom of Youth* which have stimulated the greatest controversy and the most wide-ranging, long-lasting and influential debate, and which have mirrored the educational discussions taking place in the wider world.

Fourthly, there is the creation and development of the genre of school stories, the body of fictional material, which conforms to certain rules and structures, and succeeds by repetition and ritualisation in mythifying ideas and codes. It creates an established and recognisable set of archetypes, value systems and ingredients which sanctify and perpetuate the dominant ideology. The impact of this cumulative cultural image is all the greater perhaps because everyone goes to school. However different the form and conditions of public school education from that enjoyed by the majority of the population, it is something that can be related to, and explains why the school story, as opposed, say, to the university story, reflecting an experience denied to the majority of the population, maintained mass appeal.

This study will attempt to discuss the chosen works in all four key areas. Generalisation is dangerous. As James Hilton sagely observed:

> Schooling is perhaps the most universal of all experiences, but it is also one of the most individual . . . No two schools are alike, but more than that—the school with two hundred pupils is really two hundred schools, and among them, almost certainly, are somebody's long remembered heaven and somebody else's hell.[18]

Even a brief scan of the memoirs and autobiographies of public schoolboys reveals the truth of this, for the impact of the school for good or ill is immense, occurring as it does when a boy's awareness and receptivity are at their most intense. Antony Lytton, Viscount Knebworth, enjoyed the whole of his time at Eton (1916–22), writing to his parents, 'My God! What a place Eton is! There's nothing like it in the world. You were quite right in saying that it was worth being a boy for the sake of going to Eton.'[19] Julian Grenfell too loved Eton. 'I am simply enjoying my head off here, was there ever such a place?' he wrote.[20] Alec Waugh wrote of Sherborne, 'Nearly all boys enjoy their last terms at a public school but I had a good time from the start. I enjoyed every aspect of its life.'[21] Rupert Brooke, looking back at his time at Rugby during his first year at Cambridge, said, 'I had been happier at Rugby than I can find words to say. As I looked back at five years, I seemed to see every hour golden and radiant, and always increasing in beauty as I grew more conscious; and I could not (and cannot) hope for or even imagine such happiness elsewhere.'[22]

On the other hand, Robin Maugham hated Eton, where he was bullied and made utterly wretched. 'The school was a prison in which I was sentenced to live for a fixed number of years,' and even after he had left, 'For several years I could not go near the place. I could not even drive through Slough without feeling physically sick. Even now scenes from those ghastly days disturb me.'[23] Richard Norton, Lord Grantley, recalled of Wellington, 'My whole time at Wellington was so disgusting and useless that I find myself hardly able to write about it without nausea . . . I never revisit that part of the country . . . without thinking of the detestable old school.'[24] John Betjeman recalled a life of dread at Marlborough in his verse autobiography:

> The dread of beatings! Dread of being late!
> And, greatest dread of all, the dread of games![25]

Peregrine Worsthorne was at Stowe. 'The early years were unmitigated hell. Never in later life have I suffered such terror, such loneliness, such hunger, such pain, such oppression, such injustice, or had reason to believe that human nature was so vile.'[26] A visit to Auschwitz was to remind him forcibly of Stowe.

While allowing for an individual variety of response, it is perhaps possible to refine these individual attitudes down into categories. Dr. Royston Lambert isolates five separate attitudes to school. He lists their proponents as: conformists, those who accept the ends and means of the school; ritualists, those who are not interested in or do not accept the school's aims but go along with them; retreatists, the uncommitted who do not oppose but do not accept the school; innovators, who do not like current practices and seek change; rebels, who reject the school and its structures.[27]

Those who write about their schooldays are by definition self-selecting and tend inevitably to be the conformists, the innovators and the rebels. The other categories are apathetic. The writers may be recollecting in the tranquillity of old age and the golden glow of reminiscence an idealised youth in a prelapsarian paradise, or as propagandists and mythographers seeking to etch the system into the collective consciousness of the nation. Equally, they may often be as newly emancipated young men, seeking to pay off old scores, rationalise hatred and misery, purge their soul in literary catharsis.

This leads in turn to three different kinds of literature, the conformist, which endorses the dominant ideology, the alternative, which proposes changes, and the oppositional, which proposes rejection and abolition. All the books studied fell into one or other of these three categories. There is, however, an interesting distinction to be made. Popular culture seems on the whole to have been strongly sympathetic to the public schools. High culture has contained a greater portion of condemnation and dissent. It is important not to take the evidence of malcontents as an expression of the whole reality. As Lionel Trilling wisely observed of E. M. Forster, who castigates the public schools in *The Longest Journey*:

> Even if he had not been at a disadvantage (as a day boy), it is unlikely that Forster would have been happy at his public school. Few gifted boys have been, and the literary men of our time continue the indictments which have made the English public schools a matter of controversy and even political conflict since early in the nineteenth century.[28]

It is almost invariably the case that hostility to the public school and an indictment of the system as a whole in fiction spring from unhappy personal experience of it rather than a general and detached philosophical standpoint. Similarly support for it comes from those who have been happy to conform to its rules and norms, and look backwards with delight and longing.

While it is obviously important to analyse the arguments put forward in public school fiction, to recover the context and the reality, to assess the author's intentions, it is equally important to chart its reception. This can be done in a number of ways: by reference to print runs (where available), by an analysis of reviews (which indicate the role within the literate culture of the work in question), by reference to memoirs and autobiographies (inevitably impressionistic). But most of all it can be done by the application of the reception model outlined above.

The system, as we know it, emerged with the reforms undertaken in the public schools in the nineteenth century. The unreformed public schools of the eighteenth century and the Regency period were essentially self-governing boy republics, run by a prefectorial elite, in which the teachers rarely intervened. The boys were taught classics, but otherwise lived a life in common, badly fed and unregulated. Their life was tribal, turbulent, brutal and often drunken. It was a world where only the fittest survived and in which every vice flourished: drinking, gambling, bullying, poaching, debt, profanity and prostitution.[29] The boys clung to their rights with fanatical tenacity and any attempt at infringement led to rebellion. Bullying in particular was rife. 'You have no idea how savage the boys are,' wrote James Milnes Gaskell to his mother on arriving at Eton in 1824.[30] The historian James Anthony Froude looked back on his schooldays at Westminster in the 1830s with the utmost horror. He was treated as:

> the drudge and sport of my stronger contemporaries. No one interfered: it was the rule of the Establishment, and was supposed to be good for us . . . I have had my legs set on fire to make me dance. When I had crawled to bed and to sleep I have been woke many times by the hot points of cigars burning holes in my face. I was made drunk by being forced to swallow brandy punch, which I hated. My health broke down and I had to be removed for a few months . . . When I was sent back to college, it all began again.[31]

His experience was by no means uncommon. But the public schools merely reflected the prevailing values of a dissolute aristocracy, whose world was one of hard drinking, ruinous gambling, horse racing, blood sports and prizefighting. The measure of a man was how much he could drink and how tough he was. It was an ethic that the aristocracy shared with the 'rough' working class. It is no wonder that a schoolmaster observed in 1806, 'The youth of Eton are dissipated gentlemen; those at Westminster dissipated with a little of the blackguard; and those at St. Paul's the most depraved of all.'[32]

But by the 1830s the public schools were coming under attack for their immorality, exclusivity and restricted curriculum. The rise of Evangelicalism coupled with the expansion of the middle classes literally transformed the face of society. As Harold Perkin pointed out, 'Between 1780 and 1850 the English ceased to be one of the most aggressive, brutal, rowdy, outspoken, riotous, cruel and bloodthirsty nations in the world and became one of the most inhibited, polite, orderly, tenderminded, prudish and hypocritical.'[33] The Evangelicals, characterised by an intense seriousness of purpose, immense industry, enthusiastic missionary spirit, censorious highmindedness and puritanical abstention from worldly pleasures, mounted a full-scale and successful assault on every level and aspect of society, promoting religion, education, duty and hard work, and attacking cruelty, vice and frivolity. They created a cult of respectability and conformity, and established the home as the centre of nineteenth-century life. The result was the pacification and purification of society.[34]

Inevitably they turned their attention to the schools and sought to remodel them in their own image, with the promotion of the doctrine of 'Godliness and Good Learning'. The most celebrated exemplar of change was Dr Thomas Arnold, appointed headmaster of Rugby in 1828. Under his impact the English public school became uniquely among all Western educational systems a place to train character. He was one of several headmasters who sought to apply the Evangelical influence to school but he became the most famous because of the effect of two highly influential books, Arthur Stanley's *Life and Correspondence of Dr Thomas Arnold* and Thomas Hughes's *Tom Brown's Schooldays*. The success of Hughes's book demonstrates the importance of public school fiction in the creation of the cultural image of the public school. For it was Hughes's version of Dr Arnold which became the symbol of the reformed public schools.

But at the same time as the country was being swept by respectability the middle classes were demanding admission to the inner circle of power. They wanted an intellectually respectable, morally sound, socially elevating education for their sons. The public schools provided the vital matrix for the amalgamation of upper class and middle class, widening the circle of power sufficiently to defuse the discontents of the newly rich. The children of the upper middle class joined those of the aristocracy in the public schools and were turned into gentlemen, with a common code of behaviour and belief. Elite schooling gradually replaced noble birth as the identifying badge of the ruling class, and the public school system expanded to accommodate them.

Half those institutions at present constituting the public school system were founded between 1841 and 1900.[35]

The system emerged from the fusion of the original nine great public schools, the old endowed grammar schools, which went exclusive and up-market, and the new Victorian foundations. The Public School Commission investigated the system, and its report (1864), while praising the work of Arnold and endorsing prefects, games and fagging, recommended changes, many of them implemented, in the interests of meeting the economic, spiritual and psychological needs of the upper middle class. Governing bodies were remodelled, the curriculum was improved, better teachers and improved facilities were introduced. The Headmasters' Conference was founded in 1869 as the public schools drew together into a coherent structure, with standardised administration and curriculum procedures—a structure, as Weinberg puts it, as important to Britain as the invention of the factory, for it was 'a powerful device for insulating and socializing an elite and for protecting the values of the aristocracy, moral fervour and gentle-manliness'.[36]

The mid-Victorian period saw a remarkable breed of headmasters taking the public schools by the scruff of the neck and transforming them into respectable institutions—Cotton of Marlborough, Thring of Uppingham, Benson of Wellington, Percival of Clifton, Vaughan of Harrow. The school took control of the boys' lives in a way unthinkable in the days of the unreformed public schools. Uniforms were introduced. Sport was promoted to use up their surplus energies. Religion was advanced to the centre of school life, with compulsory chapel and the weekly sermon as the high point of moral instruction. The prefects became the Praetorian Guard of the headmaster. House and school loyalties were inculcated by competitive games, school songs, school magazines and Old Boys' associations.

On the whole, boys were bored by their school work, which continued to be centred on the classics. But the classics taught boys public speaking, trained their minds in general analytical principles, instilled in them Greek and Roman virtues and gave them a common cultural perspective. They turned their energies to organised games, and by the 1890s athletics had become a mania which characterised the public schools until well after World War I. It caused critical commentators to claim that athleticism was leading to the submergence of intellectual life and the rise of philistinism. J. H. Simpson, a master at Rugby, wrote in 1900, 'A great many people think of the public schools . . . as being primarily places where boys learn to play games . . . the popular impression in this matter is broadly true.'[37] But games mania coincided with the dominance of imperialism, and the public schools became, in Mack's words, 'mints for the coining of Empire-builders'.[38] Officer training or cadet corps were introduced, and patriotism and imperialism became an integral part of every aspect of their lives. The gentlemen and sportsmen became the masters of the empire, Sudan, for instance, being described as 'a country of blacks run by blues'. Sir Reginald Furse, who controlled colonial recruitment from 1910 to 1948, specifically selected his men on the basis of character and recruited them mainly from the public schools. He wrote, 'We could not have run the show without them. In England, universities train the mind; the public schools train character and teach leadership.'[39] To have been a public school prefect Furse regarded as ideal training for colonial government. In a book on the colonial service Robert Heussler collected some of the testimonial letters used to make selections and they include such statements as 'He would be capable of dealing with men, his mind is well-balanced, his manners agreeable, and in every respect he is a perfect gentleman' and 'He would maintain the best traditions of English government over subject races . . . He is a gentleman, a man of character.'[40]

By 1900 public schools had become close-knit communities, highly disciplined, obsessed with games, fervently religious, intensely class-conscious and geared to turning out gentlemen all-rounders. To develop physical hardihood there were cold showers, cross-country runs, spartan dormitories, outside lavatories and compulsory games. But the schools also sought to give their pupils moral training, to develop self-restraint, a proper sense of values and preparation for the exercise of power.

The monastic all-male environment, the playing of games (with the ideas of team spirit, abiding by the rules and being a sporting loser), the cultivation of traditions and rituals (school songs, slang, uniforms and colours) into which all new boys had to be religiously initiated, the strict disciplinary system, the rigidly defined hierarchy through which a boy rose from fag to prefect, all aided in the creation of group loyalty, corporate spirit and elite solidarity. The emotional lives of the boys, herded together at the time of maximum sexual potency, were directed towards each other, in the form either of sex or of a platonic and essentially ennobling love. In its own way this factor too cemented the loyalty and unity of the group. There was also a code of behaviour the boys developed for themselves: no 'squealing', no stealing, co-operative preparation of work, the phlegmatic bearing of all anguish and irritations. This overlapped with and reinforced the code that was imposed on them from above.

The prefect system gave the senior boys a taste of the exercise of power and put them on their honour not to abuse it. The Public School Commission (1864) credited this system with an enormous effect on social life and national character, fostering the special characteristics the British claimed as their own: 'their capacity to govern others and control themselves, their aptitude for combining freedom with order, their public spirit, their vigour and manliness of character, their strong but not slavish respect for public opinion.'[41]

Almost unconsciously the public school boy absorbed a complete code of behaviour which would enable him to do 'the right thing' in any situation. It involved obedience to superiors, the acceptance of a position in the hierarchy, team spirit, and loyalty. It produced the gifted amateur, trained for nothing but ready for anything, who had a relaxed air of command, a sense of duty and a feeling of the obligation of the superior to his inferiors. It also involved the traditional British phlegm, reserve, understatement, unflappability, the stiff upper lip, a result of the inculcation of modesty in victory and defeat, the all-male society in which emotion was sissy, the encouragement of restraint in the exercise of power.

The public school spirit was summarised by the Rev. T. L. Papillon:

> Many a lad who leaves an English public school disgracefully ignorant of the rudiments of useful knowledge, who can speak no language but his own, and writes that imperfectly, to whom the noble literature of his country and the stirring history of his forefathers are almost a sealed book, and who has devoted a great part of his time, and nearly all his thoughts to athletic sports, yet brings away with him something beyond all price, a manly, straight-forward character, a scorn of lying and meanness, habits of obedience and command, and fearless courage. Thus equipped, he goes into the world, and bears a man's part in subduing the earth, ruling its wild folk and building up the Empire; doing many things so well that it seems a thousand pities that he was not trained to do them better, and to face the problems of race, creed and government in distant corners of the Empire with a more instructed mind. This type of citizen, however, with all its defects, has done yeoman's service to the Empire; and for much that is best in him our public schools may fairly take credit.[42]

The heroic conduct and heart-breaking sacrifice of public school boys in World War I indicated just how deep this ethos had penetrated. Of 5,588 Old Etonians who served in the war, for instance, 1,159 died and 1,469 were wounded. From even a small school like Fettes 1,094 joined up and nearly a quarter of them (246) died. Losses among junior officers, among whom public school and university men were very numerous, were devastatingly high. Five out of every nine who fought in France or Flanders were posted killed, wounded or missing. However, for all the talk of World War I as a watershed, there was comparatively little change in the public school system in the inter-war years, or indeed in the nation. When World War II broke out there were more boys in independent schools than there had been in 1914. E. C. Mack, writing of the inter-war years in 1940, concluded, 'Though there was an attempt to modernize and eliminate evils, both the key ideals and the key practices of the Victorian schools remained intact, chiefly because Conservatives willed that they should. The post-war public school was still a class institution, devoted to making leaders and statesmen out of privileged British youth.'[43]

World War II was a much more significant watershed, and afterwards the public schools began to achieve a more academic orientation, with curriculum reform and the promotion of science. They became at last the centres of academic excellence that Arnold and company had wanted. But they did so in part because the needs of the middle class had altered. The gradual dissolution of the empire and the reduction in size of the armed forces meant that far fewer public school boys were needed as officers and administrators. Instead they were drawn to industry, finance and the City. In the schools during the 1950s and 1960s fagging was phased out, beatings were reduced, the tyranny of games was broken, the cadet corps and the chapel ceased to be compulsory, uniforms were no longer universal. It was arguably as great a transformation as that of the 1830s and 1840s. By 1980 the schools stood for academic achievement, moderation in discipline and a more relaxed attitude to games and sex. In many schools co-education is even being tried. The old public school code has been diluted. The demand for public schools remains as great as ever, if not greater, particularly since the abolition of the grammar schools, and they continue to flourish. But they are now a significantly different system with different priorities from those which flourished from the 1850s to the 1950s.

The school story genre was essentially created by Thomas Hughes. Despite its precursors, Hughes's *Tom Brown's Schooldays* (1857), rapidly followed by Dean Farrar's *Eric* (1858), not only set up a range of themes, situations and archetypes which subsequent authors were to develop, but also made a major contribution to the educational debate. There was already an important distinction between the two books. Farrar's looked back to the past and the dominance of the Evangelicals; Hughes's to the future of a school system geared to athleticism and imperialism. However, in the first instance it was Farrar who had the greater influence on school story writers. In the 1860s and 1870s writers like the Rev. H. C. Adams, the Rev. T. S. Millington and Ethel Kenyon wrote in the tradition of *Eric* and were high on moral didacticism and low on patriotism and athletics.

This changed in the 1880s after the foundation of *The Boy's Own Paper* (1879), whose early success owed much to the popularity of Talbot Baines Reed's school stories. Reed succeeded in fusing the best elements of Hughes and Farrar, but his moralising was unobtrusive, his narratives were vigorous and convincing, and his boy heroes instant identification figures for the young reader. The flood of school stories in the 1880s directly reflects the upsurge of juvenile publishing in the wake of Forster's Education Act (1870) and the development of new publishing technology. Publishers pinpointed prize and gift books as a growth area, and the expansion of schooling furnished ideal subject material for them. It was also part of what E. C. Mack calls 'the greatest upsurge of passionate adoration to which the schools had ever been subjected',[44] an upsurge manifested in memoirs, histories, poems and songs, which bathed the public schools in the glow of romance and highlighted elements which were to become integral to the fiction: friendships and floggings, japes and scrapes, customs and traditions. Academic work was the significant exception. A standard format emerged for the school story. E. C. Mack summarised it:

> A boy enters school in some fear and trepidation, but usually with ambitions and schemes; suffers mildly or seriously at first from loneliness, the exactions of fag-masters, the discipline of masters and the regimentation of games; then makes a few friends and leads for a year or so a joyful irresponsible and some-times rebellious life, eventually learns duty, self-reliance, responsibility and loyalty as a prefect, qualities usually used to put down bullying or over-emphasis on athletic prowess; and finally leaves school with regret for a wider world, stamped with the seal of an institution which he has left and devoted to its welfare.[45]

Amidst the great tide of material the work of two individual literary geniuses emerged, men who did not devote their careers to the school story but produced major examples of the genre, Rudyard Kipling (*Stalky and Co.*) and P. G. Wodehouse (*Mike*). Both writers, like Hughes and Farrar, were reflecting current issues of educational debate —Kipling the necessity for military preparedness and Wodehouse the role of athleticism.

Despite the prolificity of some of the school story writers, it was an art that had to be mastered. A. C. Benson, himself a prolific writer and successful schoolmaster, reflected upon the difficulty of writing boys' stories, a difficulty which had prevented him trying it. First, the plot is a difficulty, 'The incidents of school life do not lend themselves to dramatic situations. Then, too, the trivialities of which school life is so much composed, the minuteness of the details involved, make the subject a singularly complicated one.' Second, there is boy conversation, difficult to produce because on the one hand it is concerned with small concrete facts and incidents, and on the other hand marked by, as he tactfully put it, 'Rabelaisian plainness of speech on certain subjects'. Third, the boy mind and outlook are difficult to capture: 'their credulity, their preoccupations, their conventionality, their inarticulate-ness, all these qualities are very hard to indicate'. Fourth, there is the question of the inner life, 'The nobler qualities of human nature are latent in many boys; but they are for the most part superficially ruled by an intensely strong *mauvaise honte*, which leads them to live in two worlds, and to keep the inner life very sharply and securely ruled off from the outer.' He concludes of boy attitudes: 'Only a boy could formulate these, and no boy has sufficient ease of expression to do so, or sufficient detachment both to play the part and describe it.'[46] No boy, that is, until Alec Waugh, who successfully executed all Benson's requirements for the successful school story: the detailed texture of school life, the authentic flavour of boy conversation, the boy mind and inner life—all vividly and compellingly captured and presented.

While much of the writing was for boys, there was also a new development, a body of public school fiction for adults, and it begins to emerge at a time in the 1890s and the Edwardian age of mounting criticism of the public schools, from both ends of the political spectrum. It arose from concern based variously on charges of philistinism, amateurism, excessive conformism, class exclusivity and games worship. Within this adult market there were writers, working directly from their own experience, who were critical of the public schools (Forster's *The Longest Journey* and Waugh's *The Loom of Youth*) and who were warmly supportive (Vachell's *The Hill* and Raymond's *Tell England*). But it is important to discern here the divergence between the high culture (generally hostile to the public schools) and the popular culture (broadly supportive), which was to persist until well after World War II. Within the high culture, too, there is a distinction between the alternative image (Waugh) and the oppositional (Forster). There had always been a current of criticism of the public school system and its product, but it peaked during and after World War I. Most 'serious' writers from the Great War onwards excoriated the public schools as hotbeds of homosexuality, brutality, snobbery and conformism.[47] The system was seen as symbolic and symptomatic of the mind-set which had caused the war. Lytton Strachey chose Dr Arnold as one of those Victorians eminently deserving of debunking. In *The World of William Clissold* (1926) H. G. Wells castigated the public school product as 'stiff, arrogant, profoundly ignorant, technically honourable and utterly incomprehensible to the uninitiated rest of mankind'.[48] Graham Greene equated school, prison and factory as the means by which the capitalist system sought to suppress individualism and promote the uniformity it needed to survive and expand. Writers like George Orwell, Richard Aldington and E. M. Forster kept up the attack. In *Out of Bounds* Esmond Romilly declared that he found in 'the public school system an elaborate organization for propaganda which was to produce in the minds of the boys a ruling class ideology'.[49]

But neither P. W. Musgrave nor Isabel Quigly has appreciated the full extent to which such criticisms remained part of a narrow intellectual world, a world of high-society literary salons and low-circulation magazines, rarely reaching out to or affecting the perceptions of the wider public. Of much greater significance in representing the attitude of the public to the public schools in the inter-war years were the middlebrow best-selling novels like *Tell England* (1922), and *Goodbye, Mr Chips* (1935), both of which reached far beyond the novel-reading public through their adaptation to the cinema, and the phenomenal success of Frank Richards's public school stories in the weekly magazines *The Magnet* and *The Gem*. Richards's work lies in direct line of descent from Hughes and Reed. The magazines ended with the outbreak of World War II but Richards returned to his chosen theme after the war in hardback and on television. Greyfriars lived on even after his death in 1961. Frank Richards probably had a greater influence on the popular perception of the public schools in the long run than Orwell, Forster, Aldington and Greene put together.

There can be little doubt that public school fiction created for boys going to public school a fully formed picture of what to expect. According to Alec Waugh, preparatory school boys read Talbot Baines Reed assiduously in preparation for their translation to public school.[50] Even H. E. Bates, who won a scholarship to Kettering Grammar School in 1916 after attending a 'crude industrial elementary school', had a clearly defined picture of what to expect, based on an idealised image:

> I had not read the school-stories of popular writers for nothing. I knew very well that the masters would wear black gowns and possibly mortar-boards too. The prefects would have studies in which they fried sausages and drank beer on the quiet in the middle of the night . . . I should have to learn Latin and French and a new kind of English in which words like cads and rotters and expressions like bally bounders and beastly fellows played a large part.[51]

Many boys were to be disabused of their preconceptions on their arrival but others carried on reading public school stories in *The Captain* and *The Public School Magazine*, magazines aimed specifically at a public school readership. As late as 1969 Royston Lambert found the expectations of children going away to boarding school at eleven to be 'coloured by comics and old fashioned school stories'. 'I actively expected this school to be like the things we read about in a book such as *Jennings* or *Billy Bunter*,' said a boy aged eleven, and a sixteen-year-old boy said, 'I had a romantic "Tom Brown" idea and expected to be tossed in a blanket and be instilled with school spirit, with harsh seniors pushing you around and making you fag for them all the time.'[52]

This process of conditioned expectation was the subject of a notable satire by Desmond Coke, *The Bending of a Twig* (1906). Dedicated to his old housemaster and set at Shrewsbury, the book shows Lycidas Marsh going to school, armed with the impressions provided by schoolbooks acquired by his mother. She buys him *Tom Brown, Eric, The Hill, Stalky and Co.* and *Jack Joker*, a penny dreadful. *Stalky* makes him bloodthirsty and his mother confiscates it. She also confiscates *Jack Joker*, set at Bircham College, where the French master is a nihilist and the headmaster Jack the Ripper. *Eric* moves him to tears but he is mystified by the indiscriminate deaths of good and bad boys. *Tom Brown* reminds him of 'the Vicar's sermons or the books with S.P.C.K. on their backs'. *The Hill*, with all its talk of mystic and passionate friendship, merely mystifies him, but he carefully learns all the slang. When he gets to Shrewsbury he finds it nothing like the picture in his books. He finds himself ignored rather than bullied, then mocked for his faulty slang. When he decides to fight the school bully he finds the fight has been set up to provide humour. When he confesses dramatically to an infringement of the rules for which another boy has shouldered the blame, he expects praise but finds them both landed with detention. But eventually Lycidas settles down, is accepted, rises through the school to prefect and learns to exercise power responsibly. He leaves, determined to make Shrewsbury proud of him. The success of Desmond Coke's book, widely praised in its time and now forgotten, depends on a general recognition of the common experience of public school boys in going to school, primed with impressions derived from fiction.[53]

The largest audience for public school fiction, however, remained boys who had not been and would never go to public school. For them the image was a glamorous substitute for the grim reality of their own schools, a wish-fulfilment of a particularly potent and beguiling kind. The system, ethos and values of the public schools percolated down throughout the rest of the educational system. The grammar schools were modelled on them, complete with houses, prefects, cadet corps, games, religion and patriotism, the principal difference being that they were day schools and not boarding schools. Even some of the council schools, according to Jack Common, made 'foolish attempts at imitations of it'.[54]

The aim of the elementary schools in the nineteenth century and beyond is clear. As J. J. Price wrote in *School Management and Method* (1879):

> The effect of an elementary school is to provide efficient instruction and education for children of mechanics, artisans and the poorer classes and to train them in habits of punctuality, cheerful obedience to duty, good manners and language, and of honour and truthfulness in word and act.[55]

Military drill was included in the curriculum of many schools to instil discipline. History and geography were grounded in the teaching of patriotism and good citizenship. From 1870 to the 1960s the schooling of the working class was geared to the promotion of middle-class values of discipline, thrift and hard work, to opening up the working-class child's mind to middle-class culture and giving an avenue of escape for the brightest youngsters, and to instilling the virtues of patriotism, duty and service. There was resistance from some sections of the working class, which took the form of truancy, insubordination, a stubborn resistance to being indoctrinated or improved, by the adoption of alternative values. According to Jack Common, working-class boys disliked school, which was alien to working-class life:

> It does not grow from that life; it is not 'our' school, in the sense in which other schools can be spoken of by the folk of other classes. The government forced thm on us, and the real shaping of the working class boys goes on after they are shut.[56]

It is this situation which makes boyhood reading crucial. For those who did not absorb public school values and virtues from inside the school—and some did—they certainly did so outside through their reading. In the case of middle-class boys it reinforced the ethos of the school and in the case of working-class boys it substituted for it. C. E. B. Russell and Lillian M. Russell, commenting on a lifetime's work with Lads' Clubs, noted that 'the books popular among working boys are precisely those which delight their contemporaries in the well-to-do classes'. The younger ones liked school stories, the older ones adventure stories. They added:

> No one who has studied the habits of boys will deny that they are fond of reading. Who has not seen the reading errand-boy, basket on arm, moving slowly down the street, leaning against a lamp post or more comfortably disposed on a quiet doorstep, with his eyes fixed on a green, blue or pink-tinted paper? The 'nipper' in the waiting van may be similarly engrossed. The office-boy has a bulging pocket, suggestive of printed matter surreptitiously enjoyed in moments of solitude. The boy who has a railway journey to make almost invariably lays out part of his pocket money on 'something to read in the train'.[57]

Not only were working-class boys voracious readers but their reading was voluntary, habitual and potent. In *Boy Life and Labour* (1914) Arnold Freeman made the same point. The bulk of working-class boys whom he questioned read penny dreadfuls and halfpenny comics, 'as do many boys of the middle classes'. He noted that they could be bought second-hand very cheap. In his examples of boys typical of three groups—the better class of boy worker, unskilled labour and unemployables—one of his two typical unskilled boys read *The Gem* and both his typical unemployables read school stories, one of them *The Gem.* [58]

Frederick Willis, who grew up to be a hatter and thus a member of the labour aristocracy, recalled that in his Edwardian boyhood he attended a board school in south-east London, a mixed working-class/middle-class institution where he was very happy, 'We were taught to be God-fearing, honourable, self-reliant and patriotic; to be clean and trim in our appearance, to be smart in our walk and actions, and always walk in step with a companion'. He recalled also:

> We were great readers of school stories, from which we learnt that boys of the higher class boarding-schools were courageous, honourable and chivalrous, and steeped in the traditions of the school and loyalty to the country. We tried to mould our lives on this formula. Needless to say, we fell very short of this desirable end, and I attributed our failure to the fact that we were only board-school boys and could never hope to emulate those of finer clay. Nevertheless the constant effort did us a lot of good.[59]

This reveals a fascinating dual level of involvement—aspiration to higher things but acceptance of the *status quo*. It sums up to perfection the twin process of the maintenance of the existing hierarchy and class system with everyone in his place, and the absorption of a set of elite role models and values, which between them ensured social cohesion and relative stability for a hundred years.

Notes

1 Walter E. Houghton, *The Victorian Frame of Mind* (1957), New Haven, 1979, xv.
2 Hugh Kingsmill, *After Puritanism, 1850-1900*, London, 1929, 13.
3 Nicholas Pronay and D. W. Spring (ed.), *Propaganda, Politics and Film, 1918-45*, London, 1982, 196.
4 George Orwell, *Collected Essays, Journalism and Letters*, I, Harmondsworth, 1970, 528.
5 On this argument see John MacKenzie, 'Values of imperialism', *Social History Society News Letter*, 11, 2 (autumn 1986), 3-4.
6 John Ruskin, *The Crown of Wild Olive*, II, London, 1866, 54.
7 Joan Rockwell, *Fact in Fiction: the use of literature in the systematic study of society*, London, 1974, vii, viii, 4.
8 See Tony Bennett, Graham Martin, Colin Mercer and Janet Woollacott (ed.), *Culture, Ideology and Social Process*, London, 1981, and Richard Collins, James Curran, Nicholas Garnham, Paddy Scannell, Philip Schlesinger and Colin Sparks (ed.), *Media, Culture and Society*, London, 1986.
9 Roger Jowell and Colin Airey (ed.), *British Social Attitudes—the 1984 Report*, Aldershot, 1984, 111-17.
10 Isabel Quigly, *The Heirs of Tom Brown*, London, 1982, and P. W. Musgrave, *From Brown to Bunter*, London, 1985.
11 Jeffrey Richards and Anthony Aldgate, *Best of British*, Oxford, 1983, and *Britain Can Take It*, Oxford, 1986.
12 J. S. R. Goodlad, *A Sociology of Popular Drama*, London, 1971, 7.
13 On Gramsci's ideas see Stuart Hall, 'Culture, the media and the ideological effect', in James Curran, Michael Gurevich and Janet Wollacott (ed.), *Mass

Communication and Society, London, 1979, 315–48.

14 Richard Maltby, *Harmless Entertainment*, Metuchen, N.J., and London, 1983.

15 George Macdonald Fraser (ed.), *The World of the Public School*, London, 1977, 7.

16 Alec Waugh, *Public School Life*, London, 1922, 203.

17 Eleanor Adlard (ed.), *Dear Turley*, London, 1942, 135.

18 James Hilton, *To you, Mr Chips*, London, 1940, 11–12.

19 Earl of Lytton, *Antony*, London, 1935, 44.

20 Jeanne Mackenzie, *The Children of the Souls*, London, 1986, 32.

21 Alec Waugh, *The Early Years of Alec Waugh*, London, 1962, 28.

22 Rupert Brooke, *Collected Poems, with a memoir by Edward Marsh* (1918), London, 1966, xi–xii.

23 Robin Maugham, *Escape from the Shadows*, London, 1981, 62, 79.

24 Richard Norton, Lord Grantley, *Silver Spoon*, London, 1954, 29–31.

25 John Betjeman, *Summoned by Bells*, London, 1960, 67.

26 Macdonald Fraser (ed.), *World of the Public School*, 80.

27 Royston Lambert, *The Hothouse Society*, London, 1968, 358.

28 Lionel Trilling, *E. M. Forster: a study* (1944), London, 1969, 25.

29 This is lovingly described in John Chandos, *Boys Together: English Public Schools, 1800–1864*, London, 1984.

30 Chandos, *Boys Together*, 42.

31 Waldo Hilary Dunn, *James Anthony Froude*, I, Oxford, 1961, 33.

32 Vivian Ogilvie, *The English Public School*, London, 1957, 125.

33 Harold Perkin, *The Origins of Modern English Society*, London, 1969, 280.

34 Ian Bradley, *The Call to Seriousness: the evangelical impact of the Victorians*, London, 1976.

35 On the history of the public schools see in particular Jonathan Gathorne-Hardy, *The Public School Phenomenon*, Harmondsworth, 1979; J. R. de S. Honey, *Tom Brown's Universe*, London, 1977; T. W. Bamford, *The Rise of the Public School*, London, 1967; Rupert Wilkinson, *The Prefects*, London, 1964; Ian Weinberg, *The English Public Schools*, New York, 1967; Brian Simon and Ian Bradley, *The Victorian Public School*, Dublin, 1975; Ogilvie, *The English Public School*.

36 Ian Weinberg, *The English Public Schools*, 52.

37 Gathorne-Hardy, *Public School Phenomenon*, 165.

38 Edward C. Mack, *Public Schools and British Opinion, 1780–1860*, London, 1938, 400.

39 Robert Heussler, *Yesterday's Rulers*, Oxford, 1963, 82.

40 Heussler, *Yesterday's Rulers*, 19–20.

41 Edward C. Mack, *Public Schools and British Opinion since 1860*, New York, 1941, 38.

42 Bernard Darwin, *The English Public School*, London, 1929, 21.

43 Mack, *Public Schools and British Opinion since 1860*, 372. On World War I losses see Robert Wohl, *The Generation of 1914*, Cambridge, Mass., 1979, 115.

44 Mack, *Public Schools and British Opinion since 1860*, 134.

45 Mack, *Public Schools and British Opinion since 1860*, 201–2.

46 A. C. Benson, *The Upton Letters*, London, 1905, 107–11.

47 On this subject see John Reed, *Old School Ties*, Syracuse, N.Y., 1964.

48 Reed, *Old School Ties*, 36.

49 Esmond and Giles Romilly, *Out of Bounds*, London, 1935, 214.

50 Alec Waugh, *Public School Life*, 31.

51 Graham Greene (ed.), *The Old School* (1934), Oxford, 1984, 15.

52 Lambert, *Hothouse Society*, 52–3.

53 For an appreciation of Coke's work see Isabel Quigly, *Heirs of Tom Brown*, 226–8.

54 Jack Common, *The Freedom of the Streets*, London, 1938, 62.

55 Philip McCann (ed.), *Popular Education and Socialization in the Nineteenth Century*, London, 1977, 181.
56 Common, *Freedom of the Streets*, 60–1. On working-class rejectionism see Stephen Humphries, *Hooligans or Rebels?*, Oxford, 1981.
57 C. E. B. and Lillian Russell, *Lads' Clubs*, London, 1932, 137, 145, 140–1. The character of working-class boyhood reading is confirmed by Frederick Rogers, *Labour, Life and Literature*, Brighton, 1973, 10–11, and Frederick Willis, *101 Jubilee Road*, London, 1948, 108–11.
58 Arnold Freeman, *Boy Life and Labour*, London, 1914, 144, 154–60.
59 Frederick Willis, *A Book of London Yesterdays*, London, 1960, 49, 53.

2

The making of a muscular Christian: *Tom Brown's Schooldays*

Tom Brown's Schooldays is the most famous school story ever written. It has been continuously in print since its publication in 1857 and its influence has been enormous, J. J. Findlay, Professor of Education at Manchester University, observed in 1897, 'With the exception of Pestalozzi's *Leonard and Gertrude*, *Tom Brown* is the only work of fiction which has exercised a worldwide influence on the development of education.'[1] This influence lay in the reflection, mythification and propagation of what was to become a dominant image of the public school, a place which trained character and produced Christian gentlemen. Bernard Darwin, devoting to *Tom Brown* an entire chapter in a book on the public schools in the 'English Heritage' series in 1929, wrote, 'It is often said . . . that Dickens created Christmas. In that sense it may be permissible to suggest that Hughes created . . . the public school spirit.'[2]

Precursors of *Tom Brown's Schooldays* are regularly disinterred and examined, the merits of Harriet Martineau's *The Crofton Boys* (1841) or Frank Smedley's *Frank Fairlegh* (1850) canvassed. Diligent research has even turned up two earlier schoolboy heroes called Tom Brown. But none of these books created anything like the impact that *Tom Brown's Schooldays* did.[3] Its place as the *fons et origo* of the school story remains secure. With *Tom Brown* the school story as *genre* effectively began. As early as 1861 *Blackwood's Magazine* could declare:

> The British schoolboy has become a hero. His slang has been reproduced in print . . . until it has become almost as classical as the Scotticisms of Burns, or the French that passes muster in polite society . . . The professional story-tellers rejoice in the addition of another new figure to their repertory of ready-made characters; and they put in the sharp public-school boy side by side with the clever governess and the muscular parson. The discovery is due to the author of *Tom Brown's Schooldays* . . . It is no mean triumph to have

been the Columbus of the world of schoolboy romance . . . It lay within easy reach, indeed, but was practically undiscovered.[4]

The ideological significance of *Tom Brown's Schooldays* is threefold, as it looks to the past, to the present and to the future. Firstly, it recalls, records and mythifies the Rugby of Dr Arnold, creating a selective image of Arnoldianism which was to be highly influential, and eclipsing the somewhat different reality. But on to his image of Arnoldianism Thomas Hughes grafted other concepts dear to himself and not especially associated with Arnold, the ideals of Christian Socialism, the ideas of Carlyle (work, hero worship) and a strongly marked English nationalism. In due course the work was to receive an additional and most potent imprint—that of Victorian chivalry. With the passing of time the pronounced religious element of the second half of the book, which had been Hughes's avowed object in writing it, was downgraded in favour of the games-playing and character formation of the first half, which were adduced in support of the later nineteenth-century cults of athleticism and imperialism. For *Tom Brown* is more than just a school story: it is a mirror of the changing nature and structure of Victorian values, a vital point of intersection between ideas that had been dominant and ideas that were to become so. It exists on two levels of distortion. Arnold's concept of 'Godliness and Good Learning' is passed through the filter of Hughes's commitment to muscular Christianity, and this in its turn feeds into the games mania and Empire worship of later decades.

The changing values and preoccupations of society and in particular the receding of the tide of religious faith led to the development of a critical view of the novel, summed up characteristically by P. G. Wodehouse in a piece for *The Public School Magazine* in 1902.[5] He claimed that the two halves of *Tom Brown* were written by two different authors. In Part 2, in the final cricket match, Tom Brown does a whole range of inconceivable things—he puts the visiting M.C.C. in to bat first, allows comic songs to be sung during the luncheon interval and admits including Arthur in the first eleven not on his merit as a player but because it will do him good. For Wodehouse, who took his cricket seriously, this proved conclusively that Hughes could not have written Part 2. Wodehouse reveals that in fact it was written by the committee of the Secret Society for Putting Wholesome Literature within the reach of Every Boy and Seeing that he Gets it. They had objected to Part 1 ('It contained no moral. There are scenes of violence and your hero is far from perfect') and so took over the writing of the rest of the book, apart from the fight with Slogger Williams, interpolated by Hughes as a concession by the society. This amusingly encapsulates the much debated view that something happened to

Hughes between the writing of the two parts of the book. J. M. Ludlow suggested that the death of Hughes's eldest daughter half-way through affected him so deeply as to cause him to adopt a different tone in the second half of the book, and subsequent commentators have taken up this interpretation.[6] But it is a misconceived view and one which entirely overlooks the purpose Hughes had in writing it.

Patrick Scott's researches in the Macmillan papers have put the whole subject in perspective. He uncovered Hughes's plan for the book, which shows that he had already written several of the key religious episodes before his daughter's death (Arthur praying in the dormitory and being abused, Tom getting some new ideas about the Bible, Arthur's illness and recovery, East and Tom discussing religion). The change of mood and tone had always been part of Hughes's scheme.[7] For, as he said in the preface added to the sixth edition, in response to those critics who chided him for preaching, 'My sole object in writing was to preach to boys.'

Scott argues convincingly that the book is entirely coherent and consistent if seen in terms of Tom's moral evolution from feckless and thoughtless eleven-year-old to thoughtful, mature Christian gentleman. Scott does much to eliminate the false dichotomy between the idea of Part 1 as realistic and Part 2 as pious fiction. But he perhaps overstates his case when he says that:

> The piety and highmindedness of Part 2 of *Tom Brown's Schooldays* was a true presentation of Arnold's Rugby as Hughes would have experienced it, while the gentlemanly philistinism of the first part, authentic enough in its outline, is much closer to previous literary simplification of life at Rugby School. The historian will find safer evidence of Arnold's Rugby in Part Two than in Part One, splendid as that is.[8]

It would be truer to say that the two conventions existed side by side. Many boys passed through the school uninfluenced by Dr Arnold. Bullying, drinking and poaching continued and there were punitive expulsions aimed at eliminating it.[9] Indeed, Thomas Hughes's idolised elder brother George was one of those expelled because as a prefect he had failed to punish those who had broken an Italian's plaster casts. Arnold explained to George's father that he believed that 'those praeposters who had been more active in enforcing the school routine have been unjustly treated with contempt and insult by a larger party of the boys—in fact, either bullied or cut.'[10] Gentlemanly philistinism remained a feature of some Rugby circles and indeed is celebrated by a younger contemporary of Tom Hughes, George Alfred Lawrence, who entered Rugby in 1841 and published in 1857, the same year as *Tom Brown's Schooldays*, his novel *Guy Livingstone*. The hero, first seen at Rugby, is a hard-riding sportsman, who lays an enemy out with a brass candlestick, does as little work as possible and flirts with the headmaster's wife. *Blackwood's Magazine* singled out these opening scenes at Rugby for praise for their realism.[11]

Hughes's novel needs to be seen as part of the continuing ideological battle to secure the victory of Christian gentlemanliness over other forms, particularly the Regency sporting tradition epitomised by Lawrence. In writing *Tom Brown* Hughes was consciously using the novel as a vehicle for ideas, as did so many eminent Victorians, among them F. D. Maurice (*Eustace Conway*), John Henry Newman (*Loss and Gain*), Cardinal Wiseman (*Fabiola*), James Anthony Froude (*Nemesis of Faith*), Benjamin Disraeli and Charles Kingsley. Novels were in the nineteenth century, in a way they no longer are, part of the intellectual and moral debate.

The idea of writing a story about Rugby came to Hughes when he considered what he wanted to tell his eight-year-old son Maurice about school. He thought a story would be the best way and wrote most of it in the long vacation of 1856. He told his friend J. M. Ludlow that 'he thought that good might be done by a real novel for boys—not didactic like *Sandford and Merton*—written in a right spirit but distinctly aiming at being interesting'. He showed Ludlow what he had written and Ludlow insisted that it should be published. He sent it to Alexander Macmillan, a strong supporter of the Christian Socialist movement, and Macmillan undertook to publish it.[12] The completion of the book was delayed by the death of Hughes's eldest daughter Evie from scarlet fever, but he completed it in 1857. Charles Kingsley, who saw the finished book in February 1857, wrote enthusiastically to Macmillan: 'It is an extraordinary book . . . I should have been proud to have written that book, word for word, as it stands . . . As sure as eggs are eggs, the book will pay both of you well.'[13] The book appeared anonymously, dedicated to Mrs Arnold and attributed to 'An Old Boy'. But the secret of the authorship was soon disclosed and made Hughes a celebrity.

Mention of Thomas Day's *Sandford and Merton* by Hughes is intriguing. A heavily moralistic tale of a boy's education, it was the leading children's book before *Tom Brown*. It had been read by Hughes in boyhood and had been reprinted in the 1850s as part of the growing interest in education. Gerald Redmond sees some similarities between the description of Tom's fight with Slogger Williams and that between Harry Sandford and Master Mash in *Sandford and Merton*.[14] But whatever literary influences, conscious or unconscious, were exercised on Hughes, his principal inspiration was unquestionably his own schooldays.

Hughes always insisted that *Tom Brown's Schooldays* was not autobiographical and that Tom was merely 'the commonest type of English boy of the upper middle class'.[15] But no one ever believed him. His friend, Llewellyn Davies, writing his *Dictionary of National Biography* notice, repeated Hughes's denial of identification but added gently, 'The sentiments and doings ascribed to Tom Brown were, by Hughes' account, those of the kind of boy that Hughes was'.[16] Professor John Conington, a contemporary of Hughes at Rugby, described him as 'on the whole very like Tom Brown, only not so intellectual'.[17] Thomas Arnold, Jr, the Doctor's son, recalled Tom Hughes at fifteen as:

> tall for his age; his long thin face, his sandy hair, and his length of limb, and spare frame, gave him a lankiness of aspect which was the cause, I suppose, that the boys gave him the extraordinary nickname of 'executioner'. No name could be less appropriate, for there was nothing inhuman or morose or surly in his looks, and still less in his disposition; the temper of a bully was utterly alien from him, and he was always cheerful and gay. He was one of the best runners in the school . . . all the small boys liked him because he was kind and friendly to them.[18]

It is the picture of Tom Brown. Hughes was regularly referred to in the press as Tom Brown and his election handbills in Lambeth included the words 'Vote for Tom Brown'. It is in fact perfectly clear that much of the book is autobiographical.

Hughes, the second of eight children of John and Margaret Hughes, was born at Uffington, Berkshire, in 1822 and brought up in the Vale of the White Horse. He was steeped in the countryside, in country ways and country sports, and he set much of the action of the early part of the book in that area. Hughes's father, a man of 'true popular sympathies', an old Tory paternalist, who played cricket and football with the villagers but insisted on obedience and deference, is idealised in the book as Squire Brown.

In 1833 John Hughes sent Tom to Rugby, although he did not agree with Arnold's politics, because he had faith in his character and abilities. There Tom endured fagging and bullying, but developed self-reliance, courage, sportsmanship, made friends and became captain of football and cricket. He led the school eleven in a memorable match against an M.C.C. eleven, captained by Lord Charles Russell, on 17 June 1841. The match is described in detail at the climax of the book.

The inspiration of many of the episodes and characters in *Tom Brown* is known, thanks to the tireless work of Colonel Sydney Selfe, who corresponded extensively with friends and contemporaries of Hughes to establish the facts.[19] Genuine episodes from Rugby life were woven into the text. Arnold hitting a boy in form because he believed him to be lying is based on a celebrated incident in which the Doctor flogged a boy called March wrongly for lying; he later apologised to the boy. The battle with a local landowner's gamekeepers occurred; the landowner was Boughton Leigh. The incident with the ducks actually happened to George Hughes. The praying Arthur being mocked and bullied was based on an incident involving Isaac Newton Fellowes, the future Lord Portsmouth, as Hughes revealed in a letter in 1895. The fever outbreak was modelled on an actual epidemic. Several old boys recalled roastings similar to that endured by Tom. The fight between Tom and Slogger Williams was based on a fight between Augustus Orlebar and Bulkeley Owen Jones, both later Church of England clergymen.

Many of the characters similarly had their basis in reality. Dr Arnold and his wife and the college servants (Mrs Wixie, Old Thos, Sam and Bogle), Sally Harrowell and Stumps, and Mr Benjamin Aislabie of the M.C.C. were all real-life characters. The Young Master at the end has been identified as G. E. L. Cotton. Harry 'Scud' East was based on William Patrick Adam, subsequently Liberal whip in the Commons and Governor of Madras. His nickname at school was 'Scud'. J. G. Hollway, an intimate of Hughes, wrote to Colonel Selfe, 'Flashman the bully is a painfully correct photograph of — — I won't recall his name'. Martin was based partly on H. C. 'Taxidermy' Taylor and partly on 'the wild, blue-eyed' Edwin Shapland. George Arthur has been variously attributed. *The Dictionary of National Biography* believed that he was based on Arthur Stanley, a view widely held in the nineteenth century.[20] Certainly George Arthur resembles the young Arthur Stanley in more than just his name. Stanley had arrived at Rugby at thirteen, an unathletic boy who was nicknamed 'Nancy' and scorned for not playing games. But he later earned respect for his religious beliefs and intellectual powers. Hughes had tea with Stanley, by then in the sixth form, when he first arrived at Rugby and would have imbibed the legend of the brilliant boy while there in sufficient detail to inspire his character of George Arthur. Mrs Hughes denied absolutely that Arthur was Stanley, and Colonel Selfe supported her in this, arguing that Arthur was chiefly based on Henry Walrond.[21] But Mrs Hughes claimed wrongly that Stanley and her husband had never met at Rugby, so her testimony is flawed.

Even minor characters were inspired by Hughes's Rugby contemporaries. Holmes the praeposter ('one of the best boys in the school') is Septimus Cox Holmes Hansard, son of the printer and later Rector of Bethnal Green. Osbert 'who could throw a cricket ball from the Little Side Ground over the rook trees to the Doctor's walk' is William Cotton Oswell, explorer and hunter, who accomplished a similar feat. 'Crab' Jones is Edmund 'Crab' Smyth, later a colonel in the Indian Army. 'Tadpole' Hall is George Granville Bradley, later Master of Marlborough and Dean of Westminster.

Intellectual matters play little part in *Tom Brown's Schooldays* because Thomas Hughes himself was not very academic and was not part of Dr Arnold's inner circle of the intellectual elite. But Arnold persevered with Hughes, encouraging his taste for literature and history. Hughes grew to revere him for three main reasons. First, there were his sermons and his vigorous and enthusiastic Christian commitment, the effect of which on boys Hughes faithfully reports. Second, there was his method of teaching, using Scott's novels as illustrations in his classics lessons and preaching the need for inter-class harmony and sympathy in history lessons. When he went up to Oriel College, Oxford, Hughes discovered Carlyle, saw conditions in the country for himself and was converted from Toryism to radical Liberalism, retrospectively therefore moving closer to Arnold's political and social viewpoint. Third, there was Arnold's generosity in inviting George Hughes to stay at his Lakeland holiday home at Fox Howe after he had been expelled, and writing a friendly letter of reproach rather than punishing him when Tom organised and attended a School House supper against Arnold's orders.[22]

After Oxford, Hughes was called to the bar and became in due course a QC and a Liberal MP. He became a leading member of the Christian Socialist movement, a disciple of F. D. Maurice and from 1872 to 1883 Principal of the Working Men's College. He was a stalwart of the Volunteer movement, seeing it as providing a vital bridge between the classes. An immensely attractive and likable figure, great-hearted, industrious, cheerful and enthusiastic, Hughes devoted his life to the promotion of greater sympathy between the classes on the basis of a shared Christianity. A passionate opponent of snobbery, intolerance and cruelty, he opposed colour prejudice, promoted the idea of industrial partnership and was an advocate of trade union rights. Hughes's 'childlike heart, knightly loyalty, humane geniality and simple Christian faith' made him in a sense 'the centre of the movement', said an early historian of Christian Socialism.[23] Hughes ended his days as a county court judge in Chester, after an unsuccessful attempt to start a utopian settlement of ex-public schoolboys called Rugby in the United States.[24]

Three parallel themes are explored in *Tom Brown* and they are central to Victorian culture and society. The first is Tom's socialisation into the institution, his acceptance of hierarchy, privilege and responsibility; the second is the inculcation of manliness, and the third his religious awakening. *Tom Brown* is, first of all, a classic exposition of the socialisation of the English public school boy, a detailed account of the moral and spiritual education of an ideal and idealised Christian gentleman. It fits precisely the model of socialisation outlined by Ian Weinberg.

Socialisation. In Weinberg's model the new boy is subject initially to *rites de passage*, systematic humiliations involving compulsory singing, bullying and fagging.[25] This serves 'to erase all of his former statuses, whether of family, class or preparatory school. He loses his means of defence against the institution and is a *tabula rasa* for a new "total identity" to be imprinted by the public school. Any confidence or rebelliousness is drubbed out of him.' The new boy is also instructed in the layout, lore and slang of the school, which signals his acceptance into the new community.

Once the new boys have become established they enter the middle phase of their school existence, when they have integrated into the school but not yet achieved the authority of the prefectorial elite. It is at this stage that they rebel against the authority of the older boys and the masters, and bully smaller boys. Weinberg observes, 'The boys in the middling stratum are the most troublesome because they are gaining their full physical strength and they wish to test their independence in an environment which is now familiar.' Rebellion can take different forms—withdrawal into oneself and out of the system, breaking the rules (against smoking, bounds, sexual activity) or withdrawal into intellectual pursuits and eccentricity, something which Weinberg notes is 'tolerated and perhaps even respected'.

The school has ways of dealing with rebellion, however. One is close supervision and the enforcement of rules by prefects and masters. Another is 'emphasising *superordinate* goals in daily activities', in particular loyalty to the school and house in sporting and academic competition. But it is also helped in part by the boys themselves, who develop a set of codes in order to survive, codes which 'serve to protect the inmate's self against authority, and make it easier to live a non-private life among peers'. This involves not stealing from or cheating other boys, bearing irritation with self-control, not 'squealing' on other boys and asserting 'manliness' via sport in order to define oneself as a male at a time of segregation from the opposite sex. But these norms have the effect of stabilising rather than disrupting traditional rules and procedures, and because the norms are a form of social control imposed by the boys on each other they enable headmaster and staff to keep aloof from the petty details of routine and discipline.

In due course the rebellious phase ends with acceptance into the elite, the prefects. For, despite the rebellion, the boy in general 'accepts the institution's view of him and conforms to its demands'. Boys recognise and accept the hierarchy of school society in the expectation of eventual accession to the elite.

Tom Brown thus begins with Tom's emancipation from the family and the protection of womenfolk and his emergence into a world of boys, first by playing with the village boys and then attending a private school, characterised by bullying, tale-telling, inadequate supervision and a defective educational philosophy which contrasts with that of

Rugby: 'The object of all schools is not to ram Latin and Greek into boys but to make them good English boys, good future citizens.'[26]

When the private school closes on account of fever, Tom is sent to Rugby (the year is 183–). His father, Squire Brown, meditates on what to tell Tom:

> Shall I tell him to mind his work, and say he's sent to school to make himself a good scholar? Well but he isn't sent to school for that—at any rate, not for that mainly. I don't care a straw for Greek particles or the digamma; no more does his mother . . . If he'll only turn out a brave, helpful, truthtelling Englishman and a gentleman and a Christian, that's all I want.[27]

So his advice to Tom is 'Tell the truth, keep a brave and kind heart and never listen to or say anything you wouldn't have your mother and sister hear, and you'll never feel ashamed to come home or we to see you.' So the agenda for education is clearly set out and parallels exactly Dr Arnold's statement that his avowed aim was to create 'a school of Christian gentlemen'. Arnold sought to instil in his pupils 'first, religious and moral principle; second, gentlemanly conduct; third, intellectual ability'.[28] Arnold intended that the list should be in ascending order of importance, the first two being an essential preparation for the third. Hughes, however, takes it in descending order of importance, with intellect seen as much less important than conduct. This in a sense encapsulates the distortion of Arnoldianism which *Tom Brown's Schooldays* represents.

By the end of the book Tom has reached an acceptance and understanding of his father's educational goals for him, as he tells Arthur:

> I want to be A1 at cricket and football and all other games . . . I want to carry away just as much Latin and Greek as will take me through Oxford respectably . . . I want to leave behind me the name of a fellow who never bullied a little boy or turned his back on a big one.[29]

His process of socialisation follows exactly the pattern laid down by Weinberg. First there are the *rites de passage*. East takes Tom round the school, explaining rules and practices, dress regulations and *mores*. Then there is house singing, with each new boy placed on the table in turn and made to sing a song on penalty of drinking a large mug of salt and water if he resists or breaks down. There is fagging, into which Tom enters cheerfully, and bullying, with Tom tossed in a blanket by Flashman and company on his first day, but pluckily taking it.

The middle-school phase of rebellion comes next. Discipline in School House breaks down once Old Brooke leaves. The new praeposters are either small, clever boys with neither the strength of body or character to govern (i.e. intellect without character) or big boys of the wrong sort with no sense of responsibility (i.e. strength without character). So there is bullying, as fifth-form boys of the sporting and drinking set who have age and experience but not yet authority join forces with irresponsible praeposters to tyrannise over younger boys. This leads to the celebrated roasting of Tom. But Tom and East organise resistance to the fagging, take on and fight Flashman and the bullying declines, particularly after Flashman is expelled for being found hopelessly drunk.

But Tom and East not only rebel against bullying, they also rebel against rules and authority in that demonstration of independence and muscle-flexing that Weinberg postulates. Tom and East become outlaws, 'Ishmaelites, their hands against everyone and everyone's hands against them'. They break bounds, fish illegally and, when caught, are flogged.

The eccentrics also fulfil the role perceived by Weinberg. At Rugby Diggs and Martin are loners, pursuing their interests (naturalism, chemistry) outside the usual schoolboy range, and are left alone. They also intervene, Diggs to protect Tom and East from Flashman and Martin to defend Arthur.

The school's way of dealing with rebellion are all implemented. The inculcation of house loyalty begins on the first day, when Tom participates in the big game between the School House and the rest of the school, post-game feast and sing-song. He witnesses the keynote speech of house captain, Old Brooke, with the toast: 'dear old School House—the best house of the best school in England'. This prompts one of Hughes's many homiletic asides to his reader, apologising for his excessive school patriotism, but adding, 'Would you, any of you, give a fig for a fellow who didn't believe in and stand up for his own house and his own school,' assuming a common experience in his readers.[30] The boys' code is seen in force with Tom admired for not sneaking to the masters on his ill treatment by Flashman. Indeed, Tom's conduct in the face of gross ill treatment, his acceptance and silence about it, help shame some of the bullies. Finally, there is magisterial supervision. The Doctor watches over the career of Tom and East, warns them that they are in danger of expulsion if they carry on as they are doing and rescues Tom from perdition by assigning the frail and timid new boy George Arthur to his care, causing him to blossom into a new sense of responsibility. Tom ends up as captain of cricket, pillar of the school and exponent of all the virtues and values of the public school system.

Manliness. Hughes was well aware of the boy's need to assert and demonstrate his masculinity, and his book therefore sought to advocate a particular form of manliness. The form which Hughes espoused was that which was satirically labelled 'muscular Christianity' and of which he and Charles Kingsley were the most celebrated exponents. Kingsley disliked the term but Hughes willingly embraced it, providing a very careful definition of it in *Tom Brown at Oxford*, distinguishing muscular Christians from those whom he calls mere 'musclemen':

> The only point in common between the two being, that both hold it to be a good thing to have strong and well-exercised bodies, ready to be put at the shortest notice to any work of which bodies are capable, and to do it well. Here all likeness ends; for the 'muscleman' seems to have no belief whatever as to the purposes for which his body has been given him, except some hazy idea that it is to go up and down the world with him, belabouring men and captivating women for his benefit or pleasure, at once the servant and fomenter of those fierce and brutal passions which he seems to think it a necessity, and rather a fine thing than otherwise, to indulge and obey. Whereas, so far as I know, the least of the muscular Christians has hold of the old chivalrous and Christian belief, that a man's body is given him to be trained and brought into subjection, and then used for the protection of the weak, the advancement of all righteous causes and the subduing of the earth which God has given to the children of men.[31]

This clearly points to the context within which Hughes was preaching, an ideological contest between rival versions of manliness. It was one in which indeed Hughes can be said to have joined battle with an influential fellow Rugbean, George Alfred Lawrence.

Few areas of Hughes's writing have become so controversial as Part 2, chapter 5, of *Tom Brown*, with its graphic account of the fight between Tom and Slogger Williams and its long disquisitions on the value of fighting. But passages from this chapter are regularly taken out of context to demonstrate that Hughes was progenitor of a brutal philistinism.[32] The most celebrated are:

> After all, what would life be without fighting, I should like to know? From the cradle to the grave, fighting, rightly understood, is the business, the real, highest, honestest business of every son of Man.[33]

and:

> Boys will quarrel and when they quarrel, they will sometimes fight. Fighting with fists is the natural and English way for English boys to settle their quarrels. What substitute for it is there, amongst any nation under the sun?[34]

But critics of Hughes almost invariably omit his qualifications. 'Fighting, rightly understood' is the key phrase. He goes on to give a broad definition of fighting: 'Everyone who is worth his salt has his enemies who must be beaten, be they evil thoughts and habits in himself or spiritual wickedness in high places, or Russian or border-ruffians, or Bill, Tom or Harry, who will not let him live his life in quiet till he has thrashed them.'[35] 'Struggle' might be a better word than fighting, for Hughes's fighting includes self-conquest, moral crusading, imperial defence and self-defence. His second passage continues:

> As to fighting, keep out of it if you can by all means. When time comes, if it ever should, that you have to say 'Yes' or 'No' to a challenge to fight, say 'No' if you can . . . It's proof of the highest courage and one from true Christian motives. It's quite right and justifiable if done from a simple aversion to physical pain and danger. But don't say 'No' because you fear a licking, and say or think it's because you fear God, for that's neither Christian nor honest.[36]

Now this is very far from being an unqualified endorsement of brutishness. It is a clear desire to direct man's natural aggressive instincts into proper, productive channels. Hughes advocated boxing as much for its efficacy in keeping men fit as for its use in fighting. He was himself a keen exponent and taught it at the Working Men's College. In his definition of fighting he was following his mentor, Carlyle, who wrote:

> Man is created to fight; he is perhaps best of all definable as a born soldier; his life 'a battle and a march' under the right General. It is for ever indispensable for a man to fight: now with Necessity, with Barenness, Scarcity, with Puddles, Bogs, tangled Forests, unkempt Cotton—now also with the hallucinations of his poor fellow Men.[37]

The idea that Hughes advocated merely physical courage and athletic proficiency is wholly bogus: that was the ethic of his rivals. That great set piece, the fight between Tom and Slogger Williams, is provoked by the bullying of Arthur and ends with the combatants shaking hands— the quintessence of muscular Christianity, fighting for a just cause and as a last resort. It is the promotion of an ethic of fighting which seeks to civilise and humanise the sheer brutality and cruelty of life in the unreformed public school and to counteract the neo-Regency aristocratic philistinism of Lawrence and his school of writers.

Hughes elaborated further on manliness in *The Manliness of Christ*, which he defined not just as physical courage or athletic proficiency. He defined it as tenderness and thoughtfulness for others, readiness to bear pain and even death, unswerving loyalty to truth, subordination of the human will to one's sense of duty. Tom Brown embodies these qualities exactly. Hughes adds; 'True manliness is as likely to be found in a weak as in a strong body . . . a great athlete may be a brute or a coward, while a truly manly man can be neither'.[38] Nor is manliness an exclusive attribute of the upper class. Hughes gives examples of it from all classes: imperial episodes of self-sacrifice by ordinary soldiers in the storming of Badajoz and the sinking of the *Birkenhead*, miners at Pontypridd working day and night to rescue friends, a gambler at St Louis losing his life rescuing women and children from a fire. In

Tom Brown the village boys Tom plays with are described as 'manly' and so too are Dr Arnold and Arthur's clergyman father.

This is Christian Manliness, whose emergence has been sensitively and sympathetically traced by Norman Vance.[39] It emerged from the religious upheavals of the mid-Victorian period, in particular the dispute between Kingsley and John Henry Newman about the nature of Christianity. Kingsley could not accept the rejection of the physical world that Newman was advancing, stressing instead the importance of direct Christian action in the world. He was equally opposed to the promotion of celibacy, asceticism and what he saw as 'fastidious, maundering, die-away effeminacy'. So Kingsley articulated a comprehensive alternative world view in his novels, where discussions of contemporary social and political problems rubbed shoulders with satire, moralising and *mens sana in corpore sano* propaganda. The principal elements in this world view were the promotion of physical strength, courage, health, the importance of family life and married love, the elements of duty and service to mankind and the scientific study of the natural world to discover the divine pattern of the moral universe. Hughes differed in some respects from Kingsley, and Kingsley himself differed from the mainstream of manliness advocates by laying stress on the particular importance of married love, something which undoubtedly proceeded from his own highly sexed nature. He placed rather less emphasis on the romantic male friendships that figured strongly in other manly writings, such as those of Hughes.

The ideas of Christian manliness were derived from various intellectual influences, notably Samuel Taylor Coleridge, Thomas Carlyle, Thomas Arnold and F. D. Maurice, whom Vance calls 'traditionalist Radicals'. They rejected the triumphalist gospel of material progress associated with Macaulay and asserted more important moral, spiritual and cultural values, based on the gospel of work, the worship of heroes, the celebration of God in nature, an idealised vision of the past, the promotion of cross-class sympathy. They were not revolutionaries. Arnold's prescription for revolutionaries was 'Flog the rank and file and fling the ringleaders from the Tarpeian rock'.[40] In sum, the aim of Christian Socialists was the regeneration, purification and redirection of the nation through a loving, committed and socially active Christianity, creating the kingdom of God on earth.

Christian manliness was, however, up against an older ideal of manliness, that of the Regency sporting ethic, celebrated by Pierce Egan, which involved physical prowess, courage and endurance but also drinking, gambling and brutality.[41] It was centred on such cruel pursuits as prizefighting, cock-fighting and dog-fighting. Appealing as they did to all classes, these pursuits were seen as democratic, patriotic and the source of national strength. This ethic, which linked the aristocracy and the lowest classes, was the ethic characterising the un-reformed public school. It was to be driven underground by the purification of society under the impact of Evangelical respectability, but it maintained its hold, with a chivalric veneer, in the novels of G. A. Lawrence, which highlighted war, sport and fighting, and featured hard-riding, hard-drinking, two-fisted, anti-intellectual, godless aristocratic snobs. *The Saturday Review* (12 September 1857) described Guy Livingstone as 'a hero of the iron kind, unequalled for strength of body, will and temper—in boxing and riding, a demigod to his sporting set, and heroically and Byronically overbearing and insolent to the world in general': the epitome of the muscle man.

Games. A vital role in the creation of the muscular Christian was taken by sports and games, properly organised and played.[42] This is the second key element of the book. Early on, Hughes sings the praises of backswording and wrestling, old country pursuits, which are falling into desuetude but which he wants to preserve as bulwarks of manliness, to 'try the muscles of men's bodies and the endurance of their hearts, to make them rejoice in their strength'.[43] But sport also promotes qualities of character. Hughes shows strutting, arrogant Joe Willis beaten by an older man who demonstrates the athletic skill, discipline and moderation in victory that Hughes wants to see in public school sport.

Hughes praises the old stagecoach rides at the expense of the soft and safe train travel boys now enjoy. Those rides tested endurance. Tom's endurance is also tested by the tossing and roasting he un-complainingly endures. But, more important, he takes part in games, from the very day of his arrival and immediate participation in the rugby match between the School House and the rest of the school.

'Are you ready?' 'Yes.' And away comes the ball kicked high in the air, to give the School time to rush on and catch it as it falls. And here they are amongst us. Meet them like Englishmen, you Schoolhouse boys, and charge them home. Now is the time to show what mettle is in you—and there shall be a warm seat by the hall fire, and honour, and lots of bottled beer tonight, for him who does his duty in the next half-hour. And they are well met. Again and again the cloud of their players-up gathers before our goal and comes threatening on, and Warner or Hedge, with young Brooke and the relics of the bulldogs, break through and carry the ball back; and old Brooke ranges the field like Job's warhorse, the thickest scrummage parts asunder before his rush, like the waves before a clipper's bows; his cheery voice rings over the field, and his eye is everywhere. And if these miss the ball, and it rolls dangerously in front of our goal, Crab Jones and his men have seized it and sent it away towards the sides with the unerring drop-kick. This is worth living for; the whole sum of schoolboy existence gathered up into one straining, struggling half-hour, a half-hour worth a year of common life.[44]

Old Brooke's farewell speech to the School House at the sing-song is an important statement of the value of team games:

> Why did we beat em? . . . It's because we've more reliance on one another, more of a house feeling, more fellowship than the School can have. Each of us knows and can depend on his next-hand man better—that's why we beat 'em today. We've union, they've division—there's the secret. (Cheers.)[45]

Games promote team spirit and fellowship. Brooke wants this unity kept up and therefore denounces the evils in School House, which are clearly the opposite of healthy games-playing and team spirit; bullying ('There's nothing breaks up a house like bullying'), drinking ('drinking isn't fine or *manly*, whatever some of you may think of it'; my italics) and opposition to the Doctor's attempts to suppress disreputable old customs.

The same theme recurs at the end of the book in the description of the climactic cricket match. Tom, now nineteen, is captain of cricket, a praeposter, and he talks to the Young Master about cricket:

> 'It's more than a game. It's an institution,' said Tom.
> 'Yes,' said Arthur, 'the birthright of British boys old and young, as *habeas corpus* and trial by jury are of British men.'
> 'The discipline and reliance on one another which it teaches is so valuable, I think . . . it merges the individual in the eleven; he doesn't play that he may win but that his side may.'[46]

The genuinely joyous celebrations of sport were one of the reasons for the book's continuing popularity.

Arnoldianism. The third key aspect of the book, perhaps the most significant in Hughes's eyes, was the religious and moral education of Tom under the guidance of Dr Arnold. As Hughes noted in the preface to the sixth edition, 'He taught us that life is a whole, made up of actions and thoughts and longings, great and small, noble and ignoble; therefore the only true wisdom for boy or man is to bring the whole life into obedience to Him whose world we live in, and who has purchased us with His blood.'[47]

When Tom first arrives at Rugby the Doctor's power is still not fully established. He is unpopular because of his attempts to eradicate old customs. 'There are no such bigoted holders by established forms and customs, be they never so foolish and meaningless, as English school boys,' says Hughes. There was a minority, 'often so small a one as to be countable on the fingers of your hand', totally in sympathy with the doctor's message. But 'he was looked upon with great fear and dislike by the great majority even of his own house.'[48]

But Arnold's success with Tom is to be the measure of his success with the school at large. The Doctor's first substantive appearance in the book is when he preaches in chapel and his sermon is a crucial and vivid setpiece, the first step in Tom's spiritual awakening:

> What was it that moved and held us, the rest of the three hundred reckless, childish boys, who feared the Doctor with all our hearts, and very little besides in heaven and earth; who thought more of our sets in school than of the Church of Christ and put the traditions of Rugby and the public opinion of boys in our daily life above the laws of God.

The Doctor's success lay in the image he presented, not of a man giving advice and warning from above, but:

> the warm, living voice of one who was fighting for us and by our sides and calling on us to help him and ourselves and one another.[49]

He fought against 'whoever was mean and unmanly and unrighteous in our little world' and brought home steadily to a boy the meaning of his life, depicting life as:

> a battlefield, ordained from of old, where there are no spectators but the youngest must take his side, and the stakes are life and death. And he who roused this consciousness in them, showed them at the same time, by every word he spoke in the pulpit, and by his whole daily life, how that battle was to be fought, and stood there before them their fellow soldier and the captain of their band . . . it was this thoroughness and undaunted courage which more than anything else won his way to the hearts of the great mass of those on whom he left his mark and made them believe first in him, and then in his Master. It was this quality above all others which moved such boys as our hero, who had nothing whatever remarkable about him, except excess of boyishness: by which I mean animal life in its fullest measure, good nature and honest impulses, hatred of injustice and meanness, and thoughtlessness enough to sink a three-decker.[50]

As a result of these sermons, Tom 'hardly ever left chapel on Sunday evenings without a serious resolve to stand by and follow the doctor'. This certainly provides justification for Arnold's decision to make the chapel central to school life, to take on the chaplaincy himself and to stress Christian principles as the basis of life.

The image Arnold presented was a stern one. As an Old Rugbeian, Theodore Walrond, recalled, 'In his government of the school he was undoubtedly aided by a natural sternness of aspect and manner,' which made 'all his relations with his pupils rest on a background of awe'.[51] But Hughes also contrived to soften and humanise the Doctor. His very first appearance in the book is when he and his family attend the House game and cheer the team, seeming 'as anxious as any boy for the success of the School House'. Arnold certainly encouraged games and sports for exercise and fitness but was not especially interested in them and certainly not associated with the cult of athleticism. But his appearance here was to lead to his association with the cult in later years. When Tom and 'Tadpole' Hall are lost at 'hare and hounds' and return to the school late, bedraggled and anticipating punishment, Arnold greets them kindly and concernedly, and does not punish them. Arnold is seen in the bosom of his family, carrying a wooden boat, a scene that was 'kindly and homely and comfortable'. Later still Tom joins the Arnold family for tea, and, when the Doctor arrives, 'how frank and kind and *manly* was his greeting'.[52] All this serves to round out the preacher and pedagogue as family man, sports-lover and mentor.

The Doctor is seen in action, working with the sixth form. In one vignette a gross case of bullying occurs, deserving expulsion. The Doctor sends for Holmes, a praeposter, and invokes his aid. Holmes lectures the house on bullying and the bully is beaten. Years later the bully thanks him for making a man of him by the beating, 'the turning point in his character'. He intervenes similarly and also by indirect means to save Tom.

The Doctor, who makes it his business to know about all the boys in the school, their appearance, habits, companions, becomes concerned about Tom and East in their rebellious phase. His solution is to put Tom in charge of George Arthur, a delicate, fatherless child of thirteen new to the school. The second phase of Tom's spiritual education now begins. Tom protects Arthur from bullying and is much mocked for it. When the homesick Arthur kneels to pray in the dormitory and a slipper is thrown at him, Tom retaliates on his behalf. Later Tom himself starts to pray and other boys follow suit. Hughes comments:

> It was no light act of courage in those days, my dear boys, for a little fellow to say his prayers publicly, even at Rugby. A few years later when Arnold's *manly* piety had begun to leaven the school, the tables turned; before he died, in the school-house at least, and I believe in the other house, the rule was the other way. [Italics mine.][53]

Arthur reads his Bible daily, and Tom and East start to do so too. When Arthur is recovering from a near fatal bout of fever he appeals to Tom not to use cribs in his lessons because it is not honest; Tom agrees.

The role of Arthur, much mocked in later, more secular years, is in fact crucial, for it provides the complement to Tom's healthy boyishness. Just as Arthur's influence on Tom and East is spiritually beneficial (Bible-reading, prayer), so theirs on him is physically improving (cricket, swimming, running). Arthur symbolises adult responsibility, spirituality, commitment, the necessary counterbalance to the sturdy manliness, decent instincts and robust common sense of Tom. He is almost the Soul to Tom's Body.

Arthur's influence on Tom is reflected and extended in Tom's influence on East. East admits that he has never been confirmed and does not take the sacrament. Tom persuades him of the value of the sacrament, something that makes you feel part of the great struggle for good. He sends him to see the Doctor and East returns transfigured:

> 'You can't think how kind and gentle he was, the great grim man, whom I've feared more than anybody on earth . . . I can hardly remember what he said, yet; but it seemed to spread round me like healing and strength and light, and to bear me up, and plant me on a rock, where I could hold my footing and fight for myself.'[54]

So by a combination of the Doctor's teachings, the influence of Arthur, his family background and his own innate decency Tom is transformed into an ideal Christian gentleman, unable to do anything but fight for the underdog: 'It was a necessity with him, he couldn't help it any more than he could eating or drinking. He could never play on the strongest side with any heart at football or cricket, and was sure to make friends with any boy who was unpopular or down on his luck.'[55]

At the very end of his career Tom learns from the Young Master that all along Arnold has watched over and guided him, and that separating him from East and putting him with Arthur was his means of ensuring that Tom would get 'manliness and thoughtfulness':

> Up to this time, Tom had never wholly given in to, or understood the Doctor. At first he had thoroughly feared him. For some years, he had learnt to regard him with love and respect and to think him a very great and wise and good man. But, as regarded his own position in the School, of which he was no little proud, Tom had no idea of giving anyone credit for it but himself; and truth to tell, was a very self-conceited young gentleman on the subject . . . It was a new light to him to find that, besides teaching the sixth and governing and guiding the whole school, editing classics, and writing histories, the great Headmaster had found time in those busy years to watch over the career, even of him, Tom Brown, and his particular friends—and, no doubt, of fifty other boys at the same time; and all this without taking the least credit to himself, or seeming to know, or let anyone else know, that he ever thought particularly of any boy at all. However, the Doctor's victory was complete from that moment over Tom Brown at any rate . . . there wasn't a corner of him left which didn't believe in the Doctor.[56]

Soon after, the Doctor dies and the book ends with Tom's moving visit to his tomb and his grief over the loss of the hero who had made him realise his true mission in life.

So the book enshrines the picture of Arnold as the great apostle of the Christian life. How accurate was Hughes's depiction of Arnold's views? Dean Stanley, Arnold's biographer and one of his most famous pupils, claimed that he did not recognise the life of Rugby depicted by Hughes.[57] One of Arnold's masters, James Prince Lee, later Bishop of Manchester, was horrified by the misrepresentation of Arnold's mode of dealing with boys.[58] Matthew Arnold, the Doctor's son, said, 'It gives only one side, and that not the best side, of Rugby School life, or of Arnold's character. It leaves out of view, almost wholly, the intellectual purpose of a school.'[59]

Arnold was unquestionably the most celebrated headmaster of the nineteenth century, thanks to the success of *Tom Brown's Schooldays*. But he had little to do with many of the principal changes affecting the public school during the course of the nineteenth century—the broadening of the curriculum, the introduction of compulsory games, uniformity of dress and stricter social discipline. Nor is it true that he transformed Rugby from barbarism to civilisation. The school was neither as bad under his predecessor nor as good under Arnold as apologists claimed.[60] The extent of his influence was always limited. Dean W. C. Lake, one of his elite, recorded, 'It would be a mistake to suppose that his influence materially changed the character of school life for the ordinary boy.'[61] Arthur Hugh Clough, another of the elite, wrote while there, 'Even here at Rugby . . . there is a vast deal of bad.'[62] Arnold himself was only too aware that conditions in school varied according to the character and capabilities of the prefects. In his last sermon he declared his anxiety 'that our good seems to want a principal stability: to depend so much on individuals. When everything in past years has been most promising, I have seen a great change suddenly produced after a single vacation; and what we hoped had been the real improvement of the school, was proved to have been no more than the present effect produced by a number of individuals.'[63] But even if the full weight of his 'Godliness and Good Learning' fully touched only an elite, his moral influence and character training reached further. Theodore Walrond insisted, 'Not in the universities only, but in the army and elsewhere, it came more and more to be observed that Arnold's pupils were, to a degree unusual at that time, thoughtful, manly-minded, and conscious of duty and obligation.'[64] The very evidence of the conversion of the ordinary and unintellectual Tom Hughes lends credence to that claim.

Arnold did lay stress on the training of character, and, as Jonathan Gathorne-Hardy puts it, 'School as a place to train character—a totally new concept so far—was what came to distinguish the English public school from all other Western school systems. It was what amazed and impressed foreigners—and amazes them still.'[65] Arnold's principal means of doing this was to make the chapel the focus of school life, to stress Christian values and to gear the school to the production of Christian gentlemen, with the emphasis on the Christian: 'He is not well educated who does not know the will of God or knowing it, has received no help in his education towards being inclined and enabled to do it.'[66] He was the first headmaster to take on the school chaplaincy. His ideas were set out in his sermons which became a high point of schoolboy life and were aimed at the improvement and shaping of character and outlook. He quoted with approval John Bowdler's description of public schools as 'the very seats and nurseries of vice':

> That is properly a nursery of vice where a boy unlearns the pure and honest principles which he may have received at home, and gets in their stead, others which are utterly low and base and mischievous—where he loses his modesty, his respect for truth, and his affectionateness, and becomes coarse, and false and unfeeling. That too is a nursery of vice, and most fearfully so, where vice is bold, and forward, and presuming; and goodness is timid and shy, and existing as if by sufferance—where the good, instead of setting the tone of society, and branding with disgrace those who disregard it, and themselves exposed to reproach for their goodness, and shrink before the open avowal of evil principles, which the bad are trying to make the law of the community. That is a nursery of vice where the restraints laid upon evil are considered as so much taken from liberty, and where, generally speaking, evil is more willingly screened and concealed, than detected and punished. What society would be, if men regarded the laws of God and man as a grievance, and thought liberty consisted in following to the full their proud, and selfish, and low inclination—that schools to a great extent are; and therefore, they may be well called 'the seats and nurseries of vice'.[67]

In another sermon he specifies the evils existing in schools as direct sensual wickedness, such as drunkenness, the systematic practice of falsehood, cruelty and bullying, a spirit of active disobedience, general idleness, a spirit of combination in evil.[68] Of these Arnold felt that lying and the spirit of combination were the most serious sins at Rugby, but that there was also some evidence of bullying and idleness.

The principal remedy for all this was of course religion. But, coupled with religion, he believed also in the cultivation of the intellect. He believed it to be a moral duty. 'I am quite sure that it is a most solemn duty to cultivate our understanding to the uttermost . . . I am satisfied that a neglected intellect is far oftener the cause of mischief to a man than a perverted or overvalued one,' he wrote in a letter.[69] In a sermon he said, 'You are called upon like all other persons to make yourselves, as far as you can, strong and active and healthful and patient in your bodies, yet your especial call is rather to improve your minds because it is with your minds that God calls you to work hereafter.'[70] He sought to instil a love of learning and was always most at home and most comfortable with his intellectual elite, boys like Arthur Penrhyn Stanley, Charles James Vaughan, Arthur Hugh Clough, William Charles Lake and his son, Matthew Arnold, who went on to distinguished scholarly and ecclesiastical careers, though in some cases also to loss of faith.[71]

Arnold's special efforts were reserved for his intellectual elite: 'I do enjoy the society of youths of seventeen or eighteen, for they are all alive in limbs and spirits at least, if not in mind, while in older persons the body and spirits often become languid without the mind gaining any vigour to compensate for it.'[72] But critics of Arnold, including some of the elite in later life, felt that he pushed bright boys too hard, leading to overstrain and intellectual burn-out. Dean Lake suggested, 'I have always thought that it was the average idle boy, such as those whom *Tom Brown* describes, who were most improved, and more in their after life than at school, by Arnold's training and example,' and he himself bitterly regretted in later life abandoning his friends of the cricket and football fields and devoting himself exclusively to intellectual companions like Vaughan and Stanley.[73]

Apart from the chapel, Arnold utilised existing institutions to pursue his aims. He made great use of the prefectorial system, using the sixth form as his allies, to allow his ideas to filter down. He raised the prestige, increased the salaries and improved the conditions of the teaching staff, securing their support as well. He used corporal punishment sparingly, and then only on the younger boys and for moral offences (lying, drinking, sloth). But he made regular use of punitive expulsions ('It is not necessary that this should be a school of three hundred, or even one hundred boys, but it *is* necessary that it should be a school of Christian gentlemen').[74] He encouraged games and sports, as well as nature rambles, for exercise, but not the cult of athleticism.

Arnold's significance was that he symbolised the new tone that was taking over society. His view can be summed up as 'Godliness and Good Learning' and it was a view that others besides Arnold were advancing. But his articulation of it, promoted by Dean Stanley's life, which Sir Joshua Fitch, Her Majesty's Inspector of Training Colleges, called 'one of the best biographies in our language',[75] and popularised with variations by Hughes, made Arnold the standard-bearer of the new moral earnestness and commitment to personal and social improvement which was the characterising hallmark of early and mid-Victorian society. Certainly his disciples, Vaughan, Cotton and Prince Lee, who all became headmasters, consciously advocated 'Arnoldian' ideas. The intellectual leaders of the movement were, as David Newsome put it, 'a single class stamped with an unmistakable mint mark: a combination of intellectual toughness, moral earnestness and deep spiritual conviction'.[76] This earnestness, the product of the Evangelical revival, gave Victorian England its philanthropy, its missionary zeal, its paternalism, its reformist impulse and its puritanism. As Newsome says, 'The application of the doctrine of godliness and good learning to the upbringing of boys in the public schools did much to create that breed of diligent, earnest, intellectual eminent Victorians which has left its impress on almost every aspect of the age.'[77]

Arnold's celebrated encapsulation of his aim—to instil religious and moral principle, gentlemanly conduct and intellectual ability—has been much misunderstood. Taken at face value, it has been alleged to mean an order of priorities with intellect coming last. But this is a clear contradiction of his oft-stated commitment to intellectual activity. It is an order of priority which recognises the reality of the situation. Without the first two qualities, intellectual ability is useless. But also the first two needed to be instilled as part of the campaign against the unreformed public school which Arnold found—the system of boy republics with masters and boys in open warfare, boys ruling themselves and perpetuating savagery, bullying and drunkenness. Arnold was perfectly clear about the situation he faced. He outlined it in his sermons, and if the sermons are read in conjunction with Hughes's book it is clear that in some respects the latter is almost a dramatisation of the former. Hughes vividly illustrates drunkenness, lying, bullying and the spirit of combination. The battle between good and evil Arnold discerned is fought in those terms in *Tom Brown*, with Tom epitomising the modesty, affectionateness and respect for truth that Arnold admires. In more general terms, the other aspects of Arnold's regime come out fully. The centrality of chapel and the impact of the Doctor's sermons are brought home. The value of the prefectorial system is illustrated, with Brooke and Holmes supporting and furthering the Doctor's work and with the prefectorial duties making a man of East ('he rose to the situation and burnt his cigar-cases, and gave away his pistols and pondered on the constitutional authority of the sixth and his new duties . . . ay, and no fellow ever acted up to them better').[78] The expulsion of wrongdoers is graphically demonstrated.

There are, however, some differences of emphasis. The Doctor wanted fighting stopped. But Hughes approved of it, when necessary. Rather more significant is the fact that intellectual life plays a minor role in the book, and this reflects Hughes's own experience. He was not an academic boy; his critics (Stanley, Matthew Arnold) were. So godliness plays a much greater role than good learning in *Tom Brown*. When Old Brooke says, 'I know I'd sooner win two school-house matches running than get the Balliol scholarship,' he is reflecting a feeling common among the generality of boys.[79] Hughes gave voice to it himself in an address at Rugby in 1894 at the unveiling of a memorial to William Cotton Oswell:

> Though we small boys were proud in a way of Stanley and Vaughan, of Clough and Burbidge, and other scholars and poets, we looked on them more as providential providers of extra half-holidays than with the enthusiasm of hero-worship. This we reserved for the kings of the Close, round whom clustered legends of personal encounters with drovers at the monthly cattle-fairs . . . or the navvies who were laying down the first line of the London and

North Western Railway or the game-keepers of a neighbouring squire with whom the school was in a state of open war over the right of fishing in the Avon.[80]

Academic work appears only in a short passage dealing with methods of doing the *vulgus*, a short exercise in writing a Latin or Greek verse on a set subject or in a discussion of the ethics of cribbing between Tom and East.[81] As for the rest, there is none of the joy in scholarship, intellectual enquiry or book learning that characterised the true Arnoldian. But the true Arnoldian was probably as rare as George Arthur, who goes rapidly up the school and is at its head by sixteen, but is 'no longer a boy, less of a boy in fact than Tom', who is a year older. This serious, intense intellectual, old beyond his years, is the authentic Arnoldian. But he is not the book's hero.

Hero worship. Aside from the three main threads of the story, *Tom Brown's Schooldays* has received the impress of many of the intellectual and ideological movements of the era, which Hughes himself embraced and embodied, and it is this which makes *Tom Brown's Schooldays* one of the most representative books of its age. First, there is hero worship. The nineteenth century was pre-eminently the age of hero worship, the cult defined and promoted by Thomas Carlyle, who believed that:

> Universal History, the history of what man has accomplished in this world, is at bottom the History of the Great Men who have worked here. They were the leaders of men, these great ones; the modellers, patterns, and in a wide sense creators, of whatsoever the general mass of men contrived to do or to attain; all things that we see standing, accomplished in the world are properly the outer material result, the practical realization and embodiment, of Thoughts that dwelt in the Great Men sent into the world: the soul of the whole world's history, it may justly be considered, were the history of these.[82]

It was, according to Walter E. Houghton, the product of the combination of the enthusiastic temper, the concept of the superior being, the revival of Homeric mythology and medieval balladry, the popularity of Scott and Byron, the experience of Napoleon and his age.[83] It flourished as a bulwark against the dominance of the commercial spirit, to meet the need for moral exemplars to resist or promote change, to provide symbols of an Age of Industry and Empire.

Hughes was a hero worshipper, his worship in turn being directed towards his elder brother George, Dr Arnold and F. D. Maurice. The latter he variously described as 'the best and wisest Englishman who ever lived' and 'the greatest figure since St Paul'. He wrote hero-worshipping biographies of, among others, his brother George, Dr David Livingstone and Alfred the Great. He also penned encomia to two former schoolfellows who went on to become heroes of the empire. One was William Hodson of Hodson's Horse, a hero of the Indian Mutiny, who died in action in 1857. Hughes remembered him as 'a bright, pleasant boy, fond of fun, and with abilities decidedly above the average, but of no very marked distinction, except as a runner, in which exercise . . . he was almost unequalled and showed great powers of endurance'.[84] But his heroic service and death in India made him 'a glorious Christian soldier and Englishman'. Hughes was embodying contemporary public opinion when he wrote of the Mutiny, 'In all her long and stern history, England can point to no nobler sons than these, the heroes of India in 1857.'[85]

William Cotton Oswell was a hero of Hughes's at school and after, and when he addressed Rugby on the subject of Oswell in 1894 he began by saying, 'I hope you boys in this last decade of the century are as great hero-worshippers as we were in the fourth.' Oswell struck the young Hughes as standing out from the rest 'as Hector from the ruck of Tojan princes'. It was the rare mixture of kindliness and gentleness with marvellous strength, activity and fearlessness, which made him *facile princeps* among his contemporaries. I don't believe he ever struck a small boy here, or even spoke to one in anger.'[86] Six feet tall, perfectly developed, a sporting hero, nicknamed 'The Muscleman', he served in India as collector and judge, then travelled to Africa as explorer, big game hunter and friend and companion to Livingstone. Sir Samuel Baker dubbed Oswell 'the Nimrod of South Africa, without a rival and without an enemy, the greatest hunter ever known in modern times, the truest friend and most thorough example of an English gentleman'.[87] The Old Etonian Lord Rendel described him as 'manliness without coarseness, polish without complacency, nobility without caste. May Rugby keep the mould and multiply the type.' To which Hughes adds, 'amen'.[88] It was these men of principle and action that Hughes held up as role models for the youth of Britain. They were the sort of men that Tom Brown would have grown into.

Like his creator, Tom Brown is also a hero worshipper. In the village he is devoted to handsome, intelligent Harry Winburn ('the quickest and best boy in the parish . . . the Crichton of our village'), who can wrestle, climb and run better than anyone else and gives Tom valuable wrestling lessons. At private school he has an unnamed schoolfellow hero, whom he partners in many scrapes. He looks up at Rugby to Old Brooke, and finally ends up worshipping Arnold as 'a heroworshipper who would have satisfied the soul of Thomas Carlyle'.

Ruralism. Hughes saw the true source of national strength as residing in the countryside.[89] He expressed in the opening chapters of *Tom Brown* his distaste for the transformation of the countryside in particular and society in general by industrialisation and its agent, the railways. The railways had decisively altered the old static, stable life: 'We are a vagabond nation now, that's certain . . . The Queen sets us the example—we are moving on from top to bottom.'[90] This is said in tones of deep regret, and it is perhaps one reason why he made his childhood reminiscences so vibrant. As Raymond Chapman points out, so many of the great Victorians had been children in the Regency period, and when they grew up to live in a transformed world they looked back with regret to that era, which became suffused with innocence, and imbued with qualities which the modern age seemed to be losing—order, calm, stability, unhurriedness.[91] Like Dickens, Hughes celebrates the stagecoach age, and rejoices in the old coaching days, penning an exhilarating account of Tom's journey to school by coach which remains one of the great coaching passages.

His love of the countryside, country sports and pursuits, of rural myths and legends, coupled with his regret about change, its agencies and effects, is encapsulated in one of many passages apostrophising his young readers:

Oh, young England! young England! You who are born into these racing rail-road times, when there's a Great Exhibition, or some monster sight, every year; and you can get over a couple of thousand miles of ground for three pounds ten, in a five weeks' holiday; why don't you know more of your own birth-places? You're all in the ends of the earth, it seems to me, as soon as you get your necks out of the educational collar, for Midsummer holidays, long vacations or what not . . . And when you get home for a quiet fortnight, you turn the steam off, and lie on your backs in the paternal garden, surrounded by the last batch of books from Mudie's library, and half bored to death . . . Now, in my time, when we got home by the old coach, which put us down at the cross-roads with our boxes, the first day of the holidays, and had been driven off by the family coachman, singing 'Dulce Domum' at the top of our voices, there we were, fixtures, till black Monday came round. We had to cut out our own amusements within a walk or a ride of home. And so we got to know all the country folk, and their ways and songs and stories, by heart; and went over the fields, and woods, and hills, again and again, till we made friends of them all. We were Berkshire, or Gloucestershire, or Yorkshire boys; and you're young cosmopolites, belonging to all counties and no countries.[92]

But there is more than mere nostalgia here. He sees rural sports and customs as essential to the cultivation of manliness, both physical and moral, and also to class harmony. He describes wrestling and back-swording—fighting with sticks—and laments its decline. He lovingly evokes the 'veast', the Berkshire equivalent of the Lancashire wakes, the anniversary of the local church's dedication, celebrated with eating, drinking, sports and shows. This allows him to castigate the exclusive-ness of other pastimes, 'class amusements, be they for dukes or ploughboys', which 'always become nuisances and curses to a country. The true charm of cricket and hunting is, that they are still more or less sociable and universal; there's a place for every man who will come and take part.'[93]

He sees the decline of rural sports, then, as a threat both to democracy and to manliness, and he fears that overly intellectual and refined efforts to reform the working classes will fail, increasing class division. His answer is, of course, the inculcation of muscular Christianity, as much a recipe for a moral working class as for a moral gentry:

> Don't let reformers of any sort think that they are going to lay hold of the working boys and young men of England by any educational grapnel whatever, which hasn't some *bona fide* equivalent for the games of the old country 'veast' in it; something to try the muscles of men's bodies and the endurance of their hearts, to make them rejoice in their strength. In all the new fangled comprehensive plans which I see, this is all left out; and the consequence is that your great Mechanics' Institutes end in intellectual priggism and your Christian Young Men's Societies in Religious Pharisaism . . . Life isn't all beer and skittles—but beer and skittles, or something better of the same sort, must form a good part of every Englishman's education.[94]

The proper way to approach the working class is 'to talk to them about what is really at the bottom of your hearts, and box, and run, and row with them, when you have a chance'.[95] Tom is taught rural lore by two old villagers and plays happily with village boys, 'full as manly and honest, and certainly purer, than those in a higher rank'.[96]

Squire Brown is held up as the model of a Tory populist. He believed in social hierarchy and thought loyalty and obedience to it were men's first duties. But he held other social principles, first and foremost:

> The belief that a man is to be valued wholly and solely for that which he is in himself . . . As a necessary corollary to this belief, Squire Brown held further that it didn't matter a straw whether his son associated with lord's sons or ploughman's sons, provided they were brave and honest.[97]

The squire himself had played football and gone birds-nesting with farmers and labourers, so had his father and grandfather. Tom therefore played with the village boys freely. This philosophy, of course, feeds directly into Hughes's Christian Socialism.

But there is more to Hughes's ruralism even than manliness and class harmony. This part of rural Berkshire was closely associated with and inextricably bound up in England's past, historical and mythical. It was the area where St George slew the dragon, where Wayland Smith had his cave, where Alfred defeated the Danes at the battle of Ashdown. So we have a potent combination of chivalry, Anglo-Saxon folk heroes and the victory of a Christian warrior over the forces of paganism. Together these ideas were potent in the national ideology and in Hughes's thinking. It is no coincidence that he wrote both a biography of Alfred the Great and *The Scouring of the White Horse*, devoted entirely to his native heath.

He expatiates on Saxon place names, traditions and his pride in being a West Saxon, 'I was born and bred a West Countryman, thank God! A Wessex man, a citizen of the noblest Saxon kingdom of Wessex . . . There's nothing like the old countryside for me, and no music like the fresh twang of the real old Saxon tongue.'[98] This lines Hughes up with the exponents of Anglo-Saxonism like Charles Kingsley, J. A. Froude and E. A. Freeman, who saw the Anglo-Saxons as the source of Britain's democratic institutions (Parliament, the common law), national religion (the Protestant temper) and the fighting and leadership qualities of the British race.[99] It was a central interpretative strand in English history, explaining the impulse to world rule. There is therefore a direct link between the green hills of Berkshire and the far-off foreign shores that constitute Britain's overseas empire.

On one level Hughes conforms to the influential thesis advanced by Martin Weiner that Britain's industrial decline can be traced to a state of mind best described as ruralism. Weiner sees this as the glorification of the countryside and all things rural in a deliberate rejection of urban and industrial reality by a non-industrial, non-innovative, anti-materialist patrician culture, endorsed by a gentrified bourgeoisie. The myth of England as essentially rural and essentially unchanging appealed across party lines to Conservatives and Socialists alike, and counted among its adherents such disparate figures as Rudyard Kipling, William Morris, Robert Blatchford and John Ruskin, all of whom in their different ways castigated the evils of technology, capitalism and an acquisitive industrial society. For some, however, the countryside was not only the antithesis of capitalism, it was also the antithesis of imperialism, part of the Little Englandism which saw the true destiny of the nation lying in a return to the pre-imperial rural Eden.

Not everyone saw it like that, however. For some the English inheritance of character, leadership, moral strength and democratic traditions, so rooted in the rural past of Merrie England, led inevitably to expansion overseas. It was one of the principal sources and inspirations of imperialism. Thus the English countryside, alive with the associations and lore of the past, represents stability, tradition, inspiration, home, family, history, the place from which to start forth in the divinely ordained British mission to govern the world and spread the virtues and values of Englishness and to return thence when the burden was laid down. So the two aspects of ruralism and imperialism, far from being antithetical, are mutually supportive and complementary.[100] Hughes is the perfect exemplar of this. For him there is no distinction between nation and empire, between rural England and Greater Britain.

Imperialism. Hughes was a fervent patriot, declaring proudly in Boston, Massachusetts, 'I am before all things an Englishman—a John Bull, if you will—loving Old England and feeling proud of her.'[101] He therefore saw no contradiction in praising the rich traditions of rural Wessex and the expanding empire overseas. For his closest identification is with the squirearchy, which he sees as equally the backbone of England and of the empire. 'The great army of Browns who are scattered over the whole empire on which the sun never sets and whose general diffusion, I take to be the chief cause of that empire's stability.' Why? Because 'for centuries, in their quiet, dogged, homespun way, they have been subduing the earth in most English counties, and leaving their mark in American forests and Australian uplands. Wherever the fleets and armies of England have won renown, there stalwart sons of the Browns have done yeoman's work.'[102] So empire is the context within which Hughes's heroes function. He lovingly exalts the qualities of the Browns, their fighting spirit, clannishness, quixotic temper and optimism, exactly the qualities needed to run an empire. All this struck the right chords later in the century when imperialism had become the dominant ideology, and the public schools were the nurseries of imperial administrators and officers.

At the end of *Tom Brown* Harry East departs to join a regiment in India. The Young Master tells Tom of Rugby, 'Perhaps ours is the only little corner of the British Empire which is thoroughly, wisely and strongly ruled just now,'[103] thus suggesting a model for future imperial rule, a model which was indeed followed, so that in looking back we can see that all relationships between officers and men, rulers and ruled, can be construed in the mould of teachers, prefects and fags, with the empire as Eton, Harrow and Rugby writ large.[104] Rugby itself contributed those imperial heroes lauded by Hughes, William Hodson and William Cotton Oswell, as well as the Doctor's son, William Delafield Arnold, who became Director of Education in the Punjab. Imperialism ran like a scarlet thread through Hughes's thought. In *The Manliness of Christ* he cited the wreck of the *Birkenhead*, one of the great imperial myths, to illustrate self-sacrifice, and in his defence of fighting when necessary he included 'Russians and border-ruffians'.

Chivalry. For Arnold chivalry was synonymous with feudalism, tyranny and class arrogance, all that was reactionary and needed eliminating. In 1829 he wrote, 'If I were called upon to name what spirit of evil predominantly deserved the name of Antichrist, I should name the spirit of chivalry.'[105] But by 1917 Sir Henry Newbolt was claiming that the public school system was essentially based on the codes and structures of chivalry and in 1898 J. H. Skrine, Warden of Trinity College, Glenalmond, wrote, 'With all its glory and its faults, chivalry it is again.'[106]

What happened in between was the simultaneous promotion of athleticism, muscular Christianity and chivalry by a whole raft of influential figures in literature, education and society as a code for living, and for counteracting the violence, godlessness and aristocratic selfishness of the old unreformed public school. Games, chapel and missions to the slums became key elements in the new public schools, and by the 1870s chivalry was in the air. As Mark Girouard has written:

> Actual knights in armour appear as school trophies, and abound in the form of statues or stained glass figures, especially as memorials to the Crimean, Boer or Great Wars . . . In school magazines, the articles interspersed among the ever increasing accounts of school games include ones on muscular Christianity, Kingsley, King Arthur, Tennyson's *Idylls*, chivalry and the Niebelungenlied.[107]

Hughes was steeped in the works of Walter Scott, who had been a friend of his grandmother. Indeed, Mary Ann Hughes had supplied Scott with the details of the legend of Wayland Smith's cave which he used in *Kenilworth*.[108] Arnold had used Scott's novels to teach from at Rugby. Hughes himself loved to allude to the old Spanish legend of Durandarte at Roncesvalles, which represented for him 'the beau ideal of knighthood summed up in a few words'.

> Kind in manners, fair in favour,
> Mild in temper, fierce in fight—
> Warrior, purer, gentler, braver,
> Never shall behold the light.[109]

This is the beau ideal of the public schoolboy too. Hughes installed stained glass pictures of Guinevere, Vivian, Elaine and Enid, the heroines of Tennyson's *Idylls of the King*, in his house.

Although the language of chivalry is not as prominent in *Tom Brown* as it might have been later in the century, the story was firmly annexed to the chivalric tradition by the illustrated edition of Arthur Hughes, published in 1889. The capital letter of chapter 1 had the infant Tom in helmet, sword and buckler as St George fighting the dragon. The capital of Part 2, chapter 7, had a knight in full armour kneeling to pray. The chapter dealt with East's struggle with his religious feelings and was headed by six lines from James Russell Lowell's *Vision of Sir Launfal*. The poem, by one of Hughes's favourite poets, told of a knight setting out to seek the Holy Grail and learning in a dream that the Grail is really to be found in sharing all he has with his fellow men. In Part 2, chapter 9, the illustration of Tom's visit to Arnold's tomb gives him, as Mark Girouard has pointed out, a knightly air; 'the rug over his shoulder suggests a military cloak and his attitude—pensive, bareheaded, one leg forward—is in the tradition of West's Black Prince and Watts's recent Sir Galahad'.[110]

Christian Socialism. Chivalry was a key element in Christian Socialism and a strong element in the ideology of Kingsley and Hughes. Kingsley described himself as 'a joyous knight errant' and Hughes as 'a knight of the Round Table'. Preaching before Queen Victoria, Kingsley declared, 'The age of chivalry is never past so long as there is a wrong left unredressed on earth or a man or woman left to say, "I will redress that wrong or spend my life in the attempt." '[111]

Christian Socialism, one of Hughes's abiding enthusiasms, inevitably left its imprint on *Tom Brown's Schooldays*.[112] So great was F. D. Maurice's influence on *Tom Brown*, which he read in draft, that Macmillan's reader observed that Arnold was presented as preaching Mauricean doctrines.[113] Christian Socialists sought to re-christianise the masses by promoting fellowship, human dignity and, where necessary, social reform. In particular they believed in 'co-operation, not competition' and were proposing an alternative to *laissez-faire*. They arose in response to the events of 1848. Alarmed by the revolutionary elements in Chartism, with whose broad aims they were in sympathy, they tried to propose a peaceful and constructive alternative. This alternative aimed to bring to the working classes four types of benefit: a renewal of Christian commitment, better living and working conditions and an improved education. It was hoped that this would improve cross-class sympathy and avert violent outbreaks.

The group centred on F. D. Maurice, Charles Kingsley, J. M. Ludlow and Hughes, and found practical expression in the Working Men's College, of which Maurice was the first and Hughes the second Principal. *Tom Brown's Schooldays* has been described by one commentator as 'the most important document in Christian Socialist literature . . . a social document depicting a polity in miniature as a model for national society'.[114] This is confirmed by Hughes's words in the preface to the first edition, where he quotes approvingly from the *Rugby Magazine*: 'We must bear in mind that we form a complete social body . . . a society in which by the nature of the case we must not only learn but act and live; and act and live not only as boys but as boys who will be men.'[115] So Hughes depicts both good and evil at Rugby and shows that evil can be conquered by faith, truth, manliness, co-operation and brotherly love.

When Arthur talks to Tom of his father it is clear that the Rev. Arthur was an archetypal Christian Socialist. His father had been a clergyman in a Midland town, oppressed by economic recession, strikes and crime. He had arrived there aged twenty-five, a young man, newly married, full of faith, hope and love, and inspired with 'a real whole-some Christian love for the poor, struggling, sinning men, of whom he felt himself one'. He earned 'a *manly* respect wrung from the unwilling souls of men who fancied his order their natural enemies; the fear and hatred of everyone who was false or unjust in the district, were he master or man' (my italics). He acted as mediator between master and man and strove to improve conditions, supported always by his wife. When he died during a typhus epidemic, which he characteristically strove to combat, working men carried his coffin to its grave. 'For many years afterwards the townsfolk felt the want of that brave, hopeful, loving parson and his wife, who had lived to teach them mutual forbearance and helpfulness, and had *almost* at last given them a glimpse of what this old world would be if people would live for God and each other instead of for themselves.'[116] It is evident too that George Arthur has the spirit of his father in him and becomes in a way a symbol of adult Christian Socialist responsibility. This is finally confirmed by the vision that Arthur has when seriously ill, a vision which draws on the imagery and ideas of Carlyle that so inspired the Christian Socialists—of fellowship, work and common effort. He dreams that he has died and gone to heaven and finds himself on the bank of a great river:

> On the other bank of the great river I saw men and women and children rising up pure and bright and the tears were wiped from their eyes, and they put on glory and strength, and all weariness and pain fell away. And beyond were a multitude which no man could number, and they worked at some great work; and they who rose from the river went on and joined in the work. They all worked and each worked in a different way, but all at the same work. And I saw there my father, and the men in the old town whom I knew when I was a child; many a hard stern man, who never came to church, and whom they called atheist and infidel. There they were, side by side with my father, whom I had seen toil and die for them, and women and little children, and the seal was on the foreheads of all. And I longed to see what the work was, and could not . . . Then . . . I saw myriads on this side, and they too worked, and I knew that it was the same work; and the same seal was on their foreheads. And though I saw that there was toil and anguish in the work of these . . . I longed . . . more and more to know what the work was. And as I looked, I saw my mother and my sisters, and I saw the Doctor, and you, Tom, and hundreds more whom I knew; and at last I saw myself too, and I was toiling and doing ever so little a piece of the great work.[117]

The great work is clearly that work which Arthur's father had died while performing and which Arnold also preached, the improvement of the lot of the poor, the spreading of Christian values and the improvement of class harmony. All this recalls Carlyle:

> There is a perennial nobleness, and even sacredness, in Work . . . It has been
> written, 'an endless significance lies in Work'; a man perfects himself by
> working . . . properly speaking, all true Work is Religion . . . Older than all
> preached Gospels was this unpreached, inarticulate, but ineradicable, forever-
> enduring Gospel: Work and therein have wellbeing . . . What is immethodic,
> waste, thou shalt make methodic, regulated, arrable; obedient and productive
> to thee. Wheresoever thou findest Disorder, there is thy eternal enemy;
> attack him swiftly, subdue him; make Order of him, the subject not of Chaos,
> but of Intelligence, Divinity and Thee . . . But above all, where thou findest
> Ignorance, Stupidity, Brute-Mindedness . . . attack it, I say; smite it wisely,
> unweariedly, and rest not while thou livest and it lives.[118]

Here is the same visionary quality, the same equation of work and
godly purpose, the same injunction to struggle.

Impact. The book was published on 24 April 1857. It had sold
28,000 copies by the end of 1862. By 1892 Macmillan had published
fifty-two editions and thereafter other publishers began to issue
editions.[119] It was from the first widely read. *The North British Review*
called it 'a work which everybody has read or means to read'.[120]
Charles Kingsley wrote to Hughes in June 1857 that he was promoting
the book everywhere he went but:

> I soon found how true the adage is that good wine needs no bush for every-
> one had read it already, and from everyone, from the fine lady on her throne
> to the redcoat on his cock-horse to the schoolboy on his forrum (as our
> Irish brethren call it) I have heard but one word, and that is that it is the
> jolliest book they ever read. Among a knot of redcoats at the cover-side,
> some very fast fellow said, 'If I had had such a book in my boyhood, I
> should have been a better man now!' and more than one capped his sentiment
> frankly.[121]

In 1868 Robert H. Quick compared its influence and effect with that of
Carlyle's *Sartor Resartus*.[122] Certainly eminent Victorians hastened to
read it. Holman Hunt read it with great delight. Tennyson read it aloud
to his wife while they were on a tour of northern England in 1857 and
both enjoyed it thoroughly. Walter Bagehot read it in 1858. Octavia
Hill read it soon after its publication and pronounced the book 'one of
the noblest I ever read'.[123] Dr Livingstone read it in 1865 and declared
it 'a capital book'.[124] The diarist Henry Crabb Robinson praised it but
he did not rate it higher than Harriet Martineau's *The Crofton Boys*.[125]
Sir Alexander Arbuthnot, Vice-chancellor of Calcutta University, a
contemporary of Hughes at Rugby, recalled, 'Sir Henry Montgomery
sent me out a copy in the year of the Mutiny. It was a remarkable
book and gave a very good account of life at Rugby in our day. When I
read it I was rather surprised that Tom Hughes should have been able
to write such a book. I should not have been equally surprised if George

had been the writer.'[126] Leslie Stephen read it and Hughes informed his wife, 'he is almost the most enthusiastic party about Tom Brown whom I have met—it is certainly very odd how it suits so many different folk.'[127] By 1873 Stephen could say, 'Neither the British jury nor the House of Lords nor the Church of England, nay scarcely the monarchy itself, seems to be so deeply enshrined in the bosoms of our country-men as our public schools' and his brother Fitzjames Stephen directly attributed this to '*Tom Brown* and his imitators'.[128]

The book was widely reviewed and often in the most laudatory terms. 'We hail this little work as the truest, liveliest and most sympathising description of a unique phase of English life that has yet been given to the public,' said *The Times*.[129] 'The book will be read with general pleasure,' said *The Quarterly Review*.[130] *The Edinburgh Review* thought that as a book for boys it was 'so good that hardly any praise can be too high for it'.[131] Its authenticity was particularly singled out by *The Saturday Review* and *The Edinburgh Review*.

The texture of its ideas was recognised and applauded. Reviews give a good indication of the temper of the times and why the book was so widely read. Of its Englishness *The Saturday Review* observed, 'A thoroughly English book, heartily acquiescing in English ways and tastes.'[132] Of its deep Christian faith, *The Times*: 'It is difficult to estimate the amount of good which may be done by *Tom Brown's Schooldays* . . . it is an attempt, a very noble and successful attempt, to Christianize the society of our youth through the only practicable channel—a hearty and brotherly sympathy with their feelings; a book, in short, which an English father might well wish to see in the hands of his son.'

Its manliness was praised. *The Literary Gazette* found Tom and Arthur's friendship 'very true and beautiful' and portrayed with 'a manly tenderness'.[133] *The Edinburgh Review* thought the same of the account of Arnold's death and Tom's grief ('It is a long time since we have read anything more touching and at the same time more manly'). *The Saturday Review* welcomed the writing of a boys' book by a man, complaining that since Captain Marryat's demise:

the writing of boys' books has passed into the hands of unmarried ladies . . . Women's boys, like women's men, are too likely to be of an altogether 'rose pink' and ideal type. They are very charming, no doubt, but redolent rather of surplices and choir chants than of playground and Latin grammar; while if they are allowed to have human faults, they are compelled forthwith to begin meditating over those faults, anatomizing and self-tormenting, in a fashion altogether female—harmless, possibly, and certainly natural and inevitable in girls, but in boys unnatural . . . a . . . training which may make them melancholy, superstitious or hypocritical, but will never make them men.

Its chivalry was detected. *The Literary Gazette* suggested that Tom would have sat at the Round Table 'had not chronology stood in his way', as he was 'never wanting in the cause of persecuted little boys, Rugby's substitutes for the distressed damsels of an earlier chivalry', and *The Times* noted, 'The author has devoted his best powers to the delineation of this schoolboy friendship and we believe he has shown true insight in so doing. It is in the affections and chivalrous feelings of boyhood that the true antidote is to be found to the rude and selfish violence which characterizes all masses where reciprocal duties are not clearly defined.'

Several reviewers noticed Hughes's affinity with Kingsley's ideas, but *The Times* rejected the idea of life as a struggle: 'We cannot but reject that everything high and holy should be invoked to the aid of the vulgar instinct of pugnacity, and that what Christianity command should be so recklessly confounded with that which it prohibits.'

But most of the critics concentrated on Arnold and Arnoldianism, and used the book as an excuse to discuss the role of the Doctor in general. Some gave unqualified praise. *The Literary Gazette* called it 'a living picture of a great and good man whose memory England most gratefully and justly preserves among her holiest things'. *The Saturday Review* called it a tribute to Arnold: 'of all the memorials of that truly good and great man, which the world has yet seen, this book is one of the most satisfactory to us'. Others were more critical. *Blackwood's Magazine* complained that Arnold's influence had been overrated: that the school had not been a place of disorder and irreligion before his advent, that religious and manly boys had preceded him—for instance, Spencer Thornton—and that Arnold was in fact little known to the majority of the boys.[134]

The North British Review was in fact highly critical of the products of Arnold's intellectual elite, as were *The Times* and *Edinburgh Review*. *The Times* opined:

> We believe that some of our readers will not approach without certain apprehension a story the scene of which is laid in Rugby under Dr. Arnold. The model Rugby sixth formers were apt to regard themselves as members of a semi-political, semi-sacerdotal fraternity; they exhibited an inclination to extend the monitorial system to the world, and to walk through the university at least as they did through Rugby 'with their canes' and calling out 'Silence, silence!'. Their contemporaries amused themselves with their obtrusive self-consciousness, their oppressive sense of responsibility, their conscientious tendency to entangle themselves in theological difficulties of the second magnitude, and their nervous anxiety to look after other people's moral welfare.

The Edinburgh Review spoke of an irredeemable 'priggishness' and *The North British Review* complained of lack of 'imagination and sentiment' and pointed to a 'hardness and coldness of tone': 'How is it that among so many men of undoubtedly superior talent, who have sprung from Rugby during and since Arnold's time, not one so far as we know, has been able to take hold of the *popular* mind?'[135]

The blame for this is laid squarely at Arnold's door. *The North British Review* complained that he had a single ideal for all boys, and that was 'his own concept of the perfect man', the intellectual and moral beings he turned out from his sixth form. He did not acknowledge the difference between boys but measured them by whether or not they attained his ideal. He had no sense of humour. Indeed, Arnold's fear of the boy's 'animal propensities' caused him to expel some admirable, high-spirited boys ('In fact, such lads, though they will of course lie open to temptation in virtue of their animal vigour, are usually those who are least disposed to any real vice').

Fitzjames Stephen in *The Edinburgh Review* mounted an even more comprehensive attack both on Arnold and on Hughes's depiction of him. 'Whatever benefits boys could derive from living under the care of a man of perfect honesty, deep conscientiousness, sincere and fervent piety, and an energy and courage which almost became blemishes by their excess, the Rugby boys derived from Dr Arnold.' But he had no sense of humour, he turned impressionistic boys into over-intellectualised prigs, who assess everything according to principle: 'It seems to have been his serious wish to bring boys to see a duty in every act of their lives, and to imitate his own habit of referring the most trifling matters to the most awful principles.' The Rugby boy, he said, 'Never ties his shoes without asserting a principle; when he puts on his hat he "founds himself" on an eternal truth.'

Stephen went on to say that 'no two persons could be less like each other than the real Dr. Arnold of Rugby and the Dr. Arnold of *Tom Brown's Schooldays*'. He suggested that Hughes's acquaintance with Arnold at school was comparatively slight and that he had learned to admire him later in life, 'and . . . now looks back upon him and his system through a sort of halo, shed upon them by the light of Mr. Kingsley's writings'. Stephen complained that Arnold had been transformed into an incarnation of the virtues lauded by Kingsley, which in two important aspects distorted the reality. Arnold was portrayed as a simple, sturdy soul who was 'a patron saint of athleticism'. In fact the real Arnold was 'constantly harassed and exercised' by doubts and scruples, and valued intellectual activity far more highly than sport.

Indeed, he complained further that Hughes paid no attention to the intellectual life of Rugby, giving 'the impression that it was an immense playground'. He complained that 'a boy might really infer from *Tom Brown* that he was only sent to school to play at football and that the lessons were quite a secondary consideration'. He was also worried about the prominence accorded to games, which although allegedly voluntary exerted a moral sanction: 'Even when . . . no direct force is employed to compel the boys to play at the games of the season, there is an indirect compulsion at least as inexorable. A boy may not actually be obliged to play on any particular occasion; but if he habitually abstains from doing so he becomes a social outcast and exposes himself to a very strong suspicion of being guilty of the one unpardonable sin punishable by unlimited thrashing, contempt and excommunication—namely cowardice.'

The debate which the book stimulated is reflected in the preface to the sixth edition, in which Hughes printed a letter from F. D. Maurice, greatly exercised by the bullying depicted and calling for greater magisterial supervision and the division of schools into three different classes, for boys aged from nine to twelve, from twelve to fifteen and over fifteen. Another correspondent and former school-fellow of Hughes resisted the idea of splitting boys up by age because it would not eliminate bullying: 'Bullying must be fought in other ways—by getting not only the sixth to put it down but the lower fellows to scorn it, and by eradicating mercilessly the incorrigible.'[136]

Hughes himself took up the point, made by several reviewers, about the priggishness of Rugby boys. He claimed the mark of the Rugby boys was 'their genial and hearty freshness and youthfulness of character'. But he added:

> This boyishness in the highest sense is not incompatible with seriousness—or earnestness if you like the word better. Quite the contrary. And I can well believe that casual observers, who have never been intimate with Rugby boys of the true stamp, but have met them only in the everyday society of the universities . . . may have seen a good deal more of the serious or earnest side of their characters than of any other. But the more the boy was alive in them, the less will they have been able to conceal their thoughts or their opinion of what was taking place under their noses; and if the greater part of that didn't share with their notions of what was right, very likely they showed pretty clearly that it did not, at whatever risk of being taken for young prigs.[137]

Tom Brown functioned on three different levels of readership. The first was boys intending to go to public school, for whom it served as a guide or manual. That they were Hughes's primary target was made perfectly clear in the book by the author addressing the boys direct from time to time and including untranslated Greek and Latin texts, which they were expected to understand. The picture it painted was eagerly absorbed by such boys. But its influence may have been for good or for ill. In 1913 Lord Kilbracken recalled it with gratitude and affection:

> I read *Tom Brown* for the first time about fifty-two years ago, shortly before I was sent to Rugby. The manners and customs which it describes were

already almost a quarter of a century old; many and great changes, nearly all of them for the better, had in that interval taken effect; but, as I well remember, the atmosphere, the spirit, the tradition of the place appeared to me . . . to be exactly what *Tom Brown* had led me to expect. There it was, indefinable and indescribable, but perfectly recognisable and unmistakable; and there it remains, as I hope and believe, to this day.[138]

Richard Usborne (Charterhouse) thought its influence on boys of prep.-school age wholly malign, frightening them unduly and leaving 'a nasty and unacknowledged residue'. He defined this as the inculcation in the English ruling class of the view that corporal punishment of all sorts (bullying, caning, boxing, fighting) should be bravely inflicted and bravely received:

My mother . . . gave me *Tom Brown* . . . to read before I went to my prep school, at the age of seven. It put the wind up me vertically . . . I did learn from it that school could mean my being boxed on the ear, caned, flogged, fagged, bullied, tossed in blankets, roasted in front of fires, made to sing songs solo . . . and be constantly involved in fist fights with bigger boys, velveteens and louts. I would have to endure these things bravely and without preaching, so that I 'might never bring shame or sorrow to the dear folks at home'.[139]

It had a more positive and long-lasting influence on the youthful Baron de Coubertin, who read it in French translation as a schoolboy and subsequently made a pilgrimage to Rugby before founding the modern Olympic Games in the spirit of sportsmanship the book defined.[140] In 1908 the weekly magazine *The Captain*, with a largely prep. school and public school readership, ran a competition for the twelve best books for boys ever written. They had 800 replies. *Tom Brown's Schooldays* was placed first, followed in order by *Treasure Island*, *Robinson Crusoe*, *Westward Ho!*, *The Adventures of Sherlock Holmes*, *Ivanhoe*, *King Solomon's Mines*, *Coral Island*, *The Fifth Form at St Dominic's*, *The Last of the Mohicans*, *Mr Midshipman Easy* and *J. O. Jones*.[141] It is evident that like all books boys could take from *Tom Brown* different messages. But it set a standard of behaviour, conduct and expectation which defined the public school spirit and against which people measured themselves.

The second level of readership was adults, who saw it as part of the educational debate. J. C. Cotton Minchin wrote in 1901 that Hughes 'devoted his life to the cause of the public schools and proved himself their most successful recruiting sergeant. Thanks to *Tom Brown's Schooldays*, hundreds of parents have sent their boys to public schools, who would not have done so, had that book never been written.'[142] The importance of its being read by adults is that it powerfully promoted the reformed public school as *the* vehicle for upper middle class and upper class education at a time of debate about educational forms and structures.

Third, it was read by boys who had not been and would not go to public school. As Asa Briggs observed, 'Hughes did more than any other writer to acquaint the non-public-school boy with the conditions of life and teaching at Rugby.'[143] It became and remained a favourite with such boys. A survey of juvenile reading in a variety of boys' schools, eliciting 790 replies, was published by Edward Salmon in 1888. In the boys' list of favourite books, *Tom Brown* came sixth, equal with the Bible and following *Robinson Crusoe, Swiss Family Robinson, The Pickwick Papers, Ivanhoe* and *The Boy's Own Annual.*[144] For a similar study in 1940 A. J. Jenkinson surveyed 1,570 boys in State schools aged between twelve and fifteen on their favourite books. He noted 'the remarkable popularity of *Tom Brown's Schooldays*', with twelve and thirteen-year-old boys.[145] Among twelve-year-olds, asked what they had read during one month, *Tom Brown* came fourth after *Treasure Island, Robinson Crusoe* and *David Copperfield*. Among thirteen-year-olds it was second to *Treasure Island* and just ahead of *Westward Ho!* and *The Invisible Man*. Among fourteen and fifteen-year-olds it was virtually unread. Geoffrey Trease wrote in 1948:

> Tom Brown may not be so popular now as when he was created nearly a century ago . . . but he is by no means finished. In a poll of some two thousand New Zealand schoolboys, he came third in popularity, far outstripping such formidable rivals as Beau Geste and Bulldog Drummond.[146]

For boys who could not afford to buy books—and by the inter-war years there were very cheap reprints—the book was stocked in school libraries, presented as prizes and kept also in boys' clubs. C. E. B. Russell, long-time youth worker, wrote in 1905 in a book about working-class Manchester lads of the need to stock wholesome but exciting reading in clubs and particularly recommended *Tom Brown* ('one of the noblest books ever written').[147] In 1912 a Board of Education circular recommended it, along with *Robinson Crusoe* and *Masterman Ready*, as appropriate reading for the elementary schools.[148] This allowed Hughes's values and beliefs to filter down into the State schools and to work upon the boys to complement the public school ideas and standards which masters were imposing, creating a two-way process of imposition and reception.

Individuals have testified to the book's impact upon them. The London hatter Frederick Willis, recalling his Edwardian boyhood, named *Tom Brown's Schooldays* 'one of the great literary landmarks of my boyhood', adding, 'I have re-read this quite recently and still consider it the finest moral tonic for a boy in English literature.'[149]

Its potency and poignancy continued to have an effect long after it was written. A young officer on leave from the trenches in 1917, Lieutenant William St Leger, noted in his diary that he was reading *Tom Brown* (' like Little Arthur's vision of death so much').[150]

But in addition to the book's continuous availability, the new mass media have taken *Tom Brown* and translated it into visual form. The first film version, the silent 1916 British film, directed and written by Rex Wilson, was selected for a royal command performance in 1917. Only a fragment of it has survived. There have, however, been two splendid sound versions of the story, which, while departing sometimes radically, from Hughes's plot, have remained faithful to his spirit. In 1940 Hollywood produced a version done with style, wit and spirit. The film, directed by Robert Stevenson, had a definitive Dr Arnold in Sir Cedric Hardwicke, high-principled, grave and dedicated but given a quiet sense of humour. James Lydon played Tom and Freddie Bartholomew East. In 1950 a new version was made in Britain, directed by Gordon Parry and filmed at Rugby itself. Robert Newton was an effective Dr Arnold, with John Howard Davies and John Charlesworth as Tom and East respectively. In the interests of dramatic cohesion both versions kept the Tom–Flashman feud at the centre of the action. But the American version diverged most from the original by eliminating Arthur and substituting a quarrel and estrangement between Tom and East centred on the schoolboy 'sneaking' ethic. Tom is shunned when he is believed wrongly to have 'sneaked' on Flashman. So when East is wrongfully expelled, Tom says nothing to help clear him. but they are eventually reconciled at Arnold's tomb. The British version retains Arthur, though involving Flashman until the end. Both films stressed the ideals of Arnold as defined by Hughes and the creation of a school of Christian gentlemen. B.B.C.-TV followed suit in 1981 with a vigorous serialised adaptation featuring Iain Cuthbertson as Dr Arnold, Anthony Murphy as Tom and Simon Turner as East. It dramatised only the first half of the book, centring on Flashman, memorably played by Richard Morant.

The book was a success with boys then and has remained a success with them since because of its vivid recreation of boy life, the rough-and tumble, the triumphs and disasters. Tom Brown is the perfect boyhood identification figure, an ordinary, decent, healthy, essentially unremarkable boy. It worked because Hughes loved his schooldays and conveyed that love in pulsating prose. Even more significantly, it works because, like all the best school story writers, Hughes remained a schoolboy all his life, a prize specimen of that Victorian type *puer aeternus.*[151]

Its success with adults derived from the rich mixture of ingredients, all of which could appeal to different groups at different times. Conservatives liked it because it contained enough of the hurly-burly of the unreformed public school, games and manliness to satisfy them. Progressives admired it for highlighting the role of Arnold and his commitment to Christian and moral education. Hughes was widely seen as having placed his version of this securely on the educational agenda. So much so that the book became almost a textbook for masters seeking to improve the tone and conduct of a public school. It is universally agreed that the public school ideal and spirit and the version of Arnold that prevailed in the nineteenth century was Hughes's.[152] Later in the century the proponents of athleticism and imperialism could call the book in aid.

Attacks on it are more often than not misplaced and unjust, based on misreadings, partial quotation and a misunderstanding of the context. By the end of the century two of the major elements of the book were already unfashionable and out of key with dominant ideas. The strong religious element, the preaching and sermonical approach had always been controversial. As Edward Salmon noted in 1888, 'the chief fault urged against Mr. Hughes' method is a proneness to preach'.[153] It is also perhaps this continuing commitment to robust Christian witness that explains Bernard Darwin's comment: 'I have been assured by two old Rugbeians who were separated by an interval of thirty-five years that when he came down to Rugby [Hughes] was regarded by the boys in general as a bore.'[154]

Second, there is the prominence of emotion. There are tears aplenty: Tom weeps when he realises that he has betrayed his mother's wishes for him to pray nightly, Arthur weeps over his father and over a particularly emotional passage in *The Iliad*, East weeps with the Doctor and Tom weeps at the Doctor's tomb. Open expressions of emotion were a characteristic of the Evangelical temper of the first half of the nineteenth century. Arnold would himself regularly weep in the pulpit. But Hughes's depiction of Tom's courage in resisting bullying and in fighting his corner helped to promote an entirely different public school tradition, of self-control and the stiff upper lip. Sir Harold Nicolson (Wellington) recalled:

A further quality inculcated by the Tom Brown tradition was that of self-control. It is convenient to reduce personal violence to a minimum and to subject the overt expression of the passions to some automatic discipline. In the latter half of the nineteenth century, the advocates of the public school spirit contended that this self-discipline should extend to all expressions of feeling whatsoever. Although it had been considered effective rather than unmanly for such heroes as Pitt, Fox, Nelson and even Wellington to cry in public, tears began about 1850 to be regarded as ungentleman-like. This prohibition was not until 1900 universally accepted. Lord Houghton, when told of the death of Lady Waldegrave, burst into a fit of unrestrained weeping. Tennyson used to sob passionately when reading *Maud* and expected his audience to do likewise. I have myself seen such men as Curzon and Churchill cry, quite quietly but very hard. Yet the theory became established that to display emotion was a feminine, or provincial or foreign thing to do.[155]

But to attack Hughes as wittingly or unwittingly betraying Arnold is unjust. Isabel Quigly suggests that he did, following Nicolson, who suggested that Arnold 'would, quite rightly, have regarded *Tom Brown's Schooldays* as a caricature of all that he had wished to do, and almost succeeded in doing, at Rugby'.[156] What Hughes does is to show the transformation of an ordinary, headstrong boy into a responsible, mature, committed adult, chivalrous, Christian and concerned. It is done in accordance with Arnold's emphasis on instilling moral and religious principle and gentlemanly behaviour. Tom never reaches the third stage—intellectual. But then, neither Tom nor his creator were intellectuals. Nor were the bulk of Rugby boys. As *The North British Review* rightly said in criticising Arnold's intellectual elite:

> The mass of the English world is not remarkably intellectual. A considerable capacity of observation and a fair amount of reasoning power is as much as is to be looked for in the majority of our countrymen, even in mature years. But the sound judgement which these are ultimately to develop is of later growth; and the ordinary subjects of study in the public school—and more then than now—do not, at least as they are ordinarily handled, greatly interest the boy . . . The boy in general is a well disposed animal enough—indeed as he is *now* seen—for the change within thirty years past is surprising in this respect—a very nice animal, is distinctively an animal, and whatever of character he may show will be of an animal kind.[157]

But the boys were the better for the contact with Arnold and his religious and moral ideas than otherwise. It is unlikely that a school story about an intellectual boy like Arthur would have had success. Indeed, J. E. C. Welldon's *Gerald Eversley's Friendship*, which reads rather like *Tom Brown* rewritten from Arthur's perspective, did not achieve the success of *Tom Brown*.

It is also crucial to appreciate the context within which Hughes was writing: the bid to reform the unreformed public schools and the Evangelical desire to eliminate the worse excesses of survival of the fittest, brutality, starvation, reactionary snobbism, gambling, drinking and whoring. To argue that the choice was between intellectual activity and the games-playing muscular Christianity of Hughes is to posit an entirely false and unhistorical antithesis. The choice was between aristocratic barbarism and Christian gentlemanliness. There can be no doubt that Hughes's heart was in the right place. It is surely better to see a school as a maker of Christian gentlemen, however intellectual, than as a playground for aristocratic thugs. Hughes promoted fighting but only if it had a chivalric purpose, the protection of the weak. Games did not figure excessively in the book but he advocated them for their team loyalty, for fitness and for good sportsmanship. Hughes showed his dislike of snobbery and class hatred by having Tom mix easily with the village boys and make friends with the gamekeeper 'Velveteens'. The house spirit is advocated as a vehicle for spreading decent behaviour. The role of individual character is crucial: 'In no place in the world has individual character more weight than public school'. It is essential to mould characters. Without sterling characters law and order collapses, decent standards decline and aristocratic barbarism returns. This is epitomised by the history of School House, which under Young Brooke and Old Brooke is well ordered and decent, and in between their regimes a scene of tyranny, disorder and violence. If 'Good Learning' was not always possible, Hughes cannot be blamed for choosing godliness and chivalry over aristocratic brutalism.

Nor can Hughes be blamed for changes in society after his day which led to the lessons and morals of his book being used as selectively as they have been by latter-day critics. His cultural legacy is threefold. First, he effectively defined the public school spirit, with its emphasis on the shaping of character rather than intellect, so that by the end of the century the public schools were turning out (in A. C. Benson's words) 'well-groomed, well-mannered, rational, manly boys, all taking the same view of things, all doing the same things', all conforming to the code.[158] Second, Hughes created the school story and inaugurated that succession of notable exponents that runs through Talbot Baines Reed to Frank Richards. Third, Hughes contributed notably to the idealisation of the boy. Hugh Kingsmill observed pertinently that Arnold 'would not even have understood, far less approved, the Victorian cult of Boys for boys' sake, begun in *Tom Brown's Schooldays*, but finding varied forms in *Eric*, the poems of the Etonian master Cory and Bowen's Harrow songs, down to the novels of E. F. Benson, and other connoisseurs in the charm, naturalness, animal grace etc. of the adolescent male'.[159] He is perfectly correct in both respects. Arnold was horrified by the 'evil of boy nature' and wished boys to hurry through that stage as rapidly as possible. ('My object will be, if possible, to form Christian men, for Christian boys I can scarcely hope to make. I mean that, from the naturally imperfect state of boyhood, they are not susceptible of Christian principles in their full development upon their practice, and I suspect that a low standard of morals in many respects must be tolerated amongst them.')[160]

Hughes, on the other hand, idealised the ordinary boy, like Harry East, for instance, 'frank, hearty, and good-natured, well-satisfied with himself and his position and chock-full of life and spirits'.[161] This is very much in the spirit that was to become a central thread of Victorian culture, so much so that Martin Green could with justice assert, 'It is a striking feature of late Victorian culture that its emotional focus was on boys'.[162]

Notes

1 J. J. Findlay, *Arnold of Rugby*, Cambridge, 1914, xiii.
2 Bernard Darwin, *The English Public School*, London, 1929, 157-8. Cf. also Harold Child, 'The public school in fiction', in *The Public Schools from Within*, London, 1906, 295.
3 On Brown's precursors see, for instance, P. W. Musgrave, *From Brown to Bunter*, London, 1985, 21-46; Margaret Maison, 'Tom Brown and company: scholastic novels of the 1850s', *English*, 12 (1958), 100-3; Gerald Redmond, 'Before Hughes and Kingsley: the origins and evolution of "Muscular Christianity" in English children's literature', in Charles Jenkins and Michael Green (ed.), *Sporting Fictions*, Birmingham, 1981, 8-35. The earlier Tom Browns appear in Dorothy Kilner's *First Going to School* (1804) and *The Good Child's Delight* (1819), see Redmond, p. 21.
4 *Blackwood's Magazine*, 89 (February 1861), 132.
5 Reprinted in P. G. Wodehouse, *Tales of St Austin's*, London, 1972, 157-62.
6 W. H. G. Armytage and E. C. Mack, *Thomas Hughes*, London, 1952, 88.
7 Patrick Scott, 'The school and the novel: *Tom Brown's Schooldays*', Brian Simon and Ian Bradley (ed.), *The Victorian Public School*, Dublin, 1975, 34-57.
8 Scott, 'The school and the novel', 48.
9 On conditions at Arnold's Rugby see T. W. Bamford, *Thomas Arnold*, London, 1960, Edward C. Mack, *Public Schools and British Opinion, 1780-1860*, London, 1938, 238-9; Armytage and Mack, *Thomas Hughes*, 16-17.
10 Thomas Hughes, *Memoir of a Brother*, London, 1873, 34.
11 *Blackwood's Magazine*, 89, 133.
12 The story of the writing of the book is in Armytage and Mack, *Thomas Hughes*, 86-103.
13 Armytage and Mack, *Thomas Hughes*, 89.
14 Redmond, 'Before Hughes and Kingsley'.
15 Thomas Hughes, *Tom Brown at Oxford* (1861), London, 1889, viii.
16 *Dictionary of National Biography*, II, 879.
17 Thomas Hughes, *Tom Brown's Schooldays*, London, 1913, ed. F. Sidgwick, x.
18 Thomas Arnold, *Passages from a Wandering Life*, London, 1900, 32-3.
19 Lt. Col. Sydney Selfe, *Chapters from the History of Rugby School, with notes on the characters and incidents depicted by the master hand of Thomas Hughes in Tom Brown's Schooldays*, Rugby, 1910, 114-46. Cf. also Bamford, *Thomas Arnold*, 50; Thomas Arnold, *Passages from a Wandering Life*, 33.
20 *Dictionary of National Biography*, II, 932.
21 Selfe, *Chapters*, 119.
22 In his memoirs of Rugby William Gover recalls the effect of Arnold's sermons and Arnold's fury at Rugby School boys despising town boys; see *The Parents' Review*, 6 (1895-96), 756, 759. The effects of Arnold's sermons are also recalled in Alexander Arbuthnot, *Memories of Rugby and India*, London, 1910, 35, and Katherine Lake (ed.), *Memorials of Dean William Charles Lake of Durham*, London, 1901, 8.
23 Charles E. Raven, *Christian Socialism, 1848-54* (1920), London, 1968, 130-1.
24 On his career see Armytage and Mack, *Thomas Hughes*.
25 Ian Weinberg, *The English Public Schools*, New York, 1967, 97-126. Cf. also John Wakeford, *The Cloistered Elite*, London, 1969, 128-59.

26 Thomas Hughes, *Tom Brown's Schooldays* (1857), London, 1889, 52.
27 Hughes, *Tom Brown's Schooldays*, 59.
28 Vivian Ogilvie, *The English Public School*, London, 1957, 145.
29 Thomas Hughes, *Tom Brown's Schooldays*, 255-6.
30 Hughes, *Tom Brown's Schooldays*, 102.
31 Hughes, *Tom Brown at Oxford*, 99.
32 This controversy is surveyed by George Worth, 'Of muscles and manliness: some reflections on Thomas Hughes', in James R. Kincaid and Albert J. Kuhn, *Victorian Literature and Society*, Ohio, 1984, 300-14. Cf. also Harold Nicolson's statement that Hughes believed in 'indiscriminate combat', *Good Behaviour*, London, 1956, 259.
33 Hughes, *Tom Brown's Schooldays*, 231.
34 Hughes, *Tom Brown's Schooldays*, 246.
35 Hughes, *Tom Brown's Schooldays*, 231.
36 Hughes, *Tom Brown's Schooldays*, 246.
37 Thomas Carlyle, *Past and Present*, London, 1905, 163-4.
38 Thomas Hughes, *The Manliness of Christ*, London, 1880, 21, 22, 25-6.
39 Norman Vance, *The Sinews of the Spirit*, Cambridge, 1985.
40 Matthew Arnold, *Culture and Anarchy* (1869), Cambridge, 1978, 203.
41 See J. C. Reid, *Bucks and Bruisers*, London, 1971.
42 On this whole subject see Bruce Haley, *The Healthy Body and Victorian Culture*, Cambridge, Mass., 1978.
43 Hughes, *Tom Brown's Schooldays*, 33-4.
44 Hughes, *Tom Brown's Schooldays*, 89-90.
45 Hughes, *Tom Brown's Schooldays*, 100.
46 Hughes, *Tom Brown's Schooldays*, 289.
47 Hughes, *Tom Brown's Schooldays*, xv. On Arnold and his views see Arthur P. Stanley, *The Life and Correspondence of Thomas Arnold*, 2 vols., London, 1845; Findlay, *Arnold of Rugby*; Joshua Fitch, *Thomas and Matthew Arnold and their Influence on English Education* (1897), London, 1905; T. W. Bamford, *Thomas Arnold*; David Newsome, *Godliness and Good Learning*, London, 1961.
48 Hughes, *Tom Brown's Schooldays*, 103.
49 Hughes, *Tom Brown's Schooldays*, 115.
50 Hughes, *Tom Brown's Schooldays*, 115-16.
51 *Dictionary of National Biography*, I, 587.
52 Hughes, *Tom Brown's Schooldays*, 126, 180.
53 Hughes, *Tom Brown's Schooldays*, 184-5. William Gover recalls being pelted with shoes when kneeling to pray. *Parents Review*, 6 (1895-96), 834.
54 Hughes, *Tom Brown's Schooldays*, 177-8.
55 Hughes, *Tom Brown's Schooldays*, 272.
56 Hughes, *Tom Brown's Schooldays*, 298-9.
57 Rowland E. Prothero, *Life and Letters of Dean Stanley*, I, London, 1894, 68.
58 Arthur Westcott, *Life and Letters of Brooke Foss Westcott*, London, 1903, I, 248.
59 Fitch, *Thomas and Matthew Arnold*, 105.
60 Bamford, *Thomas Arnold*, 175-90.
61 Lake, *Memorials of Dean Lake*, 17.
62 A. H. Clough, *Poems and Prose Remains*, I, London, 1896, 56.
63 Thomas Arnold, *Sermons*, V. London, 1878, 341.
64 *Dictionary of National Biography*, I, 587.
65 Jonathan Gathorne-Hardy, *The Public School Phenomenon*, Harmondsworth, 1979, 85.
66 Thomas Arnold, *Sermons*, III, 131.
67 Thomas Arnold, *Sermons*, II, 82-3.
68 Thomas Arnold, *Sermons*, V, 48-54.
69 Fitch, *Thomas and Matthew Arnold*, 90.

70 Fitch, *Thomas and Matthew Arnold*, 90.
71 On the careers of four of his disciples see Frances J. Woodward, *The Doctor's Disciples*, Oxford, 1954.
72 Newsome, *Godliness and Good Learning*, 50.
73 Lake, *Memorials of Dean Lake*, 12.
74 Fitch, *Thomas and Matthew Arnold*, 83–4. Expulsion was a favoured weapon of Arnold, his firm belief being 'the first, second and third duty of the master of a great public school is to get rid of unpromising boys', Thomas Hughes, 'Rugby School', *Great Public Schools*, London, 1889, 158.
75 Fitch, *Thomas and Matthew Arnold*, 1.
76 Newsome, *Godliness and Good Learning*, 25.
77 Newsome, *Godliness and Good Learning*, 48.
78 Hughes, *Tom Brown's Schooldays*, 296.
79 Hughes, *Tom Brown's Schooldays*, 100.
80 Hughes, *Manliness of Christ*, London, 1894, appendix, 232.
81 Hughes, *Tom Brown's Schooldays*, 211–13 (*vulgus*); 264–9 (cribbing).
82 Thomas Carlyle, *Lectures on Heroes and Hero-worship*, London, 1905, 1, 2.
83 Houghton, *Victorian Frame of Mind*, 310.
84 Thomas Hughes, 'Hodson of Hodson's House', *Fraser's Magazine*, 59 (February 1859), 128.
85 Thomas Hughes, 'Hodson', 127.
86 Hughes, *Manliness of Christ*, appendix, 231, 233.
87 Hughes, *Manliness of Christ*, appendix, 240–1.
88 Hughes, *Manliness of Christ*, appendix, 251–2.
89 On ruralism see Martin Weiner, *English Culture and the Decline of the Industrial Spirit, 1850–1980*, Cambridge, 1981, and Raymond Williams, *The Country and the City*, London, 1985.
90 Hughes, *Tom Brown's Schooldays*, 15.
91 Raymond Chapman, *The Sense of the Past in Victorian Literature*, London, 1986, 145.
92 Hughes, *Tom Brown's Schooldays*, 45.
93 Hughes, *Tom Brown's Schooldays*, 23.
94 Hughes, *Tom Brown's Schooldays*, 33–4.
95 Hughes, *Tom Brown's Schooldays*, 20–1.
96 Hughes, *Tom Brown's Schooldays*, 50.
97 Hughes, *Tom Brown's Schooldays*, 42–3.
98 Hughes, *Tom Brown's Schooldays*, 13.
99 On Anglo-Saxonism see J. W. Burrow, *A Liberal Descent*, Cambridge, 1981; Hugh McDougall, *Racial Myth in English History*, Montreal, 1982; Asa Briggs, 'Saxons, Normans and Victorians', *Collected Essays*, 2, Brighton, 1985, 218–39.
100 This is persuasively argued by J. S. Bratton, ' "Of England, Home and Duty": the image of England in Victorian and Edwardian juvenile fiction', *Imperialism and Popular Culture*, Manchester, 1986, 73–93.
101 Quoted in W. E. Winn, '*Tom Brown's Schooldays* and the development of "Muscular Christianity" ', *Church History*, 29 (1960), 71.
102 Hughes, *Tom Brown's Schooldays*, 1–2, 4.
103 Hughes, *Tom Brown's Schooldays*, 290.
104 This argument is developed in Jeffrey Richards, *Visions of Yesterday*, London, 1973.
105 Stanley, *Life of Arnold*, I, 255.
106 Mark Girouard, *The Return to Camelot*, New Haven, Conn., 1981, 170.
107 Girouard, *Return to Camelot*, 169.
108 S. M. Ellis, *Wilkie Collins, Lefanu and Others* (1931), Freeport, Conn., 1968, 217.
109 Vance, *Sinews of the Spirit*, 136.
110 Girouard, *Return to Camelot*, 168.
111 Girouard, *Return to Camelot*, 130.

112 On Christian Socialism see Torben Christensen, *Origin and History of Christian Socialism*, Aarhus, 1962, and Edward Norman, *The Victorian Christian Socialists*, Cambridge, 1987.
113 Vance, *Sinews of the Spirit*, 53.
114 A. J. Hartley, 'Christian Socialism and Victorian morality: the inner meaning of *Tom Brown's Schooldays*', *Dalhousie Review*, 49 (1969), 216, 223.
115 Hartley, 'Christian Socialism and Victorian morality', 216.
116 Hughes, *Tom Brown's Schooldays*, 195-7.
117 Hughes, *Tom Brown's Schooldays*, 259-60.
118 Carlyle, *Past and Present*, 168, 172-3. Arnold would certainly have endorsed this vision of work. *Quarterly Review*, 102 (1857), 338, stressed Arnold's dedication to work, 'of which he was a worshipper, holding labour—which of itself formed his best pleasure—to be his appointed lot on earth'.
119 The editions are discussed in Armytage and Mack, *Thomas Hughes*, 294-5.
120 *North British Review*, 28 (February 1858), 139.
121 Mrs Kingsley, *Charles Kingsley: his letters and memories of his life*, 2, London, 1880, 54.
122 Robert H. Quick, *Essays on Educational Reform* (1868), London, 1904, 488.
123 All examples given by Amy Cruse, *The Victorians and their Books*, London, 1935, 298-9.
124 W. Edward Oswell, *William Cotton Oswell*, 2, London, 1900, 88.
125 Edith J. Morley, *Henry Crabb Robinson*, London, 1933, 146.
126 Arbuthnot, *Memories of Rugby and India*, 48.
127 Armytage and Mack, *Thomas Hughes*, 89.
128 Edward C. Mack, *Public Schools and British Opinion since 1860*, New York, 1941, 134-5.
129 *The Times*, 9 October 1857.
130 *Quarterly Review*, 102 (July–October 1857), 330-54.
131 *Edinburgh Review*, 107 (January–April 1858), 172-93.
132 *Saturday Review* (3 October 1957), 313--14.
133 *Literary Gazette* (20 June 1857), 587-8.
134 *Blackwood's Magazine*, 89 (February 1861), 133--6.
135 *North British Review*, 28, 123-39.
136 Hughes, *Tom Brown's Schooldays*, ix-xii.
137 Hughes, *Tom Brown's Schooldays*, xiv.
138 Hughes, *Tom Brown's Schooldays* (1913), ix.
139 George Macdonald Fraser, *The World of the Public School*, London, 1977, 136-50.
140 P. C. McIntosh, *Sport and Society*, London, 1963, 90-3.
141 *The Captain*, 19 (1908), 90.
142 J. G. Cotton Minchin, *Our Public Schools: their influence on English history*, London, 1901, 210.
143 Asa Briggs, *Victorian People* (1954), Harmondsworth, 1977, 156.
144 Edward Salmon, *Juvenile Literature as it is*, London, 1888, 15.
145 A. J. Jenkinson, *What do Boys and Girls Read?*, London, 1940, 18.
146 Geoffrey Trease, *Tales out of School*, London, 1948, 29.
147 C. E. B. Russell, *Manchester Boys* (1905), Manchester, 1984, 29.
148 Jacqueline Rose, *The Case of Peter Pan*, London, 1985, 121.
149 Frederick Willis, *101 Jubilee Road*, London, 1948, 111.
150 Michael Moynihan, *People at War, 1914-1918*, London, 1973, 67.
151 Armytage and Mack, *Thomas Hughes*, 92; J. F. C. Harrison, *A History of the Working Men's College*, 38.
152 Edward C. Mack, *Public Schools and British Opinion, 1780-1860*, London, 1938, 325; Nicolson, *Good Behaviour*, 259; Cotton Minchin, *Our Public Schools*, 208, for instance.
153 Salmon, *Juvenile Literature*, 84.
154 Darwin, *The English Public School*, 160.
155 Nicolson, *Good Behaviour*, 260.

156 Isabel Quigly, *The Heirs of Tom Brown*, London, 1982, 49–50; Nicolson, *Good Behaviour*, 258.
157 *North British Review*, 28 (February–May 1858), 137.
158 A. C. Benson, *The Upton Letters*, London, 1905, 48.
159 Hugh Kingsmill, *Matthew Arnold*, London, 1931, 20.
160 David Newsome, *Godliness and Good Learning*, 55.
161 Hughes, *Tom Brown's Schooldays*, 74.
162 Martin Green, *Dreams of Adventure, Deeds of Empire*, London, 1979, 389.

3

Paradise lost:
Eric, or, Little by Little

Few best-sellers can have been so reviled and excoriated over the years as Dean Farrar's *Eric, or, Little by Little*. It has consistently earned such critical judgements as 'mawkishly false' (Vivian Ogilvie), 'a preposterous book' (John Rowe Townsend), 'the sort of story Dr Arnold would have written if he'd taken to drink' (Hugh Kingsmill), 'terrible warnings, soaked in nauseously cloying piety' (Roger Lancelyn Green), 'the only book that I ever wanted to lose' (Eric Ambler), 'the nightmare emanation of some morbid, introverted brain' (Edward C. Mack), 'one of the most idiotic books of the nineteenth century' (Benny Green).[1] The undoubted immortality of *Eric* is, then, as one historian has put it, very largely 'an immortality of derision'.[2]

Most tellingly, perhaps, it was disparaged by other school story writers. P. G. Wodehouse, who read *Eric* as a boy and loved it, grew critical of it in later years and mocked its style in his own school stories.[3] Talbot Baines Reed wrote disapprovingly that the Dean administered a powder of religious dogma and Christian morality, mixed with narrative 'jam' of school life. But he thought the 'powder' too aggressive, the 'jam' too insipid and the mixture as a whole nauseous to the average boy.[4] In Kipling's *Stalky and Co.* 'Ericking' is the derisive term used to describe pious behaviour. When Stalky's aunt buys him *Eric* and *St Winifred's* he seeks immediately to dispose of them to a local bookseller, only to find that they are a drug on the market.

The criticism began as soon as the book was published. Writing in *Blackwood's Magazine* in 1861, W. Lucas Collins said of the book, 'A more utter failure . . . can hardly be conceived. Seldom has a book been written with such an excellent intention, by a scholar and a gentleman, which is so painful to read.' He admitted its popularity, which he attributed to the general interest in school stories, the authority of the author as a Harrow master, and the sensationalism and 'painful and repulsive details of the story', which 'confirmed all that anxious mothers had always feared and half believed of the enormities of large schools'. But he deprecated the sensationalism ('granting the facts, we can see no sufficient motive for dragging such a miserable history into daylight') and the excessive emotionalism. Claiming that 'the popularity of *Eric* has probably lain most with mammas and sisters' and that the book was certainly not popular with schoolboys, he compared with mounting exasperation the masculinity and realism of Thomas Hughes's works with what he saw as the femininity and unreality of Farrar's, in particular *Eric* and the later *Julian Home.*

> The very names which they affect for their heroes are characteristic. Tom and his father are of the old hearty John Bull type; Eric of the modern sentimental . . . Julian again (who rejoices in a sister 'Violet' and a brother 'Cyril') in his very name conveys the notion of the melodramatic. . . . Names of such a stamp by no means coincide with the British schoolboy's notion of the beautiful. He has a much higher respect for 'Tom'. But there are several passages in both Mr. Farrar's books which look more as if they had been written by a lady, drawing upon her own innocent imagination for the sayings and doings of schoolboy life, than by a master in one of our most important public schools, who must know, or ought to know, how schoolboys really think and speak.

Quoting the passage from *Eric* in which Eric and Russell swear eternal friendship, hold hands and agree to call each other by their Christian names, Collins expostulates:

> We will venture to say that nineteen out of twenty schoolboys who read the passage would pronounce it 'bosh' and if the twentieth admired it, we should be pretty safe in setting him down as a spooney.

He dismisses vows of eternal friendship as 'confined almost exclusively to Frenchmen and young ladies' seminaries. The fellows at Harrow did not use to be do demonstrative.'[5]

The Saturday Review complained, 'We can scarcely imagine a less healthy book to put into a boy's hand', pointing to the dangers of inculcating priggishness, self-importance and a morbid self-consciousness. It criticised the over-earnestness:

> It is a novel written to exalt principles which are . . . widely adopted at public schools in the present day, and which owe much of their currency to the influence of the late Dr. Arnold. In former times, the *escapades* of schoolboys used to be looked upon and referred to principally as matter of joke . . . To Dr. Arnold and those who derived their views from him, such notions were a sort of abomination of desolation. It was one of his most favourite maxims that boys were moral agents as well as men, that they were as capable as men both of crimes and of sins, and that to speak or think lightly of their offences was to sap the very foundations of morality.

It also poured scorn on the excess emotionalism:

> Its general tone is uniformly sad and this sadness is heightened artificially. To say nothing of three more or less violent deaths, two of which involve angelic deathbeds, everything is served up with tear sauce. The boys quote hymns, and to the infinite indignation of all English readers, occasionally kiss each other.[6]

Of this review Farrar wrote from Harrow to a friend, 'I know the Saturday Wasp only too well personally. His unChristian tone will do the book no harm except that little fools here have read it and think him an oracle.'[7]

Experts on children's literature were soon expressing doubts similar to those of the critics. In 1869 Charlotte Yonge described *Eric* as 'that morbid dismal tale . . . which we hope no mother or boy ever reads, since it can answer no purpose but to make them unhappy and suspicious, besides that it enforces by numerous telling examples that the sure reward for virtue is a fatal accident'.[8] In 1888 Edward Salmon expressed grave misgivings:

> No single book for boys presents so many difficulties to the mind of the critic as *Eric* . . . its tone generally is so sorrowful and the impression it conveys is so pessimistic that it would be decidedly unwise to put it indiscriminately into any boy's hands . . . If *Eric* be accepted by any child as true to life, he would, arguing from the logic of its facts, rise from its perusal assured that, if once he went astray, retribution would have no end and penitence could never bring him peace.[9]

The author of *Eric* was one of the most influential churchmen of his day. According to *The Dictionary of National Biography* he 'exerted a vast popular influence upon the religious feelings and culture of the middle classes for fully forty years by virtue of his enthusiasm, always sincere it not always discriminating, and of his boundless industry'.[10] Frederic William Farrar (1831–1903) was born in Bombay, the son of the chaplain of the Church Missionary Society, and educated at King William's College, Isle of Man, and later King's College, London, and Trinity College, Cambridge. He became a master at Marlborough under G. E. L. Cotton in 1854, then for fifteen years (1855–71) was a housemaster at Harrow. He concluded his academic career as Master of Marlborough (1871–76), where as a reforming Head he introduced science teaching and improved the sanitary arrangements. He had been ordained in 1854 and left Marlborough to pursue a career in the Church during which he became the most popular preacher in England, and a very successful writer on religious matters, including a best-selling life of Christ. His career culminated in his appointment as Dean of Canterbury in 1895.

It is clear from his son Reginald's biography, which contains tributes from many friends and colleagues recalling his 'gentleness of disposition, his nobility of character, his manliness and love of truth', that Farrar was an immensely industrious, kind-hearted, enthusiastic, high-souled, dedicated man, devout, earnest and essentially unworldly. As a teacher he was at his best with able boys, though unwavering in his efforts to stimulate and interest all. A favourite pupil, George Russell, recalled his teaching of the fourteen-year-olds of the Remove at Harrow:

> Everyone who knows Public Schools knows that boys of that age are thorough Philistines, despising intellect and glorying in their brutal ignorance. For such creatures it was a most beneficial experience to pass into Farrar's hands. He employed all his varied resources—kindness, sympathy, sternness, rhetoric, sarcasm—in the effort to make us feel ashamed of being ignorant and anxious to know. He was ruthless in his determination to disturb what he called 'the duckweed'—the mass of sheer indolence and fatuity which pervaded his form—and to bring out and encourage the faintest signs of perception and intelligence. His contagious enthusiasm stimulated anything which we possess-ed in the way of intellectual taste or power. He taught us to love what was beautiful in literature, art and nature. He lived and moved and had his being in poetry, and was never so happy as when helping us to illustrate our Virgil or Euripides from Wordsworth and Milton.[11]

He was not a great disciplinarian. J. D. Rogers, a pupil at Marlborough, recalled:

> He gave us great liberty, rode with a very loose rein, and trusted to our moral force instead of his own vigilance. Moreover, he proclaimed all his own weak points from the housetop; thus his rooted belief that he knew boys whom he did not know led him into many blunders, for which, however, his evidently kindly meaning easily atoned; and the too great ease with which he took offence, and then forgave, looked like want of judgement, but was partly due to the unsuspecting sincerity which made him utter everything that was passing through his mind. He made up for want of firmness by excess of kindness.[12]

Farrar's Marlborough colleague, P. E. Thompson, confirmed Rogers's view but added, 'Where a question of morals were concerned, no head-master could be more prompt and severe. He consoled and encouraged the offender, but his first consideration was the welfare of the community.'[13]

That same colleague gently recalled, 'Humour was not a conspicuous quality in him,' and 'he was without the gift of small talk'.[14] In addition he adopted a grandeur of manner, partly to conceal a natural shyness, partly because he lived on a loftier plane of life and thought than the ordinary mortal. It was this grandeur of manner that struck boys most forcibly but it led to problems, as J. D. Rogers recalled:

> He was as unlike in nature to the typical schoolboy as it was possible to be. None could have ever called him 'jolly' or 'old fellow' . . . At first sight he seemed all stateliness and austerity: cold, splendid, one-sided, unattainable . . . The last sight of him revealed only an excess of sincerity, sensitiveness, candour and kindliness . . . The first quality set off and ennobled the very rare and high enthusiasm which was his most valuable teaching asset; it also accounted for some of his faults and accentuated all his faults as a schoolmaster. The last quality . . . accounted for his other faults and saved him from the effects of all his faults as a schoolmaster.[15]

His high expectations of the intellectual lives of his pupils led to frequent disappointments. Taking visitors to sixth-form studies to see his sixth form at work, he found them enjoying a repast of cocoa and roast potatoes and issued a magisterial reproof:

> I confidently expected to be able to point with pride to my sixth form boys absorbed and immersed in study of some Attic masterpiece . . . But what was my indignation, vexation and shame when I discovered them greedily engaged in ravenously devouring the semese fragments of a barbaric repast.[16]

This provoked mirth rather than regret in the boys. The authentic voice of the Victorian schoolmaster, vexed by boyish ignorance and lack of application, can be heard in the thunderous rebukes recollected by his pupils: 'your ignorance is so profound that it ossifies the very powers of scorn' or (sarcastically) 'Can any boy tell me within five hundred years the date of Joan of Arc?' He would reprehend displays of ignorance in one of his own eight children with a grave 'Antediluvian megatherium'.[17]

His seriousness, grandiloquence and lack of humour were a source of much fun for the boys. C. L. Graves, a Marlborough pupil, recalled:

> Some of the cleverest boys in the Sixth used to lay themselves out to play on his foibles and susceptibilities, yet I have good reason to believe that the most ingenious of his tormentors had all the while a warm feeling for the Headmaster whose sense of propriety they would from time to time attempt to disconcert.[18]

When he left Marlborough for Harrow, Marlborough boys spoofed him by persistently writing to him to sympathise with him about the violent physical attacks he was allegedly suffering at the hands of Harrow boys and which provoked from Farrar in a letter to a friend a frenzied outburst against such tales ('They are grotesquely and groundlessly and absolutely false and as diametrically the reverse of anything possible as they can be'), revealing at once the essential unworldliness, humourlessness emotionalism of the man.[19]

Sir Edwin Arnold, who sent his son to study under Farrar at Marlborough, provides what seems to be a balanced summation of his teaching career, speaking with gentle exactitude:

All the clever boys grew deeply attached to the patient, earnest and richly endowed man, whose smile was so sweet when an act of boyish virtue or a brilliant piece of classwork pleased him, and who was so gentle in his displeasure, and so just, even in his anger. The noisy, lazy and shallow among his pupils found him perhaps pedantic, dry and exacting for he loved hard work too well for himself to understand how distasteful it seemed to some natures. Boys are stern and keen judges of their instructors, and those who were smitten with the modern passion for athletics did not always find Farrar enthusiastic enough about cricket, football and the out of door portion of an English boy's upbringing.[20]

Farrar's works bear the clear imprint of the personality of their author in all its complexity.

Farrar was twenty-seven when he wrote *Eric*, and he dedicated it to G. E. L. Cotton, Bishop of Calcutta, formerly his headmaster at Marlborough and before that the Young Master in *Tom Brown's Schooldays*. Like Cotton, Farrar shared the aims and outlook of Thomas Arnold. Reviewing Arnold's sermons for *Macmillan's Magazine*, he pronounced them 'the best models of what school sermons ought to be' and praised Arnold 'as a model for all clergymen in this respect more than all others, that—like Canon Kingsley—he was every inch a man'. He called himself 'one of the least worthy of those who in a similar office to Arnold's own would fain have caught something of his spirit'.[21]

Farrar's novels make sense only when set firmly in the context of Evangelicalism. Evangelicalism dominated British life for the first half of the nineteenth century. The product of the eighteenth-century religious revival, it was a reaction against worldliness, rationalism and optimism. The Evangelicals believed in total commitment to Christianity, a perpetual sense of accountability for every act, an overriding seriousness of purpose and the governing principle of hard work and duty. Their style was intensely emotional, vibrantly enthusiastic and continuously introspective. All these qualities can be seen as characterising the message, structure and style of Farrar's *Eric*. The book stands as an emblem of the Evangelical Age, all the more poignant for appearing at its end, a grand synthesis of a world view that was about to be overtaken.

Farrar expounded his Evangelical faith in the sermons he preached as Master of Marlborough and which were published under the title *In the Days of thy Youth*. He believed firmly that the boy was father to the man:

> Be false and treacherous, be unjust and impure, be indolent and disobedient now, and . . . you will grow up into a useless, dangerous, degraded man. And, on the other hand, be good and faithful, be pure and honest, be brave and generous now, and then be very sure that God will make you a worthy son of the school that trained you, a worthy citizen of the nation that nurtured you; nay even more, a true child of God, a certain inheritor of the kingdom of Heaven.[22]

He quotes with approval the eighteenth-century moralist who argued, 'Virtue is the conquest of self for the benefit of others.'[23] Selfishness is seen as the source of all ills; school as the place where boys must be trained to be 'modest and manly, loyal and grateful, affectionate and courteous, humble and pure'.[24] He warns that step by step, little by little, one can rise up and attain righteousness or descend to destruction. He warns of the boy who begins term with a resolution to do better and not waste his school career:

> He begins well for the first few days; he springs up cheerfully and manfully in the morning in good time, with no lazy self-indulgent lingering; he says his prayers humbly and reverently; he kneels punctually in chapel; his lesson has been honestly prepared; he succeeds, and thinks that he is entering on a better state of things, and that this term *at last* is going to be a well-spent, and faithful and honourable one. It goes on for a few days. But it hardly needs even a temptation to make him fall away; if a temptation does come, however trivial, his good purpose slips into instant ashes, like tow at the breath of fire. But even if no special temptation comes, there is no perseverance, no solidity, no manly consistence in his brief improvement. One morning all is done a little later; the rising begins to get hurried and slovenly; the morning prayer first slurred over, then shortened, then neglected; unprepared, he meets the temptations of the day; the work is put off or done anyhow; the playtime unduly lengthened; the novel not laid aside; the duty forgotten or neglected. He sinks lower and lower, the esteem of his teachers is lost, his self-respect is wholly weakened, and so, little by little, ever little by little, the old story is renewed again, and the new term is wasted like the old.[25]

Here in sum is the underlying message of *Eric*.

Farrar firmly believed that though a man's life may be influenced, it cannot be determined, by circumstances. The individual can rise above sin, evil, temptation, by his own efforts. Self-conquest is essential: 'Selfishness . . . is the source of nearly all the ruin and misery, which devastate the world. Pride springs from it; ambition lives for it; anger leans on it; lust serves it. It is the fruitful source of disbelief.'[26] On the other hand, 'obedience, diligence, honesty, truth, kindness, purity, are your duties to God and Man'.[27] He calls on the boys to cultivate seriousness of mind, obedience and diligence, offering them as an ideal the great Puritan John Milton, whose ideal was:

to make labour and intent study his portion in this life . . . to draw inspiration from devout prayer . . . to encourage in his own soul an honest haughtiness of innocence and self-respect as to render it impossible to him to sink and plunge into the low descents of unlawful degradations; it was even without the oath of knighthood to be born with the free and gentle spirit of the Christian knight; it was to cherish that fine reservedness of natural disposition, and moral discipline.[28]

He warns them against evil words, against lies ('A man of honour could not tell a lie even if he wished'), profanity ('it is a sign of mental imbecility and social ill-breeding, no less than moral death'), uncharity ('ill-nature, gossip, spite, malice, slander, whispers, backbiting, detraction, calumny') and impurity ('the influence of such words is truly baleful; their effect often terribly permanent').[29] He warns them against evil friendships and encourages the cultivation of good friends, 'with whom you can enjoy that blessed and beautiful thing, a free, pure, noble, natural school friendship—a thing as blessed and beautiful as a low and sneaking friendship is leprous and accursed'.[30] He warns them against succumbing to the prevailing evil tone. 'The average boy, the ordinary boy, of a school, if a school have a vicious tone, catches that vicious tone, and leaves it worse himself, and worse for others.'[31] But if a few boys can set a bad tone, a few can set a good tone, and he urges them to do this. It is the characteristic missionary impulse of the Evangelical.

Farrar warns them against the dangers of athleticism. A boy who over-values athletic success can be led into vanity. Too much time spent on games is wasted time. Athleticism can lead to foolish partisanship. 'Games, however useful and delightful, are not of first-rate, not even of third, fourth or fifth—scarcely even of tenth-rate importance in comparison with higher things.'[32] But Farrar was setting his face against the trend. What would he have thought of the fact that the 1907 edition of *Eric* boasted a cover picture of a schoolboy cricketer at the wicket? This represented the triumph of the new faith of athleticism over the Evangelicalism of his youth.

In his last sermon before leaving Marlborough, Farrar outlined his view of how a boy could be happy:

> it is by diligence; it is by purity; it is by self-denial. It is by being clear of vice; clear of self-indulgence; clear of self-conceit. It is by that seriousness of mind which stands in awe and sins not; by that thoughtfulness of disposition which sets a right value on time and opportunity; by that resoluteness of purpose which shall arm you both against the sudden onslaughts and the insidious approaches of evil.[33]

All these ideas were woven into the structure and texture of *Eric*, which needs to be read alongside the sermons to appreciate its ideological purpose. The effect of such sermons on the more thoughtful and susceptible boys in Farrar's congregations is attested by George Russell:

> His exuberance of rhetoric, though in later years it offended adult audiences, awed and fascinated boys, and his solemn yet glowing appeals for righteousness and purity and moral courage left permanent dints on our hearts . . . and lives.[34]

Farrar spoke constantly of his love for his boys and sought strenuously to lead them to the Christian truth. Two terms recur constantly in his own writings and in writings about and references to him by his contemporaries—'manly' and 'earnest'. It is clear that for him the terms were interchangeable, and that what he was setting out to do was define for boys his own brand of Christian manliness, which required sober-mindedness, constant self-examination and a passionate commitment to the faith.

The hysterical virulence of attacks on *Eric* should perhaps give us pause for thought. They are inspired in part by the fact that Farrar's brand of masculinity has clashed with two other definitions which have successively provided the dominant ideology of maleness in Britain, though both have also coexisted since the nineteenth century. One is that late nineteenth-century public school gentlemanliness based on emotional restraint, the ethics of athleticism and the strong commitment to a sense of balance and proportion, all of which have become synonymous with Englishness and which were outraged by the emotionalism, super-piety and Evangelicalism of Farrar's boys. The other is that aggressively *macho* image which antedated Evangelicalism and surfaced again with the decline of the gentlemanly ideal. Real men do not weep; real men swear, smoke, gamble and drink; real men never admit that they are wrong; real men settle disagreements with their fists. The idea that they might weep, pray, declare their love for their friends or seek to eschew bad habits for the good of their immortal soul is greeted by this school of thought with disbelieving scorn. It is this version of manliness, shared in the late eighteenth and early nineteenth centuries by the aristocracy and the lower classes, that *Eric* sets out to undermine.

Eric is conceived on an epic scale, its model Milton's *Paradise Lost*, which Farrar had learned by heart as a boy. His pupil, J. D. Rogers, recalled:

> Probably he is the only nineteenth century man of letters of whom it could be said that his character was steeped and saturated in Milton. Admiration for Milton in the sense in which Farrar admired Milton exists no longer if it ever existed. Some attraction or affinity drove him towards whatever looked large and splendid, away from what looked little and sordid. That was why he preferred the desolate unearthly glory of Milton to the glorious humanity of

Shakespeare. Indeed, I think that he liked Milton, because Milton is remote from humanity, shrinks from contact with its coarser manifestations, and lets us too easily forget the facts of actual life.[35]

The book is carefully and deliberately structured to show the gradual descent of Eric through swearing, smoking, drinking, idleness and self-will to destruction. Each defeat in the moral battle is marked by the death of someone he loves (his best friend Russell, his adored younger brother Verny, his beloved mother). Eventually he too dies, having repented and received forgiveness. The battle for his soul is conducted between a series of saintly figures (Russell, Montagu, Mr Rose) and a series of evil, almost demonic figures (Barker, Ball and Brigson), exemplars of that schematic, black-and-white view of boys which Montagu Butler, headmaster of Harrow, discerned in him:

> He seemed always to have before him two haunting visions, the one of boyish innocence, the other of boyish wickedness. If to some of us he appeared sometimes to see these two great extremes out of due proportion and to be less clearsighted as to the wide region which lies between them, we were nevertheless grateful for his loving sympathy with the one and his solemn warnings to the other.[36]

With the arrival of Brigson the story specifically takes on Miltonic proportions, as Farrar heads chapter 1 of Part 2, 'Abdiel' ('Among the faithless, faithful only he'), a reference to Montagu, and later declaring that while the satanic Brigson was at Roslyn, 'the whole lower school was a Pandemonium of evil passions and despicable habits'. The story begins in sweetness and light, with the family, the countryside, purity and joy, and Eric at school continually gets glimpses of what might have been, repents time and again, is given every consideration and support by the headmaster and Mr Rose and yet, by his desire for popularity, by his stubborn pride and his basic self-centredness, he falls like Lucifer from Paradise. *Eric* stands, then, as a grand apocalyptic symphony in which Farrar brings together all his ideas and themes about school, boyhood, sin and nobility.

The eponymous hero Eric Williams, born in India, is sent to England at an early age to be raised by an aunt and her daughter. He grows into a truthful, quick-witted, sturdy, honourable, handsome boy, who at the age of twelve begins to show signs of pride and temper, and therefore needs to be sent to school. ('Beyond a certain age no boy of spirit can be safely guided by a woman's hand alone'.) His first experience of formal teaching at a local Latin school ends abruptly when the master goes mad. The only thing of value that Eric learns at the school is to mix freely and equally with boys of the lower classes ('no harm, only good, seemed to come from the intercourse'). In this

his experience parallels that of Tom Brown.

When his parents return from India, Eric is sent to Roslyn School, where he encounters all the perils and pitfalls of school life. He is bullied by the unprepossessing, spiteful and unintelligent Barker. Farrar reflects:

> Why is it that new boys are almost invariably mistreated? I have often fancied that there must be in boyhood a pseudo-instinctive cruelty . . . which no amount of civilization can entirely repress. Certain it is, that to most boys the first term is a trying ordeal. They are being tested and weighed. Their place in the general estimation is not yet fixed, and the slightest circumstances are seized upon to settle the category under which the boy is to be classed. A few apparently trivial accidents of his first few weeks at school often decide his position in the general regard for the remainder of his boyhood. And yet these are *not* accidents; they are the slight indications which give an unerring proof of the general tendencies of his character and training.[37]

Farrar tells the story of Owen, who, bullied by Barker, reports him first to his form master, Mr Gordon, and then to the headmaster, Dr Rowlands. Barker is flogged and threatened with expulsion, and for a while Owen is ostracised for 'sneaking', but the bullying ceases. However, Farrar adds, 'I do not recommend any boy to imitate Owen in this matter. It is a far better and braver thing to bear bullying with such a mixture of spirit and good humour, as in time to disarm it.'[38] He apparently sees bullying as part of the *rites de passage* of the new boy which test out his character and endurance. Eric tells no one about his treatment, and the bullying continues until his father accidentally catches Barker brutalising his son and horsewhips him.

Eric now gets to know three boys in particular, and in them Farrar carefully delineates three boy-types. Duncan is 'the most boyish of boys, intensely full of fun, good nature and vigour; with fair ability, he never got on well, because he could not be still for two minutes . . . but out of school he was the soul of every game'. Montagu is a 'thorough little gentleman', who, 'without being clever or athletic . . . managed to do very fairly both at work and at the games, and while he was too exclusive to make many *intimate* friends, everybody liked walking about or talking with him . . . In nearly all respects, his influence was thoroughly good and few boys were more generally popular.' Owen is the intellectual; 'his merit was a ceaseless diligence, in which it was doubtful whether ambition or conscientiousness had the greatest share. Reserved and thoughtful, unfitted for or indifferent to most games, he was anything but a favourite with the rest and Eric rather respected than liked him.'[39] All three become friends but it is the saintly orphan Edwin Russell whom Eric likes best, confiding to his mother that he 'loved Russell almost as well as he loved Vernon'.[40]

After bullying, Eric's next exposure is to cribbing (using translations to prepare the Latin construe). At first he scorns to use a crib and comes joint top in the examinations by his own efforts. Promoted to the Upper Fourth, he takes his turn at writing out the general crib but does not use it himself. But Eric's popularity of which he is very proud, prevents him from expressing 'a manly disapproval of the general cheating'. This moral failure becomes the first stage of his decline. For Eric is discovered in possession of the general crib by Mr Gordon and is ferociously denounced and put in detention. In reaction, Eric begins to neglect his academic work and direct all his energies to games.

When Eric is flogged by the headmaster for giggling in chapel, he becomes suffused with pride and rebelliousness. ('It was his *first* flogging, and he felt it deeply. To his proud spirit the disgrace was intolerable. At that moment, he hated Dr. Rowlands, he hated Mr. Gordon, he hated his schoolfellows, he hated everybody'.)[41] Eric becomes increasingly self-centred, neglecting his brother Vernon ('What a little bore you are') and causing his parents needless anxiety by thoughtlessly going crab-fishing and arriving back hours late for dinner. When his parents return to India and he is parted from them, he resolves, 'I *will* be a better boy, I *will* indeed; I mean to do great things, and they shall have nothing but good reports of me.'[42] But as a boarder Eric finds academic work impossible, as out of class the boys indulge permanently in games, pranks, horse-play and sometimes bullying. Eric is 'taken up' by Upton, eighteen-year-old cousin of Russell, 'immensely popular in the school for his prowess and good looks'. Upton is idolised by the small boys, whom he protects from bullying, but is a dangerous influence because of his idea of manliness, 'which he thought consisted in a fearless disregard of all school rules, and the performance of the wildest tricks'. Eric and Upton become sworn friends and Russell and Montagu discuss the 'taking up system', and agree that it is bad, expressing what is almost certainly Farrar's view, that it is bad because it reduces small boys to 'an unnatural sort of dependence', it makes them conceited and it causes jealousy in others.[43]

Next, Eric starts swearing. 'What a surly devil it is,' he declares of Mr Gordon. 'Oh, Eric, that's the first time I ever heard you swear,' says Russell, acting as the voice of Eric's conscience. 'I hope that I know the difference between what's right and what's wrong, and do let me say that you will be much happier, if you try not to yield to all the bad things round us.' Eric defends swearing. Everyone except Owen and Russell does it. But Russell's reprimand causes him to reflect:

> He knew that all his moral consciousness was fast vanishing and leaving him a bad and reckless boy. In a moment all this passed through his mind. He remembered how shocked he had been at swearing at first; and even when it became too familiar to shock him, how he determined never to fall into the

habit himself. Then he remembered how gradually it had become quite a graceful sound in his ears—a sound of entire freedom and independence of moral restraint; an open casting off, as it were, of all authority, so that he had begun to admire it, particularly in Duncan, and, above all, in his new hero Upton; and he recollected how, at last, an oath had one day slipped out in his own words, and how strange it sounded to him . . . but now that he had done it once, it became less dreadful, and gradually grew common enough, till even conscience hardly reminded him that he was doing wrong.[44]

The next stage in Eric's decline is indecency. Ball arrives at Roslyn, 'backward in work, overflowing with vanity at his supposed good looks, of mean disposition and feeble intellect, he was the very worst specimen of a boy that Eric had ever seen'. But Eric's 'silly love of universal popularity' makes him accept and tolerate the society of Ball. Ball corrupts the boys in dormitory No. 7 with his air of experience and tales of immoral doings at his previous school. When he first uses indecent words Eric, though shocked, remains silent. Farrar apostrophises him in a celebrated and characteristic passage:

> Now, Eric, now or never! Life and death, ruin and salvation, corruption and purity, are perhaps in the balance together, and the scale of your destiny may hang on a single word of yours. Speak out, boy! Tell these fellows that unseemly words wound your conscience; tell them that they are ruinous, sinful, damnable; speak out and save yourself and the rest. Virtue is strong and beautiful, Eric, and vice is downcast in her awful presence. Lose your purity of heart, Eric, and you have lost a jewel which the whole world, if it were 'one entire and perfect chrysolite', cannot replace. Good spirits guard that young boy, and give him grace in this his hour of trial! Open his eyes that he may see the fiery horses and the fiery chariots of the angels who would defend him, and the dark array of spiritual foes who throng around his bed. Point a pitying finger to the yawning abyss of shame, ruin, and despair, that even now perhaps is being cleft under his feet. Show him the garlands of the present and the past, withering at the touch of the Erinnys in the future. In pity, in pity, show him the canker which he is introducing into the sap of the tree of life, which shall cause its roots to be hereafter as bitterness, and its blossom to go up as dust.
>
> But the sense of sin was on Eric's mind. How *could* he speak? Was not his own language sometimes profane? How—how could he profess to reprove another boy on the ground of morality, when he himself said and did things less dangerous perhaps, but equally forbidden? For half an hour, in an agony of struggle with himself, Eric lay silent. Since Ball's last words nobody had spoken. They were going to sleep. It was too late to speak now, Eric thought. The moment passed by for ever; Eric had listened without objection to foul words, and the irreparable harm was done.[45]

Eric discusses the situation with Russell and Montagu, and Russell reveals he spoke out against indecent words and stamped them out in his dormitory. Montagu also attacks indecency, regarding it as 'blackguardly and in bad taste'. So the religious and social sanctions are invoked here, just as in Farrar's sermons.

There is more to this than just swearing. Indecency is worse. Jonathan Gathorne-Hardy has identified the particular sin under discussion as masturbation.[46] The clue comes in Russell's reminder to Eric that Dr Rowlands had warned them against such indecency in his lecture on Kibroth-Hattavaah, the place of burial in the Book of Numbers for those guilty of sensual lust. Farrar launches into a passionate lamentation:

> Kibroth-Hattavaah! Many and many a young Englishman has perished there! Many and many a happy English boy, the jewel of his mother's heart—brave and beautiful and strong—lies buried there. Very pale their shadows rise before us—the shadows of your young brothers who have sinned and suffered. From the sea and the sod, from foreign graves and English churchyards, they start up and throng around us in the paleness of their fall. May every school-boy who reads this page be warned by the waving of their wasted hands, from that burning marle of passion where they found nothing but shame and ruin, polluted affections, and an early grave.[47]

Eric's decline continues apace. Caught doing amateur theatricals after lights-out, Eric is caned by the Head. 'He burned not with remorse or regret, but with shame and violent indignation, and listened, with an affectation of stubborn indifference, to Dr. Rowlands's warnings.'[48] Rowlands warns him against Upton, and so Eric cultivates his friend-ship out of defiance. 'Any attempt on the part of masters to interfere in the friendships of boys is usually unsuccessful,' says Farrar sadly.[49]

The concerned schoolmaster Mr Rose has Eric for supper, encourages him, prays for him, and for a while Eric is better, 'full of the strongest resolutions and earnestly praised amendment for the future'. 'But when the hours of temptation come, his good intentions melted away.' When 'Gordon is a surly devil' is written on the blackboard, everyone believes Eric guilty. He refuses to own up and the headmaster withdraws all the boys' privileges. Eric is sent to Coventry by the boys, Russell, Owen, Montagu, Duncan, Wright and Mr Rose alone maintain-ing his innocence. Eric 'with firm manly bearing' agrees to stand school trial for the offence. Russell defends Eric in the trial and proves Barker guilty. Barker is made to run the gauntlet, flogged and expelled. Russell, however, forgives Barker, prays for him and is the only boy to see him off with one last kind word. The death of Russell provides the dramatic climax to Part 1.

Upton teaches Eric to smoke. They believe it to be 'manly'. But then Eric and his friends are trapped on a rock by the incoming tide and Russell is injured trying to jump to safety. Eric swims across to protect him while Montagu goes for help. Delirious, Russell moans,

'Dear Eric, don't smoke.' Russell is returned to the school, seriously ill, his leg is amputated and, amid tears, prayers and fervent protestations of love, he dies. In a highly charged and entirely convincing passage Eric reproaches himself ('How odious seemed all the vice which he had seen and partaken in'). The effect on Montagu of Russell's death is also profound. He turns his heart to God and becomes 'nobler and manlier' than before. His father, a gentleman and a scholar, had taught him the principles of refinement and good taste but had paid little attention to godliness. Now Montagu, without losing his winning gracefulness, adds 'a touching earnestness'. He has found the essential ingredient of life and becomes one of the chosen, taking over the role of Russell in the book and at the school.[50]

During the holidays the chastened Eric writes to Mr Rose, wondering if it is right to bring his younger brother Vernon to the school and expose him to all the evils and temptations he has undergone. Mr Rose replies in terms Farrar himself used in a sermon:

> The true preparation for life, the true basis of a manly character, is not to have been ignorant of evil, but to have known it and avoided it; not to have been sheltered from temptation; but to have passed through it and over-come it by God's help . . . The ruin of human souls can never be achieved by enemies from without unless they be aided by traitors from within.[51]

Part 2 begins a year later. Memories of Russell grow dim, the good resolutions fade and Eric resumes his bad habits. It happens gradually, not without inward struggle and remorse, but by degrees the struggles grow weaker. Eric is now sixteen, high in the fifth form and captain of the school eleven. His school work has fallen off but he is 'the acknowledged leader and champion in matters requiring boldness and courage'. His head continues to be turned by popularity ('favour of man led to forgetfulness of God'). Eric neglects Vernon, who falls into bad company, in particular that of Brigson, expelled from one of the worst managed schools in Ireland and let loose on the boys of Roslyn. 'Never did some of the Roslyn boys, to their dying day, forget the deep, intolerable, unfathomable flood of moral turpitude and iniquity which he bore with him; a flood which seemed irresistible.'[52] Brigson, a bully and self-appointed leader of the lower school, orders that no work be done outside the classroom and teaches the small boys to cheat, lie and disobey their masters. Owen is head of the school but 'he was so little of a boy that he had no sympathy with the others and little authority over them'. Farrar attributes the deteriorating state of affairs to the absence of the prefect system from the school. Montagu does what he can to resist the spread of corruption but he stands alone. As a result Brigson gets his minions to harass Montagu constantly until finally he catches small boys wrecking his room, thrashes them and thrashes Brigson. But Brigson's hold on the lower school remains strong. The upper school divides into two groups, the games players under Eric and Duncan, who are not interested in anything but games, and the intellectuals, under Montagu, who actively seek to counteract the malign influence of Brigson. Farrar is making clear his view of athleticism here, as an obsessive state which loses sight of issues of real importance.

Eric now 'takes up' the bright, high-spirited Charlie Wildney, nicknaming him 'sunbeam' ('he's a very nice little fellow, a regular devil'). His fierce disregard of the rules makes Wildney an object of general admiration. Duncan, Eric and Wildney smoke in their study. They sneak out of school to buy beer from a nearby pub. Wildney is caught and flogged, but does not name his associates. Both Montagu and Mr Rose try to persuade Eric to mend his ways but in vain. All decent boys now shun Eric, despising him as a boy who would do anything for popularity. Eric is thrown back on the company of Ball and even of Brigson. Brigson forms 'the anti-muffs' to meet at the Jolly Herring to smoke and drink. The pub is raided by two masters, and Eric and Wildney escape back to school. There Eric, slightly the worse for drink, defies Mr Rose and breaks his cane when Mr Rose lays it across his back.

Eric's brother Vernon remonstrates with him for the way he has treated Mr Rose, telling him that he was also caught at the pub, and Mr Rose has been talking to him and praying for him. Eric is so moved that he goes to the headmaster, confesses all and makes a public apology to Mr Rose. Brigson's power is finally broken when he organises a 'crusting' (pelting with bread crusts) of Mr Rose. When Mr Rose confronts him, Brigson denies organising it, is flogged, breaks down and begs for mercy. 'Miserable coward,' thunders Mr Rose, and proceeds to flog all the others involved. This act decisively establishes Mr Rose's authority. ('Mr Rose's noble moral influence gained tenfold strength from the respect and wholesome fear that he then inspired.')[53] The boys now all cheer Mr Rose and reject Brigson as coward and liar, and Brigson gets his father to remove him from the school.

Eric's decline, however, continues. When little Wright, encouraged by Montagu, tries to stamp out cribbing in the lower forms, Eric boxes his ears. Montagu and Owen, out walking, see Eric, Wildney, with whom Eric is now 'infatuated', and a few others smoking pipes and drinking brandy. Duncan, although a friend of Eric, does not join in. His rough honesty and good sense prevent him, and as he gets older he gets 'steadier, more diligent, more thoughtful, more manly', a perfect example of Farrar's ideal of a boy standing out against corruption. Eric and Wildney begin to show more clearly the signs of drinking. Eric fights Montagu when he tries to break up a study drinking session.

Eric and Wildney steal pigeons from Gordon's house as a lark and have a celebratory carouse. Eventually they turn up drunk at roll call and are sentenced to be publicly expelled. Eric begs the headmaster for a second chance, and because of his rescue of Russell the Head relents and allows them to stay. Rose, Vernon, Montagu, Owen and Duncan all intercede for Eric. Tearfully Vernon and Eric pray together, kiss and go for walks along the sands. Eric and Wildney are flogged and gated and bear their punishment in 'a manly and penitent way'. Eric begins to act as a force for good, unanimity begins to prevail again at school, and Eric and Montagu are reconciled. Vernon falls to his death while out collecting birds' eggs from a cliff nest. Eric, consumed with grief, determines to continue the process of reform ('I *must* be a better boy'). But his sins catch up with him when Billy, landlord of the Jolly Herring, reports that Brigson never paid the bill for their feasts. Eric manages to raise the money to pay the bill. But then Billy threatens to reveal his involvement in the pigeon theft unless he is paid £5. Eric is sorely tempted to steal the cricket fund money but resists. He has terrifying conscience-stricken dreams.

In the only sporting scene in the entire book, Eric plays cricket for the first time since Vernon's death and triumphs:

> It was long since he had stood before the wicket, but now he was there, looking like a beautiful picture as the sunlight streamed over him, and made his fair hair shine like gold. In the triumph of success his sorrows were flung to the winds, and his blue eyes sparkled with interest and joy.[54]

It is his last moment of happiness at Roslyn. It is discovered that the cricket fund money has been stolen, suspicion falls on Eric and he runs away to sea as a cabin boy on a trading schooner. On board he suffers the ultimate torment of being thrust into the midst of the working classes:

> The whole life of the ship was odious to him. His sense of refinement was exquisitely keen, and now to be called Bill, and kicked and cuffed about by these gross-minded men, and hear their rough, coarse, drunken talk and sometimes endure their still more intolerable patronage, filled him with deeply-seated loathing.[55]

Ill and brutalised, he is unable to work and is flogged into insensibility by the captain. Farrar goes into rhapsodies of horror describing it:

> Now Eric knew for the first time the awful reality of intense pain; he had determined to utter no sound, to give no sign; but when the horrible rope fell on him, grinding across his back and making his body literally creak under the blow, he quivered like an aspen-leaf in every limb, and could not suppress the harrowing murmur, 'O God, help me, help me.' Again the rope whistled in the air, again it grided across the boy's naked back, and once more the crimson

furrow bore witness to the violent laceration. A sharp shriek of inexpressible agony rang from his lips so shrill, so heartrending, that it sounded long in the memory of all who heard it. But the brute who administered the torture was untouched. Once more, and again, the rope rose and fell, and under its mark the blood first dribbled, and then streamed from the white and tender skin.[56]

Eventually, ragged, filthy and sick, he escapes and makes his way to his aunt's, where he is welcomed and tended, but his constitution has been fatally undermined by starvation and ill treatment. Montagu and Wildney, sent for by his aunt, reveal that Eric has been cleared of suspicion of theft of the cricket fund. Billy stole it. Eric is transformed:

> Every trace of reacklessness and arrogance had passed, every stain of passion had been removed; every particle of hardness had been calcined in the flame of trial. All was gentleness, love and dependence, in the once bright, impetuous, self-willed boy; it seemed as though the lightning of God's anger had shattered and swept away all that was evil in his heart and life, and left all his true excellence . . . pure and unscathed.[57]

But there is worse to come. News arrives that Mrs Williams, already affected by Vernon's death, has died of grief on learning of Eric's disgrace. Eric shrieks and swoons, but recovers in time to die, confident of forgiveness. In a postscript we learn that Montagu has become an MP and the 'best loved landlord for miles around', Owen a fellow of Trinity, Upton and Wildney army officers and Brigson—of all things— a policeman.

The success of *Eric* prompted Farrar to essay another school story, *St Winifred's, or, The World of School* (1862), a book which Reginald Farrar thought superior to *Eric*. It was influenced more than *Eric* by his experiences at both Harrow and Marlborough. Reginald Farrar believed that, though it had less effect than *Eric*, it was 'truer to the real life of boys and has been less open to criticism'.[58] In fact it essentially reworks *Eric*, though with fewer deaths and tears and a happier ending. The characters, elements and motifs of the book all recall those of *Eric*, with the individual characters having direct counterparts. Montagu becomes Power; Owen, Daubeny; Duncan, Henderson; Wildney, Wilton; and Eric, Kenrick. Like Roslyn, St Winifred's is modelled on Farrar's own school, King William's College, though with fagging and prefects added, to bring it more into line with the reformed public school.

The central character is Walter Evson, who comes to St Winifred's, survives bullying, disgrace and being sent to Coventry, to become a hero when he rescues friends trapped on a nearby mountain. First Walter and then his friend, Kenrick, are subjected to the same trials, temptations and decline as Eric. But both are rescued and survive to become Farrar's model boys, 'strenuous, diligent, modest, earnest, kind', though Kenrick, like Eric, loses his mother. Kenrick is rescued from drowning by Walter, who is also instrumental in effecting his moral redemption. Like Eric, Walter too has a younger brother, Charlie, who does not die at school but heroically suffers prolonged bullying, his saintly fortitude prefiguring his eventual death as a missionary in the South Seas. This time there is only one deathbed scene, that of Daubeny, who dies of brain fever brought on by overwork. The influence of *Tom Brown's Schooldays* can clearly be seen in the episode of the frail Arthur Eden, whom Walter takes under his wing and protects, fighting the bullying Harpour on his behalf, just as Tom took on Slogger Williams.

Eric, however, remained the book by which Farrar was to become best known as a boys' writer. It was first published in November 1858 and ran through thirty-six editions in Farrar's lifetime, the second coming within a month of the first. An illustrated edition appeared in 1889. According to Farrar, *Eric* had sold 60,000 copies by 1894 and *St Winifred's* 43,000.[59] *Eric* remained in print for many years and was reprinted in 1971. As late as 1931 B.B.C. radio broadcast a serious adaptation of it.

Parents certainly approved of it, for Farrar's book created a vogue for the name Eric, making *Eric* along with Hugh Walpole's *Jeremy at Crale*, the only public school story measurably to influence the nomenclature of British children. Among the unlikely recipients of the name were Eric Gill and Eric Blair. The educational and religious authorities were on the whole well disposed to the book and it turned up regularly as a school and Sunday school prize.

But what did boys make of it? This will depend very much on the circumstances under which it was read and on the nature of the boy reading it. As a boy P. G. Wodehouse read and loved it, and F. Anstey, author of the delightful satire *Vice Versa*, read it and 'accepted it as a lifelike presentment of what went on at public schools'.[60] Edward Salmon's 1888 survey of boys' favourite books put *St Winifred's* tenth (with eleven preferences) and *Eric* twenty-fourth (with six).[61] *The Captain's* survey of the twelve best books for boys, which put *Tom Brown's Schooldays* first, put *Eric* sixteenth and *St Winifred's* twenty-third. *The Fifth Form at St Dominic's* came ninth and *Stalky and Co.* nineteenth, which provides an interesting perspective on boy choice.[62]

Farrar almost certainly wrote with public school boys in mind, hence the presence of untranslated Latin and Greek in the text. But this was no barrier to readers of other classes. Frank Richards regularly included Latin in his stories, with an avowedly lower middle-class and working-class readership, arguing that what boys did not understand they merely skipped. So the story is likely to have reached via prizes and libraries a wider audience.

Not all boys received *Eric* in the spirit in which it was offered. Kipling recalled that during his own schooldays there was a boy (almost certainly himself) 'who had to tell stories night after night in the Dormitory and when his stock ran out he fell back on a book called *Eric or Little by Little* as comic literature and read it till the gas was turned off. The boys laughed abominably.'[63] It is significant that while it was widely read at Harrow when Farrar was there, the most popular characters with the boys were Duncan and Wildney, the most obviously 'boyish' of the pupils at Roslyn and the most easily adopted as identification figures.[64] W. MacQueen Pope, recalling a late Victorian boyhood, reckoned that 'the old pi books' were on their way out and the 'egregious' *Eric* was rejected as unbelievable.[65]

But a significant minority of boys did accept the book in the spirit in which it was offered and were deeply moved. Reginald Farrar recalled:

> Hardly a week passed since *Eric* was first published without my father receiving from all parts of the English-speaking world—from India, from the colonies and from America—letters from earnest men who were not ashamed to write and confess with gratitude that the reading of *Eric* marked a turning point in their lives, and that its lessons had been with them an abiding influence for good.[66]

Reginald Farrar printed a selection of these letters. Bishop Magee of Peterborough wrote on his deathbed in 1883 that *Eric* 'has been the salvation of my son'. A Cambridge student wrote in 1874, 'I can fairly say that I have never gained so much from all that I have ever heard or read or that has ever happened to me as I have from that book.' A boy who had recently left Shrewsbury School wrote in 1902, 'It was through reading *Eric* that I first learned to hate sin, and ever since that time, about four years ago I have tried to live a pure, brave and true life at school; and I have tried to help others to do the same, and I know in some cases by God's help I have not failed'.[67] Even more significant is the testimony of the curate of Hunslet parish church, writing in 1901:

> During some years of work in E. London and here on the outskirts of Leeds, I have tried to do something by way of getting boys to read books of the healthy sort. And I have repeatedly noticed that both among the very poor of London, and among the better sort of working folk here, boys have always been enthusiastic in praise of *Eric* and *St Winifred's*. I confess that this has surprised me, and I always feared that the clothing of the stories would make them somewhat difficult for the less educated. But I have found myself altogether mistaken.[68]

It is likely that this impact on all classes of reader was substantially diminished as an increasingly secularised twentieth century left the religiosity and fervent Evangelicalism of the early and mid-Victorian period far behind, and as *Eric* became simply the subject of sophisticated mockery, with no voices raised in its defence. But as late as the 1920s *Eric* could still move a boy. Len Wormull, recalling his boyhood reading, noted, 'My predilection for the school-story began with *Eric* . . . Old-fashioned and over-sentimental, yes, but how I loved, and cried over, this tale of Roslyn School. Others in the genre quickly followed, mostly from the public library.'[69]

It is time *Eric* was looked at dispassionately and returned to its historical context. Criticism of the book over the years has come under six general headings. First of all, it has been consistently compared unfavourably with *Tom Brown's Schooldays*. The verdict of Ian Hay, himself a former schoolmaster (Fettes, Durham School), and author of *Pip* and *Housemaster*, may stand for the many voices asserting the essential inferiority of *Eric* to *Tom*. Writing in 1914, he asserted:

> We accept all the incidents in *Tom Brown* without question. We never dream of doubting that they occurred . . . Arthur, we admit, is a rare bird, but he is credible. Even East's religious difficulties . . . are made convincing. The reason is that *Tom Brown* contains nothing that is alien from . . . schoolboy human nature. It is the real thing all through . . . Details may have changed, but the essentials are the same . . . Not so at all times with *Eric* . . . Here we miss the robust philistinism of the eternal schoolboy, and the atmosphere of reality which pervades *Tom Brown*. We feel that we are not *living* a story but merely reading it. *Eric* does not ring true . . . None of us desires to scoff at true piety or moral loftiness, but we feel instinctively that in *Eric* these virtues are somewhat indecently paraded. The schoolboy is essentially a matter-of-fact animal, and extremely reticent. He is not usually concerned with the state of his soul, and never under any circumstances anxious to discuss the matters; and above all he abhors the preacher and the prig. *Eric* . . . is priggish from start to finish.[70]

So regular and consistent were the attacks on *Eric* and so unfavourable the comparisons with *Tom Brown* that Reginald Farrar felt the need to tackle them head-on in the biography of his father:

> For the discerning critic, these books, each admirable in its own *genre*, no more challenge comparison than do the works of Fra Angelico and Frith. *Tom Brown's Schooldays* is the work of a realist, and no book more true to the life of the schoolboy has been, or is likely to be, written. It gives an incomparable picture of the average public schoolboy—healthy, athletic, chock-full of animal spirits, morally sound at the core, common-sense, if also common-place . . . We get nothing but good by reading the book; yet healthy and excellent as is its tone, we are not profoundly touched to finer issues by it. *Eric* and *St. Winifred's* are of a wholly different strain, and no one of enlightened literary judgement would attempt to compare them with the above. They are the work of an idealist, and of one who never wrote

without a definite moral purpose. If . . . you dislike idealism, and cannot tolerate books written 'with a purpose'—*Eric* and *St. Winifred's* are not for you. No cynic . . . was ever wholly in sympathy with Farrar's work; and the clever modern public-school boy is but too often an amateur of cynicism, [who] . . . detests emotion, sneers at it in others, and stoically suppresses it in himself.[71]

There is a good deal of justice in what Farrar writes. But the contrast is perhaps over-drawn. For Hughes and Farrar had much in common. They were in fact friends. Both were men of liberal political sympathies, of deep Christian belief, of personal kindness and of immense industry. Both had sat at the feet of and been strongly influenced by F. D. Maurice. Both men in fact named sons after Maurice. Both men revered Arnold and in many ways, as David Newsome has perceptively pointed out, '*Eric* . . . , although it makes no reference to Arnold or to Rugby, is a truer reflection of Arnold's ideals than Thomas Hughes's master-piece.'[72] The desire for earnest, grave and grown-up boys, the view of life as a battle between good and evil, the emotionalism, the stress on gentlemanliness, intellectual commitment and religious faith, the down-grading of athleticism, the defence of the prefectorial system, all bear the authentic stamp of Arnold.

Both Hughes and Farrar wrote with the avowed intention of preaching. In the preface to the twenty-fourth edition of *Eric* Farrar declared that 'The story of *Eric* was written with but one single object—the vivid inculcation of inward purity and moral purpose, by the history of a boy, who, in spite of the inherent nobleness of his disposition, falls into all folly and wickedness, until he has learnt to seek help from above.' Both Hughes and Farrar clearly had sermons in mind, as is evident, if *Tom Brown* and *Eric* are read in conjunction with the sermons of Arnold and Farrar. Indeed, so close in Farrar's mind were his books and his sermons that one of his Marlborough sermons actually adapts the description of a storm at sea from *St Winifred's*.

The difference between Hughes and Farrar is essentially one of temperament and standpoint. Hughes was dealing with the triumphant evolution of a thoughtless, cheerful, healthy, ordinary English boy into a caring and committed Christian gentleman. He had an optimistic view of boys, as of life, and his standpoint was one of identification with the boys. He had been at school a generous, open-hearted, games-playing, non-academic boy, and he remained one all his life. Farrar, on the other hand, even when a boy, had been what he always remained, a serious-minded, grave, hard-working, knowledge-hungry adult, with no time for games, frivolity or japes. As his schoolmate E. S. Beesly recalled, 'He was already as a boy what he was afterwards as a school-master, "a preacher of righteousness".'[73] So his book dealt with the gradual, inevitable decline of a thoughtless, cheerful, healthy, ordinary English boy into a runaway and a drunkard, seduced by his love of popularity and a too easy-going nature. His essentially pessimistic view of boy nature emerges in his sermons:

> Is not the condition of most of you . . . this? You have indeed sinned; you have gone astray and done wickedly; you have sometimes offended with your tongue; the thoughts of your heart are sometimes very evil; you are but too conscious of many weaknesses, many transgressions. You know that you are not yet what you should be, what you might be, what you yet hope to be.[74]

Farrar's viewpoint is not that of the average schoolboy; it is that of the schoolmaster. It is not surprising therefore that the voice of school-masterly experience creeps into the book from time to time. When the master of the Latin school goes mad, Farrar notes sadly, 'The perpetual annoyance caused to his refined mind by the coarseness of clumsy or spiteful boys had gradually unhinged his intellect.'[75] An anecdote of J. D. Rogers demonstrates how feelingly Farrar penned these words:

> At a certain history lesson, after the whole form had failed to answer some trifling question, Farrar fairly flung the reins down and broke into the follow-ing oration: 'My dear boys! I am profoundly discouraged! For fifteen years of my life I have been letting down a bucket into an empty well and drawing it up again! For fifteen years of my life I have been pouring out water upon the arid sand!' Then he gathered up his books and fled.[76]

The Rev. Henry Gordon, though a brilliant teacher, is quick-tempered, imperious and new to the profession, and thus 'had not yet learned the practical lesson . . . that to trust young boys to any great extent is really to increase their temptations.'[77]

Farrar's ideal master is Mr Rose, 'a far truer and deeper Christian' than Gordon. Rose 'lived in and for the boys alone and his whole life was one long self-devotion to their service and interests':

> Many a weary hour had he toiled for them in private, when his weak frame was harassed by suffering; many a sleepless night had he wrestled for them in prayer, when, for their sakes, his own many troubles were laid aside. Work on, Walter Rose, and He who seeth a secret will reward you openly! but expect no gratitude from those for whose salvation you, like the great tenderhearted apostle, would almost be ready to wish yourself accursed.[78]

The second criticism is that the picture of school life at Roslyn is sensationalised and violently over-drawn. This was alleged at the time of publication and has been echoed since. Edward Salmon declared in 1888, 'Its first object is to expose some of the evils of the public school system but it is hardly conceivable that a state of things so utterly bad as that which prevailed at Roslyn ever existed in any single school.'[79]

But in fact the book is an absolutely authentic picture of King William's College, Isle of Man, whose lovingly described scenery is such a feature of *Eric*. As Patrick Scott has shown, the layout and routines of Roslyn are exactly those of King William's and Farrar drew directly on episodes from his own schooldays. The death of Vernon Williams, for instance, is modelled on that of Robert Woodhouse, a King William's pupil in Farrar's time, who fell to his death climbing for birds' eggs. The teaching and organisational methods were to some extent modelled on Harrow and Marlborough. But the basic tone and state of events are these of the King William's College of his boyhood. He peopled the school with masters and boys modelled on people he had known at the college and at Harrow.[80]

Farrar claimed in his preface, 'To the best of my belief, the things here dealt with are not theories, but realities; not imagination, but facts.' It is clear, then, that *Eric* is almost as much autobiographical reminiscence as *Tom Brown*. Farrar revealed to his friend E. S. Beesly that Montagu, Owen and Russell were based on Harrow boys he knew, and that 'Wildney is a little boy named W — — who was really introduced to me as "a very nice little fellow—a regular devil". He brutalised himself by drink, was expelled and went to sea.'[81] Ball was based on a boy at King William's College and it seems clear that Brigson was too. George Russell recognised Mr Rose and Mr Gordon as accurate portraits of masters at Harrow:

> Of Mr. Rose I will say no more than that he was an excellent schoomaster and a most true saint, and that to his influence and warnings many a man can, in the long retrospect, trace his escape from moral ruin. He died the death of the Just ten years ago. Mr. Gordon is now a decorous Dean, but . . . he was the most brilliant, the most irregular and the most fascinating of teachers. He spoilt me for a whole quarter. I loved him for it then, and I thank him even now.[82]

When *Eric* was read at King William's and the opinion expressed that it would injure the school, Farrar wrote:

> Even if so, I am not to blame—for the picture, as far as it is one, is highly flattered. KWC has no Mr. Rose, or even Mr. Gordon—or Dr. Rowlands. KWC had *certainly* no Russell or Owen; and the things that did go on there are really far worse than I have described.[83]

As Reginald Farrar demonstrates, the early part of *Eric* is entirely autobiographical.[84] Farrar was himself sent back from India to England with his older brother Henry, to whom he was devoted. They lodged with two maiden aunts at Aylesbury and Farrar went to the local Latin school. When he was eight, his parents returned from India, took a house at Castletown on the Isle of Man and sent Farrar and his brother to King William's College for the first three years as day boys, and later, after the return of the parents to India, as boarders, with the head-master, the Rev. Mr Dixon. At King William's Farrar's thirst for know-ledge was slaked by omnivorous reading. By the age of sixteen he had read Hooker's *Ecclesiastical Polity*, Prideaux's *Connections between the Old and New Testaments* and Coleridge's *Aids to Reflection*. He and his friends eagerly discussed classical texts and Reginald Farrar noted, 'The young cynic of today derides the boys of *Eric* and *St Winifred's* who are represented as eagerly discussing out of school the characters of Homeric heroes; but the fact remains that the more intelligent boys of that epoch, being precluded from such lofty themes as cricket averages . . . *did* find interest in discussing the "shop" of their school classics.'[85] This is confirmed by the evidence that among Farrar's contemporaries at King William's were Edward Spencer Beesly (1831–1905), later Professor of History and Latin at London University; Thomas Edward Brown (1830–1897), the Manx poet and for thirty years Second Master at Clifton College; Thomas Fowler (1832–1904), Professor of Logic and Vice-chancellor of Oxford University, and James Maurice Wilson (1836–1931), son of the first Principal of King William's College and headmaster of Clifton College (1879–90). This parade of erudition would confirm Farrar's belief that circumstances did not dictate character but vice versa, and men like this overcame the appalling conditions, cruelty, bad teaching and poor food to live to a productive and distinguished old age.

Two of Farrar's contemporaries confirmed exactly the picture of the school that he painted. Wilson wrote that *Eric* 'was no caricature of this school':

> The bullying and cruelty which we both suffered in the first two years was almost incredible . . . I doubt whether any school could have been . . . worse. I am speaking of course only of the boarders and only of the Principal's House. The day boys only suffered from bad teaching—teaching I imagine almost as bad as it could be. But we suffered from dirt and slovenliness, from insufficient food, from horrible bullying and indecencies indescribable. We took it all as a matter of course and never complained at home . . . It was a lawless, dirty, degraded life, and few survived it without real damage.[86]

Wilson recalled being kicked, cuffed, beaten and sometimes stripped naked and forced to run the gauntlet of older boys, who flicked him with the corners of wet towels. The outdoor life was their 'only salvation'—rambling, exploring, climbing, birds'-nesting. He reckons that effectively he educated himself with a group of like-minded friends in his last two years.

Beesly, who was Farrar's study mate, also recalled spartan conditions, poor teaching, frugal meals and no decent library:

> The moral tone, at the beginning of my time, was neither better nor worse than in most schools, but in the course of the year it was much injured by some new arrivals. Farrar's influence was always exercised on the side of all that was honourable, high-minded, humane and refined. He was . . . a shining example and a support to all who were well-inclined.[87]

The third area of complaint came from the days of the public school spirit. Harold Child, noting in 1906 that *Tom Brown* had 'expounded and so helped vastly to create' the public school spirit, observed that it was almost wholly absent from *Eric* and *St Winifred's*:

> There is no trace here of the public school spirit; the school is nothing; the individual character is everything. The books, intended, we presume, to counteract the muscular element that many held too prominent in *Tom Brown*, miss their mark, presenting an ideal so far from that in favour that they have become the laughing stock of most schoolboys and the butt of all later writers in public school stories.[88]

Absence of the public school spirit also means absence of games, the prefectorial system and team spirit and too much emphasis on religion and introspection. But it is absurd to criticise the book on these grounds, for Roslyn is a pre-Arnoldian public school, the epitome of the old unreformed system, and could not be expected to boast the features of Arnold's Rugby. King William's College, Castletown, in Farrar's time did not have a prefect system. 'The law of the strongest prevailed,' recalled E. S. Beesly. This was something Farrar deeply regretted, extolling the prefect system in *Eric*:

> Had the monitorial system existed, that contagion could have been effectually checked; but, as it was, brute force had unlimited authority. Ill indeed are those informed who raise a cry, and join in the ignorant abuse of that noble safeguard of English schools. Any who have had personal and intimate experience of how schools work *with* it and *without* it, know what a Palladium it is of happiness and morality; how it prevents bullying, upholds manliness, is the bulwark of discipline, and makes boys more earnest and thoughtful, often at the most critical periods of their lives, by enlisting all their sympathies and interests on the side of the honourable and the just.[89]

There was also no organised or compulsory games. Farrar himself was never a cricketer, and, although fond of football and a fine swimmer, gained his greatest pleasure from rambling and climbing. The book reflects this.

But, even more important, the 1830s, when Farrar was at school, were the era of Evangelicalism. The school had a regime of 'the narrowest evangelical type'. Farrar's father was an Evangelical and Farrar himself, despite his increasingly liberal religious views and the storm of controversy that attended his 'Eternal Hope' sermons when he preached of a God of Love rather than everlasting hell-fire, remained always of an Evangelical temper. For him religious faith was infinitely more important than the public school spirit and the book faithfully reflects that viewpoint.

The fourth criticism is that the boys depicted in the book are unrealistic. Andrew Lang claimed of Farrar's books that the boys:

> are not real boys. They are too good when they are good, and when they are bad, they are not perhaps too bad . . . but they are bad in the wrong way. They are bad with a mannish and conscious vice, whereas even bad boys seem to sin less consciously and after a ferocious fashion of their own.[90]

A non-conformist critic observed:

> If Mr. Farrar has been in the habit of meeting such boys as he describes we can only say that a most kind and indulgent fate has not permitted us the same advantage. Young gentlemen who do nothing but walk about their school playgrounds with their arms round one another's necks, discussing the various responsibilities of a Christian's duty, deserve to be caged and kept for public exhibition. Boys and girls who are perpetually stopping in the middle of their play to say prayers and sing hymns are simply nauseating.[91]

This is funny but it is simply not true. Farrar himself and his immediate circle at school were just the kind of serious-minded, earnest, responsible and pious scholars, impatient of frivolity, devoted to learning, unshakable in their commitment to purity and Christian faith, that Farrar sought continuously to turn his pupils at Harrow and Marlborough into through his books and his sermons. Speaking from experience, Harold Child (Winchester) wrote:

> The Farrar type of boy . . . is not so rare as might be supposed. When the writer was in his first term at a public school, the three in authority in his dormitory set upon and severely mauled a prefect of another room who came in on some errand. Released, the victim retired to fasten his collar and brush his hair; which done, he returned, went solemnly to each of his aggressors and held out his hand, saying, 'Goodnight, X; I bear you no malice.' He may, of course, have learnt it out of *Eric* or *St. Winifred's* but since he was at least seventeen at the time, he must have been rarely faithful to early formed ideals. Dean Farrar's school stories, then, possibly contain more truth than is commonly allowed.[92]

Unquestionably there will have been more boys able to identify with Tom Brown but that does not mean that there were not public school boys like Russell and Montagu just as there were boys like Wildney and Duncan.

Closely associated with the question of authentic boys is the allegation of excess emotionalism. Hugh Kingsmill called *Eric* 'the most luxuriant example' of mid-Victorian emotionalism over the young, and Farrar 'the most extreme exponent of mid-Victorian emotionalism'.[93] Farrar himself admitted subsequently in a letter to E. S. Beesly, 'the lacrimosity is, I know, too much, and arises from the state of mind in which I wrote it'.[94] Farrar was grieving over the sudden death of his beloved mother when he wrote and tears came easily. Her death remained a permanent sorrow to him as he felt he had not always displayed his love for her sufficiently during her life-time. The passion poured into the deathbed scenes in *Eric* are part of his personal catharsis, the means of purging his own grief and re-assuring himself of the benevolence of God and the reality of eternal life. When he writes of Eric's grief, 'Reader, if ever the life has been cut short which you most dearly loved, if ever you have been made to feel absolutely lonely in the world, then, and only then, will you appreciate the depth of his affliction,' he was writing from the heart.[95]

Certainly tears are constant in *Eric*. Eric weeps when he is bullied, unjustly beaten, when he quarrels with Mr Rose and with Montagu, when he is reprimanded by his brother, when Mr Rose forgives him, when he is not expelled, when he goes to sea and when he returns home. Tears are copiously shed around the deathbeds of Russell and Eric and the corpse of Verny. These deaths have a permanent effect on Montagu, turning him into a serious, earnest boy. Eric himself also foresakes smoking, determines to work hard and be worthy of his friend. But then, deathbeds were a staple of Victorian literature, and in particular children's deaths.[96] One only has to think of the deaths of Little Nell, Smike, Paul Dombey and Jo the crossing sweeper in Dickens, of Helen Burns in *Jane Eyre*, of Little Willie Carlyle in *East Lynne.* They were vehicles for repentance, reconciliation and redemption. But they also served as a formalisation of the process of grief, for death itself was a more permanent fact of life in the Victorian era than today, particularly the death of children. Its frequency did not make the grief any easier to bear. One again has only to recall the tragedy of the sudden death from meningitis of Archbishop Benson's brilliant elder son Martin or of Thomas Hughes's daughter Evie while he was writing *Tom Brown's Schooldays* or the supremely tragic deaths of the five daughters of Archbishop Tait from scarlet fever within the space of six weeks. But the Victorians derived comfort from their religious faith and from the transformation of the tragic event into a dramatic set piece.

Russell, Eric and Montagu constantly express their love for each other. Montagu, estranged from Eric, reflects, 'He little knows how I love him and yearn for the Eric I once knew—Eric the fairhaired.'[97] Russell and Eric agree to call each other by their Christian names. ('And the two boys squeezed each other's hands and looked into each other's faces and silently promised that they would be loving friends for ever.')[98] Russell, injured and unconscious, is held up by Eric, who 'felt *then* how deeply he had loved him, how much he owed him; and no mother could have nursed a child more tenderly than he did his fainting friend'.[99]

Mr Rose also demonstrates an emotional involvement with his boys, praying with them and for them, and is prostrated with grief at Eric's death. Alien as it may seem to readers of a later era, this emotionalism of both boys and adults has its roots in reality. Hugh Kingsmill admits:

> In the years before and merging into adolescence boys indulge secretly in many brief but intense adorations; and a death or an accident produces among the young a mass emotion of the same order. An instance of each occurred at the writer's preparatory school; and still more extraordinary was the leave taking of a popular master who shook hands with the assembled boys in rotation and embraced them. Many of the boys wept without restraint.[100]

David Newsome wrote of the 'tendency to emotionalism and to passionate friendship' in the early Victorian period:

> The doctrine of the stiff upper lip was no part of the public school code of the Arnoldian period . . . Tears were usual, the expected consequence of reproof. There was not a dry eye in the Wellington Chapel when Benson preached his farewell sermon. Headmasters and assistant masters occasionally wept together in the course of a difference of opinion. And the word 'Love' was more frequently on their lips, used with real sincerity. The association between master and pupil seems to have often been very intimate, admitting expressions of emotion on both sides.[101]

Adolescent boys may have continued to be emotional in private. But public displays of emotion became taboo. The gentlemanly ideal, good form, came to consist of unemotional behaviour. The periodical *London Quarterly* declared in 1869:

> Good Society hates scenes, votes every eccentricity of manner and demonstrativeness of demeanour bad form; the schools have followed suit and the ideal of deportment which an Eton or Harrow boy proposes to himself is of pure passionless exterior . . . The Etonian has schooled himself into undemonstrativeness persistently and well.[102]

The comment is interesting in that it suggests that the schools were mirroring a social trend, which they seem so often to have done, reacting to the outside world and to society in a very sensitive and responsive way.

When Ian Hay observes that the spectacle of Eric and Russell sitting by the sea 'looking into each others eyes and silently promising they will be loving friends for ever' makes the undemonstrative young Briton physically unwell' and, again, 'Russell's illness and death bed deliveries are an outrage on schoolboy reserve,' he is reflecting an entirely different reality from the one Farrar had experienced.[103] The stiff upper lip had triumphed, the result partly of the exaltation of athleticism, with its concomitant need for self-control, team spirit, modesty in victory and defeat, partly the needs of the empire for administrators able to display *sang-froid* in the face of tight corners and the excesses of excitable natives, and partly the decline of Evangelicalism with its exuberant displays of emotion.

Lastly there is the charge that Farrar promoted sexual anxiety. The nineteenth century was undoubtedly greatly concerned about masturbation. Dr Alex Comfort wrote:

> It was the young, as the traditional victims of precept and the age group chiefly concerned, who suffered most of their elders' anxiety, as it spread from the medical profession to parents, school teachers and nannies—among whom the scrupulous and timid developed a new bogey and the sadistically inclined a new pretext for severity and anxiety-production. The upright and anti-sexual schoolmaster who was not consciously sadistic, but was consciously anxious, set about doing one's duty—but often the unconscious, and the intoxication of his own eloquence, take over.[104]

He quotes the Kibroth-Hattavaah passage from *Eric* in support of this view. It is evident that like many headmasters Farrar was concerned about moral pollution among his boys. But neither his sermons nor his books demonstrate an obsession with it. The Kibroth-Hattavaah passage is unique in *Eric*, a book of some 368 pages. The sins Eric actually commits are smoking, drinking, swearing, theft, idleness and thoughtlessness. Sex is mainly remarkable by its absence, as indeed it is from *Tom Brown*. Even if the conventions of the day had permitted him to write about it in detail, it is doubtful whether he could have brought himself to do so.

Virtually all the objections lodged against *Eric* can be seen, therefore, to be without real substance. There were such schools as Roslyn and such boys as Farrar depicts. The emotionalism and absence of school spirit, the emphasis on moral self-examination and the low priority accorded to athletics reflects Farrar's own experience and the age which had shaped him. The criticism in the end boils down to the fact that the critics do not like or agree with Farrar's opinions, and that is no basis for making dispassionate historical judgements.

In recent years some voices have been raised in defence of *Eric*. Gillian Avery argued that the scorn heaped on *Eric* is largely undeserved and that Farrar's books are 'eloquent, sometimes moving . . . and are an interesting study in the deep feelings that adolescent boys undoubtedly do have and which it has been customary of more recent years to suppress in school fiction'.[105] Mary Hobbs called *Eric* 'a remarkably penetrating study of adolescence and an invaluable document on nineteenth-century education'.[106] Patrick Scott, in his careful, thorough and fair-minded study, concludes that Farrar's novels 'far from being melodramatic and fictional . . . are factual documents, even auto-biographical in content' and that they had been subjected to attack in part owing to his florid, rhetorical style, which has gone out of fashion, and in part because he fell foul of two powerful lobbies.[107] At the time of publication the old guard who did not want the public schools reformed along Christian lines attacked it, and later 'the bland faith in the essential decency of boy-nature of the New Guard—the Ian Hays and Desmond Cokes—stopped Farrar's novels from ever acquiring an acceptable image'. All three of these champions of *Eric* are right. Styles of writing change. Farrar was a marvellously vivid story-teller with a great sense of pace, a sensuous love of words and a talent for description. Either you like it or you do not. I love it. Sometimes he was melodramatic, sometimes he was sentimental; both were key characteristics of the literary output of his age. Sometimes he erred in recording how boys would speak to one another, but not always and far less often than he has been criticised for. He was psycho-logically accurate in charting Eric's decline and downfall, as after each failure he tries genuinely and determinedly to make a fresh start, reproaching himself, each time his resolve undermined by his desire for popularity. The depiction of the centrality of ups and downs within schoolboy friendships also carries an authentic ring. It is absurd to condemn Farrar for embodying the ideas, attitudes and prejudices of his age. His only fault was that he outlived his age, and that can happen to any of us.

Notes

1 Vivian Ogilvie, *The English Public School*, London, 1957, 183; John Rowe Townsend, *Written for Children*, Harmondsworth, 1983, 115; Hugh Kingsmill, *After Puritanism, 1850–1900*, London, 1929; Roger Lancelyn Green, *Tellers of Tales*, London, 1965, 231; Eric Ambler, *Here Lies Eric Ambler*, London, 1985, 32; Edward C. Mack, *Public Schools and British Opinion since 1860*, New York, 1941, 17; Benny Green, *P. G. Wodehouse*, London, 1981, 14.
2 Percy Muir, *English Children's Books, 1600–1900* (1954), London, 1979, 115.
3 Frances Donaldson, *P. G. Wodehouse*, London, 1982, 66.

4 Stanley Morison, *Talbot Baines Reed*, Cambridge, 1960.
5 *Blackwood's Magazine*, 89 (February 1861), 131–48.
6 *Saturday Review*, 6 November 1858, 453–4.
7 Reginald Farrar, *The Life of Frederic William Farrar*, London, 1904, 75.
8 Charlotte M. Yonge, 'Children's literature', *Macmillan's Magazine*, 20 (July 1869), 454.
9 Edward Salmon, *Juvenile Literature as it is*, London, 1888, 90-3.
10 *Dictionary of National Biography*, Twentieth Century Supplement, 2627.
11 G. W. E. Russell, *Sketches and Snapshots*, London, 1910, 234-5.
12 J. D. Rogers, 'Dean Farrar as headmaster', *Cornhill Magazine*, n.s., 14 (1903), 604.
13 Reginald Farrar, *Life of Farrar*, 153.
14 Reginald Farrar, *Life of Farrar*, 150, 155.
15 Rogers, 'Farrar as headmaster', 607.
16 Farrar, *Life of Farrar*, 176.
17 Farrar, *Life of Farrar*, 86, 184.
18 Farrar, *Life of Farrar*, 170.
19 Farrar, *Life of Farrar*, 128.
20 Farrar, *Life of Farrar*, 33.
21 F. W. Farrar, 'Thomas Arnold, D.D.', *Macmillan's Magazine*, 37 (April 1878), 456-9.
22 F. W. Farrar, *In the Days of thy Youth* (1876), London, 1896, 18.
23 Farrar, *In the Days of thy Youth*, 23.
24 Farrar, *In the Days of thy Youth*, 194.
25 Farrar, *In the Days of thy Youth*, 183-4.
26 Farrar, *In the Days of thy Youth*, 110.
27 Farrar, *In the Days of thy Youth*, 137.
28 Farrar, *In the Days of thy Youth*, 294.
29 Farrar, *In the Days of thy Youth*, 32-8.
30 Farrar, *In the Days of thy Youth*, 304.
31 Farrar, *In the Days of thy Youth*, 347.
32 Farrar, *In the Days of thy Youth*, 371.
33 Farrar, *In the Days of thy Youth*, 394-5.
34 G. W. E. Russell, *Sketches and Snapshots*, 235-6.
35 J. D. Rogers, 'Dean Farrar as headmaster', 598.
36 Farrar, *Life of Farrar*, 140.
37 F. W. Farrar, *Eric, or, Little by Little* (1858), London, 1907, 26-7.
38 Farrar, *Eric*, 31.
39 Farrar, *Eric*, 29-30.
40 Farrar, *Eric*, 39.
41 Farrar, *Eric*, 59.
42 Farrar, *Eric*, 67.
43 Farrar, *Eric*, 78-80.
44 Farrar, *Eric*, 82.
45 Farrar, *Eric*, 87-9.
46 Jonathan Gathorne-Hardy, *The Public School Phenomenon*, Harmondsworth, 1979, 96.
47 Farrar, *Eric*, 94.
48 Farrar, *Eric*, 104.
49 Farrar, *Eric*, 105.
50 Farrar, *Eric*, 174.
51 Farrar, *Eric*, 183.
52 Farrar, *Eric*, 187.
53 Farrar, *Eric*, 240.
54 Farrar, *Eric*, 321.
55 Farrar, *Eric*, 337.
56 Farrar, *Eric*, 340.
57 Farrar, *Eric*, 356.

58 Farrar, *Life of Farrar*, 73.
59 Farrar, *St Winifred's* (1862), London, 1907, x.
60 Frances Donaldson, *P. G. Wodehouse*, London, 1983, 66; F. Anstey, *A Long Retrospect*, London, 1936, 58.
61 Edward Salmon, *Juvenile Literature as it is*, 15.
62 *The Captain*, 19 (1908), 90.
63 Rudyard Kipling, *Land and Sea Tales for Scouts and Guides*, London, 1923, 267.
64 Farrar, *Life of Farrar*, 75.
65 W. MacQueen-Pope, *Back Numbers*, London, 1954, 194.
66 Farrar, *Life of Farrar*, 74.
67 Farrar, *Life of Farrar*, 78–82.
68 Farrar, *Life of Farrar*, 79.
69 *The Friars Chronicles*, 18 (summer 1986), 59.
70 Ian Hay, *The Lighter Side of School Life*, Edinburgh, 1923, 148–50.
71 Farrar, *Life of Farrar*, 72–3.
72 David Newsome, *Godliness and Good Learning*, London, 1961, 37.
73 Farrar, *Life of Farrar*, 18.
74 Farrar, *In the Days of thy Youth*, 249.
75 Farrar, *Eric*, 8.
76 Rogers, 'Dean Farrar as headmaster', 606.
77 Farrar, *Eric*, 45.
78 Farrar, *Eric*, 231–2.
79 Salmon, *Juvenile Literature*, 90.
80 Patrick Scott, 'The school novels of Dean Farrar', *British Journal of Educational Studies*, 19 (1971), 163–82.
81 Farrar, *Life of Farrar*, 75–6.
82 G. W. E. Russell, *Collections and Recollections*, London, 1896, 486.
83 Farrar, *Life of Farrar*, 75–6.
84 Farrar, *Life of Farrar*, 2.
85 Farrar, *Life of Farrar*, 14.
86 James M. Wilson, *An Autobiography 1863–1931*, London, 1932, 8, 10, 12, 18.
87 Farrar, *Life of Farrar*, 17–18.
88 Harold Child, 'The public school in fiction', *The Public Schools from Within*, London, 1906, 295.
89 Farrar, *Eric*, 189.
90 Andrew Lang, *Adventures among Books*, London, 1905, 309.
91 G. M. Young, *Victorian Essays*, Oxford, 1962, 159.
92 Harold Child, 'The public school in fiction', 296.
93 Kingsmill, *After Puritanism*, 14, 30.
94 Farrar, *Life of Farrar*, 75.
95 Farrar, *Eric*, 171–2.
96 See John Reed, *Victorian Conventions*, Ohio, 1985, 156–71.
97 Farrar, *Eric*, 244.
98 Farrar, *Eric*, 47.
99 Farrar, *Eric*, 152.
100 Kingsmill, *After Puritanism*, 36.
101 Newsome, *Godliness and Good Learning*, 83–4.
102 Peter T. Cominos, 'Late Victorian sexual respectability and the social system', *International Review of Social History*, 8 (1963), 42.
103 Hay, *The Lighter Side of School Life*, 153.
104 Alex Comfort, *The Anxiety Makers*, London, 1967, 90. On anxieties about masturbation see R. P. Neuman, 'Masturbation, madness and the modern concept of childhood and adolescence', *Journal of Social History*, 8 (1975), 1–27.
105 Gillian Avery, *Nineteenth Century Children*, London, 1965, 146.
106 Mary Hobbs, 'Fair play for Eric', *Times Literary Supplement*, 30 November 1967.
107 Scott, 'School novels of Dean Farrar', 177–80.

4

The perfection of the formula: *The Fifth Form at St Dominic's*

After *Tom Brown's Schooldays* and *Eric* there was a gap of some thirty years before the next major development. There were school stories by writers like the Rev. T. S. Millington, the Rev. H. C. Adams and Ethel Kenyon, but their principal influence was Farrar rather than Hughes. They were set mainly in small private schools rather than in large public schools, were low on games and patriotism and high on moral didacticism.[1] But none of them made anything like the impact of *Tom Brown*, or *Eric*. The great leap forward came with the arrival of *The Boy's Own Paper* and the stories of Talbot Baines Reed.

The work of Reed represents the triumphant fusion of the twin traditions of Hughes and Farrar into a blend palatable to the later Victorian boy. 'Very few people have written schoolboy stories for schoolboys anything like so well,' said Harvey Darton, and Ian Hay declared of his stories, 'in their own particular line, they have never been bettered.'[2] Reed created the formula that many writers were subsequently to follow.

Reed's stories became one of the principal attractions of *The Boy's Own Paper*, which represents a new phenomenon in the history of school stories—the weekly magazine.[3] *The Boy's Own Paper* was launched by the Religious Tract Society and became the longest-running juvenile periodical in history. The society, a conservative and evangelical body, founded in 1799, published a wide variety of religious literature (sermons, books, pamphlets, commentaries, tracts, periodicals). Its 1850 catalogue had included 4,363 different items. It had been producing material specifically for children since 1814. But in the 1870s it became increasingly concerned about the host of sensationalist 'penny dreadfuls' that were forming a large part of the juvenile literature market. An R.T.S. report asked, 'schools are multiplied everywhere, but what are boys to read out of school hours?'[4] This multiplication of schools was the result of the sanctioning of a nation-wide system of

elementary education by the 1870 Education Act, and it convinced the
society there was a wide potential readership for a boys' weekly paper.
In 1878 the society decided to launch one, specifically to counteract
the effects of the 'penny dreadfuls'. The 1879 report of the R.T.S.
declared, 'The urgent need of such a periodical had been long and
deeply felt. Juvenile crime was being largely stimulated by the
pernicious literature circulated among our lads. Judges, magistrates,
schoolmasters, prison chaplains, and others were deploring the existence
of the evil, and calling loudly for a remedy but none seemed to be
forthcoming.'[5] A committee was set up to investigate the feasibility of
the project and an editor was appointed under the supervision of the
Rev. James Macaulay, a senior member of the R.T.S. and editor of
The Leisure Hour and *Sunday at Home.* The new editor, who was to be
the major influence on the development of the paper, was George
Andrew Hutchison, a Liberal, a prolific writer and editor, and a man
of impeccable religious credentials. For twelve years he had edited
Night and Day, a magazine for the boys of Dr Barnardo's Homes. He
was a lifelong worker for the Sunday school movement and edited
The Sunday School World. He also edited, concurrently with *The
Boy's Own Paper*, *The Toilers of the Deep*, the magazine of the Royal
National Mission to Deep Sea Fishermen, and *The Baptist*, the weekly
family paper of the Baptist Church. Harvey Darton characterised him
as an ideal editor ('unobtrusive . . . thorough, determined, without
dogmatism, always alive and keen, and . . . equably sane') and claimed
that he had 'a stronger indirect influence on English boyhood than any
man of his time'.[6] He guided the fortunes of *The Boy's Own Paper*, or
B.O.P., as it was affectionately known, from 1879 to 1912. An early
prospectus for the magazine announced:

> Its editors understand boyhood well, enter heartily into its pursuits and
> pleasures. True religion, in their view, is a spirit pervading all life, in work,
> in play; and in this conviction, rather than any purpose of direct doctrinal
> teaching, this tone is given to the Paper.[7]

But there were regular complaints from the society that there was too
much fiction. An R.T.S. resolution in 1884, for instance, suggested that
it was in the best interests of their youthful readers 'to give more
prominence to Christian truth and influence'.[8] Hutchison fought
constantly and successfully to avoid an excess of overt moralising,
preferring to suggest, encourage and imply through fiction, travel and
sport rather than hector and lecture as from the pulpit. The *B.O.P.*
aimed to cast its net wide, its inaugural advertisement declaring:

> It is intended not only to provide the lads of our own families and schools
> with wholesome, elevating reading, but to supplant, if possible, some of the
> literature the injurious effect of which all so sincerely deplore. In order that

the new paper may achieve what is desired for it, the prompt and hearty co-operation of ministers and parents, schoolmasters and teachers, and indeed of the friends of youth generally, is necessary. *The Boy's Own Paper* should be introduced into every home and school—should be circulated by employers in their shops and factories—should be given away largely through our ragged schools and juvenile missions—and, in short, should be brought well before the attention of every boy in the land.[9]

The *B.O.P.* was issued weekly at a penny, with a monthly version which bound the weekly parts in a special wrapper. A bound volume of the year's issues was produced as *The Boy's Own Annual*. Jack Cox, the last editor of the *B.O.P.*, suggested that the society had its eye on two different markets:

> The weekly issue was eagerly bought by schoolboys, office boys, apprentices and cadets; read and re-read, passed from hand to hand, loaned out and seized back, until it was grubby and falling apart. Family readers subscribed in more dignified style to the monthly; but often they sought both issues— the weekly to give away, the monthly to keep for leisurely re-reading and later reference.[10]

Incidental evidence—for instance, from the letter columns of the *B.O.P.*—suggests that this remit was being to some extent met. A letter in 1879 from a branch of the technical department of the Post Office in Scotland revealed that out of eighty-four lads on the staff, sixty-three took the *B.O.P.* weekly and five monthly.[11] In a handwriting competition for under-elevens in 1890, seventeen pupils from the Harrow Green Board School were awarded certificates.[12] Dr Gordon Stables, the resident medic, addressed one of his articles specifically to working boys: 'Although I may be accused sometimes of writing only for school "chaps" and young Eton "toffs", I really have all classes, high and low, in my mind, while I give advice. And I have a soft side even to mill-hands and miners.'[13] He canvasses the evils of smoking, drinking and gambling and the virtues of fresh air and cold tubs. In 1929 at a lunch to celebrate the *B.O.P.*'s jubilee, the Prime Minister, Stanley Baldwin, spoke of the pleasure that both he and the Labour leader, Ramsay MacDonald, had derived from the *B.O.P.*, and their wide divergence of background (Old Harrovian scion of a Shropshire business family and the illegitimate son of Scottish crofting stock) is an indication of the widespread appeal of the paper.[14]

The *B.O.P.*, an appealing mix of fiction and articles on sport, nature, travel, hobbies and fitness, was an immediate success. Profits from the first year exceeded £2,000 and by 1888 had reached £4,000. In the late 1880s the print run was 500,000 copies a week and since it was considered that two or three boys read each copy, the actual readership was estimated to be in the region of 1¼ million. The print run rose eventually to 665,000.[15] But by the end of the century profits were declining. In 1894 they totalled only £291, and in 1896 the magazine made a loss. But in 1899 profits were again up to £1,600. Patrick Dunae has suggested that the decline in profits did not necessarily signal a loss of popularity, because the *B.O.P.* maintained a high cost of production due to the quality of paper and illustrations.[16] In 1893, for instance, of £7,748 gross profit, £6,000 went in production costs. Nevertheless the *B.O.P.* began to face stiff competition from *Chums*, launched by Cassell's in 1892, and *The Captain*, launched by Newnes in 1899. Throughout the Edwardian period the circulation remained at 400,000 copies. But the paper now relied on a subsidy from the R.T.S. to keep going and its main readership seems to have become largely public school and middle-class boys, as evidenced by the fact that it became a monthly publication only in 1913.

Although G. A. Hutchison ran the work of W. H. G. Kingston, R. M. Ballantyne and Jules Verne in the *B.O.P.*, his greatest discovery was undoubtedly Talbot Baines Reed.[17] Reed's family was closely involved with the R.T.S. His father, Sir Charles, was a member from 1864 until his death in 1881, and his brother, the Rev. Charles Edward Reed, was one of the organising committee of the *B.O.P.* Talbot Baines Reed, then twenty-six, had already written articles for the periodical press and was an obvious candidate to recruit. His first article, 'My first football match', by 'an Old Boy', appeared in the first issue of the *B.O.P.* (18 January 1879). Thereafter he contributed short stories about Parkhurst School, historical sketches on 'Boys of English history' and sketches of 'Boys we have known', creating the standard repertoire of schoolboy types who were to constitute the stock company of fiction: the sneak, the sulky boy, the easy-going boy, the untidy boy, the duffer, the dandy, the growler, the bully, the scapegrace, etc. He also reported annually on the Oxford and Cambridge boat race.

When Hutchison urged him to try his hand at a school serial, he produced *The Adventures of a Three Guinea Watch*, which the *B.O.P.* ran in 1880–81, and thereafter he confined himself to serials, writing a dozen in fourteen years. All were published in book form but Reed made nothing from this, having transferred the copyright of the stories to the R.T.S. for a nominal fee because of his belief in their work. 'The new Talbot Baines Reed' became a major attraction of the *B.O.P.* and was eagerly looked forward to by readers.

Reed was the best kind of Victorian, a man of high principle, enormous industry, strong social conscience, earnest endeavour and a robust sense of humour. His friend John Sime called him 'the very ideal of a chivalrous English gentleman'.[18] He was an eminent Victorian from a family of eminent Victorians, the son of Sir Charles Reed (1819–81), Liberal M.P., chairman of the London School Board and active committee member of the British and Foreign Bible Society, and grandsom of the Rev. Andrew Reed (1787-1862), a Congregationalist minister, a hymn writer of distinction and the founder of orphanages, asylums and hospitals for incurables.

Talbot, known familiarly as 'Tibby', was born in Hackney in 1852, one of five brothers, the eldest of whom, Charles Edward, was also a Congregationalist minister and secretary of the British and Foreign Bible Society. From 1864 to 1868 'Tibby' attended the City of London School, where his brother had been school captain and largely responsible for starting cricket and football. It was a day school, but he fused his experience there with the boarding school tradition of the previous literature, particularly *Tom Brown* and *Eric*, when he wrote his own stories, and achieved such success that public school boys regularly pronounced the stories authentic. G. A. Hutchison confirmed that 'so realistic were Mr. Reed's descriptions of the minutest details of public-school life, that on the appearance of the stories in our pages we were sure to receive letters from readers in different parts of the country, asserting that their own particular schools had been manifestly described, and asking whether the writer was this or that Old Boy whom they remembered.'[19]

Reed loved his schooldays and seems to have successfully combined both academic work and sport. 'We did work,' he recalled. 'Have we forgotten the old Doctor's speech to the boys on Prize Day? Or the new Doctor's Greek Testament class? Or the tussle for the Latin verse prize in the Sixth? Or the tears we shed over Hecuba and Andromache?'[20] But sport was equally important to him. Ten years after leaving, he wrote to the school magazine, reprehending the lack of a football or cricket club at the school:

> Is there no one left who can recall the days when the City School was deemed a force not unworthy to range itself against St. Paul's, King's College, University School, or Christ's Hospital? when, amid the cries of 'bravo, City', from hundreds of spectators, our ball flew over the goal of the Blackheath School; or our bats punished the bowling of Bruce Castle; and when our sports were run after, and our 'quarter mile' a famous event . . . The credit of the school is at stake. Unless the fellows do something to remedy matters the name of a City School Man will come to be a term of reproach rather than of honour.[21]

A contemporary recalled that as a schoolboy 'He was a handsome boy, strong and well-proportioned, with a frank, open face, black hair, and lively dark eyes, fresh complexion, full of life and vigour, and with a clear, ringing voice.' He was 'A1 in football', a good all-rounder in cricket and in sport as in everything', his temper and performance were always equable and reliable'.[22]

Generosity of character, athletic prowess and intellectual vivacity marked his school career. Leaving school, he joined the family type-founding business, rising eventually to be its managing director. He grew to love the old art of typefounding and wrote a classic work on its history. He was a lifelong Liberal, but most of all his life was animated by his Christian faith. His old school friend recalled:

> Reed was a true follower of Christ, but without any cant or feeble sentimentality in his religion. He had a dread of anything sensational in religious services or exercises, and was particularly careful that his feelings should not run away with his reason. For this cause, the simple, cheerful Puritanism in which he had been brought up was eminently suited to his simple, manly character and disposition, but he could always recognise and sympathise with what was best in all forms of religion. It may truly be said that he had no enemies—not even himself—except in so far as in working for others he did not spare his strength.[23]

Reed believed in the fundamental principles of co-operation and help:

> The strong fellows should look after the weak, the active must look after the lazy, the merry must cheer up the dull, the sharp must lend a helping hand to the duffer. Pull together, in all your learning, playing and praying.[24]

In politics, religion and personality he resembled Thomas Hughes. An optimistic, manly Christian, he was a devoted family man (married at twenty-four to the daughter of an Irish judge and father of four children). He was a keen sportsman ('a fair shot', a strong swimmer who had won the Royal Humane Society Medal at seventeen for saving a cousin from drowning). He was a selfless worker for others (deacon of the Congregational Church, strong supporter of philanthropic enterprises, he devoted all his spare time to writing for boys). He shared with Hughes the singular characteristic of remaining a lifelong boy. His friend John Sime spoke of him possessing 'the healthy freshness of heart of boyhood' and G. A. Hutchison wrote, 'He was to the last a real boy amongst boys—never seeming so happy as when thinking or planning for the lads or actually in their company. His heart remained young, despite the burden incident to manhood.[25] Reed's workaholic regime, however, undermined his health. He contracted consumption and died at the age of forty-one on 28 November 1893, universally lamented.

By general consent, his most famous story, though not necessarily his best, was *The Fifth Form at St Dominic's*, serialised in the *B.O.P.* in 1881–82 and published in book form in 1887. It remained in print until 1948, was reissued in 1951 and again in 1971. It is currently out of print. The story was filmed in Britain in 1921 with Ralph Forbes and Maurice Thompson as the brothers Oliver and Stephen Greenfield.

The Fifth Form at St Dominic's interweaves four narrative strands, against the background of the rivalry of the fifth and sixth forms at the eponymous school. The first strand centres on the friendship of the fifth-formers Horace 'Wray' Wraysford and Oliver Greenfield, a friendship not marked by extravagant protestations of love as in Hughes and Farrar but more intense than those in Wodehouse. The boys received careful and well rounded characterisation. 'Wray' is a 'handsome, jovial-looking boy of sixteen—one of the best "all-round" men in the Fifth or indeed in the School'. Reed makes it clear that he is not only certain to be in the school eleven against the county and to win the mile and the hurdles at the athletic sports, but he is deemed likely to carry off the Nightingale scholarship. So he maintains a perfect balance between sport and scholarship. His best friend is Oliver Greenfield, 'quieter and more lazy and more solemn. Some say he has a temper and others that he is selfish; and generally he is not the most popular boy in St Dominic's. Wraysford, however, sticks to him through thick and thin and declares that . . . he is one of the best fellows in the school and one of the cleverest.'

A crisis arises when, during a quarrel, the unpopular prefect Edward Loman strikes Oliver in front of the fifth form and Oliver will not fight. He is defended out of loyalty by Wraysford and by Anthony Pembury, the whimsical, crippled editor of the fifth-form magazine. But the rest of the fifth form shun him, believing him to have 'shown the white feather'. Oliver explains that he has been trying to curb his temper and will not be drawn into needless fighting, and Reed comments:

> The reader will no doubt already have decided in his own mind whether Oliver Greenfield did rightly or wrongly in putting his hands into his pockets instead of using them to knock Loman down. It certainly did not seem to have done him much good at the time. He had lost the esteem of his comrades, he had lost the very temper he had been trying to keep—twenty times since the event—and no one gave him credit for anything but 'the better part of valour' in the whole affair. And yet that one effort of self-restraint was not altogether unmanly. At least, so thought Wraysford that night, as he lay meditating upon his friend's troubles, and found himself liking him nonetheless for this latest piece of eccentricity.[26]

Reed is expanding here on Hughes's philosophy. Fighting for its own sake is not a good thing but fighting for a cause is essential. Such a cause occurs later when Loman, the publican Ben Cripps and a group of drunken tavern louts are preparing to throw Oliver's brother Stephen into the river. Oliver and Wray wade into them and beat them ('A pair of well-trained athletic schoolboys, with a plucky youngster to help them, are a match any day for twice the number of half-tipsy cads'). When Stephen explains that they had tried to force Stephen to join in drinking, smoking and card-playing Oliver challenges Loman to a fight, and this time Loman refuses.

Oliver and Wraysford both enter for the Nightingale scholarship. The examination paper is stolen and suspicion falls on Oliver, who had been seen near the headmaster's study. He is sent to coventry by the other boys: 'It must be said of the Dominicans—and I think it may be said of a good many English public school boys—that however foolish they may have been in other respects, however riotous, however jealous of one another, however well-satisfied with themselves, a point of honour was a point of honour which they all took seriously to heart.'[27] Greenfield retaliates by cutting everyone in return, including Wray, who is hurt by this but confused by the situation. Oliver wins the scholarship against Wraysford and Loman, but is hissed on prize day when he receives it. Oliver, Wray and Loman then all sit for the Waterston exhibition. After it, Wraysford goes to Oliver and effects a reconciliation:

> Oh! the happiness of that precious quarter of an hour when the veil that has divided two faithful friends is suddenly dashed aside, and they rush one to the other, calling themselves every imaginable bad name in the dictionary, insisting to the verge of quarrelling that it was all their fault, and no fault at all of the other, far too rapturous to talk ordinary common sense, and far too forgetful of everything to remember that they are saying the same thing over and over again every few minutes. 'The falling out of faithful friends'— as the old copybooks say in elegant Virgilian Latin—'renewing is of love'. And so it was with Oliver and Wraysford.[28]

The centrality of schoolboy friendship looks back to Hughes and Farrar and the friendships of Tom and East, Eric and Russell, and forward to those stories like *The Hill* which were to anatomise it in greater detail.

Oliver wins the Waterston, confounding the theory of his cheating, and then the missing exam paper is found in a volume of Juvenal belonging to Loman. He denies ever having seen it before, but Oliver is restored to general favour. He is reinstated in the school eleven, from which he had been dropped, and distinguishes himself in a game in which St Dominic's are beaten by the county but not disgraced. Oliver's story is essentially a celebration of heroic individualism. It is about being true to yourself, sticking to your principles against all the odds and seeing it through. It recalls the progress and development of Tom Brown.

The second theme of the book, the contrast and counterpoint, the decline and fall of Edward Loman, echoes *Eric*. Loman, like Eric, declines little by little. He is in the toils of the unscrupulous publican Ben Cripps, who, instructing 'the young gentlemen' in billiards, entices them into drinking, gambling and borrowing. As he gets deeper into debt and more desperate, Loman begins to tell lies, a moment of crucial revelation:

> Loman was amazed at himself. He had suddenly made up his mind to tell one lie. But here they were following one after another, as if had told nothing but lies all his life! Alas, there was not drawing back, either.[29]

His debt mounts as he tries to retrieve the situation by betting and finally he owes £35. He takes to drinking heavily. He beats up young Stephen Greenfield when he refuses to fag for him. He steals the Nightingale paper to assure himself of the £50 scholarship but fails when another paper is substituted. His academic work and his sport suffer as he becomes increasingly despairing. He is sacked as a monitor for going to the pub. He borrows from Wray and Oliver to help pay off his debts, but when he cannot muster the full amount Cripps writes to the headmaster, exposing him. Loman flees the school, is found by Oliver desperately ill with rheumatic fever, confesses all and purges his sins. He is sent to Australia to farm for four or five years and to recover his physical and moral health. Oliver is the only boy to shake hands with him when he leaves, demonstrating his Christian principles, and directly emulating Russell and Barker at Roslyn. So, as so often, the empire provides the place for black sheep to make good. Five years later, having pulled himself together, he returns to take up a career in the law. Loman's story is well told and demonstrates without undue moralising the downward spiral of gambling, drinking and deception.

The third theme centres on the school career of Stephen Greenfield, Oliver's younger brother. He arrives as a new boy and we thus see the school and its customs through fresh eyes. A hoax exam paper is perpetrated on him; he fags for Loman. The tribal life of the 'guinea pigs' and the 'tadpoles', two rival groups of small boys, is vividly described: their battles with the monitors and each other, their indignation meetings, their feasts, their strike against fagging and their general exuberance. Stephen finds himself at home at St Dominic's after about a fortnight:

> He was not one of those exuberant, irresponsible boys who take their class-fellows by storm, and rise to the top of the tree almost as soon as they touch the bottom. Stephen . . . was not a very clever boy, or a very dashing boy, and yet somehow he managed to get his footing among his comrades in the Fourth Junior, and particularly among his fellow Guinea-Pigs. He had fought Master Bramble six times in three days during his second week, and was engaged to fight him again every Tuesday, Thursday and Friday during the term. He had also taken the chair at one indignation meeting against the monitors, and spoken in favour of a resolution at another. He had distributed brandy-balls in a most handsome manner to his particular adherents, and he

had been the means of carrying away no less than two blankets from the next dormitory. This was pretty good for a fortnight. Add to this that he had remained steadily at the bottom of his class during the entire period, and that he had received an 'impot' from Mr. Rastle, and it will easily be understood that he soon gained favour among his fellows.[30]

Stephen starts using cribs, settles down into a 'slough of idleness', but Mr Rastle, his form master, invites him to tea, offers to help him and urges him to pray when in trouble, in one of the few overt references to Christianity. This talk has the same effect on him as one of Arnold's sermons on Tom Brown; Stephen eschews cribs and seeks to become a more diligent student. A similar impression is made when the head-master, Dr Senior, chastens the juniors about their strike, visits the fourth form to test them, exposes their ignorance and warns them:

> If you try, and work hard, and stick like men to your lessons, you will know more than you do know; and when you do know more you will see that the best way for little boys to get on is not by giving themselves ridiculous airs, but by doing their duty steadily in class, and living at peace with one another, and submitting quietly to the discipline of the school. Don't let me hear any more of this recent nonsense. You'll be going off in a day or two for the holidays. Take my advice, and think over what I have said; and next term let me see you in your right minds, determined to work hard and do your part honestly for the credit of the good old school.[31]

The Doctor's strictures only increase the boys' veneration for him. During the holidays Wraysford saves Stephen from drowning when their boat is swept over the weir. Stephen falls innocently into visiting the pub and is in danger of going the same way as Loman. But after his rescue by Oliver and Wraysford from the pub thugs, Oliver reports his conduct to the Head, and in sobered mood Stephen is moved by one of the Head's sermons on the theme of 'Forgetting those things which are behind—reaching forth unto those things which are before' and resolves to mend his ways. A fatherly talk with the Doctor completes the cure. He stands by Oliver during his period 'in Coventry'. So Stephen arrives a high-spirited, mindless boy, integrates, goes through the phase of withdrawal and rebellion, and overcomes it with the help of Oliver, the advice of the Head and the friendly concern of Mr Rastle.

The fourth theme centres on the role of Tony Pembury, lame, sarcastic and non-sporting, but eccentric, individualist and a survivor. Pembury is one of the few who stand by and defend Oliver in a display of solidarity with a fellow outsider. He launches the fifth form's magazine, *The Dominican*, to rival the dull, unreadable *Sixth Form Magazine*. It causes a sensation, exacerbating the rivalry of the two forms. Pembury has help with the first issue but has to do the whole of the second when the others default ('With the body of a cripple, he had the heart of a lion, and difficulties only made him more dauntless'). The Doctor advises Pembury to remove the more offensive personal allusions but allows the magazine to continue, providing Pembury with a role and a distinctive niche in the life of the school. The last chapter of the book, five years after the events recounted, sees Pembury now a newspaper editor, Oliver a barrister, Wraysford a college tutor and Stephen now captain of cricket, hero and model of the school, demonstrating that the child is father of the man.

Vivid and readable, *St Dominic's* formed the prototype school story, creating a sense of lived school life, with much on games and friendship and rather less on lessons. But then, for the majority of boys lessons are much less significant in the scale of priorities than friendships and social activities. Any other form of story would be untrue to the majority of boys' lives and would therefore carry less weight and credibility. Most important, the boys are realistic depictions, boys for the 1880s as Hughes's were for the 1850s. As Reed's friend John Sime recalled, this was one of his strengths:

> He sympathised with the troubles and joys, he understood the temptations and fathomed the motives that sway and mould boy character. His boy heroes are neither prigs nor milksops, but in their strength and weakness they are the stuff which ultimately. makes our best citizens and fathers; they are the boys who, later in life, with healthy minds in healthy bodies have made the British Empire what it is.[32]

G. A. Hutchison claimed:

> These boys of St. Dominic's, even the best of them, are very human—neither angels, nor monstrosities, but, for the most part, ardent, impulsive, out-and-out, work-a-day lads; with the faults and failings of inexperience and impetuosity, no doubt, but with that moral grit and downright honesty of purpose that we still believe, the distinguishing mark of the true British public school boy . . . such boys stand at the antipodes alike of the unreal abstractions of an effeminate sentimentalism—the paragons who prate platitudes and die young—and of the morbid specimens of youthful infamy only too frequently paraded by the equally unreal sensationalism of to-day to meet the cravings of a vitiated taste.[33]

The influence of both Hughes and Farrar on Reed is clear. From *Eric* comes the gradual destruction of Loman and the machinations of the unscrupulous publican. From *St Winifred's*, where Walter Evson is sent to Coventry and given a silent reception when he wins the high jump, comes the ostracisation of Oliver and his reception on prize day. It seems likely too that the dramatic stranding and rescuing of the boys from a mountain top in *The Clock House at Fellsgarth* was also inspired by *St Winifred's*. From *Tom Brown* comes the discussion of a rationale for fighting, the principled stand of Oliver (both authors have a chapter entitled 'The turn of the tide'), the socialisation of young Stephen and the effects of the headmaster's sermon. Similarly, in *The Cock House*, *Tom Brown* seems to have been the inspiration for the first-night singing of the new boys, the captain's speech, the games and the big fight between Corder and Brinkman. The eccentric Rollitt, who protects younger boys from bullying, looks to have been modelled on Diggs.

Reed was unashamedly writing moral fables. As G. A. Hutchison put it in his preface to the book-length version of *St Dominic's*, 'Our prayer is that God may abundantly bless the book to the building up in our schools and families of strong Christian characters who in the after days shall do valiant service for Christ and humanity.'[34] But Reed was also writing out of his own experience about real boys and without the full weight of ideological baggage that Hughes carried. He was certainly concerned to tell a story which would show boys acting according to principle. The fall of Loman, the rescue of Stephen and the conduct of Oliver all reinforce this theme.

Reed does not overemphasise games, for we are not yet in the full spate of athleticism. The Sixth *v.* the School cricket match and the School *v.* the County rugby match are both described in full but an earlier cricket match is omitted, because, as Reed observes, 'the reader will probably be far more interested in the incidents of the Sixth versus School match when it comes off'.[35] Scholarships, the production of the school magazine and friendships are as important as sport, unlike in Wodehouse, where sport is dominant. As might be expected, Reed endorses fagging, the prefectorial system and house loyalty. Although he foregrounds certain characters, he is concerned to provide a cross-section of school life and to see it in the round, much in the way *Grange Hill* does for the modern comprehensive. The serial format of the *B.O.P.*, the parallel plot lines, the large cast of characters, all emphasise the similarity of structure and approach. However, the work of Reed as a whole, although he rings the changes and maintains a consistent freshness, liveliness and interest, does suggest that there is truth in the treatment made by both Alec Waugh and P. G. Wodehouse that the problem with schools is that nothing ever happens.[36] Certainly things do happen, but within a restricted range of events and recurrently, so that one tends to find that Reed's work is a matter of themes and variations. *The Cock House at Fellsgarth*, while concentrating more on juniors than on seniors, reworks almost all the elements of *St Dominic's*—the rivalry of the two sides, vicissitudes of new boy, suspected theft, a sending to Coventry, a rescue from drowning, a strike—with some new elements (the school clubs, running the tuck shop, climbing Hawk's Pike). Because it concentrates more on small boys *The Cock House* has less psychological depth and development, remaining more incident-based and less character-based than *St Dominic's*. But this does not make it any the less truthful. The 'Guinea Pigs' and 'Tadpoles' rivalry and the rough-and-tumble life of the juniors, so brilliantly captured in *St Dominic's*, was reworked with variations in *The Cock House of Fellsgarth* (the rivalry of the Classical and Modern juniors), *Tom, Dick and Harry* (the rivalry of boarders and day boys) and *The Willoughby Captains* (rivalry of Welch's House and Parratt's House juniors). Alec Waugh recognised the realism of this portraiture of small boys, though seeing the picture more reminiscent of the prep. school than the public school proper:

> The smallest boys do resemble the 'Tadpoles' . . . In spite of frequent visits to the bath room their hands and collars are continually smeared with ink; when they go for walks at least one of them falls into the ditch . . . they are all dog-eared except at meal-times and at the start of the morning's work. And they have the same attitude to life. They are continually forming rival gangs; they are on the brink of feuds and jealousies. They side against one another. Each boy in turn becomes the object of general dislike.[37]

Isabel Quigly has pointed out that the plot of *St Dominic's* shows how many of the incidents and patterns of events in Reed's stories became standard in the *genre*: 'The stolen exam paper, the innocent wrongly accused, his suffering, proud loneliness and final triumph, the boating accident, the runaway lost in a storm, rescued by the boy he had wronged and brought back to the school half dead.'[38] They certainly recurred in the work of Frank Richards, Reed's most illustrious successor. But even before the great days of *The Magnet* a flock of formula writers—Hylton Cleaver, Harold Avery, Gunby Hadath, John G. Rowe, Kent Carr, Richard Bird—writing both in periodicals and in books, endlessly reproduced, disseminated and perpetuated the characters, incidents and ideology of Reed.

How was *The Fifth Form at St Dominic's* received? W. MacQueen Pope, writing of the reading tastes of lower middle-class non-public school boys in the late Victorian and Edwardian eras, called *St Dominic's* 'a classic' and recalled:

> Boys adored it, partly because of its well-told tale, and partly because the school it depicted represented their ideal of what a school should be, and partly because it was totally unlike their own—it represented to them a scholastic Heaven.[39]

Reed's work was much in demand for prizes. My own copy of *Fifth Form at St Dominic's* was presented to Henry Burridge for attendance and good conduct at Barnoldswick Church Sunday School, 20 August 1905.

Edward Salmon, writing in 1888, noted the recent popularity of Reed and observed that 'there should be a considerable future before him in the line he has adopted. He tells a story well and naturally, and is thoroughly conversant with every phase of boy-life.'[40] In his questionnaire about boys' favourite reading, no Reed title is specifically mentioned among the books but *The Boy's Own Annual*, whose star writer he was, emerged as fifth favourite and among magazines outstandingly the most popular, garnering 404 votes. Its nearest rival, *Tit Bits*, managed a mere 27.[41]

In 1899 the *B.O.P.* ran a competition to discover who were the twelve favourite authors to have appeared in its pages. A hundred and twenty-one names figured in the nominations. Dr Gordon Stables emerged as favourite, with 187 votes. Reed came ninth, with 111. But all those ahead of Reed were current *B.O.P.* authors and Reed's work had not appeared in the paper since his death six years before.[42]

The competition in *The Captain* (1908) for the twelve best-ever books for boys, based on 800 entries, placed *Fifth Form at St Dominic's* ninth. But only two others of the twelve titles were school stories: *Tom Brown's Schooldays* (first) and *J. O. Jones*, by *The Captain's* editor, R. S. Warren-Bell (twelfth).[43] A. J. Jenkinson's survey of 1,570 boys in 1940 only covered 'adult' authors read and this did not include Reed. But the *B.O.P.* was by now well down the table of preference in magazines. With 304 secondary school boys of twelve-plus, the *B.O.P.* came fourteenth (with fourteen votes) in the order of preference, with *Wizard* (150), *Hotspur* (145) and *Rover* (132) first choices. With 211 boys of thirteen-plus *B.O.P.* came tenth with nineteen votes, and with 250 boys of fourteen-plus, eleventh, with thirteen votes. It was read on the whole by respectable, better-class boys. Of elementary school boys, none mentioned the *B.O.P.*[44] Clearly by 1940 the great days of the *B.O.P.*'s mass appeal were long over, and it is likely that World War I saw the watershed when competition, first from *Chums* and *Captain*, later from *Gem* and *Magnet* and later still from *Wizard*, *Hotspur* and *Rover*, eroded its readership. Nevertheless it carried on until 1967, the venerable survivor of a distant age.

But Reed's work remained for many a vivid and prized memory. J. Howard Whitehouse, educationalist, author and Liberal M.P., recalled in 1935:

> I should place first amongst books which gave a natural picture of school life the tales of Talbot Baines Reed . . . The value and charm of his stories arise from the fact that he loved and understood boys, and that in his tales he has given us types which are true to life, and written with such charm that old and young find joy in his pages. The things which his boys did are things which we should all have done if we had the opportunity. His boys talk as all boys talk at a certain age . . . I was a youth when Talbot Baines Reed's

stories first appeared in the *Boy's Own Paper*, a paper which did much for the boys of England . . . How well I remember counting the days between the monthly parts of the *Boy's Own Paper* when such a story as 'A Dog with a Bad Name' was appearing in its pages. I had an order with a local bookseller for the paper, and on the 24th of every month I was his first customer to get my paper. I used to think he was a particularly wicked and offensive man, because he had the monthly parts in stock before the 24th, but refused to sell them until that day.[45]

Sir Compton Mackenzie (St Paul's) also testified to the compulsive power of Reed, though he preferred *The Cock House of Fellsgarth* to *St Dominic's* and recalled 'lying on that sofa in the dining room and reading the *Boy's Own Paper*' in which *The Cock House* was being serialised. He recalled accurately that it told 'the story of the feud between the Classical side and the Modern side at a public school, and significantly the chaps in the Classical side were all decent chaps and the chaps in the Modern side were a pretty caddish lot . . . Wally Wheatfield, D'Arcy, Ashby and Fisher II were the spirited Classical juniors. Percy Wheatfield (Wally's twin brother), Cash, Cottle, Lickford and one whose name I have forgotton (I have not read the book for nearly forty years) were the equally spirited Modern juniors. The only criticism I had to make of *The Cock House* was that instead of the "right-o" of my time (the O.K. of today) the chaps said, "all serene". I could not understand how the author of such a jolly good story could suppose that boys ever said "all serene".'[46]

Alec Waugh introduced a subtle distinction, suggesting that the preparatory school was much more like the public school of this fictional tradition than the actual public school. He claimed that 'Talbot Baines Reed is only read by boys of under thirteen; and boys of under thirteen have moulded themselves after his image'.[47] If this is true, it still confirms the influence of Reed in shaping perceptions and providing role models.

The Boy's Own Paper, and with it the stories of Talbot Baines Reed, became a prime vehicle for the popularisation of the public school ethos. According to E. C. Mack, in the fifteen years between 1855 and 1870 *Beeton's Boys' Annual* contained only eight to ten pieces about schools, of which five were about public schools.[48] The *B.O.P.* published twenty-four such pieces in three years. He concluded that the *B.O.P.* authors, in particular Talbot Baines Reed and R. Hope Moncrieff, 'had . . . completely mastered the art of writing specifically for adolescents'. They preached, but indirectly, and aimed for authenticity in their picture of boys and school life. 'The heroes are plain, simple boys who hate singularities and subtleties and who, although they seldom grow ecstatic or sentimental about the public school system, accept unquestioningly the ritual and standards of their schools.'[49] There seems little reason to dispute Mack's conclusion that the *B.O.P.* was one of the most powerful exponents of the public school ideal, unconsciously absorbed by generations of boys.

Notes

1 On these writers see P. W. Musgrave, *From Brown to Bunter*, London, 1985, 92-111.
2 F. J. Harvey Darton, *Children's Books in England* (1932), Cambridge, 1982, 301; Ian Hay, *The Lighter Side of School Life*, Edinburgh, 1923, 160.
3 On *The Boys's Own Paper* see Patrick Dunae, 'British Juvenile Literature in an Age of Empire, 1880-1914', Manchester University Ph.D. thesis, 1975, 81-129, and Patrick Dunae, '*Boy's Own Paper*: origins and editorial policies', *Private Library*, 9 (1976), 123-58, in particular. Also Jack Cox, *Take a Cold Tub, Sir! The story of the* Boy's Own Paper, Guildford, 1982.
4 Dunae, '*Boy's Own Paper*', 126.
5 S. G. Green, *The Story of the Religious Tract Society*, London, 1899, 127.
6 Harvey Darton, *Children's Books*, 299.
7 Stanley Morison, *Talbot Baines Reed, Author, Bibliographer, Typefounder*, Cambridge, 1960, 15.
8 Dunae, '*Boy's Own Paper*', 145.
9 Dunae, '*Boy's Own Paper*', 132.
10 Cox, *Cold Tub*, 22.
11 Musgrave, *From Brown to Bunter*, 142.
12 Philip Warner (ed.), *Best of British Pluck*, London, 1976, 6.
13 Warner (ed.), *British Pluck*, 96-8.
14 *The Times*, 19 January 1929.
15 Dunae, '*Boy's Own Paper*', 133-4.
16 Dunae, '*Boy's Own Paper*', 147.
17 On Reed's life and work see Morison, *Reed*.
18 Talbot Baines Reed, *Kilgorman* (1895), London, 1906, preface, xxiv.
19 Talbot Baines Reed, *A Book of Short Stories*, London, 1901, introductory sketch, 24.
20 Morison, *Reed*, 4.
21 Morison, *Reed*, 4-5.
22 Reed, *Short Stories*, 12, 14.
23 Reed, *Short Stories*, 18.
24 Morison, *Reed*, 72.
25 Reed, *Kilgorman*, viii; Reed, *Short Stories*, 26.
26 Talbot Baines Reed, *The Fifth Form at St Dominic's* (1887), London, 1905, 89.
27 Reed, *St Dominic's*, 224.
28 Reed, *St Dominic's*, 294.
29 Reed, *St Dominic's*, 105.
30 Reed, *St Dominic's*, 90-91.
31 Reed, *St Dominic's*, 166-7.
32 Reed, *Kilgorman*, viii.
33 Reed, *St Dominic's*, introduction, 6-7.
34 Reed, *St Dominic's*, introduction, 8.
35 Reed, *St Dominic's*, 79.
36 P. G. Wodehouse, 'School stories', *Public School Magazine*, 8 (1901), 125; Alec Waugh, *The Loom of Youth*, 184.
37 Alec Waugh, *Public School Life*, London, 1922, 31.
38 Isabel Quigly, *The Heirs of Tom Brown*, London, 1982, 83.
39 W. MacQueen Pope, *Twenty Shillings in the Pound*, London, 1948, 92.
40 Edward Salmon, *Juvenile Literature as it is*, London, 1888, 100.

41 Salmon, *Juvenile Literature*, 15.
42 *Boy's Own Paper*, 21 (1899), 415. The top twelve were Dr Gordon Stables (187), the Rev. A. N. Malan (185), G. Manville Fenn (173), Jules Verne (165), David Ker (159), G. A. Henty (158), Paul Blake (138), Harold Avery (125), Talbot Baines Reed (111), A. R. Hope (97), A. Colbeck (74), J. Dawtrey (73).
43 *The Captain*, 19 (1908), 90.
44 A. J. Jenkinson, *What do Boys and Girls Read?*, London, 1940, 64-75.
45 J. Howard Whitehouse, *Education*, London, 1935, 154-6.
46 Compton MacKenzie, *My Life and Times—Octave One* (1883-91), London, 1963, 240.
47 Alec Waugh, *Public School Life*, 31.
48 Edward C. Mack, *Public Schools and British Opinion since 1860*, New York, 1941, 149.
49 Mack, *Public Schools*, 150.

5

The triumph of athleticism: *Mike*

From the 1850s organised sports were a feature of the English public schools and during the 1860s, 1870s and 1880s they were transformed into an obsession which bred an entire philosophy (athleticism), given historical sanction by the popularisation of an alleged aphorism of the Duke of Wellington that 'the battle of Waterloo was won on the playing fields of Eton'. The concepts of gentleman and sportsman became interchangeable through the public schools, and the revived chivalry of the nineteenth century fed directly into the athleticism cult. The word 'cult' is used here advisedly, for athleticism had its gods and heroes, its rituals and its hymns, and it was invested with the kind of religious fervour that Arnold had sought to channel into Christian commitment.[1]

It was not Arnold but a coterie of celebrated mid-Victorian headmasters like C. J. Vaughan of Harrow, G. E. L. Cotton of Marlborough and Edward Thring of Uppingham who promoted games at school. Organised games were introduced in part to counteract the effect of less wholesome leisure activities of public school boys such as stone-throwing, poaching, birds-nesting and, at Marlborough, beating frogs to death. But also, against a general background of vandalism and indiscipline, it was a potent means of social control and character-forming. It was seen as an ideal way of putting into effect Arnold's desire to shape character.. It directed energy and aggression into productive channels. It promoted manliness and chivalry through the ideas of team spirit, leadership, loyalty, bravery, fair play, modesty in victory and humility in defeat.

By the end of the century games were compulsory and athleticism was dominant. This athleticism informed the regimes of the later Victorian headmasters. The priorities of H. H. Almond of Loretto were 'First—character; second—physique; third—intelligence; fourth—manners; fifth—information.'[2] As a corollary anti-intellectualism was rife, and intellectuals came to be seen as essentially unmanly. As one commentator wrote in 1872, 'A nation of effeminate, enfeebled book-worms scarcely forms the most effective bulwark of a nation's liberties.'[3] But in fact these poor despised creatures of culture and intellect were just as indispensable to the nation to guard its soul as the gentlemen sportsmen were to defend its heart.

The games-playing ideology was sustained by a structure of ritual and symbolism—the prestigious old-boys' matches and the house matches, the sporting housemasters and even more the schoolboy sports heroes—'the bloods'—who provided role models. Benefactors endowed sports facilities. School magazines kept up a stream of pro-paganda. There was the system of colours and of costume, tasselled caps, sashes, scarves and flamboyant blazers—the Uppingham XV even carried riding crops—dress and privilege gradings as stratified, formalised, detailed and intricate as those of the Byzantine court in its heyday. The loyalty inculcated, the aspirations fostered and the role models provided remained with many boys for ever.

Then there were the school songs, the hymns of the games cult, chanted ritually and characterised by J. A. Mangan as a 'unique mixture of emotionalism, innocence, myopia and rigidity'.[4] He singles out as the particular virtues promoted: loyalty, masculinity, patriotism and decency. Edward Bowen's songs sum it up. Bowen, a Harrow master, was another of the boy-men so prominent in this study, a man, who according to Dr Cyril Norwood, 'kept the eternal boy alive within his own breast to the very end'.[5] Bowen's 'Forty Years On' invoked the blessings of the Deity on the new cult:

> God give us bases to guard and beleaguer,
> Games to play out, whether earnest or fun,
> Fights for the fearless and goals for the eager,
> Twenty and Thirty and Forty Years On.

The complex of ideas that athleticism involved is perfectly exemplified in the Sedbergh cricket song:

> If you've England in your veins
> And can take a little pains
> In the sunny summer weather when to stay indoors is sin,
> If you've got a bit of muscle,
> And enjoy a manly tussle,
> Then go and put your flannels on and let the fun begin.
>
> You must leave your honoured self
> In the shed, upon the shelf,
> Nor think about your average but do your level best.
> Keep your temper and be jolly,
> And away with melancholy,

And shut your mouth and play the game
And never mind the rest!

Let the lazy talk of luck,
It was persevering pluck,
That saved the day for Waterloo and made the winning run,
And the men with most of that'll
Be the men to fight the battle,
For a match is never lost, my boy, until a match is won.

So be worthy of your race,
Fellow countrymen of Grace,
And be faithful to the willow as your fathers were of yore,
For there's nothing in creation,
To compare with the sensation
Of dismissing a half-volley to the boundary for four!

And hail to the name
Of the brave old game;
Wherever men are English and the flag's unfurled,
And you will there find cricket
And the willow and the wicket
And there's not a game to lick it
In the whole wide world.

The whole philosophy could be summed up in three words 'Play the game'. Montagu Butler, at a dinner given by Harrovians to celebrate his eightieth birthday, declared, 'Whether it be a matter of cricket . . . or politics or professional engagements, there is hardly any motto which I would more confidently commend than "Play the Game".'[6] This morality was synonymous with that of the chivalric knight—magnanimity in victory, dignity in defeat, hatred of injustice, decency and modesty in all things. As *The Marlburian* declared in 1867, 'A truly chivalrous football-player . . . was never yet guilty of lying or deceit or meanness, whether of word or action.'[7] Both foreign and domestic commentators identified athleticism as so central to the national ideology that many were prepared to attribute the nineteenth-century pre-eminence of the British empire to that games-playing code.[8]

It is no coincidence that many of the sports-promoting head-masters were great enthusiasts for the empire. The rise of the empire put a premium on authority, discipline, team spirit and physical hardi-hood, and the public schools became, in the words of E. C. Mack, 'mints for the coining of Empire builders'.[9] The doctrine of imperialism as developed by the late Victorian imperial visionaries was in one sense but chivalry writ large, with the British as the elect, bringing to the underprivileged peoples of the world fair play and good government.

The climacteric of all this chivalry and sportsmanship was provided by the Great War. It was in a sense the inevitable, tragic fulfilment of the nineteenth century's heroic ideal. So often had the poetry equated war with sport, so deeply had a generation been inculcated with the ideals of physical preparedness, duty and honour, and so potent was the image of the glorious death of the 'Happy Warrior' that the declaration of war against the ogre Germany in defence of 'gallant little Belgium' was greeted with jubilation, and exhilarated young men flocked to the colours in their thousands. It comes as no surprise in this context to learn that at the Somme in 1916 Captain W. P. Nevill produced a football and he and his company of the East Surreys dribbled it into battle, where most of them were killed. 'True to the land that bore them, the Surreys play the game,' said a commemorative poem.[10]

Athleticism was entrenched by a combination of factors. First, there was nostalgic romanticism. F. W. Farrar, no friend of athleticism, memorably captured this tone in one of his sermons to his Marlborough boys:

> Perhaps as you faint on the arid plains of India, perhaps as you toil in the dingy back streets of great cities, amid haunts of poverty and crime—may come the memory of sunny cricket grounds where once you played. Like a draught of clear water in a desert—like that sparkling cup which his warriors brought to David from the well which he had loved in boyhood—you will drink of the innocent delight of these schooldays.[11]

The image is of athleticism as the inspiration for imperial service and urban social work, an abiding and sustaining memory in later life.

In addition, there was the press glamorisation of schoolboy sporting stars, the continuing popularity of the literature of manliness and moral puritanism, the belief that games-playing reduced the incidence of vice. Edmond Warre, headmaster of Eton, thought that games were 'a panacea for all moral delinquencies'.[12] Finally there were parental priorities. Games rather than intellectual activities helped to produce the gentleman all-rounder, and Squire Brown's priorities were still those of most parents.

Athleticism may have achieved a climacteric in the Great War but it is not true to say that it vanished at the end of it. It continued in schools with scarcely diminished vigour until World War II. The difference was that it was now under much more systematic attack. Highbrow and serious literature attacked it remorselessly. Educational reforms and the demands of a national examination system increased academic competition and forced the public schools to increase the amount of attention they paid to academic work. From the 1920s there was a consensus of opinion in English education on the side of individualism. The Second World War was followed by the dissolution of the empire. The diminishing need for imperial administrators and officers in the armed forces made athleticism less necessary as a governing philosophy.

The triumph of athleticism is perfectly expressed in the school stories of P. G. Wodehouse. Wodehouse remained a schoolboy all his days. J. B. Priestley's view was that 'this man who lived so long, wrote so much, earned several fortunes, was really a schoolboy. He was of course no ordinary schoolboy, but a brilliant, super de luxe, schoolboy. This explains what he wrote, how he behaved, why he succeeded.'[13] Indeed, Benny Green believes he was probably the perfect Edwardian schoolboy, by virtue of his 'combination of sporting ability, academic curiosity and a congenitally eupeptic disposition'.[14]

Born in 1881 in Guildford, Wodehouse was the son of a colonial magistrate serving in Hong Kong.[15] He was sent to school at Dulwich College (1894–1900), a period which he described in his autobiography as 'six years of unbroken bliss'.[16] Nicknamed Podge, he was on the classical side but was deeply involved in all kinds of activities. His friend William Townend described him as 'one of the most important boys in the school'.[17] He was a fine cricketer, a noted fast bowler, a good footballer and a keen boxer. He made both the school first eleven (for two years) and first fifteen (for one) but he missed the Public Schools Boxing Competition at Aldershot through illness. He was a prefect, and edited and contributed to the school magazine, *The Alleynian*. His abiding passion was for games. His academic attainments were by comparison unspectacular. He came twenty-fourth out of twenty-five in the classical sixth-form exams in 1899, though he rose to thirteenth in 1900, his last year.[18] As his school report for the summer term of 1899 recorded:

> He has spent too much thought upon his cricket and the winning of colours. He is a most impractical boy . . . he is often forgetful; he finds difficulties in the most simple things and asks absurd questions, whereas he can understand the more difficult things . . . He has the most distorted ideas about wit and humour . . . notwithstanding, he has a genuine interest in literature and can often talk with much enthusiasm and good sense about it . . . One is obliged to like him in spite of his vagaries.[19]

It is probable that the single most ecstatic moment of his life came on 3 June 1899, when he took seven wickets in Dulwich's trouncing of Tonbridge. His passion for school sports long survived his leaving Dulwich, and he followed the fortunes of the school teams with obsessive fervour, writing in 1946 to Townend, 'Isn't it odd when one ought to be worrying about the state of the world and one's troubles generally, that the only thing one can think of nowadays is that Dulwich looks like winning all its school matches.'[20]

For all his sporting commitment and his own admission, 'I was pretty friendly with everyone,' it is clear from the school report that

Wodehouse was something of an eccentric, and like all eccentrics he was basically a shy boy who lived in a world of imagination. He never came to terms with the real world, probably never even wanted to. He retreated into a world of books, read voraciously (Conan Doyle, Kipling and W. S. Gilbert were particular favourites) and from his early school days wanted to be a writer. Townend, his closest schoolfriend, who shared a study with him, recalled, 'We talked incessantly about books and writing. Plum's talk was exhilarating. I had never known such talk. Even at the age of seventeen he could discuss lucidly writers of whom I had never heard.'[21] Already, at school, he had written a series of 'outrageously funny' comic plays modelled on Greek tragedy dealing with boys and masters. In due course he was to create his own timeless world, essentially an Edwardian musical comedy neverland of brainless young men-about-town, fearsome aunts, impeccable butlers and dotty aristocrats.

Wodehouse's blissful schooldays ended in 1900. His family's financial circumstances made university impossible and he went into the Hong Kong and Shanghai Bank in Lombard Street as a clerk. He hated it and turned to writing for solace and escape. During his two years at the bank he had eighty items published in a variety of periodicals, and in September 1902 he finally escaped from the bank and took up journalism full-time, joining *The Globe* to write a humorous column. He was embarked on the career that would make him one of the best-loved comic writers in the language. His first stories, however, were public school stories. 'I first started writing public school stories because it was the only atmosphere I knew at all,' he said later.[22] He had sold a story to *The Public School Magazine* for half a guinea in February 1900. It became, along with *The Captain*, the chief outlet for his public school material. *The Public School Magazine* had been launched by Adam and Charles Black in 1898. It was so popular that George Newnes launched a rival, *The Captain*, in 1900, aimed at public and prep. school boys. *The Captain* was the inspiration of R. S. Warren-Bell, himself a schoolmaster and writer of school stories. He became its first editor, with the celebrated cricketer C. B. Fry as athletics editor. Fry recalled Wodehouse's stories as being 'a great success'.[23] *The Public School Magazine* succumbed to the competition in 1902 and *The Captain* became Wodehouse's principal outlet, paying him £50 for *The Gold Bat*, for instance.[24]

Between 1902 and 1909 Wodehouse published six public school novels, *The Pothunters* (1902), *A Prefect's Uncle* (1903), *The Gold Bat* (1904), *The Head of Kay's* (1905), *The White Feather* (1907) and *Mike* (1909). A collection of short stories and comic pieces was issued under the title of *Tales of St Austin's* (1903). All the novels had begun life as serials in *The Captain*, apart from the first, which appeared in

The Public School Magazine between January and March 1902.

Wodehouse had steeped himself in public school fiction as a child. He recalled in 1955:

> As a child, of course, I read *Eric* and *St. Winifred's* and the Talbot Baines Reed stories in the *B.O.P.* I loved them all. I think it is only later that one grows critical of *Eric* and *St. Winifred's* . . . *Tom Brown*, fine. Also *Vice Versa*.[25]

He expanded on his views of approach to the public school story in an anonymous article contributed to *The Public School Magazine*.[26] He described the public school story as 'far more difficult to write than any other story' because you cannot use the great mainstays of fiction— love and adventure. 'The worst of school life from the point of view of the writer is that nothing ever happens. There is no light and shade. The atmosphere of school is all of one colour.' He complained that public school speech was rarely captured authentically. 'Rudyard Kipling went near it, a gallant pioneer of the ideal, but even the conversation of Stalky and Co. leaves something unsaid.' For Wodehouse *Stalky* and *Eric* represented the two extremes. His complaint about Farrar was essentially his excess. He felt *Eric* and *St Winifred's* not improbable, 'merely probabilities somewhat richly flavoured for ordinary consumption.' He criticised the amount of space devoted to drink, commenting on Farrar's novels, 'alcoholic stimulants flow like water and a perfectly sober character is distinctly the exception'. Perhaps most of all he disliked the emotionalism. In *Mike* Wodehouse refers to *Eric*: 'Like Eric, he burned not with shame and remorse but with rage and all that sort of thing,'[27] indicating the typical stiff-upper-lip distaste for dealing with strong emotions.

On the other hand Wodehouse did owe something of his inspiration to *Stalky*. Contemporary critics were quick to point to the influence of 'Stalkyism' on his stories, though one reviewer conceded, 'no writer of school tales has so much vigour and realistic spirit as Mr. P. G. Wodehouse.'[28] Richard Usborne points to direct parallels 'between the turning off of the gas-main (*Stalky*) and the ringing of the fire bell (*Mike*); Sergeant Foxy in *Stalky* and the school sergeant in *Mike* . . . ; the masters King and Downing; the angry squire fussing about his pheasants in *Stalky* and the ditto in *The Pothunters*'.[29]

But Wodehouse's ideal school stories and his greatest influence were those of Barry Pain, notably the novel *Graeme and Cyril*, which first appeared as a serial in *Chums*, and the story 'The kindness of the Celestial'. Of *Graeme and Cyril* he noted that 'the atmosphere is just the right atmosphere, the various characters are life-like and the crowning praise of all, there is no bully'.[30] Both stories feature Cyprian Langsdyke, 'the most cleverly drawn character that can be found in the whole range of school fiction'. In fact Langsdyke—nicknamed 'The Celestial' because of his narrow Chinese eyes, with his lofty air, witty speech, reference to boys as 'my children', a character who was 'much more athletic than he looked, was reputed to be clever but whimsical, and known to be unruly'[31]—was clearly the inspiration for Psmith. Wodehouse pronounced 'The kindness of the Celestial' 'the best school story that has ever been written', arguing that the 'excellence of the story lies more in the telling thereof than in the plot'.[32] The story tells how Langsdyke decides to be kind to a master who is hard on him and treats him with exaggerated courtesy and reasonableness, perplexing and infuriating his victim. Psmith does much the same in *Mike*.

As the prime example of 'a really bad school story' Wodehouse nominated J. E. C. Welldon's *Gerald Eversley's Friendship*. He sends it up, though misremembers the finale, recalling wrongly that Gerald dies at school:

> Deaths in school stories are a mistake . . . The worst thing that ought to happen to your hero is the loss of the form prize or his being run out against M.C.C. There should be a rule to the effect that noone under the age of twenty-one be permitted to die, unless he can get the whole affair finished in a space of time not exceeding two minutes. In any case the death should not be described.[33]

His dislike of excessive emotionalism and religiosity lay behind his satirical piece on *Tom Brown's Schooldays*, which demonstrated that Hughes had written only the first half, and the second had been written by the committee of the Secret Society for Putting Wholesome Literature within the Reach of every Boy and Seeing that he Gets it.

But Wodehouse pronounced Talbot Baines Reed 'the most successful of schoolboy writers, in that he wrote a great many stories, and all of them good, some infinitely better than others but none weak.' He singled out *Tom, Dick and Harry* as Reed's best, 'as nearly perfect as it is possible for a school story to be'. Reed's picture of Low Heath School he thought 'nearer to that of a real school than any of the many other schools of fiction with the exception of Kipling's "Coll." and Barry Pain's "Desford".'[34] Wodehouse would particularly have enjoyed the fact that the boys of the school were known as 'Low Heathen'. Indeed, it is likely that Wodehouse got the idea for *The Head of Kay's* from *Tom, Dick and Harry*, in which Harry Tempest, slighted and humiliated by a master, loses interest in being house captain and allows the house to become unruly. Sheen getting his scholarship and no applause in *The White Feather* recalls Oliver's fate in *The Fifth Form at St Dominic's*. The election shennanigans in *The White Feather* and the mass walk-out of boys in *Mike* both suggest the inspiration of *The Willoughby Captains*.

In writing specifically for the boys' magazine market Wodehouse studied his sources carefully and found that he could supply what was needed. Subsequent critical judgements of the tales have varied. Wodehouse's biographer, Frances Donaldson, thought them 'extraordinarily good'.[35] Anthony Powell enjoyed them.[36] Owen Dudley Edwards declared *The White Feather* 'a signal triumph'.[37] Alec Waugh thought *Mike* 'delightful' and George Orwell proclaimed *Mike* 'one of the best "light" school stories in English'.[38] Richard Usborne, the most sedulous and devoted of Wodehouse's chroniclers, felt the stories to be 'good yarns' but added, 'there is not much reason why anybody should want to read these stories for the first time now, except as interesting Wodehouse juvenilia.'[39] Wodehouse himself thought the stories the work of an amateur and not worth critical study.[40] Nevertheless, apart from *Mike*, which was already in print, they were all reprinted in hardback in 1972 and are currently available in Penguin.

The truth is that they are apprentice works but are immensely readable, reflecting not only Wodehouse's reading but also his own schooldays. Several of the stories were set at Wrykyn School, which Bill Townend recognised as Dulwich:

> Wrykyn . . . is Dulwich, a Dulwich situated not in a London suburb but in the country. But whereas the boys of Wrykyn are practically all boarders, Dulwich . . . though with a few large boarding houses . . . is in the main a day school; nevertheless elderly men who were at Dulwich between the years 1895 and 1901 will recognise and appreciate Plum's masterly delineation of the life we lived so long ago.[41]

Benny Green's view that the school stories are radical and heretical and that 'deep derision is . . . flung at the conventions of school fiction from the first',[42] echoing as it does E. C. Mack's view that Wodehouse is 'derisive and negativistic', seems to me a fundamental misjudgement, mistaking form for content.[43] Certainly Wodehouse gently mocks some of the conventions of the older school stories but he does so because they fail to reflect the contemporary public school reality and the new code of behaviour and belief. This takes the form of claiming that he is writing about reality as distinct from fiction, thus lending his message even greater weight. Wodehouse consistently distances himself from the emotional excesses of his predecessors, the better to convey his essential message—the validity of the new orthodoxy.

Where the boys in Farrar's novels regularly and extravagantly express their love of each other, Wodehouse takes a different view of schoolboy friendships. In *A Prefect's Uncle*, writing of Norris and his friend Gethryn, nicknamed 'The Bishop', he says:

> Norris was the head of Jephson's house and he and the Bishop were very good friends, in a casual sort of way. If they did not see one another for a

couple of days, neither of them broke his heart. Whenever, on the other hand, they did meet, they were always glad, and always had plenty to talk about. Most school friendships are of that description.[44]

This directly echoes Barry Pain's description of the friendship of Graeme and Cyril:

It was not a sentimental attachment, but it was nonetheless real. It would frequently happen that days would pass without Graeme and Cyril seeing anything of each other; they were by no means inseparables. Yet whenever Cyril found himself in any difficulty he always went to Graeme to get him out of it; Graeme was equally ready to share his best fortune and his worst with Cyril.[45]

In the avoidance of emotionalism Wodehouse was as much reflecting his own age as Farrar had been. But this austere avoidance of emotion does mean that *A Prefect's Uncle*, the tale of a schoolboy shunned by his fellows, lacks the intensity and power of the similar situation in *The Fifth Form at St Dominic's*.

Wodehouse's technique of disparaging what he considers bad fictional practice but then conveying an unexceptionable moral is exemplified by *The White Feather*. When Drummond rejects the offer of the disgraced Sheen to box for the house:

It seemed to him that Sheen, as he expressed it to himself, was trying to 'do the boy hero'. In the school library, which had been stocked during the dark ages, when that type of story was popular, there were numerous school stories in which the hero retrieved a rocky reputation by thrashing the bully, displaying in the encounter an intuitive but overwhelming skill with his fists. Drummond could not help feeling that Sheen must have been reading one of these stories. It was all very fine and noble of him to want to show that he was No Coward After All, like Leo Cholmondeley or whatever his beastly name was in *The Lads of St. Ethelberta's* or some such piffling book; but, thought Drummond in his cold, practical way, what about the house?[46]

Later in the same book, Wodehouse comments:

In stories, as Mr. Anstey has pointed out, the hero is never long without his chance of retrieving his reputation. A mad bull comes into the school grounds, and he alone (the hero, not the bull) is calm. Or is there a fire, and whose is that pale and gesticulating form at the upper window? The bully's, of course. And who is that climbing nimbly up the Virginia creeper? Why, the hero. Who else? Three hearty cheers for the plucky hero. But in real life opportunities for distinguishing oneself are less frequent.[47]

For all this, Wodehouse invariably gets his heroes to do heroic things, if less melodramatically than some previous writers. For *The White*

Feather tells the conventional enough tale of Sheen, a timid boy, working for a scholarship and no good at sport, who backs off during a fight between school and town boys. He is sent to Coventry by his schoolfellows and to redeem his honour learns to box and wins the Public School Boxing Competition at Aldershot. It is nothing more nor less than a schoolboy version of A. E. W. Mason's imperial classic *The Four Feathers*, in which a coward re-established his self-respect and his reputation by secretly performing acts of great daring. It is treated perfectly seriously by Wodehouse and effectively endorses the dominant public school ideology.

The last and by common consent the best of Wodehouse's school stories, *Mike*, was published by A. and C. Black as a single volume in 1909. It had previously appeared as two serial stories, 'Jackson junior' and 'The lost lambs', in *The Captain. Mike* was reprinted in 1910, 1916, 1919, 1924 and 1925. The second half was reissued as *Enter Psmith* in 1935. The whole story was reissued with some minimal revisions (alteration of some now arcane slang words and updating of the names of famous cricketers) as two volumes, *Mike at Wrykyn* and *Mike and Psmith*, in 1953, and remains in print.

Michael Jackson, the eponymous hero of *Mike*, is the youngest of four cricketing brothers and a cricketing genius. The Jackson family was inspired by the real-life Foster family, which produced seven brothers who played for Worcestershire, a clear case of truth being stranger than fiction. Mike is seen as a typical public schoolboy:

> Except on the cricket field, where he was a natural genius, he was just ordinary. He resembled ninety per cent of other members of English public schools. He had some virtues and a good many defects. He was as obstinate as a mule, though people whom he liked could do as they pleased with him. He was good-tempered as a general thing, but occasionally his temper could be of the worst, and had, in his childhood, been the subject of much adverse comment among his aunts. He was rigidly truthful, where the issue concerned only himself. Where it was a case of saving a friend, he was prepared to act in a manner reminiscent of an American expert witness. He had, in addition, one good quality without any defect to balance it. He was always ready to help people.[48]

At fifteen Mike goes to Wrykyn, where he establishes himself rapidly as a cricketer and a boy with a genius for 'ragging'. He is drafted into the first eleven at short notice to play M.C.C. and makes such an impression that his elder brother Bob is dropped to make way for him. Chivalrously Mike fakes a wrist injury to allow Bob to play and later regains his own place for the match against the Incogniti where there is a chicken-pox outbreak at the school. When it comes to the big match of the year, against Ripton, Bob is again selected, but, discovering the story of Mike's sacrifice for him, wants to reciprocate. Mike will not allow it. But Jimmy Wyatt is caught breaking bounds, removed from the school and replaced in the team by Mike, who wins the match for Wrykyn. Wyatt is sent to the London and Oriental Bank, which Wodehouse clearly feels—from bitter experience—to be the most appalling fate that can befall a public school boy.[49] Wyatt writes a rueful account of his first day to Mike, who eventually arranges for his father to get Jimmy a job as a sheep rancher in Argentina.

Two years pass and Mike is to be captain of cricket at Wrykyn but he gets a terrible school report, which contains echoes of Wodehouse's own: 'The boy has genuine ability which he declines to use in the smallest degree . . . An abnormal proficiency at games has apparently destroyed all desire in him to realise the more serious issues of life.'[50] His father removes him from Wrykyn and sends him to Sedleigh, a school with no sporting reputation but which has just got a Balliol scholarship. Mike is heartbroken, and he determines like Achilles to sulk in his tent and play no cricket for Sedleigh. He is befriended by the languid, immaculate, monocled Psmith, just removed from Eton because of bad reports, who calls everyone 'comrade' and has decided to become a socialist. ('It's a great scheme. You ought to be one. You work for the equal distribution of property and start by collaring all you can and sitting on it.')[51] Mike and Psmith take over a study earmarked for someone else, sweet-talk the housemaster into letting them keep it and successfully fight off attempts to evict them.

Mike secretly plays cricket for a village team but joins an informal house match of Outwood's against Downing's to humiliate Mr Downing, who kept him in because of a rag. It ends with Mike 227 not out, Outwood's victorious and Downing's not even getting in to bat. Mike, however, refuses to play for the school team. Adair, the cricket captain, who wants Mike to, is so incensed by this refusal that he decides to fight him. Adair is beaten but Mike is purged of his ill temper. ('The fight . . . had the result which most fights have, if they are fought fairly and until one side has had enough.') Psmith urges Mike to play, revealing that he too is an expert cricketer, and was on the verge of getting into the Eton first eleven when he was withdrawn. Like Mike, he had shown his resentment by refusing to play for Sedleigh. But now he has changed his mind, and through him Mike and Adair are reconciled. Meanwhile Mr Downing becomes convinced that Mike has painted his bull terrier, Sammy, and denounces him to the headmaster. Psmith confesses to the prank in order to save Mike. But both of them are reprieved when a visiting old boy confesses to the deed. Mike is cleared, arranges for Sedleigh to play Wrykyn and helps his new school to victory.

Mike shows Wodehouse at his most assured and contains characteristic verbal felicities:

> There would have been serious trouble between David and Jonathan if either had persisted in dropping catches off the other's bowling.[52]

> Somewhere in the world the sun was shining, birds were twittering; somewhere in the world lambkins frisked and peasants sang blithely at their toil (flat, perhaps, but still blithely), but to Mike at that moment the sky was black, and an icy wind blew over the face of the earth.[53]

Psmith's first appearance is couched in the mature Wodehouse style:

> A very long, thin youth, with a solemn face and immaculate clothes, was leaning against the mantlepiece. As Mike entered, he fumbled in his top left waistcoat pocket, produced an eyeglass attached to a cord, and fixed it in his right eye. With the help of this aid to vision he inspected Mike in silence for a while, then, having flicked an invisible speck of dust from the left sleeve of his coat, he spoke. 'Hullo,' he said. He spoke in a tired voice.
>
> 'Hullo,' said Mike.
>
> 'Take a seat,' said the immaculate one. 'If you don't mind dirtying your bags, that's to say. Personally I don't see any prospect of ever sitting down in this place. It looks to me as if they meant to use these chairs as mustard-and-cress beds. A Nursery Garden in the Home. That sort of idea. My name,' he added pensively, 'is Smith. What's yours?'
>
> 'Jackson,' said Mike.
>
> 'Are you the Bully, the Pride of the School, or the Boy who is Led Astray and Takes to Drink in Chapter Sixteen?'
>
> 'The last, for choice,' said Mike, 'but I've only just arrived, so I don't know.'
>
> 'The boy—what will he become? Are you new here too, then?'
>
> 'Yes. Why, are you new?'
>
> 'Do I look as if I belonged here? I'm the latest import. Sit down on yonder settee, and I will tell you the painful story of my life. By the way, before I start there's just one thing. If ever you have occasion to write to me, would you mind sticking a P at the beginning of my name? P-s-m-i-t-h. See? There are too many Smiths, and I don't care for Smythe. My father's content to worry along in the old-fashioned way, but I've decided to strike out a fresh line. I shall found a new dynasty. The resolve came to me unexpectedly this morning. I jotted it down on the back of an envelope. In conversation you may address me as Rupert (though I hope you won't), or simply Smith, the P not being sounded. Cp. the name Zbysco, in which the Z is given a similar miss-in-baulk. See?'[54]

But Wodehouse was clearly beginning to repeat himself. Mike being out of dorm and pretending to the investigating housemaster that he too is investigating the noise is taken from *The Head of Kay's*. The comic account of schoolmaster Downing followed Sherlock Holmes's methods to track down the boy guilty of painting his dog is a broader reworking of the similar idea of Mr Thompson tracking down the person who stole the school cup in *The Pothunters*. The riot between schoolboys and town hooligans, ending up with a policeman being pushed accidentally into a pool, is reworked from *The White Feather*. Adair asserting his authority by fighting recalcitrants is developed from *The Head of Kay's*.

With the appearance of Psmith, however, the story suddenly bursts into life and takes off with that distinctive Wodehouse love of word play, allusion, circumlocution, creative juxtaposition, persiflage and banter. Evelyn Waugh was perfectly correct when he said, 'One can date exactly the first moment when he was touched by the sacred flame. It occurs half way through *Mike* . . . Psmith appears and the light is kindled which has burned with growing brilliancy for half a century.'[55] Psmith is Wodehouse Man fully formed and the authentic Wodehouse idiom is born. The character, according to Wodehouse, was inspired by Rupert D'Oyly Carte, Wykehamist son of the impresario. It was a debt Wodehouse acknowledged by christening Psmith Rupert.[56]

But Psmith had his progenitors in the pages of the earlier novels. As early as *The Pothunters* there is Charteris, whom Usborne thinks a self-portrait of Wodehouse.[57] He is nicknamed 'The Alderman', calls people 'my son', is garrulous, edits and largely writes the unofficial school magazine *The Glow Worm*, plays the banjo, uses literary allusions in conversation and is a complete mystery to the masters. But he also speaks in a vein of facetiously theatrical melodrama, as when Jim Thomson asks to borrow his notes and he replies, 'Kill my father and burn my ancestral home, and I will look on and smile. But touch my notes and you rouse the British Lion.' Later he says things like 'It passes out of the realm of the merely impudent into the boundless empyrean of pure cheek.' This sounds like Psmith in embryo. Even Jimmy Wyatt in the first half of *Mike* looks like a preliminary sketch for Psmith. He talks to Mike in pure Psmithese about his imminent expulsion:

> The boot. The swift and sudden boot. I shall be sorry to part with you, but I'm afraid it's a case of 'au revoir, my little Hyacinth'. We shall meet at Philippi. This is my Moscow. To-morrow I shall go into the night with one long, choking sob. Years hence a white-haired bank clerk will tap at your door when you're a prosperous professional cricketer with your photograph in *Wisden*. That'll be me . . . I'll tell you all the latest news when I come back. Where are my slippers? Ha, 'tis well! Lead on, then, minions, I follow.[58]

But Psmith also bears the clear imprint of Barry Pain's Cyprian Langsdyke, probably his true fictional progenitor.

In *Mike* Wodehouse carries on a subtextual debate with his precursors in the genre, gently setting them straight and modifying their picture from his own experience. Wodehouse's regime, the obverse of Farrar's, is that of the stiff upper lip, self-deprecating comments and lack of emotion. Wodehouse therefore rejects the idea of public displays of heroic self-sacrifice. Bob Jackson, finding that Mike has sacrificed his place in the team for him, wants to reciprocate, 'but he had the public school boy's terror of seeming to pose or do anything theatrical. He would have done a good deal to put matters right but he could *not* do the self-sacrificing young hero business. It would not be in the picture. These things, if they are to be done at school, have to be carried through stealthily.'[59] Wodehouse rejects melodramatic and inauthentic depictions of sporting prowess:

> In stories of the 'Not Really a Duffer' type where the nervous new boy who has been found crying in the boot room over the photograph of his sister contrives to get an innings in a game, nobody suspects that he is really a prodigy till he hits the Bully's first ball out of the ground for six.[60]

But the principal target here is emotional excess rather than sporting heroism. For Mike, after all, gets 277 not out in the house match and wins the crucial final match at Sedleigh against Wrykyn.

Adair, the captain of football and cricket at Sedleigh, is the object of Wodehouse's attention and carefully drawn. Adair is not naturally clever, got into the sixth form by determination and hard work, made himself good at sport by study, application and promotion of natural advantages. 'A boy of Adair's type is always a force in a school' as an example, an inspiration and a leader. But Wodehouse goes on:

> He had that passionate fondness for his school which every boy is popularly supposed to have, but which really is implanted in about one in every thousand. The average public-school boy *likes* his school. He hopes it will lick Bedford at footer and Malvern at cricket, but rather bets it won't. He is sorry to leave, and he likes going back at the end of the holidays but as for any passionate, deep-seated love of the place, he would think it bad form than otherwise. If anybody came up to him, slapped him on the back, and cried, 'Come along, Jenkins, old boy! Play up for the old school, Jenkins! The dear old school! The old place you love so!' he would feel seriously ill. Adair is the exception. To Adair, Sedleigh was almost a religion.[61]

This passage encapsulates the horror of overt emotionalism that the latter-day public school boy endorsed and echoes Kipling's depiction of the Westward Ho! boys' rejection of the 'jelly-bellied flag-flapper' who sought to articulate and verbalise their innermost patriotic feelings. As a matter of fact, for Wodehouse Dulwich was almost a religion too. But it has to be remembered that he is here effectively a boy writing for boys. The concept of 'bad form' is central. It is bad form to show emotion. Boys in fact often say the opposite of what they feel. Love of the school is simply something, like love of country, that you not only do not talk about but if it is mentioned may even overtly scorn.

Wodehouse rejects the traditional concept of the bully. Writing of Stone and Robinson, he says:

> Small boys whom they had occasion to kick, either from pure high spirits or as a punishment for some slip from the narrow path which the ideal small boy should tread, regarded Stone and Robinson as bullies of the genuine *Eric* and *St. Winifred's* brand.

But he is anxious to set the record straight from his own experience:

> There was as a matter of fact nothing much wrong with Stone and Robinson. They were just ordinary raggers of the type found in every public school, small and large. They were absolutely free from brain. They had a certain amount of muscle and a vast store of animal spirits. They looked on school life purely as a vehicle for ragging. The Stones and Robinsons are the swash-bucklers of the school world.[62]

Wodehouse mocks the idea of public schoolboys in the toils of villainous publicans. The publican's threat in *Mike* to denounce Jellicoe to the headmaster for debt, an episode which occurs both in *Eric* and in *The Fifth Form at St Dominic's*, turns out to be a practical joke. The publican is demanding payment not for drink or gambling debts but for damage caused by Jellicoe's two Aberdeen terriers, something Wodehouse considers a far more likely misdemeanour.

But, while outdated conventions are scorned, Wodehouse's stories are profoundly supportive of the public school code and spirit as it had emerged in the second half of the nineteenth century. When Mike refuses to turn out for house fielding and is caned, he is lectured by Jimmy Wyatt:

> I say, I don't want to jaw—I'm one of those quiet chaps with strong, silent natures; you may have noticed it—but I must put in a well-chosen word at this juncture. Don't pretend to be dropping off to sleep. Sit up and listen to what your kind old uncle's got to say to you about manners and deport-ment. Otherwise, blood as you are at cricket, you'll have a rotten time here. There are some things you simply can't do; and one of them is bunking a thing when you're put down for it. It doesn't matter who it is puts you down. If he's captain, you've got to obey him. That's discipline, that 'ere is. The speaker then paused, and took a sip of water from the carafe which stood at his elbow. Cheers from the audience and a voice 'Hear! Hear!'[63]

The bantering tone sugars but does not undermine the endorsement of team spirit and order. When Mike taxes Wyatt with breaking bounds, Wyatt informs him:

There are two sorts of discipline at school. One you can break if you feel like taking risks; the other you mustn't ever break. I don't know why, but it isn't done. Until you learn that, you can never hope to be the perfect Wrykinian like me.[64]

'That night,' Wodehouse tells us, 'for the first time in his life, Mike went to sleep with a clear idea of what the public school spirit, of which so much is talked and written, really meant.'

This is paralleled at the end of the second half, where it is—of all people—Psmith who lectures Mike on playing the game. It is done in his characteristically diffident fashion but is all the more impressive as an endorsement of the system, coming from him:

Comrade Adair's rather a stoutish fellow in his way. I'm not much on the 'Play up for the old school, Jones' game, but everyone to his taste. I shouldn't have thought anybody would get overwhelmingly attached to this abode of wrath, but Comrade Adair seems to have done it. He's all for giving Sedleigh a much-needed boost-up. It's not a bad idea in its way. I don't see why one shouldn't humour him. Apparently he's been sweating since early childhood to buck the school up. And as he's leaving at the end of the term, it mightn't be a scaly scheme to give him a bit of a send-off, if possible, by making the cricket season a bit of a banger. As a start, why not drop him a line to say that you'll play against the M.C.C. tomorrow?[65]

For all their humour, Wodehouse's stories were a true product of the age of athleticism. His scale of priorities was set out in a humorous piece called 'Work':

Work is supposed to be the centre round which school life revolves—the hub of the school wheel, the lode star of the schoolboy's existence, and a great many other things. 'You come to school to work' is the formula used by masters when sentencing a victim to the wailing and gnashing of teeth provided by two hours' extra tuition on a hot afternoon. In this, I think, they err, and my opinion is backed up by numerous scholars of my acquaintance . . . The ambition of every human new-boy is surely to become like J. Essop of the first eleven, who can hit a ball over two ponds, a wood and seven villages, rather than to resemble that pale young student, Mill-Stuart, who though he can speak Sanscrit like a native of Sanscritia, couldn't score a single off a slow long-hop. And this ambition is a laudable one. For the athlete is the product of nature—a step towards the more perfect type of animal, while the soldier is the outcome of artificiality. What, I ask, does the scholar gain, either morally or physically, or in any other way, by knowing who was tribune of the people in 284 B.C. or what is the precise difference between the various constructions of *cum*?[66]

Academic work plays very little part in his stories. Sport is the measure of a boy. The stories are littered with sporting aphorisms. Beckford

School 'gauged a fellow's character principally by his abilities in the cricket and football fields'.[67] Wodehouse tells us, 'To be a good wicket keeper much may be forgiven,' or 'There are few pleasanter or more thrilling moments in one's school career than the first over of a big match.'[68] In *Mike* he tells us, 'Cricket is the great safety valve. If you like the game, and are in a position to play it at least twice a week, life can never be entirely grey.'[69]

Sport is now totally dominant, as it was not in *Eric, Tom Brown* or *St Dominic's*. The stories are structured around vivid descriptions of cricket, rugby, boxing and athletics. *The Pothunters* opens for no very pressing narrative reason with the Public Schools Boxing Championship at Aldershot, and involves the inter-house cross-country and school athletic sports. Football, cricket and boxing dominate *The Gold Bat*. Conversation is entirely about house and school matches, team selection, tactics and post-match analysis. The plot centres on the desire of Trevor, the energetic Wrykyn rugger captain, to win the big match against Ripton. He is handicapped by a disruptive campaign mounted by a secret society trying to secure the reinstatement in the team of Rand-Brown, dropped by Trevor for funk. The campaign turns out to be organised by games-hating Ruthven, blackmailed by Rand-Brown into helping him because he had found out that Ruthven had sneaked on a boy for gambling and got him expelled. Trevor takes on and beats Rand-Brown in a fist fight and eventually both Rand-Brown and Ruthven are expelled for smoking. The division between vice and virtue is absolutely clear: the rotters are bad sportsmen or non-sportsmen, the heroes are decent sportsmen. Sport takes on a moral dimension, and, for all the humour of Wodehouse's comments on schoolboy smoking, we are left in little doubt about his basic disapproval of the activity:

> To smoke at school is to insult the divine weed. When you are obliged to smoke in odd corners, fearing every moment that you will be discovered, the whole meaning, poetry, romance of a pipe vanishes, and you become like those lost beings who smoke when they are running to catch trains. The boy who smokes at school is bound to come to a bad end. He will degenerate gradually into a person that plays dominoes in the smoking-rooms of A.B.C. shops with friends who wear bowler hats and frock coats.[70]

Sport is central to school morale. It is used to help restore house order, *esprit de corps* and tone in *Head of Kay's*. Success in sport indicates the return of order, harmony and discipline to the house. Sport is thus seen as morally valuable. It makes a man of Sheen in *The White Feather*. Sheen imbibes the philosophy of Joe Bevan, who teaches him boxing, and this philosophy varies very little from that of Thomas Hughes's celebrated 'fighting' passage in *Tom Brown*:

He began to understand that the world is a place where every man has to look after himself, and that it is the stronger hand that wins. That sentence from *Hamlet* which Joe Bevan was so fond of quoting practically summed up the whole duty of man-and-boy too. One should not seek quarrels, but, 'being in', one should do one's best to ensure that one's opponent thought twice in future before seeking them.[71]

The boxing lessons give Sheen something he previously lacked: self-confidence. His academic work improves, too.

The elements which Mangan sees as integral to athleticism are all to be found in Wodehouse. First, there are the prestigious matches, and Wodehouse builds his stories towards them. In particular for Wrykyn the annual match with Ripton is the highlight of the season and features in *The Gold Bat, Mike* and *The White Feather*. Matches against a visiting M.C.C. side crop up frequently. In *Mike* Sedleigh is in a parlous sporting state because it cannot get prestige matches, and when Mike arranges a match with Wrykyn it is a memorable day in the school's history and the climactic event of the book.

Second, there is the role of sporting house masters and masters. A recurrent theme is bad masters who cannot keep order and the tone of whose houses is poor. Almost invariably they are non-sporting. In *The Gold Bat* Wodehouse comments:

> There is usually one house in every school of the black sheep sort and, if you go to the root of the matter, you will generally find that the fault is with the master of the house. A house-master who enters into the life of his house, coaches them in games—if an athlete—or, if not an athlete, watches the games, umpiring the cricket and refereeing at football, never finds much difficulty in keeping order.[72]

Mr Dexter in *The Gold Bat* spends the whole time of the big cricket match prowling the back lanes looking for boys smoking instead of supporting his house. Mr Kay in *Head of Kay's* is a fussy, nervous creature, uninterested in sport, and because he does not back up his head boy, Robert Fenn, his house is in a state of disorder and low morale.

Third, there is the colours system. Anxiety about selection permeates the stories. The rivalry of Bob and Mike Jackson for a place in the Wrykyn first eleven and the problems it created are no doubt authentic and capture something of the feeling of Wodehouse himself, who from 1897 to 1899 was in the Dulwich second fifteen, unable to get his first fifteen colours because of the presence of his brother Armine in the senior team.[73] Mike's sacrifice of his team place to his brother is all the nobler because of his anxiety to get it. Mike, when he gets his colours, is quietly jubilant:

He was sorry for Bob, but he would not have been human (which he certainly was) if the triumph of having won through at last into the first eleven had not dwarfed commiseration. It had been his one ambition and now he had achieved it.[74]

Fourth, house loyalty is a motif binding the stories together, rather less prominent in *Mike*, where school loyalty is at the centre, made all the potent by Mike's forcible removal to Sedleigh. 'Mike's heart bled for Wrykyn,' writes Wodehouse. The story is about Mike overcoming his resentment and learning to play for Sedleigh. House loyalty, however, is the central theme of *The Head of Kay's*. Bob Fenn, cricketer of genius and head of Kay's, lacking the backing of his house master, fails to restore order and is superseded by Kennedy of Blackburn's, himself heartbroken at being transferred.

> From the first day at Eckleton he had been taught the simple creed of the Blackburnite, that Eckleton was the finest school in the three kingdoms, and that Blackburn's was the finest house in the finest school . . . He could have endured leaving all this when his time at school was up, for that would have been the natural result of the passing of the years. But to be transplanted abruptly and with a wrench from his native soil was too much. He went upstairs to pack, suffering from as severe an attack of the blues as any youth of eighteen had experienced since blues were first invented.[75]

Fenn refuses to co-operate with Kennedy, and sulks. Senior day-room boys rebel, refusing to turn out in the football team, and Kennedy asserts his authority by beating the ringleader, Walton, in a fight. But Fenn and Kennedy are reconciled, and together restore tone and order. The success of the house is demonstrated by their reaching the final of the house football cup competition, losing to Blackburn's, and winning the athletics.

Lastly, the stories abound in schoolboy sporting heroes, 'the bloods', who provide role models for the readers: Allan Gethryn in *A Prefect's Uncle*, Robert Fenn in *The Head of Kay's*, Trevor in *The Gold Bat* and supremely Mike. *A Prefect's Uncle*, for instance, combines a story of house morale and schoolboy honour. Allan Gethryn is asked by the headmaster of Beckford to try to 'buck up' Leicester's house, to raise its tone. But he is embarrassed by the arrival of his fourteen-year-old uncle, Reginald Farnie, much expelled, supercilious and self-possessed. Farnie leads rags, takes up with bad-hats and eventually steals money. Gethryn absents himself from the M.C.C. match in order to sort out the theft and to save his uncle from expulsion. Honour prevents him from explaining, and he is disgraced and dropped from the school team. A round-robin is organised to drop him as house captain. Whereupon he drops all those who signed, raises a new team and leads it to victory in the house cricket cup. Reinstated in the school rugger team, he scores the winning goal in the match against Charchester. *Mike* was Wodehouse's final venture into public school fiction, and marked the end of his literary apprenticeship. Mike's superseding by Psmith in the second half of the novel indicates the future direction of Wodehouse's work, away from Victorian schools and into Edwardian clubland.

Notes

1 On athleticism see J. A. Mangan, *Athleticism in the Victorian and Edwardian Public School*, Cambridge, 1981.
2 Mangan, *Athleticism*, 55.
3 Mangan, *Athleticism*, 189.
4 Mangan, *Athleticism*, 181.
5 Cyril Norwood, *The English Tradition of Education*, London, 1929, 69.
6 Mangan, *Athleticism*, 200-1.
7 Jonathan Gathorne-Hardy, *The Public School Phenomenon*, Harmondsworth, 1979, 161.
8 See, for instance, Rudolf Kircher, *Fair Play*, London, 1928.
9 Edward C. Mack, *Public Schools and British Opinion, 1780-1860*, London, 1938, 400.
10 Mark Girouard, *The Return to Camelot: Chivalry and the English Gentleman*, New Haven and London, 1981, pp. 276-93.
11 F. W. Farrar, *In the Days of thy Youth*, London, 1892, 372.
12 Patrick Dunae, 'British Juvenile Literature in an Age of Empire, 1880-1914', Manchester University Ph.D. thesis, 1975, 267.
13 J. B. Priestley, *English Humour*, London, 1976, 108.
14 Benny Green, *P. G. Wodehouse: a literary biography*, London, 1981, 33.
15 On Wodehouse's life and work see Frances Donaldson, *P. G. Wodehouse*, London, 1983; Richard Usborne, *Wodehouse at Work to the End*, Harmondsworth, 1978; Benny Green, *Wodehouse*; Owen Dudley Edwards, *P. G. Wodehouse: a critical and historical essay*, London, 1977; David A. Jasen, *P. G. Wodehouse: a portrait of a master*, London, 1981.
16 P. G. Wodehouse, *Wodehouse on Wodehouse*, Harmondsworth, 1981, 474.
17 Jasen, *Wodehouse*, 18.
18 Jasen, *Wodehouse*, 16.
19 Donaldson, *Wodehouse*, 52-3.
20 Green, *Wodehouse*, 33.
21 Jasen, *Wodehouse*, 17-18.
22 Donaldson, *Wodehouse*, 57.
23 C. B. Fry, *Life worth Living* (1939), London, 1986, 152-5.
24 Jasen, *Wodehouse*, 23.
25 Donaldson, *Wodehouse*, 66.
26 P. G. Wodehouse, 'School stories', *Public School Magazine*, 8 (August 1901), 125-8. Its provenance has been established by Usborne, *Wodehouse*, 67.
27 P. G. Wodehouse, *Mike*, London, 1925, 28.
28 *Times Literary Supplement*, 11 November 1904. References to 'Stalkyism' come in reviews of *A Prefect's Uncle* (*T.L.S.*, 20 November 1903) and *The Gold Bat* (*T.L.S.* 11 November 1904).
29 Usborne, *Wodehouse*, 77-8.
30 Wodehouse, 'School stories', 126.
31 Barry Pain, *The Kindness of the Celestial and other Stories*, London, 1.
32 Wodehouse, 'School stories', 126.
33 Wodehouse, 'School stories', 127.

34 Wodehouse, 'School stories', 128.
35 Donaldson, *Wodehouse*, 66.
36 Donaldson, *Wodehouse*, 16.
37 Dudley Edwards, *Wodehouse*, 15.
38 Alec Waugh, *Public School Life*, London, 1922, 17; George Orwell, *Collected Essays, Journalism and Letters*, 3, Harmondsworth, 1982, 394.
39 Usborne, *Wodehouse*, 69.
40 Usborne, *Wodehouse*, 15.
41 Wodehouse, *Wodehouse*, 242.
42 Green, *Wodehouse*, 14.
43 Edward C. Mack, *The Public Schools and British Opinion since 1860*, New York, 1941, 344.
44 P. G. Wodehouse, *A Prefect's Uncle*, London, 1972, 22.
45 Barry Pain, *Graeme and Cyril*, London, 1894, 184.
46 P. G. Wodehouse, *The White Feather*, London, 1972, 107.
47 Wodehouse, *The White Feather*, 112.
48 Wodehouse, *Mike*, 238-9.
49 Mike and Psmith end up in a bank in *Psmith in the City*.
50 Wodehouse, *Mike*, 173.
51 Wodehouse, *Mike*, 98.
52 Wodehouse, *Mike*, 98.
53 Wodehouse, *Mike*, 173.
54 Wodehouse, *Mike*, 178-9.
55 Donaldson, *Wodehouse*, 2.
56 Green, *Wodehouse*, 27.
57 Usborne, *Wodehouse*, 77.
58 Wodehouse, *Mike*, 141.
59 Wodehouse, *Mike*, 126.
60 Wodehouse, *Mike*, 276-7.
61 Wodehouse, *Mike*, 202-4.
62 Wodehouse, *Mike*, 222.
63 Wodehouse, *Mike*, 112-3.
64 Wodehouse, *Mike*, 113.
65 Wodehouse, *Mike*, 311.
66 P. G. Wodehouse, *Tales of St Austin's*, London, 1972, 135.
67 Wodehouse, *A Prefect's Uncle*, 10.
68 Wodehouse, *A Prefect's Uncle*, 15, 60.
69 Wodehouse, *Mike*, 213.
70 P. G. Wodehouse, *The Gold Bat*, London, 1911, 229.
71 Wodehouse, *The White Feather*, 66.
72 Wodehouse, *The Gold Bat*, 19.
73 Jasen, *Wodehouse*, 15.
74 Wodehouse, *Mike*, 106.
75 P. G. Wodehouse, *The Head of Kay's*, London, 1974, 65.

Soldiers of the Queen:
Stalky and Co.

Perhaps the most celebrated and talented writer to turn his attention to the school story was Rudyard Kipling. But, being Kipling, he did not produce what might have been expected, partly because of his maverick temperament, partly because of his personal experience and partly because of the context in which he wrote. So far we have been examining stories written in conformity with the dominant ideology, mainstream tales which even if they had rejected the traditions and conventions of earlier eras were in tune with their own. But there were alternative and oppositional views. The alternatives sought to reform the public schools; the oppositionals, to destroy them. Chief among the alternative views was that of Kipling, who was in so many ways a supporter of the dominant ideology.[1]

The dominant ideology in Britain from the 1870s to the 1940s was imperialism and its laureate was Rudyard Kipling. The acquisition of the empire for economic, strategic and prestige reasons was followed by the articulation of a philosophy of altruistic imperialism, compounded of the Protestant work ethic and a Calvinistic belief in the British as an elect, chosen to confer on the underprivileged races of the world peace, order, justice and good government. Men like Curzon, Balfour and Milner who believed with Lord Rosebery that the British empire was 'the greatest secular agency for Good that the world has ever seen' defined a form of imperialism that was a sacred trust, based squarely on service, discipline, duty and work. The voices of Carlyle, Tennyson, Kingsley, Ruskin, Disraeli, Henley, Froude and Stevenson could be heard advocating the imperial mission. But the greatest celebrant of work, discipline and empire was Kipling. In his poems and stories he set out the nature of the imperial obligation. In *Song of the English* he eloquently summarised the objectives:

Keep ye the Law—be swift in all obedience—
Clear the land of evil, drive the road and bridge the ford.
Make ye sure to each his own
That he reap where he hath sown
By the peace among our peoples let men know we serve the Lord![2]

Kipling sang the praises of the engineers and District Officers, of Indian Civil Servants and common soldiers. In particular he admired the legion of subalterns, 'boys in age, men in character, blessed with the adventurous ardour and audacity of youth'.

But even as he captured the hearts of the nation with his imperial sagas, concern was growing about Britain's status as a world power. The rapid industrialisation of Germany and America in particular, the decline in the birth rate and the changes in the nature of warfare all contrived to focus attention on the fragility of Britain's pre-eminence. This anxiety found expression in a literature of invasion, with Britain subject to attack from a variety of enemies. But increasingly the principal enemy was seen to be Germany.[3]

Successive Royal Commissions pointed out that Britain's system of technical education and scientific research was lagging badly behind her competitors, and in the last decades of the century increasing attention was paid to the education system. The Boer War, with its military disasters, inefficiency, corruption and mismanagement dramatically highlighted this problem and precipitated major investigations into Britain's military, political, administrative and educational structures, intensifying what G. R. Searle calls 'the quest for national efficiency'. Its mainspring was 'an attempt to discredit the habits, beliefs and institutions that put the British at a handicap in their competition with foreigners'.[4]

Kipling had already sounded a sombre note of warning in his poem 'Recessional' during the heady self-congratulation of Queen Victoria's diamond jubilee in 1897, and Leo Amery later described the Boer War as 'the nation's Recessional after all the pomp and show of the year of the Jubilee'. Kipling also turned his poetic skills to the lessons of the war, writing bitterly 'The islanders', which, when it was published in January 1902, with its disparaging reference: 'Then ye returned to your trinkets; then ye contented your souls/With the flannelled fools at the wicket or the muddied oafs at the goals', furnished leader writers and speech makers with a ready-made text. Kipling castigated the lack of training and preparedness for war. He called for the sending forth of:

men, not children or servants, tempered and taught to the end;
Cleansed of servile panic, slow to dread or despise,
Humble because of knowledge, mighty by sacrifice.[5]

Inevitably a crucial element of the educational debate centred on the code, role and curriculum of the public schools and in this fiction was to play an important part. As E. C. Mack noted, 'Between 1890 . . . and 1914 the novel began to play a leading, if not the leading part, in the controversy over public school education.'[6]

It was the public schools that supplied the officers and administrators who ran the empire. In 'The brushwood boy' (1895) Kipling detailed the life of his ideal subaltern and stressed the vital role of his public school in shaping him. Georgie Cottar is the subaltern supreme, innocent, modest, virginal, industrious and dedicated.[7] His career is followed from 'rumple-collared, dusty-hatted fag' to blossom 'into full glory as head of the school, ex-officio captain of games; head of his house, where he and his lieutenants preserved discipline and decency . . . general arbiter in the quarrels that spring up among the touchy Sixth— and intimate friend and ally of the Head himself . . . Above all, he was responsible for that thing called the tone of the school, and few realise with what passionate devotion a certain type of boy throws himself into this work.'[8] The sort of school that produced Georgie is economically summed up by Kipling: 'For the rest, the school was not encouraged to dwell on its emotions, but rather to keep in hard condition, avoid false quantities and to enter the army direct.'

At Sandhurst he rises in similar fashion, winning respect for his modesty and diligence, and acting in accord with his public school training, which had taught him how many were the 'things no fellow can do'. Thence to India, where he wins the love of his men by teaching them boxing and cross-country running:

> The men united in adoring Cottar and their way of showing it was by sparing him all the trouble that men knew how to make for an unloved officer. He sought popularity as little as he had sought it at school, and therefore it came to him.[9]

He does not interest himself in women, black or white, but studies to improve himself in his job. He shows his efficiency as adjutant and his gallantry on a field campaign which brings him the D.S.O. and a captaincy. But throughout all this the school analogy is clear. 'Cottar stood in the same relation to the colonel as he had to his old Head in England,' Kipling tells us, and in his dealings with the privates 'He did not forget the difference between a dazed and sulky junior of the upper school and a bewildered, browbeaten lump of a private fresh from the depot was very small indeed.'[10]

There is a mystical dimension to all this too, so often associated with imperialism in the works of Haggard, Buchan and Doyle, as well. Cottar has a dream life, vivid and noble, in which he sees the girl whom he eventually meets and will marry, and who (it turns out) has also dreamed of him. It is the dreamer, the mystic within the ideal soldier, the soul that vivifies and animates the fit and perfectly co-ordinated body of empire.

Cottar represents two other traditions. He is nicknamed Galahad by his fellow officers, locating him at once in the revived chivalry, and he is called 'Boy' by the woman he eventually marries. Steven Marcus noted, 'Boy is one of the sacred words of the English language; boyhood is, or for one hundred and fifty years was, a priestly state or condition; and the literature of boys and boyhood has had, for a secularized age, something of the aura of doctrinal or holy writ.'[11]

But essential to it all is the public school training. Some thought that perfect as it stood. Geoffrey Drage, for instance, argued in *Eton and the Empire* (1890) that the empire was held together by the patriotism, piety and obedience to superiors taught at Eton. But this was not the view held by all. Herbert Branston Gray, former headmaster of Louth Grammar School and of Bradfield College, penned, according to E. C. Mack, 'the bitterest and most thorough criticism from within that the public schools ever received'.[12] A passionate believer in the British empire, he felt that the public schools were letting it down and were mirroring society at large, which he characterised by lack of preparedness, insularity and complacency. In *The Public Schools and the Empire* (1913) he denounced the rigid conformism of the public school boy ('Life . . . is entirely subordinated to system . . . His public conduct and manners, down to the minutest detail, are prescribed for the young boy. Everybody must, within limits, do whatever anybody else does'), the dominance of athleticism ('the insane . . . mind-numbing, unwholesome cult of games worship') and the fostering of narrow, intense school patriotism, lacking the wider imperial dimension. On the other hand, he was in favour of discipline and morality, supporting the prefect system, military training and religious and ethical instruction. But he wanted a reformed curriculum, broadened to include science, education to be a combination of humanistic and naturalistic knowledge and the clear objective of turning out democratic and enlightened boys, fit for the demands of a new age. If public schools could not do it, he suggested their replacement by day schools.[13] In his principal criticisms he echoes Kipling, though in their respective remedies they would have parted company.

The events of the Boer War sharpened the debate about the public schools, highlighting three different positions: the progressives, who called for reform (better teacher training, increased emphasis on science and modern languages, less emphasis on games and character); the reactionaries, who wanted a return to the ideals of Arnold, stressing the value of the classics, and the development of the intellectual and moral interests of the boy; and the conservatives, who advocated no change at all.

Characteristically Kipling fitted none of these groups, though all of them could have found something in his views that they could endorse, along with much which they would wish to reject. Kipling certainly saw himself contributing to the debate. In his autobiography he described how the idea came to him 'for some tracts and parables on the education of the young', adding, 'It is still read and I maintain it is a truly valuable collection of texts.'[14] It seems likely that a visit in 1894 to his old school for the ceremonies marking the retirement of the headmaster, Cormell Price, sparked off the idea of reworking his schooldays at Westward Ho! He originally included a passage based on them in 'The brushwood boy' but later deleted it. Then in 1897–99 he wrote ten stories which were published in *The Windsor Magazine* in Britain and *McClure's Magazine* in the U.S.A. Later nine of them were published in book form as *Stalky and Co.* He was dissatisfied with the first story, 'Stalky', but it later appeared in *Land and Sea Tales for Scouts and Guides*, and four other Stalky stories, written later, appeared in other collections (*Regulus, The United Idolators, The Propagation of Knowledge, The Satisfaction of a Gentleman*).[15]

The setting of the stories is the United Services College (U.S.C.) at Westward Ho! in Devon and its surrounds. The central figures are the trio who inhabit study No. 5, Arthur Lionel Corkran ('Stalky'), Willie McTurk ('Turkey') and Reggie (no surname) ('Beetle'), respectively the resourceful and respected leader, the cool and sardonic son of an Irish baronet and the enthusiastic, bespectacled literary man. The three of them are natural rebels and set themselves against authority in a permanent war with the masters, and Kipling uses them as a vehicle to attack the previous school story orthodoxies.

First, he attacked the public school spirit as propounded in *Tom Brown's Schooldays* and as funnelled into the cult of athleticism. Kipling was to make his scorn of the games cult clear in 'The islanders'. In this he was lining up alongside such unlikely figures as Dean Farrar and A. C. Benson ('There is no tendency which ought to be more carefully watched and guarded than our present athletic ideals which have taken so firm a hold of the country'),[16] though in each case the motive was different. Farrar saw games as a distraction from religion, Benson from intellectual pursuits, Kipling from proper preparation for war. Kipling shows Stalky and Co. having absolutely no time for house spirit or school spirit and refusing to take part in games. They cheerfully break bounds, smoke and collaborate on their prep. They defy the prefects and gull the masters. This causes dismay to the house masters, as Kipling writes of Mr Prout:

> Boys that he understood attended house matches and could be accounted for at any moment. But he had heard McTurk openly deride cricket—even

house matches; Beetle's views on the honour of the house he knew were incendiary; and he could never tell when the soft and smiling Stalky was laughing at him.[17]

When a cadet corps is set up Stalky insists on its drilling behind closed doors, and when they are lectured on patriotism by a visiting M.P. the corps promptly disbands. Kipling recalled that at Westward Ho! the corps was seen as 'playing at soldiers', which was unacceptable to those training to be real ones.[18] In *Stalky and Co.* the boys' view is 'We're to get into the army or get out . . . All the rest is flumdiddle.'[19]

Second, Kipling attacked the evangelical introspection and excessive piety of *Eric*, which are a source of permanent mockery and the standard against which they gleefully measure their misdeeds. When Stalky's maiden aunt gives him copies of *Eric* and *St Winifred's* for his sixteenth birthday McTurk orders them disposed of. But when the Bideford bookseller will offer only ninepence for the two, since they are a drug on the market, the boys read *Eric* aloud for fun. When asked to protect young Clewer from bullying, McTurk says, 'We ain't goin' to have any beastly Erickin'. Do you want to walk about with your arm around his neck?' When Beetle, Stalky and McTurk are reported by a new master for stealing, McTurk observes, 'They spent all their time stealing at St. Winifred's, when they weren't praying or getting drunk in pubs.' 'I wonder what they'd say at St. Winifred's or The World of School,' laughs Stalky when he hears how Beetle has wrecked Mr King's study. 'Didn't I "Eric" 'em splendidly?' shrieks Beetle after doing a solemn speech about immorality before the prefect's meeting.[20]

When *Stalky and Co.* came out in book form (6 October 1899), Dean Farrar, deeply offended, wrote to Kipling about the disparaging of his work. Kipling replied graciously:

> I can assert honestly that it was no part of my intention to try to injure you with gratuitous insult. Your years and your position in the English Church alike forbid the thought of that.[21]

But he added of the books:

> It would be impossible to write any sketch of schoolboy life of twenty years ago without in some way alluding to their influence and also that there are boys, ignorant, vulgar-minded it may be, who take less interest in the moral teachings of the two books than in their divergencies from the facts of schoolboy life as boys know those today.[22]

In place of the spirit of Hughes and Farrar, Kipling preached his own philosophy, which had in mind the future, the need to prepare for war and for the defence of the empire. Padre Gillett expresses the Kipling view: 'Boys educate each other . . . more than we can or dare,'[23] and the life of guerilla warfare against the masters that the boys lead imbues them with the initiative, courage, resourcefulness and self-discipline that they will need when they are defending the frontiers of the empire.

It is the acquisition of these characteristics which is the principal theme of the stories. It is therefore odd that Kipling should have omitted from the collection 'Stalky', which explains how Arthur Lionel Corkran got his nickname. 'Stalky' meant in school slang 'clever, well considered and wily' as applied to plans of action, and the story shows Corkran displaying these qualities when a group of boys from the Coll., planning to drive off a local farmer's bullocks as a lark, are caught, owing, as Stalky scornfully points out, to incompetent planning. Stalky stages their rescue with military precision and imprisons the yokels, then gains credit for releasing the yokels from their imprisonment.

'In ambush' is a perfect example of how Stalky and Co. contrive to wrong-foot the masters while acting the innocent. Beetle, Stalky and McTurk have a lair in the furze behind the college where they smoke secretly. Prout, King and school sergeant, 'Foxy', seek to trap them. But by reporting a gamekeeper for shooting a vixen the Co. have won from the local J.P., Colonel Dabney, the right to go on to his land (usually out of bounds). Thus the trio contrive to trap Prout, King and Foxy into trespassing and get them taken up as poachers by Dabney's men. When the trio are reported to the Head for breaking bounds they are triumphantly ready to explain the situation. 'They were learning . . . the lesson of their race, which is to put away all emotion and entrap the alien at the proper time,' says Kipling.[24]

In 'Slaves of the Lamp' Part I, when Mr King orders them out of their study and into the form room for making a noise while rehearsing *Aladdin*, Stalky gets revenge by a stratagem. He uses his catapult on a local carrier, who loudly and drunkenly denounces the college. When King reprimands him, the carrier pelts King's study with rocks, creating damage which is considerably enhanced by the gleeful Beetle. The trio also pretend to be thieves in order to fool a new master, Mason, who is permanently embarassed by them thereafter. 'An unsavoury interlude' occurs when the trio prefer to go bathing rather than attend a house match. Mr King suggests that Prout's house never wash, and King's house mock the alleged smell. So Stalky inserts a dead cat in the rafters over King's house, stinking the place out. In 'The impressionists' when Prout, catching them collaborating over their prep., insists that they do it in the form room, they lure him into believing that there is systematic money-lending going on in the house, playing on his concern for house tone. Their attentions are also directed against officious prefects. In 'The last term', they contrive to embarrass the senior prefect of King's house, Tulke, by paying a local waitress to kiss him in a Bideford street. When a prefects' meeting is called to warn them about their behaviour, they solemnly indict Tulke for public immorality. They also cover their return to school late for roll call by cutting off the school's gas supply and extinguishing the lights.

It is not just a matter of military manoeuvres. There are intellectual battles too. In 'The propagation of knowledge' Beetle coaches the others for exams, feeding them information culled from his omnivorous reading. They rag Mr King, the Shakespeare-loving English master, by an elaborate game of baiting him with the Baconian origin of the plays. In 'The last term' they alter the Latin prose exam paper at the printer's, making nonsense of the questions so that they can put it about that Mr King was drunk when he set it. Kipling defends the principle of collaborative prep. in his autobiography, claiming that he taught Turkey all the French he knew and Turkey tried to teach him and Stalky Latin. 'There is much to be said for this system, if you want a boy to learn anything, because he will remember what he gets from an equal where his master's words are forgotten.'[25] Stalky himself testified to Kipling's transferring his reading from penny dreadfuls to the works of Carlyle, Ruskin and Whitman.[26]

The trio's apparent anarchy and rebelliousness are qualified by a strong sense of justice and retribution. In 'The moral reformers' the padre asks them to stop the bullying of Clewer by two seventeen-year-olds, sent for six months' cramming to get them into Sandhurst. So Stalky and McTurk lure them into a trap by pretending to bully Beetle and encouraging them to join in. They tie them up, inflict on the bullies all the torments they have inflicted on Clewer, shave off half their moustaches and reduce them to tears. This episode has prompted many over-fastidious critics to enter a tut-tutting *caveat* at excessive brutality. Perhaps these critics have never been bullied. But the bulk of Kipling's readers, including this critic, will have felt that the bullies are getting their just deserts. Their fate is not simply a just retribution but a salutary warning not to abuse physical strength and superiority.

Kipling's was an unforgiving nature. He showed this even in his school career. When the ferociously sadistic school chaplain, Campbell, preached a lachrymose sermon of farewell, asking pardon for any misdeeds, and some of the boys were inclined to forgive him, Kipling brusquely declared, 'Two years of bullying is not paid for with half an hour's blubbering in a pulpit.'[27] A kind of Old Testament retribution was a recurrent feature of all Kipling's work. In *Stalky* it takes the form of the working out of fantasy revenges for past slights. The tormenting of the two bullies almost certainly derives from Kipling's desire to pay back retrospectively those who bullied him in his first year at United Services College. Kipling does not go into the nature of the bullying but Dunsterville, declaring that 'life was certainly very rough and bullying was rampant' in the early years of the school, argues that he 'must have been perpetually black and blue' during this time. He details some of the cruel and wanton acts of savagery indulged in and reflects, 'Criminal lunatics must have been boys once and consequently one may assume that among any large group of boys there must be some embryo criminal lunatics. On no other assumption could one account for forms of bullying that are just infliction of mere pain.'[28] Crofts, who, as Mr King, is depicted as quick-tempered, sarcastic and keen on house loyalty, was an inspiring teacher, who allowed Kipling the run of his library, gave him a present when he left and corresponded with him in India. His treatment of Kipling was in part a way of keeping the precocious genius from getting too big for his boots, as Kipling later acknowledged.[29] But he could not resist getting Beetle to wreck King's study in final revenge for the numberless public put-downs.

The boys have a real but deep patriotism, whose nature is revealed in a key and much-quoted story, 'The flag of their country', when a visiting Tory M.P. addresses the boys on the subject of patriotism, duty and service by waving the flag at them, earning Stalky's contemptuous description of 'jelly-bellied flag-flapper'. Kipling notes:

> Now the reserve of a boy is tenfold deeper than the reserve of a maid, she being made for one end only by blind Nature, but man for several. With a large and healthy hand, he tore down these veils, and trampled them under the well-intentioned feet of eloquence. In a raucous voice he cried aloud little matters like the hope of Honour and the dream of Glory, that boys do not discuss even with their most intimate equals; cheerfully assuming that, till he spoke, they had never considered these possibilities. He pointed them to shining goals, with fingers which smudged out all radiance on all horizons. He profaned the most secret places of their souls with outcries and gesticulations. He bade them consider the deeds of their ancestors in such fashion that they were flushed to their tingling ears. Some of them—the rending voice cut a frozen stillness—might have had relatives who perished in defence of their country. (They thought, not a few of them, of an old sword in a passage, or above a breakfast-room table, seen and fingered by stealth since they could walk.) He adjured them to emulate those illustrious examples; and they looked all ways in their extreme discomfort.[30]

There is here a clear rejection of the jingoism with which thoughtless and superficial commentators so often label Kipling and the recognition of a higher patriotism. As Kipling says, the flag represented for the boys a feeling which was 'shut up, sacred, apart'. They needed no lectures on duty. After all, 80 per cent of them had been born abroad, 'in camp, cantonment or upon the high seas'. Seventy-nine per cent were sons of serving officers. The bulk of them were set on following their fathers' careers. 'Don't you want to die for your giddy country?' asks McTurk. 'Not if I can jolly well avoid it,' says Stalky.[31] No empty, futile gestures for them—but sensible, practical professional soldiering, inspired, nonetheless, by a sense of duty and calling, too deep for mere words.

Kipling's description of the boys' sense of outrage is entirely accurate, confirmed by such practised observers as Dr Cyril Norwood ('Most boys at public schools and elsewhere have their ideals, but they do not talk about them') and A. C. Benson ('In one way, too, a boy's sense of reverence is very strong; he dislikes the feelings which lie deep being dragged habitually to the surface').[32] This desire not to disclose or talk about inmost feelings also probably explains a puzzle about Kipling himself as a boy. He penned 'Ave imperatrix!' to celebrate Queen Victoria's survival of an assassination attempt. Kipling's two closest school friends disagreed over its intention: Beresford thought it was intended in part as a spoof, Dunsterville believed it wholly genuine in its feelings. It seems likely that Kipling, knowing of Beresford's cynicism and not wanting to admit to deep patriotic feelings, let him think it was a spoof, whereas it was the first stirring of the imperial muse. Certainly he was to quote from it approvingly in a later work.[33]

The final ingredient in the training of the future soldiers of the Queen was the close male camaraderie, unspoken but running through the stories, as a functional and emotional bond. The trio complement each other and back each other up as a unit. Dunsterville believed that the trio was formidable because of their different talents, Beresford supplying 'extraordinary mature judgement combined with a malicious ingenuity', Kipling contributing 'the enormous asset of knowledge—intuitive and acquired' and Dunsterville himself providing leadership.[34] They also gave each other friendship, loyalty and protection.

The end result of this school training is the production of serving officers of distinction. That this is Kipling's message is made clear from the clues planted throughout. During the course of 'The flag of his country' he continually alludes to the fates of those boys drilling with Stalky: Hogan, killed in Burma; Perowne, shot in equatorial Africa by his own men; Wake Minor, a Bimbashi in the Egyptian Army before he is thirty. In 'A little prep.' recent old boys, now army officers, return and are given a hero's welcome. One of them recounts the gallant death of another recent old boy, and the school takes pride in the fact that nine old boys have died in the service of their country. The last story, 'Slaves of the lamp' Part 2, shows the boys ten to fifteen years on at a reunion, still answering to their school nicknames ('Pussy', 'Tertius' and 'Abanazar') and reminiscing about school. The talk turns to Stalky, now in India, and one of them tells how Stalky got embroiled with fuzzy-wuzzies five miles into the interior of the Sudan and 'conducted a masterly retreat and wiped up eight of 'em'. Another tells how Stalky pulled his men through a 'frontier row' in India. Stalky contrived to break up the federation of two traditionally hostile tribes by setting them at each other's throats, using the same trick he had played at school with the drunken carter. Kipling comments, 'India's full of Stalkies—Cheltenham and Haileybury and Marlborough chaps—that we don't know anything about, and the surprises will begin when there is really a big row on.'[35]

There is no doubt that Stalky is the best kind of soldier, a blend of training and instinct. The worst kind is demonstrated in 'The honours of war' (1911), which involves Lieutenant Colonel 'Stalky' Corkran in another schoolboy exploit. Wontner is Stalky's antithesis, an Oxford intellectual, constantly lecturing on the theories of Clausewitz. He is threatening to ruin two young subalterns for ragging him, contrary to army regulations. So Stalky lures him into ragging them back, thus effectively undermining his case.

Despite the stress on out-of-lesson activities, the increasingly conservative Kipling later moderated his attitude to concede the value of classics. 'Regulus' (1908) is based on the idea of getting Latin wrong. The Latin is in fact got horrendously wrong, the kind of idea Frank Richards regularly had fun with in the Bunter stories. But there is a moral. The class are reading the story of Regulus, the Roman general captured by the Carthaginians, sent on an embassy to Rome to ask for peace. He strongly advises the Romans against making terms and is put to death by his captors.

Winton, an earnest, conscientious boy, suddenly breaks out, releasing a mouse in the drawing class. He is given lines, and that means missing rugby, which in turns means a caning from the captain of games. Winton apologises to the drawing master but refuses his offer to let him off lines. He insists on taking his medicine (both the lines and the caning), although he fears it will count against him and hamper his career. Instead, he gets his first fifteen cap and is made a sub-prefect, earning from Stalky the nickname 'Regulus'. This demonstrates the value of classics in character-forming.

Kipling offered something to all sides in the education controversy. The conservatives could seize on his emphasis on character formation. Radicals could take comfort from his rejection of both athleticism and Evangelicalism. Even the Arnoldians, with whom he has least in common, could endorse his homily on the value of classics. But, as always, Kipling was his own man, responding to events, engaging with orthodoxies, articulating his own distinctive and unapologetic world view.

For *Stalky and Co.* is not just about school or even education; it is, like all his work, related to his larger world view. Kipling was an adherent of the 'thin crust of civilisation' school, which believed that society stood on the brink and was prevented from going over the edge into the abyss by the forces of social control—religion, law, custom, convention and morality. These all added up to what he called 'The Law', which essentially consisted of rules of conduct for the maintenance of both the moral and the social order, and which transcended all other codes.[36]

He embodied this code in the much parodied but central 'If', which lauds coolness, self-confidence, modesty, determination, generosity of spirit and a commitment to work. It also involved loyalty to friends, keeping promises and respect for authority. Stalky epitomises 'The Law', and his real-life original went off to play the 'Great Game' in central Asia. We can see the embryonic players of the 'Great Game' emerging in the japes and rags at Westward Ho!

The need for an ultimate power to prevent cosmic chaos is filled by the Head, who appears in this Jove-like role from the outset and whose authority the trio, for all their anarchic tendencies, respect. When they are reported for trespassing on Colonel Dabney's grounds and explain the truth of the situation, the headmaster accepts their explanation and then canes them for fooling the masters. 'I swear I'll pray for the Head tonight,' says Beetle admiringly, and this refrain is repeated. The Head beats them for spoofing Prout in 'The impressionists' and the new master, Mason, in 'Slaves of the lamp'. They accept it with good grace. When the school discover in 'A little prep.' that the Head has saved a boy's life from diphtheria by sucking out the poison through a tube, the entire school cheer him and he canes them for insolence. ('Here was a man to be reverenced.')

Kipling believed in the importance of religious forms, not in the theological truth of any particular religion but in its ritual aspects, which provide a cohesive bond. This is clear in particular in 'The united idolators', where the boys, deeply infected by the Uncle Remus stories, speak in chants derived from Joel Chandler Harris. ('Ingle-go-jang, my joy, my joy! Ingle-go-jang, my joy!') The two houses fight over rival idols, Brer Terrapin and Tar Baby, which they worship and parade, to the horror of a temporary master, who does not understand boys.

Uniquely it is possible to examine in some detail the true nature of Kipling's schooldays and the way in which he transmuted them from the raw material of his stories. For they are clearly recalled through the filter of his subsequent experiences in India, his encounter with soldiers and District Officers and his concern about the state of world affairs. We can compare the stories with his own account, both in his autobiography (*Something of Myself*) and a piece on 'An English school', originally written in 1893 and later included in *Land and Sea Tales for Scouts and Guides*. But in addition the memoirs of Major General Lionel Dunsterville, the original of Stalky (*Stalky's Reminiscences*), and the fascinating and detailed *Schooldays with Kipling* by George C. Beresford, the original of McTurk, throw invaluable light on those years at U.S.C.[37] What is remarkable about these books is the way in which they mirror exactly the characteristics discerned in his school-mates by Kipling. Stalky was 'our commander-in-chief', characterised by his 'infernal impersonality . . . He saw not only us but himself from the outside.' Beresford, he thought, possessed 'an invincible detach-ment far beyond mere insolence—towards all the world; and a tongue, when he used it, dipped in some Irish blue acid. Moreover, he spoke sincerely of the masters as "ushers".'[38] It is surely of Beresford too that Kipling is speaking in 'An English school' when he talks of a Ruskin-reading study-mate who was 'the only boy in the school who had a genuine contempt for his masters'.[39]

The stories are in part autobiographical, in part wish-fulfilment, and in part educational tract, and to that extent resemble *Tom Brown* and *Eric* almost exactly. The characters in them are almost without exception based on real people. Stalky was Major General Lionel Charles Dunsterville (1865–1946), at school nicknamed 'Blobbs', who left United Services College in 1883 for Sandhurst. He later served in Waziristan, on the North West Frontier, in China and the Great War, was a renowned leader of irregular frontier forces, after his retirement wrote several volumes of reminiscence and became first president of the Kipling Society, founded in 1927. McTurk was George Charles Beresford (1865–1938), son of an army officer from County Leitrim. He left U.S.C. shortly after Kipling to join the Royal Indian Civil Engineering College at Cooper's Hill. He went on to become a civil engineer in India but returned home because of his health. Later he joined the Fabian Society, exhibited at the Royal Academy and earned distinction as a photographer and antique dealer. He was a founder member of the Kipling Society. Beetle is Kipling himself. Kipling was best known at school by the nickname 'Gigger', from his spectacles (gig lamps), but at one time had been called 'Beetle' because he looked like one—dark, round-shouldered, heavy-browed. Other boys too were based on reality. Brigadier General S. M. 'Tuppenny' Edwards, C.B., C.M.G., D.S.O., Major General J. C. 'Potiphar' Rimington, C.B., C.S.I., and Major General S. H. 'Tiddley Winks' Powell, C.B., are the originals of Dick Four, Pussy Abanazar and Tertius. 'The Infant' was General Sir George Roos-Keppel. J. P. Hogan, killed in Burma, was R. A. T. Drury. Stettson, the boy the head saved from diphtheria, was probably Docker, a day boy.[40]

The staff were all based on real characters. The headmaster, 'Proosian' Bates, was Cormell Price, headmaster of U.S.C. Mr Prout was based on the suspicious, humourless, narrow-minded house master M. H. Pugh, constantly prowling and prying, which, according to

Dunsterville, made him easy to entrap. King was based on the quick-tempered, sarcastic but brilliant Latin and English teacher William Carr Crofts, a flavour of whose teaching technique is conveyed in 'Regulus', though Kipling seems to have incorporated elements of another Latin teacher, F. W. Haslam. The amiable, easy-going chaplain, the Rev. John Gillett, was modelled on the Rev. George Willes, Hartopp on the sympathetic and enthusiastic Herbert Arthur Evans, who formed the Natural History Society and organised amateur theatricals. 'Foxy' was Sergeant Major George Schofield (1839–1907). Even 'Rabbit's Eggs' was authentic, a local carrier given the nickname by Dunsterville because of his claim to have discovered some rabbits' eggs. Dunsterville described him as 'a dull-witted peasant who was frequently under the influence of drink.'[41]

The United Services College had been founded in 1874 by a group of retired army officers with sons destined for the forces who could not afford the fees at public schools. Financial stringency was its hallmark, and this showed in spartan living conditions, and the perennial shortage of food that Kipling, Dunsterville and Beresford complain of. It was in Kipling's words 'a caste school', 75 per cent of whose members had been born overseas and intended to follow their fathers into the services. The school song reflected this:

> Far from the dear old country,
> Old Boys have fought and bled,
> Their names will be missed on the roll-call list,
> For they're numbered with the dead.
> Their country called them and they fought
> For an Empire's liberty,
> And found the deathless fame they sought
> At the U.S.C.[42]

The founders were fortunate to secure the services as headmaster of Cormell Price, head of the modern side at Haileybury and a man with a record of getting boys into the services. Price took with him some of the Haileybury boys and acquired a group of tough misfits who had been expelled by other places like Cheltenham, Sherborne and Marlborough. He was a member of the circle of William Morris and Edward Burne-Jones, Kipling's uncle by marriage, and that and its cheapness ensured Kipling's entry.

Kipling arrived at the age of twelve in 1878 and was badly bullied for a year and a half. But he became friendly with Beresford, in whom he found a fellow soul who shared his aesthetic inclinations. Eventually they teamed up with Dunsterville and took over study No. 5. From the outset Kipling was an outsider. He was at a school geared to turning out army officers but was himself never destined for the forces. His chronic short-sightedness and lack of co-ordination led to his being excused games. Already moustached at fifteen, he read voraciously, being given the run of their libraries by both Price and Crofts. In his last term the school chaplain, Willes, entertained him over pipes and whisky to late-night discussions about life and art. Like all misfits, he made life easier by becoming a 'character'. Despite not playing sport, his cleverness, his humour and his ability at verbal duels made him an outstanding figure in that small community. 'What will Gigger say?' was a consideration with the upper boys in his last term, and Beresford acknowledged that Kipling had a civilising effect on the school; the early atmosphere of bullying and rowdiness was moderated by his lethal sarcasm and ridicule.[43] Thanks to him, intellectual activities were not seen as inferior to games or athletics, quite a triumph in such a surrounding. For U.S.C. was far from an intellectual environment. 'The Coll. had few ideas,' says Beresford, 'It circulated round Virgil and tuck and games and bathing.'[44]

Nevertheless, Kipling edited the school magazine, founded and ran the Debating and Literary Society. He acted. He read voraciously. He wrote poetry endlessly. He was able to pronounce on anything. What he did not do was apply himself to his academic work. He was essentially educated outside rather than inside the classroom. But he applied himself when it suited him. His report for the last winter term, January–March 1882, shows him top of the school in English, fifth in the first Latin set, fourteenth in French and bottom in maths. He did learn something from his masters, acknowledging the Head's instruction in precis-writing for influencing his prose and also the importance of Crofts. 'Under him I came to feel that words could be used as weapons, for he did me the honour to talk at me plentifully; and our year in—year out form-room bickerings gave us both something to play with. One learns more from a good scholar in a rage than from a score of lucid and laborious drudges.' In retrospect, too, Crofts' legacy was prized: 'C. taught me to loathe Horace for two years; to forget him for twenty, and then to love him for the rest of my days and through many a sleepless night.'[45]

Intellectual activities are certainly not absent from *Stalky and Co.* and are more in evidence than in most school stories (the verbal duels with King, Beetle coaching his chums in examinations, Beetle immersing himself in the delights of the Head's library), but there is an important aspect of Kipling's school career which has been firmly suppressed in the stories. At school he was an aesthete, 'a bit under the tyranny of the Burne-Jones outlook and under the influence of that set and surroundings'. Beresford and Dunsterville shared Kipling's tastes, Beresford by inclination and Dunsterville out of perversity. He took up unfashionable stances as a matter of course—for instance, preaching

Liberal views among the predominantly Conservative boys. Dunsterville recalled that study No. 5 became a shrine to aetheticism. 'We took great pains over the aesthetic adornment of our study, the scheme being based on an olive-green, and some grey-blue paint with which we did some remarkable stencilling.'[46]

The trio began to collect curios, haunting the Bideford shops— Wedgwood teapots, terra-cotta figurines, Worcester cups and saucers, old glass pictures, Chinese paintings, Sèvres vases, stained glass, carved oak panels. Periodically Stalky would auction the lot and they would start again. Swinburne, Ruskin and Whitman were read aloud in the study. They even flew a banner decorated with sunflowers and lilies, the symbol of the aesthetic movement, from their window. Mr Pugh, 'who always liked to be thought the hearty, muscular, out-of-doors, five-mile-an-hour heel-and-toe roadster', was appalled and insisted it be taken down.[47] It is likely that this aestheticism is what led the un-imaginative Pugh to suspect Kipling of homosexuality, something which incensed Kipling when he learned of it after he had left U.S.C. But of his aestheticism Beresford recalled:

> Our schoolfellows bore no resentment with regard to aestheticism, as any-thing that Gigger did 'went'. It was obvious to them that all was meant for their entertainment and each development of the 'arty' pose was welcomed, even encouraged, as affording material for humour.[48]

Kipling's poetry at this time had nothing of war, empire and nation, and none of the interest in machinery he developed later. According to Beresford, it centred in those days on the individual, his struggles and triumphs, his dreams and his failures.[49] The exception was the celebratory poem on Queen Victoria's survival from assassination, 'Ave imperatrix!':

> For we are bred to do your will,
> By land and sea, wherever flies
> The Flag, to fight and follow still
> And work your empire's destinies.

How true was the picture of life that Kipling painted in *Stalky and Co.*? Kipling, Beresford and Dunsterville did have a hut in the furze, where they smoked, read and plotted. It is generally agreed that the portrait of Stalky is accurate. Beresford certainly thought so:

> Stalky, the veritable Stalky, was a unique schoolboy, and really had a mind and aspirations like those of the boy in *Stalky and Co.*, though in actual performance the real-life character was a somewhat watered down version of the brilliant being that was, in part, the fabrication of Gigger's brain.[50]

Dunsterville wrote self-deprecatingly, '*Stalky and Co.* is a work of fiction and not an historical record. Stalky himself was never quite so clever as portrayed in the book, and the book makes no mention of the many times when he was let down.'[51] But he later told Lord Birkenhead, 'We were rather like that, but not quite so clever. The events described are actual events, in most cases, but very much written up. Some of the events really concerned others and not us three.'[52] Nevertheless his account of the plots rings true:

> Our earlier escapades were on the lines of simple buffoonery, but we soon evolved on to a higher plane of astute plotting on more intellectual lines, the essence of each plot being that it should leave our adversaries with nothing to hit back at. The culmination of the plot was the appearance of the elusive criminals in the pleasing pose of injured innocence.[53]

Dunsterville's view of the masters was that they were 'a tyrannical lot of old men . . . who hated boys and wanted to make them miserable. So I, in my turn, tried to make them miserable.' Beresford believed this too ('We were at school to fight the masters'), added to which he was contemptuous of them.[54]

Dunsterville delighted in ingenious stunts, practical jokes, what is today called 'winding people up'. He would deliberately adopt opposing views from the majority of the company he was in. 'Stalky was always against the accepted code, the conventional standard of conduct and entered into long arguments to prove that all our assumptions and ethics were wrong and that everything should be done the other way round.'[55] Always short of money and always hungry, he constantly devised schemes and expedients to raise food and cash. He did as little book learning as possible. He would delight in conning masters into thinking he was cribbing and then revealing that he was not. He would cut chapel and sneak back into the chapel procession unobserved; he would set boys against each other by stratagems and then reveal his schemes to them and have a good laugh. 'I think that in all our villainies we did try as far as possible to amuse ourselves without injuring anyone,' he recalled.[56]

He attributed his 'stalkiness' to his unhappy early experiences. He had had a miserable childhood and was badly bullied when he first arrived at U.S.C. He believed that 'the life of perpetual suspense that I led during those harrowing years probably taught me a great deal of cunning. Like a hunted animal, I had to keep all my senses perpetually on the alert to escape from the toils of the hunter.'[57]

Many of the episodes elaborated and embroidered in *Stalky* were certainly authentic.[58] Kipling himself recalled the visits of recent old boys, now subalterns, who entranced the boys with tales of army life, the arrival of news of old boys killed in action, the Head saving the life of a boy with diphtheria, the army class being allowed to smoke, the sea bathing, the mockery of *Eric*, the school magazine. The craze for

Uncle Remus was also authentic, as Kipling reported in a letter to Joel Chandler Harris.[59] The study performance of *Aladdin* occurred, as did bacon fat being tipped from a study window on a boy beneath. All this found its way into *Stalky*. Kipling does not mention, but Dunsterville and Beresford both do, an episode when by brilliant ingenuity Beresford laid hands on the form English Literature examination paper, devised by Crofts with the main aim of showing up Kipling's ignorance of Milton.[60] Together they ensured that Kipling got all the answers up and came top, to Crofts' mystification and horror. This is transmuted by Kipling into the episode of altering the Latin examination paper to humiliate Crofts, perhaps because the original episode looked to the mature Kipling too much like dishonesty, though Beresford and Dunsterville both see it as a jape pure and simple.

Dunsterville's sense of seeing them all from the outside, seasoned with a self-deprecating sense of humour, comes over in his own book in his comments in the preface to Beresford's book: 'We were only a lot of potty little schoolboys with playful ingenuity perhaps rather unusually highly developed.'[61] He says that, in telling us what Kipling thought, Beresford 'really gives us what Beresford thinks Kipling would have thought if he had thought as Beresford thought.'

How far was Kipling a participant in the japes and scrapes? A schoolfellow of those days, H. M. Swanwick, wrote in 1937:

> It always amused us that he should have become so fervidly the prophet of Action and the laureate of the Deed; for as a boy—and I never knew him after—he was a bookworm entirely, absorbed in the life of books, unathletic, unsociable, and—sad to say—decidedly fat.[62]

Beresford also recalled Kipling not being adventurous, not breaking bounds, indulging in no acts of rebellion and danger, though he approved of and blessed such activities in others. He apparently had a horror of being caned, though when safely beyond its range defended corporal punishment. ('A cut or two, given with no malice but as a reminder, can correct and keep corrected a false quantity or a wandering mind, more completely than any amount of explanation.')[63] This is a perfect example of Kipling's transmutation of reality into myth, for he depicts the bold outlaws Stalky and Co. cheerfully enduring beatings from the Head because the ideological thrust of the stories demanded it. But already, at school, Kipling saw himself and the other two as heroic outsiders. In his *Schoolboy Lyrics*, privately published by his parents, he wrote:

> We scouted all, both great and small—
> We were a dusky crew;
> And each boy's hand was against us raised,
> 'Gainst me and the Other Two.[64]

He was, of course, exactly the sort of boy who might be expected to become the prophet of action and the laureate of the deed; the celebrant of those things that were far beyond his reach and which he could never experience at first hand. If he was short-sighted, unco-ordinated, over-weight, intellectual and aesthetic, he found vicarious pleasure in the genuine exploits of Stalky and prided himself in being his lieutenant.

Kipling rapidly came to revere and romanticise U.S.C., calling it 'a school before its time' in his autobiography and declaring in 'An English school', 'Of all things in the world, there is nothing excepting a good mother, so worthy of honour as a good school.'[65] He dedicated *Stalky and Co.* to Cormell Price. He saw U.S.C. as the nursery of those he had come in India to revere—the subalterns, engineers and administrators, 'the sons of Martha'. As early as 1893 he was writing of the school, 'Surely it must be better to turn out men who do real work than men who write about what they think about what other people have done or ought to do.'[66] But the latter was exactly what Kipling himself did. Then the man who forbade the discussion of sport in study No. 5 recalls wistfully, 'Very few things that the world can offer can make up for having missed a place in the First Fifteen.'[67] The school's arch-intellectual, in 'The last term' he contemptuously described the prefect Tulke as 'a smallish white-haired boy, of the type that must be promoted on account of its intellect, and ever afterwards appeals to the Head to support his authority when zeal has outrun discretion.'[68] His position is one of total identification with the men of action.

As a picture of boys, R. F. Moss noted, *Stalky and Co.* was convincing on one level but 'he concentrates on the highs rather than the lows of boyhood'.[69] So the high-jinks, rebellions and exclusive male clique were there, but the emotional volatility, identity crises, depressions and sexual exploration were not. But Kipling and the others are certainly recognisable in the portraits in *Stalky and Co.* In 1893 Kipling observed, 'How little the character of the man differs from that of the boy of sixteen or seventeen.'[70] This was clearly true of Dunsterville, who went on to be a brilliant unorthodox soldier, and of Beresford, who became a cynical and waspish painter and antique-dealer. It was equally true of Kipling, who in many ways remained the curious, enthusiastic, literary schoolboy, 'Gigger' of Westward Ho! Here is another case of the lifelong boy writing for boys. 'Above all, Mr. Kipling knows the heart of a boy,' wrote Ian Hay admiringly.[71] Curiously, the schoolboy Kipling, with his thick moustache, heavy smoking, precocious mentality, and his claim at sixteen to be twenty-six in everything but age, who seems in some ways so much older than his contemporaries, a man among boys, rapidly became, as he grew older, a boy among men. It can be seen in his marriage to an older woman who mothered and protected him; in his love of gadgetry, fads and crazes; his delight in the company of children; his robust and self-conscious philistinism; his use of dated schoolboy slang in speech and letters; and his idealisation of men of action. Revealingly, General A. S. Little recalled that when he was head prefect at Westward Ho! he and another boy were detailed to escort the twenty-nine-year-old author on his return visit to the school and Kipling seemed to them younger than themselves ('I recollect his decidedly boyish outlook on things') and they found his schoolboy slang and enthusiasms rather wearing.[72]

Dunsterville too was anxious to correct the idea that Kipling was never really a boy at all, writing in 1936:

> Such an idea is quite erroneous. Although it is true that at the age of fourteen he had the mind of a man of thirty, he managed in some inexplicable way to counterbalance this by extreme boyishness. He took as keen a delight as any of us in our youthful adventures and was always bubbling over with mirth and the joy of living.[73]

For all the accuracy of many of the portraits in *Stalky and Co.*, the higher ideological needs of the stories wrought a transformation in one character—the headmaster. In reality Cormell Price was a Liberal, an anti-imperialist, with aesthetic leanings, who rarely used the cane. But he adhered to the prevailing code of chivalry, regularly describing conduct he did not approve of as 'not knightly'.[74] Beresford added, 'It was well known that he took his stand on the life well lived and frowned on the race for mere wealth at the sacrifice of virtue and nobility.'[75] Kipling revered him, speaking in 'An English school' of 'the perfect judgement, knowledge of boys, patience and above all, power, that the Head must have had' and in *Something of Myself*, 'Many of us loved the Head for what he had done for us, but I owed him more than all of them put together; and I think I loved him even more than they did.'[76] But in *Stalky and Co.* he appears as the formidable, all-seeing, all-knowing 'Prooshian' Bates, a flogger and a robust imperialist. Kipling had already transmogrified him mentally into a pillar of the empire, declaring in 1894 at the retirement celebrations, 'All that the College—all that Mr. Price—has ever aimed at was to make men able to make and keep Empires'.[77] In fact his job was to prepare boys for Sandhurst, which was rather different. But Kipling's belief in individual character and initiative had to be reconciled with his belief in order and 'The Law' and this was done by investing Price retrospectively with divine majesty as the ultimate source of order and authority. The school set out to train army officers and in the view of Dunsterville and Kipling succeeded. Looking back, Dunsterville believed that the school motto, 'Fear God and honour the King', was absorbed by the boys and many followed the Second Commandment: 'Don't to anything mean. Don't let anyone down.' Kipling felt the same. 'The school motto was "Fear God, Honour the King", and so the men she made went out to Boerland and Zululand and India and Burma and Cyprus and Hong Kong, and lived and died as gentlemen and officers.'[78] Kipling set into verse at the head of *Stalky and Co.* the virtues that the boys were taught: obedience, common sense, service, hard work.

Stalky and Co., published by Macmillan in 1899, had sold 47,000 copies by 1910 and 181,000 by 1932.[79] What was the reaction to the book? It seems to have been read as widely by adults as by children, and opinion was sharply divided. The daily papers were in general favourable, and typical of the approving comments were those in *The Athenaeum* (14 October 1899):

> Most English boys—and most Englishmen who have anything of the boy still in them—will rejoice in *Stalky and Co.* Boys will declare that the book is 'spiffing' and if they read it in school hours—a not impossible fact—will have to keep a handkerchief ready to stuff into their mouths to prevent their laughter attracting the attention of the form-master. Mr. Kipling himself has every reason to feel proud of the success with which he has photographed the English public-school boy's talk and sentiments. Mr. Kipling, with that marvellous memory of his, recalls his schooldays as in themselves they really were. He sees the British boy, with his infinite capacity for fun, his finite capacity for insubordination, his coarseness in word and act, modified by an ultra-sensitive delicacy of feeling in certain directions. *Stalky and Co.* is almost a complete treatise on the strategy and tactics of the British schoolboy.[80]

But there was also a storm of criticism. The reaction in mandarin literary circles was one of pious horror. H. G. Wells called Stalky and Co. 'mucky little sadists'.[81] Somerset Maugham declared, 'a more odious picture of school life can seldom have been drawn'.[82] George Sampson called it 'an unpleasant book about unpleasant boys in an unpleasant school'.[83] Henry James thought it 'deplorable'.[84] The most concentrated and celebrated attack came in *The Contemporary Review* (December 1899), where in an article called 'The voice of the hooligan' Robert Buchanan lamented the decline of philanthropy, decency and morality in society and culture and its replacement by jingoism, philistinism and exploitation. He pointed to Kipling as the key representative of this hateful new age and focused on *Stalky* with unalloyed horror. 'Only the spoiled child of an utterly brutalized public could possibly have written *Stalky and Co.* or, having written it, have dared to publish it.' He described the trio as 'hideous little men' and went on, 'it is simply impossible to show by mere quotations the horrible vileness of the book describing the lives of these three small fiends in human likeness . . . The vulgarity, the brutality, the savagery reeks on every page.'[85]

Sir Walter Besant, long-time champion of Kipling, came to his defence in *The Contemporary Review* (January 1900), pointing to the realism of his characters and his writing, his power as a storyteller, his humanity and his wide appeal: 'Rudyard Kipling is the first of story-tellers to whom it has been granted to speak, while he still lives, to the hundred millions of those who read the Anglo-Saxon tongue . . . He is loved by old and young in every class and in every country where his language is the language of the folk.' He is, says Besant, the poet of an empire construed as 'the most profound sense of responsibility'.[86]

Those actively involved in education and the educational debate were also concerned. A. C. Benson, the former Eton house master, thought it 'amazing' in its cleverness, freshness and originality, but thought that 'it is not a fair picture of school life at all'. The masters were portrayed with 'remorseless fidelity' but the school and the boys untypical. He saw Stalky and Co. as caricatures: 'highly coloured, fantastic, horribly human and yet somehow grotesque . . . My own experience is that no boys could keep so easily on so high a level of originality and sagacity.' He also adds an interesting comment on the absence of sex from their activities:

> The difficulty to my mind is to imagine boys so lawless, so unbridled, so fond at intervals of low delights, who are yet so obviously wholesome-minded and manly. I can humbly say that it is my belief, confirmed by experience, that boys of so unconventional and daring a type would not be content without dipping into darker pleasures.[87]

He ends by saying that he has talked to a good many boys who have read the book: 'They have all been amused, interested, delighted. But they say frankly that the boys are not like any boys they ever knew.' J. Howard Whitehouse was much more severe, dismissing the stories as 'a farrago of rubbish and vulgarity' and Stalky and Co. as standing 'aloof from the boyhood of the world, without beauty, innocence or health, a herd of youthful Yahoos, with the language and habits of Bedlam'.[88] Venerable W. M. Sinclair, Archdeacon of London, chairing the coming-of-age dinner of the *B.O.P.* in 1899, declined to accept *Stalky and Co.* as 'a just and true picture of schoolboy life of to-day, or of any recent period'.[89]

One criticism that was regularly and with some justice made was that United Services College was not a typical school. This is true. It had no fagging, no chapel building, no cadet corps, no parades and no uniforms. Harold Child (Winchester) proclaimed it 'almost as unfaithful to the average school as either of Dean Farrar's [books]',[90] in particular in the absence of house and school loyalty, and H. B. Gray thought it 'breezy but in the eyes of most public school men unfamiliar'.[91] Nevertheless *Stalky* played a crucial role in the development of public school fiction. As E. C. Mack says:

> The new self-consciousness with regard to the meaning and importance of
> the public schools, the revival of serious adult concern over adolescence as
> a result of the development of modern psychology, the extension of the
> boundaries of the novel under French influence, and above all the example
> of *Stalky and Co.* in 1899 combined to encourage public school men and
> others to turn their experience and knowledge of school life to fictional
> use.[92]

Still today, fifty-five years after his death, Kipling divides people as
fiercely as he did when *Stalky and Co.* was published. It is formidable
testimony to the piercing individuality, painful relevance and mesmeric
power of his genius.

Notes

1 On Kipling's life and work see Charles Carrington, *Rudyard Kipling: his life
and work* (1955), Harmondsworth, 1970; Lord Birkenhead, *Rudyard Kipling*,
London, 1978; Angus Wilson, *The Strange Ride of Rudyard Kipling*, London,
1977; John Gross, *The Age of Kipling*, New York, 1972; Philip Mason,
Kipling: the glass, the shadow and the fire, London, 1975; Andrew Rutherford
(ed.), *Kipling's Mind and Art*, Edinburgh, 1964.

2 Rudyard Kipling, *Verse* (Definitive Edition), London, 1960, 169.

3 I. F. Clarke, *Voices Prophesying War, 1763–1984*, London, 1966.

4 G. R. Searle, *The Quest for National Efficiency*, Oxford, 1971. Cf. also
Bernard Semmel, *Imperialism and Social Reform*, London, 1960.

5 Kipling, *Verse*, 301–4.

6 Edward C. Mack, *Public Schools and British Opinion since 1860*, New York,
1941, 186.

7 Rudyard Kipling, 'The brushwood boy', *The Day's Work*, London, 1898,
338–81.

8 Kipling, 'The brushwood boy', 344–5.

9 Kipling, 'The brushwood boy', 349.

10 Kipling, 'The brushwood boy', 349.

11 Steven Marcus, 'Stalky and Co.', *Representations*, New York, 1975, 65.

12 Mack, *Public Schools*, 288.

13 H. B. Gray, *The Public Schools and the Empire*, London, 1913.

14 Rudyard Kipling, *Something of Myself* (1937), Harmondsworth, 1977, 102.

15 'Regulus' was collected in *A Diversity of Creatures* (1917); 'The united
idolators' and 'The propagation of knowledge' in *Debits and Credits* (1926),
and 'The satisfaction of a gentleman' along with all the others in *The Complete
Stalky and Co.* (1929).

16 A. C. Benson, *The Schoolmaster*, London, 1908, 96.

17 Rudyard Kipling, *Stalky and Co.* (1899), London, 1922, 13.

18 Rudyard Kipling, 'An English school', *Land and Sea Tales for Scouts and
Guides*, London, 1923, 264.

19 Kipling, *Stalky and Co.*, 166.

20 Kipling, *Stalky and Co.*, 64, 137, 49, 239.

21 Angus Wilson, *Strange Ride of Rudyard Kipling*, 71.

22 Birkenhead, *Rudyard Kipling*, 203.

23 Kipling, *Stalky and Co.*, 157.

24 Kipling, *Stalky and Co.*, 26.

25 Kipling, *Something of Myself*, 25.

26 L. C. Dunsterville, *Stalky's Reminiscences*, London, 1930, 43.
27 George C. Beresford, *Schooldays with Kipling*, London, 1936, 235.
28 Dunsterville, *Stalky's Reminiscences*, 30-1.
29 Kipling, *Something of Myself*, 31.
30 Kipling, *Stalky and Co.*, 212.
31 Kipling, *Stalky and Co.*, 201.
32 Cyril Norwood, *The English Tradition of Education*, London, 1929, 59; Benson, *The Schoolmaster*, 130.
33 Beresford, *Schooldays*, 289-93, 14; Kipling, *Land and Sea Tales*, 276.
34 Dunsterville, *Stalky's Reminiscences*, 25.
35 Kipling, *Stalky and Co.*, 271.
36 On this subject see in particular Noel Annan, 'Kipling's place in the history of ideas', in Andrew Rutherford (ed.), *Kipling's Mind and Art*, Edinburgh, 1964, 97-125.
37 Dunsterville, *Stalky's Reminiscences*, 43-58; Beresford, *Schooldays*.
38 Kipling, *Something of Myself*, 25.
39 Kipling, *Land and Sea Tales*, 274.
40 The identification of minor characters is established by Roger Lancelyn Green, *The Readers's Guide to Rudyard Kipling's Work—Stalky and Co.* (Kipling Society, 1961) and *Kipling and the Children*, London, 1965, 51-73.
41 Dunsterville, *Stalky's Reminiscences*, 45.
42 Major H. A. Tapp, *United Services College, 1874-1911*, Aldershot, 1933, 45.
43 Beresford, *Schooldays*, 262.
44 Beresford, *Schooldays*, 262.
45 Kipling, *Something of Myself*, 288-9.
46 Dunsterville, *Stalky's Reminiscences*, 46.
47 Beresford, *Schooldays*, 201.
48 Beresford, *Schooldays*, 202.
49 Beresford, *Schooldays*, 278-86.
50 Beresford, *Schooldays*, 140.
51 Dunsterville, *Stalky's Reminiscences*, 25.
52 Birkenhead, *Rudyard Kipling*, 43.
53 Dunsterville, *Stalky's Reminiscences*, 26.
54 Dunsterville, *Stalky's Reminiscences*, 50; Beresford, *Schooldays*, 51.
55 Beresford, *Schooldays*, 141.
56 Dunsterville, *Stalky's Reminiscences*, 53.
57 Dunsterville, *Stalky's Reminiscences*, 30-1.
58 On this subject see Lancelyn Green, *Kipling and the Children*, 51-73; Kipling, *Land and Sea Tales*, 255-76.
59 Lancelyn Green, *Kipling and the Children*, 166.
60 Beresford, *Schooldays*, 303-14; Dunsterville, *Stalky's Reminiscences*, 48-9.
61 Beresford, *Schooldays*, 15.
62 Birkenhead, *Rudyard Kipling*, 56.
63 Kipling, *Land and Sea Tales*, 286.
64 Rudyard Kipling, *Early Verse*, ed. Andrew Rutherford, Oxford, 1986, 45.
65 Kipling, *Something of Myself*, 21; *Land and Sea Tales*, 255.
66 Kipling, *Land and Sea Tales*, 258.
67 Kipling, *Land and Sea Tales*, 265.
68 Kipling, *Stalky and Co.*, 222.
69 R. F. Moss, *Rudyard Kipling and the Fiction of Adolescence*, London, 1982, 125.
70 Kipling, *Land and Sea Tales*, 274.
71 Ian Hay, *The Lighter Side of School Life*, Edinburgh, 1923, 159.
72 Birkenhead, *Rudyard Kipling*, 153-4.
73 Lancelyn Green, *Kipling and the Children*, 59-60.
74 Beresford, *Schooldays*, 95.
75 Beresford, *Schooldays*, 154.
76 Kipling, *Land and Sea Tales*, 257-8; Kipling, *Something of Myself*, 32.

77 Wilson, *Strange Ride of Rudyard Kipling*, 69.
78 Dunsterville, *Stalky's Reminiscences*, 53; Kipling, *Land and Sea Tales*, 260.
79 *T.P.'s Weekly*, 4 November 1910; *Sunday Times*, 3 January 1932.
80 Roger Lancelyn Green (ed.), *Kipling: the critical heritage*, London, 1971, 515–16.
81 H. G. Wells, *Experiment in Autobiography*, 2 (1934), London, 1966, 760.
82 Carrington, *Kipling*, 355.
83 Lancelyn Green, *Kipling and the Children*, 160.
84 Mason, *Kipling*, 44.
85 Lancelyn Green, *Kipling: the critical heritage*, 245.
86 Lancelyn Green, *Kipling: the critical heritage*, 255–6.
87 A. C. Benson, *The Upton Letters*, London, 1905, 98–106.
88 J. Howard Whitehouse, *Education*, London, 1935, 166–7.
89 *Boy's Own Paper*, 22 (1899–1900), 216.
90 Harold Child, 'The public school in fiction', in *The Public Schools from Within*, (ed. unnamed), London, 1906, 298.
91 Gray, *The Public Schools and the Empire*, 162.
92 Mack, *Public Schools*, 187.

7

'Only connect':
The Longest Journey

The reformation of the public schools in the mid-nineteenth century had ushered in a period of intense admiration for the system, reflected in *Tom Brown's Schooldays*, the novels of Talbot Baines Reed and the stories of Frank Richards. The Public Schools Commission of 1864 had set the tone when it reported:

> It is not easy to estimate the degree to which the English people are indebted to the schools for the qualities on which they pique themselves, their aptitude for combining freedom with order, their public spirit, their vigour and manliness of character, their strong but not slavish respect for public opinion, their love of healthy sports and exercise. These schools . . . have had perhaps the largest share in moulding the character of an English gentleman.[1]

Self-control, games worship, manliness, public service—here are the essentials of the English public school gentleman. But this archetype and the system which bred him came under attack first during the Boer War and later during the Great War. This period saw a decisive split in reactions to the system. Popular culture continued to see the public school gentleman as an ideal.[2] But high culture came to depict the public schools as hotbeds of snobbery, philistinism and homosexuality, as promoters of conformism and authoritarianism, as defenders of an outdated curriculum which did not prepare people for the real world and as bastions of anti-democratic tendencies which threatened the well-being of the nation. 'At school I lived in a Fascist state,' said W. H. Auden, evoking the classic inter-war high culture response to the public schools.[3] The result, it has been suggested, was that Britain fell behind in the industrial, military and foreign policy fields, its nineteenth-century pre-eminence undermined by an outdated and devitalising code of behaviour.[4]

Novels like Samuel Butler's *The Way of all Flesh* (1903), Compton Mackenzie's *Sinister Street* (1913), Somerset Maugham's *Of Human*

Bondage (1915), H. G. Wells's *The World of William Clissold* (1926) and Richard Aldington's *Death of a Hero* (1929) consciously depicted the public school as a microcosm of society and the source of all that was wrong with it, in particular the production of a ruling caste that was repressed and repressive.[5]

Novels and memoirs criticised spartan conditions, severe discipline, compulsory sport, corporal punishment, bullying, humiliation and most of all suppression of individuality. Homosexuality was deemed to flourish because of the idealisation of Greek culture and society, the enforced intimacy of boys herded together and the lack of outlets for burgeoning sexuality. The system was said to leave boys emotionally, intellectually and psychologically unfitted for life.

It was E. M. Forster's *The Longest Journey* which, according to John Reed, was 'the first truly modern criticism of the public school by a major novelist'.[6] It represents the classic example of an oppositional text. Forster's principal concern was with the suppression of emotion. In *Notes on the English Character* he wrote of public school men, 'They go forth with well-developed bodies, fairly developed minds and undeveloped hearts.'[7] British reserve and rigidity, he believed, were neither inherent nor accidental but the product of an educational philosophy which stressed subordination and strict authoritarianism. 'It is not that the Englishman can't feel—it is that he is afraid to feel. He has been taught at his public school that feeling is bad form. He must not express great joy or sorrow, or even open his mouth too wide when he talks—his pipe might fall out if he did. He must bottle up his emotions, or let them out only on a very special occasion.'[8] As a result the national character, taking its lead from the public schools, is incomplete. The contrast and conflict of values between the cold, correct, emotionally repressed, classic English type and the liberated, uninhibited free souls, able without restraint to love and be loved, runs through virtually all his work. In a sense he wrote the same novel five times over and then gave up novel-writing for good. 'Only connect' was his recipe not only for personal happiness but also for national well-being. For it is in *A Passage to India* precisely the public school qualities of the typical administrator and of the Anglo-Indian mentality that are undermining the Raj. For what it precluded was the things that Forster valued most—sympathy, humanity, brotherhood and love. As a matter of fact, the emotional and sexual repression which was seen as a weakness in public school education by Forster and the writers like George Orwell and Graham Greene who followed his lead may well have been a central dynamic of imperial expansion, acting as a crucial energising agent. This is persuasively argued by Ronald Hyam, who sees in conquest, exploration and ceaseless proconsular activity the sublimation of the sex drive.[9]

Forster's view, however, became the liberal orthodoxy. In 'What I believe', in 1939, Forster elaborated his feelings into a creed:

> Tolerance, good temper and sympathy—they are what matter really, and if the human race is not to collapse they must come to the front before long . . . I believe in personal relationships . . . I hate the idea of causes, and if I had to choose between betraying my country and betraying my friend, I hope I would have the guts to betray my country . . . What is good in people—and consequently in the world—is their insistence on creation, their belief in friendship and loyalty for their own sakes . . . I believe in aristocracy . . . not an aristocracy of power based upon rank and influence, but an aristocracy of the sensitive, the considerate and the plucky. Its members are to be found in all nations and classes . . . They represent the true human tradition, the one permanent victory of our queer race over cruelty and chaos.[10]

Not surprisingly, this places him at the opposite end of the spectrum from Kipling, who saw the victory over cruelty and chaos in duty, service, work and self-control as subsumed into that mystical concept, the British empire, whose administrative agents in India he heroised and mythified as Forster criticised and undermined them.

Forster's philosophy was already being elaborated in *The Longest Journey* (1907). Its title derives from Shelley's poem *Epipsychidion* and stresses the importance of loving all mankind, an idea directly expressed in the book by Stewart Ansell, who is the voice of intellectual truth. It was Forster's own favourite among his novels and earned the approbation of such literary critics as Lionel Trilling ('Perhaps the most brilliant, the most dramatic and the most passionate of his works') and J. B. Beer ('His most intense achievement').[11]

Unlike the previous stories discussed in this study, this one is about a master, but a master who is in many ways still a boy. The central character is Rickie Elliott, congenitally lame, the son of a hated father and an adored mother, raised in 'the grey monotony' of the suburbs, orphaned at fifteen. He finds intellectual awakening and release from the mental and physical confines of suburbia at Cambridge, where he makes sympathetic friends, develops literary aspirations and is attracted to Agnes Pembroke, sister of the schoolmaster Herbert. Following the death of her fiance, Gerald Dawes, in a football match, Rickie, who cherishes an idealised view of love and of women, marries Agnes. His stories having been rejected by a publisher, he is drawn into the arid life of schoolmastering at Sawston. His relationship with Agnes, however, proves empty, superficial and unrewarding. There is no meeting of minds, no engagement of the emotions, and symbolically the fruit of their union, a girl, is born crippled and dies after a short illness.

On a visit to his aunt, Mrs Failing, in Wiltshire, Rickie discovers that he has a half-brother, Stephen Wonham, who is very much his antithesis—robustly healthy, physical and 'pagan'. But, believing Stephen to be the son of his hated father, he agrees to Agnes's insistence that the relationship be concealed. When Stephen discovers the truth and turns up in Sawston, Agnes believes he intends to blackmail them and tries to buy him off. Affronted, Stephen leaves. Rickie learns not only that Stephen has been thrown out by Mrs Failing, largely as a result of Agnes's machinations, but also that he is the son of Rickie's mother and not his father. Rickie leaves Agnes and Sawston for Stephen and Wiltshire. He is killed there saving a drunken Stephen from the wheels of a train. The novel ends with Rickie's stories achieving posthumous recognition.

The book is divided into three parts—Cambridge, Sawston and Wiltshire, each of which represents a significant world view. Sawston, the public school, stands for the world of conformity, repression and lovelessness, epitomised by Herbert and Agnes Pembroke. For Forster, Sawston stands for the public school system as a whole and the empire it has bred, a regimented, loveless place of conformity and authoritarianism. Sawston, a seventeenth-century grammar school, founded by tradesmen, had been transformed in the nineteenth century into a conventional public school. ('It aimed at producing the average Englishman and to a very great extent it succeeded.')

Herbert Pembroke is seen by Forster as a typical public school master. He believes above all in organisation, and he is constantly developing and refining the organisation and traditions of the school:

> The school caps, with their elaborate symbolism, were his; his the many-tinted bathing-drawers, that showed how far a boy could swim; his the hierarchy of jerseys and blazers. It was he who instituted Bounds, and Call, and the two sorts of exercise paper, and the three sorts of caning, and *The Sawstonian*, the bi-terminal magazine.[12]

He it was who organised the day boys into a house and promoted their *esprit de corps*. ('Through the House one learns patriotism for the school, just as through the school one learns patriotism for the country'.) He embodies the conventional values of the public schools. Herbert's opening address to the boys begins, 'School is the world in miniature,' and he urges them to be 'patriotic, athletic, learned and religious', linking the honour of house, school and nation. ('It seemed that only a short ladder lay between the preparation room and the Anglo-Saxon hegemony of the globe'.)[13]

Forster illustrates what he considers the distorted set of priorities in his account of the choice of house master for Dunwood House at Sawston. The choice lies between prosaic, narrow, organisation-minded Pembroke and Mr Jackson, 'the only first-class intellect in the school', an inspired teacher who regularly gets scholarships at university for the best boys but cannot keep order. Pembroke gets the house. But he lacks a wife: 'He had always intended to marry when he could afford it; and once he had been in love, violently in love, but had laid the passion aside and told it to wait till a more convenient season,' further evidence of his inadequacy in the Forsterian scale of values. He arranges for Agnes to marry Rickie and for them to assist him in running the house. Rickie identifies with the bewildered and lonely new boys:

> They, like himself, must enter the beneficent machine, and learn the value of *esprit de corps*. Good luck attend them—Good luck and a happy release. For his heart would have them not in these cubicles and dormitories but each in his own dear home, amongst faces and things that he knew.[14]

What is wrong with Herbert? He is kind, unselfish, charitable, courteous, but Rickie (and Forster) conclude that he is stupid in the sense that 'his whole life was coloured by contempt for the intellect'. Herbert was interested only in success, and 'for this reason Humanity, and perhaps such other tribunals as there may be, would assuredly reject him'.

But Rickie gradually falls into the pattern that Herbert has set. He begins by wanting to be friends with the boys and inspire them with his own enthusiasm. But instead he becomes a martinet:

> It was so much simpler to be severe. He grasped the school regulations and insisted on prompt obedience to them. He adopted the doctrine of collective responsibility. When one boy was late, he punished the whole form . . . As a teacher he was rather dull. He curbed his enthusiasms, finding that they distracted his attention.[15]

He supports Herbert in his plan to reduce the number of day boys and increase the boarders, as a move to turn Sawston into a 'gimcrack Eton' gathers pace. His marriage also proves unsatisfactory. The relationship is amiable enough but lacking in depth. It had not been the fulfilment he expected. He was conscious of yearning for something more. 'He valued emotion—not for itself, but because it is the only final path to intimacy—she, ever robust and practical, always discouraged him.'[16]

Rickie becomes concerned about the life of the school, and in a discussion with his wife which is the philosophical centre of the book articulates his view, recalling his own schooldays and comparing them with life at Sawston:

> There was very little bullying at my school. There was simply an atmosphere of unkindness, which no discipline can dispel. It's not what people do to you, but what they mean that hurts . . . Physical pain doesn't hurt—at least not what I call hurt—if a man hits you by accident or in play. But just a little tap, when you know it comes from hatred, is too terrible. Boys do hate one another: I remember it and see it again. They can make strong isolated friend-

> ships, but of general good fellowship they haven't a notion . . . I do not approve of the boarding house system . . . What is the good of throwing boys so much together? Isn't it building their lives on a wrong basis? They don't understand each other. I wish they did, but they don't. They don't realise that human beings are simply marvellous. When they do, the whole of life changes and you get true things. But don't pretend you've got it before you have. Patriotism and *esprit de corps* are all very well, but masters a little forget that they must grow from a sentiment. They cannot create one. Cannot—cannot—cannot. I never cared a straw for England, until I cared for Englishmen, and boys can't love the school when they hate each other.[17]

This is Forster speaking from the heart and from experience. He goes on to contrast school with Cambridge ('these are the magic years'), where good fellowship and the true life of the intellect flourish, and home and 'the sweet family life which nurses up a boy until he can salute his equals'. His wife rejects his ideas. ('Boys ought to rough it or they never grow up into men . . . and you're wrong about patriotism. It can, can, can create a sentiment').

Rickie's view of the boarding system is borne out by the boy Varden. Although his mother wants to keep him at home, Pembroke insists that he board, and his year of boarding turns him into a sanctimonious prig. Unpopular and unpleasant, he is bullied and becomes ill. He survives and recovers but leaves, changed for the worse by boarding.

The ideal life, the life of ideas, intellect and the mind is represented by Cambridge. The novel opens in Rickie's rooms in Cambridge, where he is discussing philosophy with his friends:

> A year ago he had known none of these joys. He had crept cold and friendless and ignorant out of a great public school, preparing for a silent and solitary journey and praying as a highest favour that he might be left alone. Cambridge had not answered his prayer. She had taken and soothed him, and warmed him, and had laughed at him a little, saying that he must not be so tragic yet awhile, for his boyhood had been but a dusty corridor that led to the spacious halls of youth. In one year he had made many friends and learned much, and he might learn even more.[18]

He loves Cambridge and returns after vacations with joy. But it is a presage of the future that the Pembrokes should interrupt the philosophy colloquium and that Rickie's friends should flee from the Pembrokes. Cambridge is symbolised by Stewart Ansell, Rickie's closest friend, his conscience, the voice of disinterested truth, whom he admires and whose ideas influence him. Ansell refuses to be introduced to Agnes. Ansell, the son of a grocer whose father has spared no expense to give him a good education, discusses ideas brilliantly but is much less good on people. He strongly opposes Rickie's marriage to Agnes, realising that he is seeking an impossible ideal and that she is marrying him partly as a replacement for Gerald and partly because she thinks he is going to be a famous writer. Ansell advises against the marriage: 'Man wants to love mankind; Woman wants to love one man.'

Wiltshire is the third symbolic setting, the natural life, the life of freedom, love and truth, and liberation of the spirit. Rural England, and in particular Cadbury Rings, represent the old free pagan spirit. Rickie is drawn to the pagan. His stories, contained in a volume called 'Pan's Pipes', are about pagan themes. He declares to the disgust of Herbert, 'We've been nearly as great as the Greeks.'[19] He reads Theocritus and reveres Plato, whose works Herbert thinks disturb and confuse boys.

In Wiltshire Rickie meets the symbol of this third world, Stephen Wonham. Wonham is Natural Man. Rickie sees him as 'a man dowered with coarse kindliness and rustic strength, a kind of cynical ploughboy'. He had been expelled from public school for stealing, a potent rejection of the system and its ideas. He drinks and is violent, sleeps under the stars, gratifies his instincts when they arise. Ansell sees him as a sort of Greek god, 'frank, proud and beautiful'. When the Elliots reject him, suspecting blackmail, Ansell defends him: 'Why did he come here? Because he thought you would love him, and was ready to love you.' Ansell sees clearly that Wonham is the real thing. ('He knows more than we do. He knows everything.') Ansell wants to rescue Rickie from 'that ghastly woman'. He it is who makes a scene and reveals the true story of Stephen's birth, setting Rickie on the road to choosing Stephen over Agnes. Rickie, discovering that Stephen is not the son of his hated father, realises his duty to Stephen as his mother's son and grows to love him. ('On the banks of the grey torment of life, love is the only flower.')

Rickie asks Stephen to stay with him at Dunwood House but Stephen asks Rickie to go away with him to Wiltshire. Rickie goes, attracted by Stephen's directness, naturalness, muscularity and the fact that he is the embodiment of his mother. But Rickie remains torn between the three lives—Cambridge, Sawston and Wiltshire—and this situation is resolved by his death, saving Stephen from a train, the ultimate expression of love.

The story is, like so many of the school stories, a blend of autobiography, ideology and wish fulfilment, and it directly reflects Forster's own life and experience. Edward Morgan Forster (1879–1970), whose father died of consumption when he was ten months old, was raised by his mother 'Lily', to whom he remained passionately devoted all his life. This is reflected in Rickie's devotion to his mother. In his boyhood Forster was devoted to a succession of garden boys, in particular one called Ansell, 'his first and never-forgotten friend'.

Ansell is the name he gives to Rickie's closest friend. Forster was sent first to prep. school and then to Tonbridge as a day boy in 1893. Day boys were made to feel socially inferior, something that comes out clearly in *The Longest Journey*. 'It is not plain how much Forster was physically bullied at school,' says his biographer, P. N. Furbank. 'He must have been so to some extent, for one of his schoolmates when questioned about him in the 1950's, said, "Forster? The writer? Yes, I remember him. A little cissy. We took it out of him, I can tell you" . . . Whatever the truth about his miseries, no doubt what wounded him most was the general atmosphere of unkindness.'[20] This is certainly the attitude conveyed in Rickie's account of his own schooldays.

Forster wrote in 1933, 'School was the unhappiest time of my life, and the worst trick it ever played on me was to pretend it was the world in miniature. For it hindered me from discovering how lovely and delightful and kind the world can be.'[21] The depiction of Sawston is clearly modelled on that of Tonbridge. Its layout and hitory are identical. Its transformation in the nineteenth century was completed by the headmaster Dr Joseph Wood, who arrived just before Forster, wooed socially desirable parents, built grand new buildings, promoted *esprit de corps* through a volunteer rifle force, new houses and colours, and a new school song:

> Here shall Tonbridge flourish, here shall manhood be,
> Serving God and Country, ruling land and sea.
> . . . Choose we, for life's battle, harp or sword or pen,
> Perish every laggard, let us all be men.[22]

This distilled the essence of the message he expounded regularly in his sermons and strongly suggests that here is the prototype of Herbert Pembroke. Forster joined the classical side at Tonbridge, and the only master to inspire him was Isaac Smedley, a brilliant teacher unable to keep order and clearly the prototype of Mr Jackson in *The Longest Journey*.

When Forster went up to King's College, Cambridge, in 1897 he found the experience totally liberating. He fell in love with Cambridge, which gave him friends, stimulating conversation, the awakening of the mind. In his biography of Goldsworthy Lowes Dickinson, Forster recalled his own feelings:

> He had no idea what Cambridge meant—and I remember having the same lack of comprehension about the place myself when my own turn came to go up there. It seems too good to be real. That the public school is not infinite and eternal, that there is something more compelling in life than team-work and more vital than cricket, that firmness, self-complacency and fatuity do not between them compose the whole armour of man, that lessons may have to

do with leisure and grammar with literature—it is difficult for an inexperienced boy to grasp truth so revolutionary.[23]

Forster joined the Apostles, then under the influence of the philosopher G. E. Moore, who valued above all else 'the pleasures of human intercourse' and 'the enjoyment of beautiful objects'. It was a philosophy Forster found immensely congenial. *The Longest Journey*'s dedication *Fratribus* is a reference to the Apostles, and the opening scenes of the book recreate one of their conversations. Ansell is a blend of A. R. Ainsworth, a disciple of Moore and, more important, of Hugh Meredith, the brilliant and good-looking undergraduate who became Forster's closest friend. The Wiltshire section of the book was inspired by Forster's love of the countryside, his walking tours and in particular his visits to Figsbury Rings, Iron Age earthworks, where he met a lone shepherd who offered him a smoke of his pipe and whom he idealised as a remarkable human being.

Of all Forster's books, *The Longest Journey* was written with the greatest ease. In 1960 he recalled that he based the book on a notebook he kept at the time. He was inspired to explore several ideas: the idea of facing up to reality, the ideals of the public school, the concepts of Cambridge and Wiltshire, and Shelley's doctrine of love for all mankind.[24] In his world view all are related.

But it is more than just a book of ideas, it is also a book of wish fulfilment. There is a clear sub-text to *The Longest Journey*. Beneath the philosophical generalisations, the allegory and the symbolism, it is implicitly a homosexual love story. Forster at this time was an inhibited homosexual, not yet able to discuss the real thing that interested him— male love. In 1910 he was writing, 'However gross my desires, I find I shall never satisfy them for the fear of annoying others,' and in 1911 he complains that he cannot write because of 'weariness of the only subject that I both can and may treat—the love of man for woman and vice versa'.[25]

His depictions of marriage showed it increasingly as stultifying, arid and passionless. But after leaving Cambridge he had embarked on a love affair with his adored Hugh Meredith, a matter of kisses and embraces merely, but his first such experience and the beginning of a career of committed homosexuality. Once he had resolved completely the uncertainty about his own sexual identity, he ceased to write novels. The creative tension that had quickened the novels to life was stilled. In 1964 he confided to his diary, 'I should have been a more famous writer if I had written more or rather published more but sex has prevented the latter.'[26] He channelled much of his energy into sex, his fictional writing from 1922 to 1958 being confined to homosexual short stories 'not to express myself but to excite myself'. They were published after his death but have been described by Jeffrey Meyers as 'puerile, pathetic, sentimental and thoroughly unimaginative fantasies'.[27]

In 1907 he was not yet able to write what he wanted and he transformed the sexual element into a philosophical, social and metaphysical novel, enabling him to discuss a number of themes. It was his favourite novel because it is his classical exposition of them. But Forster scrupulously plants clues for the sub-text. Rickie is lame, like Philip Carey in *Of Human Bondage*, the creation of another homosexual writer, Somerset Maugham. In both cases it is a physical symbol of an emotional cripple, haunted by homosexuality. Rickie is declared by his friend Tilliard to be 'a little effeminate' and Tilliard believes marriage will make him 'responsible and manly'. Rickie reads Theocritus and reveres Plato, two of the key figures in the Victorian homosexual's library. Rickie hates his father and is devoted to his mother. Rickie is attracted to the idea of marriage and aroused by the sight of Agnes with Gerald Dawes, who had bullied him at school. But the language makes it clear that the actual attraction is to Dawes. Dawes is described as 'a young man who had the figure of a Greek athlete and the face of an English one. He was fair and clean-shaven and his colourless hair was cut rather short . . . Just where he began to be beautiful the clothes started. Round his neck went an up and down collar and a mauve-and-gold tie, and the rest of his limbs were hidden by a grey lounge suit, carefully creased in the right places.'[28] This is the language of desire, the desire to feast the eyes on the naked beauty of this latter-day Greek god. The description of the repulsion of Agnes and Rickie from Stephen because of the discovery that he is the illegitimate offspring of Rickie's hated father sounds in its vehemence far more like the recognition and rejection of homosexuality: 'He was illicit, abnormal, worse than a man diseased.' The attraction of Rickie to Stephen is partly due to the fact that Stephen contains the essence of Rickie's mother and partly because he is a rough, earthy countryman, a well known homosexual ideal of middle and upper-class men who can find satisfaction only with proletarians, and in Forster's case manifested in affairs with tram conductors, bus drivers and policemen. Stephen's expulsion from public school admittedly points to a higher social status but this is much less significant than his role as an idealised roughneck.

Forster is here dramatising the ideas of Edward Carpenter. Under the influence of Walt Whitman Carpenter had propounded a coherent view of male comradeship as a counterbalance to materialism, as the means of spiritualising democracy, of obtaining harmony with nature and bridging class barriers. Carpenter rejected the contemporary meaning of civilisation which he saw as based on property and bourgeois respectability, and stressed the spiritual side of male–male relations.

Indeed, the relationship of Edward Carpenter, sensitive, educated, upper-middle-class socialist and homosexual theorist, and working-class George Merrill, child of nature and the earth, who set up house together in rural bliss might almost be said to provide the model for that of Rickie and his 'brother' Stephen.[29]

This philosophy similarly informs the view of Stewart Ansell. He detests Agnes, partly because she wins Rickie from him and partly because he believes she is neither serious nor truthful, nor worthy of him. But he also elaborates a basically anti-woman philosophy, elevating Man and male–male relationships to a higher spiritual and intellectual level than the biological relations with woman:

> Man wants to love mankind; woman wants to love one man. When she has him her work is over. She is the emissary of Nature, and Nature's bidding has been fulfilled. But man does not care a damn for Nature—or at least only a very little damn. He cares for one hundred things besides, and the more civilized he is the more he will care for these other hundred things, and demand not only a wife and children, but also friends, and work, and spiritual freedom. I believe you to be extraordinarily civilized.[30]

Rickie writes back taking Ansell's letter as an admission of love:

> You couldn't know. I don't know for a moment. But this letter of yours is the most wonderful thing that has ever happened to me yet—more wonderful . . . than the moment when Agnes promised to marry me. I always knew you liked me, but I never knew how much until this letter.[31]

He insists that he loves Ansell as well and as much as his wife and that she can never come between them.

Rickie dies in the end because the tensions between his various dreams and desires is unresolved. Death and posthumous fame as a writer is the kind of adolescent fantasy the unfulfilled Forster may well have been entertaining.

It is fascinating to compare this novel with the subsequent explicitly homosexual *Maurice*, written in 1913 but not published until 1971 after Forster's death.[32] *Maurice* is in fact the novel lurking beneath the surface of *The Longest Journey*. *The Longest Journey*'s sub-text is of Rickie falling in love with Ansell in Cambridge but only realising it after he becomes engaged to Agnes, to whom he is attracted by an ideal of romance and marriage rather than any real desire. The marriage fails and he falls in love with the ideal friend, the rough countryman Stephen. In *Maurice* Maurice (= Rickie) falls in love with Clive (= Ansell). Clive, who is basically heterosexual but is experimenting with homosexuality, marries, becomes dull and conventional, and ends the relationship with Maurice. After trying to cure his condition, Maurice accepts it, falls in love with and finds happiness with the gamekeeper Alec

Scudder.

There are certain differences from *The Longest Journey* in that Maurice Hall is unlike Forster in all but his homosexuality. He is deliberately made by Forster into a very ordinary, unimaginative, rugby-playing public schoolboy, who becomes a stockbroker. But the Maurice–Clive relationship is based on Forster's own with Meredith, and Clive's eventual withdrawal from Maurice's life is reflected in Meredith's indifference to *Maurice*, which Forster found hurtful.[33] Forster, however, charts from his own experience Maurice's awakening realisation of his true feelings. At school he dreams of the ideal perfect friend, whom he would die for and who would die for him. He adores certain boys at his school (Sunnington). Then at university he falls for Clive Durham, his adoration growing against a background of adolescent ragging and theological discussion. They both read Plato's *Symposium*, *vade mecum* of Victorian homosexuals, but when Durham professes his love for Maurice, Maurice's 'suburban soul' is shocked:

> On rot! . . . Durham, you're an Englishman, I'm another. Don't talk nonsense. I'm not offended because I know you don't mean it, but it's the only subject absolutely beyond the limit as you know, it's the worst crime in the calendar, and you must never mention it again.[34]

But he overcomes his distaste. Clive and Maurice enjoy a university idyll, inspired by the Forsterian idea of the undeveloped heart being awakened by love and the familiar nineteenth-century ideal of temperate male love being the highest form of affection. It is a matter of kisses and embraces, passionate protestations and philosophical discussions, but no more. However, Forster settles in the end for the second kind of homosexual relationship, which merges emotional commitment with full sexual expression. Maurice falls for Scudder the gamekeeper, who climbs into his bedroom one night and introduces him to sex. Eventually they settle down together. Originally there had been an epilogue showing Maurice and Alec, having run away to the greenwood, happily growing old together as woodcutters. Forster wisely dropped it when friends found it ludicrous. This is the key to the explanation of why *Maurice* is so much less satisfactory a work than *The Longest Journey*, despite the fact that the account of Maurice and Clive's realisation of their feelings for one another has a painful truthfulness about it. The Alec–Maurice relationship is pure moonshine. Forster had no idea how a working-class character like Scudder would talk or behave. Forster admitted in a letter to Lowes Dickinson that wish fulfilment lay behind *Maurice*, and that fact weakens it. The appearance of Maurice in Clive's bedroom, climbing through a window to confess his love, and Alec's appearance in Maurice's bedroom in similar circumstances, have a dreamlike unreality about them which accords ill with the realistic tone of much of the narrative. Lytton Strachey, who liked the first part, was critical of the second half, perceptively opining, 'As you describe it, I should be inclined to diagnose Maurice's state as simply lust and sentiment . . . I should have prophesied a rupture after six months—chiefly as a result of lack of common interests owing to class differences.'[35]

Even the Clive–Maurice relationship has its comic side. The boys talk Edwardian slang ('Are you ragging or was your vac. really beastly, Durham?') and they persist in calling each other by their surnames as they stroke each other's hair in the first access of passion. It is hard to escape the impression that what we are seeing here is Harry Wharton and Frank Nugent of Greyfriars realising the 'true' nature of their friendship, for Maurice undoubtedly reads in part like the sort of novel Frank Richards might have written if he had suddenly and dramatically 'come out' as a homosexual. In the last analysis *Maurice* is one-dimensional and, for much of its length, dated and unconvincing. *The Longest Journey* is a much richer, multi-layered text, exploring Forster's philosophy in greater depth than was possible in *Maurice*.

The Longest Journey came out on 16 April 1907 and like Forster's first novel, *Where Angels Fear to Tread*, was a critical rather than a financial success. It was published by Blackwood's in an edition of 1,587 copies. It received respectful, if sometimes puzzled reviews. 'Easily the most striking novel published lately,' said *The Evening Standard*. 'Brilliant,' was the view of *The Times Literary Supplement* and *The Manchester Guardian*. Many reviewers found it 'clever' (*Tribune, Times Literary Supplement, Standard*). Only *Outlook* was totally hostile ('the most impossible book we have read for many years'). Forster's writing, his ideas, his drawing of atmosphere and character were widely praised, but there was criticism of the construction and of the excessive number of deaths and amount of cruelty, a reflection of Forster's own savagery about his unresolved sexual identity. *Maurice* significantly has a happier ending. Several reviewers found it 'elusive' (*The World, The Nation, The Daily News*), suggesting the existence of the sub-text, and there is an intriguing clue in *The Evening Standard*'s suspicion that the initials E. M. Forster might conceal a female author. Some declared it a book for the few rather than the many (*Birmingham Daily Post, The Daily News*) and all the evidence indicates that this was elite, oppositional fiction and in it we can see the inter-war high-culture image of public schools well and truly launched.[36]

But the dominance of the cultural image of the public school in literature at the expense of other forms of schooling and the articulate-ness of its opponents have led to a disproportionate amount of blame being attached to the public schools for inculcating attributes which are not in fact specific to them. Public schools were regularly condemned for promoting homosexuality, misogynism, anti-intellectualism, conformism and snobbery. But such criticisms are for the most part misplaced. On the one hand, public schools reflect the ideas, attitudes and structures of society at large, and, on the other, they share the characteristics of other 'total institutions', such as prisons and the armed forces, all-male communities enclosed and cut off from the outside world.

The claim that public schools turn people into homosexuals cannot be supported. Firstly, 95 per cent of adolescent males masturbate by fifteen, sometimes alone, sometimes in company. This applies to public school and non-public school boys alike. Psychologists tell us that all adolescent boys go through a homosexual phase, whether inside public schools or outside. Sexual experimentation is part of growing up. Secondly, there is clear evidence that many constitutionally homosexual men had no sexual experience at school, and conversely that many heterosexual men did have some homosexual experience in boyhood.[37] Public schools may produce greater sensitisation to homosexual instincts and situations because of the boarding situation but a recent report concludes that there is 'no evidence that homosexual activity was widespread' in boarding schools.[38]

The idea that public schools promote a contemptuous attitude towards women should also be seen in perspective. Macho masculine attitudes are by no means confined to public schools but equally characterise working-class teenage males, as all sociological and psychological studies of young male groups reveal a view of women almost indistinguishable from that ascribed to public school boys. This suggests that the public schools simply reflect more widely held social attitudes.

To attack the public schools for not producing intellectuals is unrealistic. Boys of all classes are for the most part unintellectual and do not have scholarly interests. But it is perhaps better to occupy them in games and to train their character rather than to allow them unrestrained free expression, with the consequent dangers of heedless hedonism or alienate them by a drily intellectual diet.

A. C. Benson famously lamented the lack of originality and unthinking conformism which he found in public schoolboys:

> I declare it makes me very sad sometimes to see these well-groomed, well-mannered, rational, manly boys all taking the same view of things, all doing the same things, smiling politely at the eccentricity of anyone who finds matter for serious interest in books, in art or music, perfectly correct, perfectly complacent, with no irregularities or angular preferences of their own; with no admiration for anything but athletic success and no contempt for anything but originality of ideas. They are so nice, so gentlemanly, so easy to get on with; and yet, in another region, they are so dull, so unimaginative, so narrow-minded.[39]

But most people conform. It makes life so much easier. L. P. Hartley (Eton) noted:

> In most of us the instinct towards conformity was strong enough to assimilate unpalatable experience, or reject it without too much disturbance of the nervous centres. I was law-abiding and industrious and so missed the important and exciting side of school life which consists of being at odds with authority . . . I had neither the spirit nor the inclination to 'rag' the masters . . . I deplore this timidity but I am glad I did not try to overcome it, for the role of revolutionary would not have suited me and I profited more by sitting receptive at the feet of my pastors and masters than I should have done by buzzing, mosquito-like, about their ears.[40]

It must be admitted that given the elite nature and class base of these institutions, snobbery was inescapable. But, in context, Orwell saw England as the most class-ridden country under the sun. The country gets the schools it requires. They are reflective as well as generative, and they can change when dominant values and structures change. For the public school is the microcosm of society and a sensitive barometer of change in society. It reflects what society wants of it, absorbs intellectual currents arising outside the public schools, and thus has in turn mirrored the ethos and needs of the dissolute Regency aristocracy, the Evangelical middle class, the imperialist elite and latterly the business plutocracy.

When all is said and done, boys in public schools are adolescents and, like all adolescents in all schools, chafe at restrictions on their freedom, seek to discover their sexual identities, try to make friends and establish themselves in their community and peer groups. All schools have bullies, misfits and conformists. The principal difference between State schools and public schools is that the latter are boarding schools, and that might in certain circumstances exacerbate the problems of adolescence. Equally, of course, many adolescents are unhappy at home and in conflict with their parents and only too glad to get away from them. For such boys, public schools may be a welcome haven.

Notes

1 Edward C. Mack, *Public Schools and British Opinion since 1860*, New York, 1941, 38.
2 On the continuance of the gentlemanly ideal see, for instance, Jeffrey Richards, *Visions of Yesterday*, London, 1973.
3 Graham Greene (ed.), *The Old School* (1934), Oxford, 1984, 9.
4 See, for instance, Martin J. Weiner, *English Culture and the Decline of the Industrial Spirit, 1850–1980*, Cambridge, 1981, and Corelli Barnett, *The Collapse of British Power*, London, 1972.
5 The hostile literature is surveyed in John Reed, *Old School Ties*, Syracuse,

N.Y., 1964.
6 Reed, *Old School Ties*, 135.
7 E. M. Forster, *Abinger Harvest*, London, 1936, 12.
8 Forster, *Abinger Harvest*, 5.
9 Ronald Hyam, *Britain's Imperial Century*, London, 1976, 135–48, and Ronald Hyam, 'Empire and sexual opportunity', *Journal of Imperial and Commonwealth History*, 14 (January 1986), 34–89.
10 E. M. Forster, *Two Cheers for Democracy*, London, 1951, 77-85.
11 Lionel Trilling, *E. M. Forster: a study* (1944), London, 1969, 67; J. B. Beer, *The Achievement of E. M. Forster*, London, 1968, 77.
12 E. M. Forster, *The Longest Journey* (1907), Harmondsworth, 1985, 48.
13 Forster, *Longest Journey*, 161.
14 Forster, *Longest Journey*, 163-4.
15 Forster, *Longest Journey*, 169.
16 Forster, *Longest Journey*, 171-2.
17 Forster, *Longest Journey*, 173-4.
18 Forster, *Longest Journey*, 10.
19 Forster, *Longest Journey*, 51.
20 P. N. Furbank, *E. M. Forster: a life*, I, London, 1977, 42.
21 Furbank, *Forster*, 48.
22 D. C. Somervell, *A History of Tonbridge School*, London, 1947, 98–105.
23 Frederick Crews, *E. M. Forster: the perils of humanism*, Princeton, N.J., 1962, 39.
24 E. M. Forster, *The Longest Journey*, Oxford 1960, introduction, ix-x.
25 Furbank, *E. M. Forster*, 183, 199.
26 E. M. Forster, *The Life to Come and other Stories*, Harmondsworth, 1984, introduction, 16.
27 Jeffrey Meyers, *Homosexuality and Literature, 1890-1930*, London, 1977, 110.
28 Forster, *Longest Journey*, 40.
29 See Sheila Rowbotham and Jeffrey Weeks, *Socialism and the New Life: the personal and sexual politics of Edward Carpenter and Havelock Ellis*, London, 1977, and Jeffrey Weeks, *Coming Out: homosexual politics from the nineteenth century to the present*, London, 1977, 68–83.
30 Forster, *Longest Journey*, 86-7.
31 Forster, *Longest Journey*, 88.
32 On homosexuality in Forster's work see Meyers, *Homosexuality*, 90–110, and A. O. J. Cockshut, *Man and Woman: a study of love and the novel, 1740-1940*, London, 1977, 169–81.
33 E. M. Forster, *Selected Letters*, I. ed. Mary Lago and P. N. Furbank, London, 1983, 229.
34 E. M. Forster, *Maurice*, Harmondsworth, 1983, 56.
35 Furbank, *Forster: a life*, II, London, 1978, 15.
36 The reviews are collected in Philip Gardner (ed.), *E. M. Forster: the critical heritage*, 1973, London, 65-100.
37 Geoffrey Walford, *Life in Public Schools*, London, 1986, 230-2.
38 Royston Lambert, Roger Bullock and Spencer Millham, *Chance of a Lifetime?*, London, 1975, 256-7.
39 A. C. Benson, *The Upton Letters*, London, 1905, 48.
40 Graham Greene (ed.), *The Old School*, 79-80.

8

David and Jonathan:
The Hill

The triumph of Freudianism, while in one regard it has been illuminating in explaining the nature of human relationships, has in another sense been restricting. It has reduced everything to sex. Yet, for a thousand years, a clear distinction was made between love and desire. Medieval philosophers and theologians, anxious always to classify and tabulate the varieties of human experience, listed a number of different kinds of love, between men and women, and between men and men, ranging from pure sexual desire to the noblest spiritual bond which in its striving for perfection mirrored Man's relationship with God.

In many ways the twentieth century is an anomaly in its pursuit for female equality, in its encouragement of male–female friendship and in its automatic post-Freudian suspicion of intense emotional relationships between men. Manly love has been an integral part of Western culture for 2,000 years, taken over from the Greeks by the Christians and purged by them of physicality. Its central text can be seen as the celebrated lament of David for Jonathan in 2 Samuel I, 26: 'I am distressed for thee, my brother Jonathan; very pleasant hast thou been to me; thy love for me was wonderful, passing the love of women.' This statement contains three elements: first, it constituted a form of brotherhood but of a spiritual rather than a physical kind; second, it involved notions of service and sacrifice, frequently death on behalf of the beloved; third, it is higher than and different from rather than a substitute for the love of women. The difference lies essentially in the fact that the love of women is sexual and therefore inferior; the love of a man for a man is noble, spiritual, transcendant and free from the tincture of base desire, something passing the love of women.

For 2,000 years male pair bonding was at the heart of the emotional life of the West. Romantic love between males was given literary warrant by classical Greek thought and medieval chivalry, in both of which nineteenth-century culture was steeped. The situation was complicated by the fact that nineteenth-century homosexual propagandists like Edward Carpenter and John Addington Symonds drew on the same corpus of material to justify their loves, which included the physical as well as the spiritual. But the old idea continued to prevail, as expressed by Charles, Lord Metcalfe, who wrote of 'the joys . . . in the pure love which exists between man and man, which cannot I think, be surpassed by the more alloyed attachment between the opposite sexes, to which the name of love is generally applied.'[1] Charles Kingsley, the great celebrant of married love, wrote to his wife, 'Remember, the man is the stronger vessel. There is something awful, spiritual, in man's love for each other . . . Had you been a man we should have been like David and Jonathan.'[2]

This points us towards the explanation. Victorian England, like ancient Greece or the medieval West, was a male-dominated society. For the upper middle class, life revolved around all-male institutions: public schools, university, the armed forces, the Church, Parliament, clubs and the City. Marriage tended to be deferred for social and economic reasons. Professor Henry Fawcett declared in 1865:

> As a general rule a man does not marry in the middle and upper classes unless he believes that he shall at any rate be able to give his children as good an education as he himself received, and be also able to place them in a social position, similar to that which he himself occupies. The majority of men are accustomed to some particular style of living, and they generally refrain from marriage if the increased expenses of married life would compel them to live in a manner which would not give them what has been aptly termed 'their habitual standard of comfort'.[3]

Women were sidelined, exploited as sex objects or worshipped as goddesses. For true emotional fulfilment, the intensity of personal relationships not supplied by parents, women or children, many men became enthusiastic proponents of male comradeship and male love as the central factor of their existence. Among them were clergymen, schoolmasters, dons and army officers, who were regularly bachelors and looked on male love as finer, nobler and more fulfilling than any other, just as ancient Greece and the early medieval West had, and for the same reasons. The consensus clearly was that manly love was essentially spiritual. It was a central strand in 'manliness', and manliness is at the heart of the value system of the public schools.

A number of different kinds of love could be found at public school. When E. M. Forster was urging 'only connect' and citing the public school as a loveless place, he was perhaps reflecting the perspective of the shy day boy. There will have been a good deal of 'connecting' of all kinds going on in the boarding houses of his old school. The different forms of love could be found singly, successively or simultaneously in adolescent relationships. There is romantic friendship, which is chaste, uplifting and emotionally fulfilling. There is hero worship, which involves the adoration of an idealised role model and the projection of self on to that model. It is now generally accepted that adolescent boys go through a homosexual phase and that it may or may not involve physical relations. But equally some boys remain ignorant of sexual feelings until after their schooldays. To reduce all adolescent relationships to sex is unnecessarily restricting and impoverishing. Love is a highly complex thing. A schoolboy's first experience of love can be one of the most intense of his life. As Benjamin Disraeli memorably recorded:

> At school, friendship is a passion. It entrances the being; it tears the soul. All loves of after-life can never bring its rapture or its wretchedness; no bliss so absorbing, no pangs of jealousy or despair so crushing or so keen! What tenderness and devotion; what illimitable confidence; what infinite revelations of inmost thoughts; what ecstatic present and romantic future; what bitter estrangements and what melting reconciliations; what scenes of wild recrimination, agitating explanations, passionate correspondence; what insane sensitiveness, and what frantic sensitivity; what earthquakes of the heart and whirlwinds of the soul are confined in that simple phrase, a schoolboy's friendship! 'Tis some indefinite recollection of these mystic passages of their young emotions that makes grey-haired men mourn over the memory of their schoolboy days.[4]

The official approved brand of love was manly love and its inculcation began early. In their lessons, their reading, the sermons they heard in chapel, public school boys were prepared for close male friendships. Spiritual love between males, comradeship, validated by Greek and medieval models, centred on admiration for their manliness—courage, virtue, skill, beauty, honour—was beamed at them from all sides. It channelled, directed and shaped the inherent and instinctive romanticism of the adolescent male. Alec Waugh described this state perfectly in *Public School Life*:

> A boy of seventeen is passing through a highly romantic period. His emotions are searching for a focus. He is filled with wild, impossible loyalties. He longs to surrender himself to some lost cause. He hungers for adventures. On occasions he even goes so far as to express himself in verse, an indiscretion that he will never subsequently commit. And what focus does a Public School provide for this eager emotionalism? There are the fierce contests of the football field, but they are, when all is said and done, the business of life, the cause for his existence. They are an enthusiasm he shares with three hundred others; he is, in fact, in love with love; he does not see a girl of his own age, his own class, from one end of the term to the other; it is in human nature to accept the second best.[5]

But national concern about schoolboy friendships began to be expressed in the 1880s, the decade which saw the celebrated Labouchere amendment to the Criminal Law Amendment Act of 1885, which effectively brought all forms of homosexual activity within the scope of the law, the beginning of the scientific definition and formulation of the condition of homosexuality and the breaking of the Cleveland Street scandal around a male brothel frequented by notable figures of the day.[6] The increasing concern about and attention paid to the question of homosexuality nationally flowed down to the schools. By 1900 many leading public schools officially or unofficially prohibited associations between boys from different forms or different houses. But such associations went underground rather than disappearing. This development represented a decisive break with the attitude which had prevailed previously in the public schools. G. E. L. Cotton, headmaster of Marlborough, had preached a sermon in 1857 extolling schoolboy friendships, especially those between older and younger boys, quoting John 13, 23, with reference to the disciple 'whom Jesus loved' and who leaned on his bosom. Cotton argued that unselfish love should inform such friendships and through them the boys would be brought nearer to God.[7] Similarly in *Tom Brown's Schooldays* a friendship between Tom and the younger George Arthur is encouraged by Dr Arnold to benefit them both. Dean Farrar, author of *Eric*, wrote in a later book, *St Winifred's or the World of School*, 'Of all earthly friendships few are more beautiful or in some respects more touching than a friendship between two boys.'[8] Both Hughes and Farrar, founding fathers of the school story, highlighted intense friendships but were careful to distinguish them from more fleshly and reprehensible associations, whose existence they recognised. The friendship they were endorsing was exclusively of the manly, improving and spiritual kind.

The one reference to sex in *Tom Brown* is guarded but, given Hughes's candour, clear. Tom and East are ordered to fag for a sixthformer by his pet, and they rough the boy up. 'He was one of miserable little pretty white-handed, curly-headed boys, petted and pampered by some of the big fellows, who wrote their verses for them, taught them to drink and use bad language and did all they could to spoil them for everything in this world and the next.' Hughes adds a footnote: 'A kind and wise critic, an old Rugboean, notes here in the margin: "The small friend system was not so utterly bad from 1841 to 1847." Before that, too, there were many noble friendships between big and little boys, but I can't strike out the passage; many boys will know why it is left in.' Tom declares of the small boy, 'Worst sort we breed. Thank goodness, no big fellow ever took to petting me.'[9] This unhealthy and unwholesome conduct is contrasted with Tom's pure and manly love for Arthur, which wells up when he sees Arthur on his sick bed: 'Never till that moment had he felt how his little chum had twined himself round his heart-strings.'[10]

F. W. Farrar begins his novel *Julian Home* (1859) with an account of the friendship of Julian and Hugh Lillyston at Horton School:

> They were continually together and never tired of each other's society; and at last when their tutor, observing and thoroughly approving of the friendship, put them in the same room, the school began in fun to call them Achilles and Patroclus, Damon and Pythias, Orestes and Pylades, David and Jonathan, Theseus and Pirithous, and as many other names of *paria amicorum* as they could remember . . . Lillyston instructed Julian in the mysteries of fives, racquets, football and cricket, until he became an adept at them all; and Julian, in return, gave Lillyston very efficient help in work, and inspired him with intellectual tastes for which he felt no little gratitude in after days . . . I am glad to dwell on such a picture, knowing, O Holy Friendship, how awfully a schoolboy can sometimes *desecrate* thy name![11]

It is clear that Farrar is propagandising for spiritual friendship in the full awareness of what was darkly called 'beastliness' among boys.

It is against this background that we can see the importance of and the interpretation provided by the role models from Greek and medieval culture. The literature of Greece, in which public schoolboys of the Victorian age were steeped, was rich in pairs of male friends, the test of whose friendship was to offer or to sacrifice their lives for love of the other: Orestes and Pylades, Damon and Pythias, Nisus and Euryalus, Achilles and Patroclus, Theseus and Pirithous, Hercules and Hylas. Whether in their original Greek setting they were Platonic lovers or Aristotelian friends, for the nineteenth century they were idealised chivalric comrades, the counterparts of David and Jonathan as exemplars of loving brotherhood. Victorian public schools, like Victorian society in general, became just as saturated in the legends, images and ethos of chivalry as those of ancient Greece. The chivalric code was reformulated to provide a living and meaningful code of behaviour for nineteenth-century gentlemen, who were seen as the embodiments of bravery, loyalty and courtesy, modesty, purity and honour. The classic stories of medieval romance, among them Roland and Oliver, Amis and Amile and the Round Table, were endlessly retold. J. H. Skrine, Warden of Trinity College, Glenalmond, wrote in 1898 of public school life, 'Chivalry it is again and this is the reason why the life of the school has romance.'[12] He probably did not have in mind romantic love between older and younger boys, but Alec Waugh, writing from first-hand experience, invoked chivalric imagery when describing it. It was, he recalled:

> A particular kind of love; an idealistic, un-self-seeking, Platonic love; a love that is based on service and devotion, that has a kinship with the love practised by the troubadours in the medieval courts of love. The very nature

of the emotion precludes all possibility of personal satisfaction. Such satisfaction, such gratification, would be a desecration of one's own high feelings. Such malpractices as one might enjoy were on a different level of emotion.[13]

In such love, different strands of teaching, thought and feeling overlap. It is only in recent years that serious, systematic, scholarly study has been undertaken of sex and love in public schools. In his authoritative analysis of boarding and public schools in the 1960s Royston Lambert stressed that the situation was 'much more complex and varied' than the old canard of the unqualified link between the public schools and homosexuality.[14] Lambert stresses the importance of sex:

> To the adolescents of thirteen and over who form the vast majority of boarders, the development, control and fulfilment of their sexual energies is a matter of overriding personal importance and a subject which pervades the talk, the imagery, the humour and the activity of the communal underlife.[15]

Nevertheless boys distinguish clearly between that and comradeship: 'The majority . . . stress the closeness and warmth of the all-male community where deep and lasting friendships are made (with no homosexual connotations) and society is not divided by sexual competitiveness'.[16] One seventeen-year-old boy at an independent school observed, 'Girls couldn't create this sense of community and comradeship—real affection and loyalty to each other. A marvellous sense of togetherness and teamwork.'[17] The absence of women can also lead to shyness and unease in their company, ignorance of them, *macho* behaviour (dirty jokes, filthy language). Two principal reactions result: to idealise women as pure, unattainable objects of adoration or to regard them as merely sex objects. But what is rarely pointed out is that such behaviour is common among non-public school and non-boarding school boys and youths. A number of authoritative studies of working-class adolescent males have pointed to the characteristic obsession with sex, the all-male groups, the swaggering macho attitudes, suggesting a wider cultural provenance for such a mind set.[18]

Lambert concluded, 'single sex . . . boarding definitely stimulates the pupils' homosexual instincts and their perception of it as a sexual response and an "ethos" '.[19] But he added that schools were not hotbeds of sexual activity, that many boys exercised self-control and repressed their feelings and that there was probably a good deal more homosexual talk than homosexual activity. But there are strong differences between and within schools:

> Boys in single sex boarding schools are always individually sensitized to and more aware of homosexuality than others, but the collective behaviour and the life of the schools may show little discernible trace of it. The causes of

the homosexual behaviour and life of schools are therefore much more subtle and complex than most boarders think: it is subtle compounds of social structure, tradition, and even the alchemy of individual personalities which work on the conditioning single-sex situation of some schools and activate the homosexuality latent in them.[20]

Two forces powerfully shape the incidence and kind of homosexuality. One is official policy, which can be tolerant, repressive or manipulative, sometimes all three. (By manipulative is meant a situation in which masters recognise the need for emotional relationships and seek to utilise them for good.) The other is pupils' attitudes, which can be repressive or tolerant or actively supportive. In some schools, homosexuality is frowned on by the boys. In a majority of schools, pupil society is 'tolerant always of emotional relationships, often of sex between contemporaries, less often of sex between older and junior boys if accompanied by emotion, but never of sex between older and junior boys in which the older one enforced his desire on the younger.'[21] In another group of schools, homosexual relationships are encouraged and any other form of behaviour is deviation. Pupil norms can change, and within two or three years homosexuality can change from being fashionable to being barely tolerated, or the reverse.

Sexual activity usually centres on mutual masturbation as part of young boys' exploration of their bodies and themselves. 'Most boys experience some physical activity with others at some stage in their school career, usually as junior boys,' declares Lambert. This may continue up to sixth-form level. But 'for many boys aged fifteen and more it is . . . the emotional side which dominates frequently unaccompanied by the mutual physical activities catalogued above'.[22] Some junior boys trade on their attractiveness, to become school 'tarts'. These relationships are 'seldom accompanied by physical sex but in some cases generate stylized codes of conduct and rituals reminiscent of medieval courtly love'.[23] The evidence suggests that serious sexual activity in the upper reaches of the school is confined to a small minority. Lambert, concludes, 'it is unlikely that more than a minority will be permanently homosexual after they leave'.[24] The psychiatrist Anthony Storr takes the same view:

> There is little evidence to suppose that public school life does in fact breed homosexuals. Whether or not one believes that the factors causing a predominantly homosexual inclination in adult life are genetic or environmental, there is no doubt that these factors have made their main impact long before a boy is old enough to enter public school; in most cases, before he goes to preparatory school. Whilst homosexual contacts at public school may postpone the development of heterosexual interest, or serve to bring out or underline a latent homosexual inclination, there is little reason to fear that such

contacts will have much permanent effect in altering the direction of a boy's sexual interests.[25]

Although evidence from the past is necessarily anecdotal and impressionistic, it strongly confirms the picture arrived at by Lambert's research. In some schools—a minority—homosexual activity was frowned on by boys and master alike. United Services College, Westward Ho! was one such. In his autobiography Kipling commented:

> Naturally Westward Ho! was brutal enough, but setting aside the foul speech that a boy ought to learn early and put behind him by his seventeenth year, it was clean with a cleanliness that I have never heard of in any other school. I remember no cases of even suspected perversion, and am inclined to the theory that if masters did not suspect them, and show that they suspected, there would not be quite so many elsewhere. Talking things over with Cormell Price afterwards, he confessed that his own prophylactic against certain unclean microbes was to 'send us to bed dead tired'. Hence the wideness of our bounds and his deaf ear towards our incessant riots and wars.[26]

General Dunsterville confirmed Kipling's impression, proclaiming U.S.C. 'a notably clean school in every sense of that word'.[27] This is directly reflected in *Stalky and Co.* in the absence of any reference to sex.

There was in more schools a good deal of sexual frolicking among younger boys, in some cases an extension of bullying, in others an expression of adolescent coltishness, in yet more a ritualisation of ways of relieving adolescent sexual tension. Sensitive and fastidious boys were repelled by this kind of behaviour. John Addington Symonds, who was at Harrow between 1854 and 1858, was extremely unhappy there, detested games, disliked competition, was perpetually unwell and was regarded as 'uncomradely and unclubbable' by his companions. He wrote:

> Every boy of good looks had a female name, and was recognised either as a public prostitute or as some big fellow's 'bitch' . . . The talk in the dormitories and studies was incredibly obscene. Here and there one could not avoid seeing acts of onanism, mutual masturbation, the sports of naked boys in bed together. There was no refinement, no sentiment, no passion; nothing but animal lust in these occurrences. They filled me with disgust and loathing.[28]

During his first half the 'beasts' tried to seduce him and failed, and he remained 'in fact and act free from this contamination'.

The philosopher and historian Goldsworthy Lowes Dickinson, at Charterhouse from 1874 to 1881, proclaimed his house 'a hothouse of vice' but declared that he 'wasn't interested in it and didn't attend to it. As I write there comes back to me a picture in the room where we changed for exercise, of a bigger boy masturbating against a smaller, amid a crowd of admirers. I passed on feeling awkward but otherwise indifferent.' He too was deeply unhappy at school, feeling 'alone as I have never been alone since, physically unfit, mentally undeveloped' and with 'not one of those passionate friendships or loves which redeem school for many boys'.[29]

Brian Inglis, who was at Shrewsbury in the 1920s, recalled that opinion about physical relationships was mixed among the boys:

> there was some impression that, like smoking, that sort of thing was bad for training. But in a monastic institution of this kind furtive sexual exploration was inevitably as common as the limited privacy allowed it to be. There were few 'queers' in the adult sense; it was sexuality rather than homosexuality.[30]

The writer and radio producer Hallam Tennyson, a self-proclaimed pacifist and Marxist, found Eton in the 1930s 'humming with sexual activity'. For eighteen months he had a relationship with Miles, 'a lean athletic boy of my age', which consisted of mutual masturbation. ('There was no guilt, no emotion; it was uncomplicated, wholly monogamous and curbed only by the exigencies of training'.) When the existence of a mutual masturbation club was discovered, a list of 200 names was eventually produced by investigation and the authorities called a halt. 'Parents were summoned and trod the streets with grave aspect, and one boy, a peer, was sacked for sodomy. The scandal subsided.' But Tennyson also testifies to the localised nature of such behaviour. His cousin Harold, two divisions above him, experienced nothing of it and claimed his reports were exaggerated, 'which seems to show how local and temporary such phases are, and how dangerous it is to generalise from them'.[31] The existence of cycles of beastliness, eras of puritanism and hedonism in the life of the same school, is confirmed by E. F. Benson (Marlborough), who writes in *David Blaize* of school fads and fashions:

> Morals are subject to the same strict but changeable etiquette; for years perhaps the most admirable tone characterises a house, then another code obtains, and Satan himself might be staggered by the result.[32]

Then there are those romantic friendships, 'that love too deep for words or touch' as Betjeman called it, recalling his Marlborough schooldays. These were in the majority. Giles Romilly, whose chief emotion had hitherto been one of acute and interminable boredom, found his life at Wellington in the 1930s lit up by love:

> For though completely innocent, and shocked at the idea of relations between people of the same sex, and not knowing even in what such relations consisted, I began to fall in love with boys younger than myself. This was more of a

pastime than anything else, and it was a very good one. It gave a flavour to meals and chapels and lectures, it coloured my existence out of school, which became an endless manoeuvring for glances, an incessant insincere agitation of the heart, a rapid fluctuation between wistful bitterness and triumph. It also gave me material for a diary, and a subject for conversation of which neither I nor my friends ever tired.[33]

T. C. Worsley, who was at Marlborough in the 1920s, and was a keen and capable cricketer, so detested the scatalogical and sexual talk of the other boys that he travelled in a separate compartment to away matches to avoid it. He recalled his devotion to the cricket captain, nicknamed from his handsome Greek profile 'Bacchus':

Bacchus had engaged my affections to an absurd and exclusive degree. I thought of no one else. I didn't think of him, let me say, in any sexual connection. I didn't at that time even know I could. But I was content only in his company—I might almost say, alive only when with him. And since cricket was the centre of his life, as of mine—in the holidays as well as in the term—that summer when he took possession of my feelings had been idyllic.[34]

Wilfrid Blunt, who was at Marlborough from 1914 to 1920 and was a total misfit in school, hating games and the corps, was in fact very happy. His happiness lay in his love of the countryside and in his romantic friendships. He described in his autobiography his adoration of two boys, whom he calls 'Walter Paxton' and 'Francis Temple-Benson':

On my side a kind of worship that was amply rewarded by a shy smile on the staircase, a few words exchanged in the dormitory, an unforgettable duet with Paxton in 'Canning's Room'; a game or two of fives with Temple-Benson and with him also a picnic on Martinsell.

But these friendships were totally innocent. Blunt, ignorant of the facts of life, only vaguely aware of sex, recalled of those times:

The tone in Canning's was—outwardly at all events—in general so 'pure' that I did not really understand the whispered, sniggering references to certain arcane practices alleged to take place in the denser thickets of Manton Coppice. At Marlborough nobody ever tried to seduce me.[35]

The idea that homosexuals are created by the public schools is not borne out by the memoirs of a number of eminent self-confessed homosexuals. John Addington Symonds and Goldsworthy Lowes Dickinson had no sexual relationships at school and were repelled by the general atmosphere of lewdness. T. C. Worsley did not become aware of his sexual orientation until after he had left Marlborough. J. R. Ackerley (1896–1967), for many years literary editor of *The*

Listener and in adult life a promiscuous homosexual, found himself at Rossall 'more repelled than attracted to sex, which seemed to me a furtive, guilty, soiling thing, nothing to do with these feelings I had not yet experienced, but about which I was already writing a lot of dreadful sentimental verse, called romance and love'. Apart from a few 'furtive fumblings', he had no physical contact with anyone and remained a virgin until he went up to Cambridge.[36] All four men became aware of their homosexuality only after leaving school.

Conversely, heterosexuals testify to the lack of permanent effect upon them of homosexual flirtations. Louis MacNeice, recalling Marlborough in the 1920s, noted that:

> Nearly all the elder boys had their mild homosexual romances—an occasion for billets and giggling and elaborately engineered rendezvous—I picked on a dark-haired boy of sixteen who had large grey feminine eyes and asked him illicitly to tea. I then wrote a poem about Circe on a marble balcony.[37]

But his heterosexuality asserted itself as soon as he left school. Cecil Day Lewis, who arrived at Sherborne in 1917,

> was initiated early into what schoolmasters call 'immorality' . . . My own disposition to join the herd, together with a natural sensuousness which was ripe to become sensuality, and my total ignorance of the 'facts of life', made me a destined victim . . . I had taken to vice like a duck to water, but it ran off me like water from a duck's back—in the sense that it was not to warp my normal heterosexual responses later.[38]

Yet school could encourage a 'homosexual ethos'. This has been famously commented on by Robert Graves and Cyril Connolly. Graves (1895-1985) was intensely unhappy at Charterhouse. ('From the moment I arrived at school I suffered an oppression of spirit that I hesitate now to recall in its full intensity'.) The school consisted of 600 boys, whose 'chief interests were games and romantic friendships. School work was despised by everyone.' As a scholarly boy who liked academic work he felt out of it. As a sexually innocent boy he detested the bawdy talk. He was at odds with the masters and the 'bloods' throughout. He resigned from the O.T.C., was not outstanding at games, was permanently short of money and was believed wrongly to be a German Jew. On all these counts he was detested, suffered from bullying and came close to a nervous breakdown. He took up boxing and this provided him with some protection. But school was also made bearable by love. Graves draws an important distinction between amorousness ('a sentimental falling in love with younger boys') and eroticism ('adolescent lust'):

> The intimacy . . . that frequently took place was practically never between

an elder boy and the object of his affection, for that would have spoiled the romantic illusion, which was heterosexually cast. It was between boys of the same age who were not in love, but used each other coldly as convenient sex instruments. So the atmosphere was always heavy with romance of a very conventional early-Victorian type, yet complicated by cynicism and foulness.[39]

Interestingly, an eighteen-year-old public schoolboy who spoke to Lambert in the 1960s made the same point, stressing the difference between sex life and emotional love life, the former secret, the latter openly discussed and common.[40]

At Charterhouse Graves fell in love with 'Dick', three years younger than himself and 'exceptionally intelligent and fine spirited'. But he was 'unconscious of sexual feeling'. It was a deeply romantic affair. Warned by one master to end it, he refused, insisting it was chaste and based on a shared interest in books. Graves was by now writing poetry and editing the school magazine, *The Carthusian* ('Poetry and Dick were now the only two things that really mattered'). Graves retained his devotion to Dick, through regularly exchanged letters, when he joined up and was serving on the western front. It was there that he read that Dick (now sixteen) had been taken to court for soliciting a Canadian corporal who had promptly given him in charge. Graves was shattered and decided Dick must have been driven mad by the war. He concluded bitterly:

> In English preparatory and public schools romance is necessarily homosexual. The opposite sex is despised and hated, treated as something obscene. Many boys never recover from this perversion. I only recovered by a shock at the age of twenty-one. For every one born homosexual, there are at least ten permanent pseudo-homosexuals, made by the public school system. And nine out of ten are as honourably chaste and sentimental as I was.[41]

Cyril Connolly (1903–74) who was at Eton from 1918 to 1922, was unhappy in his first few years at Eton. At fifteen he was 'dirty, inky, miserable, untidy, a bad fag, a coward at games, lazy at work, unpopular with my masters and superiors, anxious to curry favour and bully when I dared'.[42] He blossomed in his last two years, finding his feet in a group of aesthetes and noncomformists. Love was his consolation, and he was in love with a succession of boys:

> I had never even been kissed, and love was an ideal based on the exhibitionism of the only-child. It meant a desire to lay my personality at someone's feet as a puppy deposits a slobbery ball; it meant a non-stop daydream, a planning of surprises, an exchange of confidences, a giving of presents, an agony of expectation, a delirium of impatience, ending with the premonition of boredom more drastic than the loneliness which it set out to cure. I was now

entering adolescence and for long was to suffer from that disfiguring ailment. My sense of values was to be affected, my emotions falsified, my mind put out of focus, my idea of reality imposed on reality and where they did not tally, reality would be cut to fit.[43]

Connolly was a classic case of public school conditioning, a conditioning so complete that he believed himself to be homosexual and was surprised to discover in 1927 that he was not and to begin pursuing the opposite sex. He described homosexuality as 'the forbidden tree around which our little Eden dizzily revolved'. Work was not valued and the boys' lives centred on popularity and relationships. Yet they were relationships of a singular purity, for when he left at eighteen and a half, Connolly observed, 'I had never had sexual intercourse, I had never masturbated.'[44]

Literature before World War I tended to be of the kind Lambert describes as manipulative, recognising the emotional relationships and seeking to define and channel them in acceptable directions. The most celebrated example of public school romance is Horace Annesley Vachell's *The Hill: a romance of friendship* (1905). It was an immediate best-seller, garnering a wealth of praise: 'the best book about schoolboys since *Tom Brown*' (*Daily News*); 'no better school story has ever been written' (*Literary World*); 'quite the best story of school life which our generation has produced' (*The Tablet*). It was thought to be true to life: 'for psychological insight and clearness of characterisation it may be put beside the few masterpieces of literature about adolescence' (*Pall Mall Gazette*); 'This is really public school life which is described' (*Manchester Guardian*). It was deemed to be 'manly': 'of the same manly and inspiring type as Tom Hughes' famous book' (*The Scotsman*); 'a fine, wholesome and thoroughly manly novel' (*Ladies' Field*).

Vachell's first best-seller had been *Brothers*, and he described that and *The Hill* as his 'heavenly twins'. For ten years they remained best-sellers, but, although they sold neck and neck, Vachell received ten letters about *The Hill* for every one about *Brothers*. In 1937 he recorded that he was still receiving letters from young people about *The Hill*.[45] *The Hill* went through nine editions in 1905 and had gone through twenty-one in 1914.

Alec Waugh testifies to the role of *The Hill* in institutionalising romantic friendship:

> The schoolboy has read *The Hill*. He expects every Verney to find a Desmond. So much has been written about the lasting friendships of school life. Every boy must have his 'special friend'. Why should he be any different from his fellows?[46]

The Hill charts the course of John Verney's career at Harrow, from his arrival and the introduction of the new boy to customs, traditions, slang and rituals, through ragging, prep. and sport to his leaving with a scholarship to Christchurch, Oxford. But the heart of the story is the love of shy, scholarly and religious John—son of a parson who died in the service of the poor and nephew of a famous Old Harrovian explorer— for handsome, aristocratic Harry Desmond, son of a Cabinet Minister and the product of several generations of Harrovians. It is Desmond who clearly incarnates that 'harmony of strenuousness and sentiment' that Vachell sees as the essence of public school life. Desmond is nick-named 'Caesar' but Verney 'Jonathan' because of his devotion to Desmond, thus invoking the archetypal male relationship, David and Jonathan. Very early on Verney is seized by 'a wild and unreasonable yearning for this boy's friendship'. Initially he worships at a distance, but then after a house match tells Desmond he dislikes Scaife because Scaife likes Desmond and is not good enough for him. 'You've stuck me on a pedestal,' says Harry. 'Yes,' says John.

> For a moment, they stood alone, ten thousand leagues from Harrow, alone in those sublimated spaces where soul meets soul unfettered by flesh. After-wards, not then, John knew that this was so. He met the real Desmond for the first time, and Desmond met the real John in a thoroughfare other than that which leads to the Manor, other than that which leads to any house built by human hands, upon the shining highway of Heaven.[47]

This passage clearly establishes the relationship as mystical, spiritual, transcending flesh, beyond the love of women, the ultimate, perfect, infrangible male friendship. In a celebrated and much quoted passage, which underlines the spirituality of the relationship, Desmond comes to realise his love for Verney, when Verney is singing before the school:

> John was singing like a lark, with a lark's spontaneous delight in singing, with an ease and self-abandonment which charmed eye almost as much as ear. Higher and higher rose the clear, sexless notes, till two of them met and mingled in a triumphant trill. To Desmond, that trill was the answer to the quavering troubled cadences of the first verse; the vindication of the spirit soaring upwards unfettered by the flesh—the pure spirit, not released from the pitiful human clay without a fierce struggle. At that moment Desmond loved the singer—the singer who called to him out of heaven, who summoned his friend to join him, to see what he saw—'the vision splendid'.[48]

Anyone who doubts the authenticity of this account should note the testimony of Wilfrid Blunt, who recalled how he fell in love with Rupert Goodall at Marlborough:

For me it began at a precise moment one evening at the beginning of that February. It was the custom, a fortnight or so after the start of the term, for new boys to stand up and sing for the entertainment of their dormitory. The songs chosen usually ranged from music-hall ditties to hardy perennials such as 'John Peel' . . . Goodall . . . chose Sterndale Bennett's 'Maydew' and sang it in the purest soprano imaginable. Everyone felt awkward—awkward as one feels when an improper story has been told in unsuitable company . . . As for me, I was captivated. I knew that he must be my friend. It was what in other circumstances would be called 'love at first sight'. Or perhaps I should say 'at first *sound*'.[49]

Desmond and Verney confess their feelings for each other and become firm friends. Desmond defends Verney from bullying. They go for walks together, hours 'which he came to regard as perhaps the most delightful hours spent at Harrow'. The relationship is put under strain when Desmond wants John to stop swotting for the Shakespeare Medal. But John's sense of duty makes him refuse and he wins the medal.

Then Verney engages in battle for Harry's soul with Reginald 'Demon' Scaife, a brilliant sportsman but bad-hat who leads Desmond into evil ways. Scaife likes Desmond 'better than any fellow at Harrow' and is jealous of Verney. Scaife 'gambled . . . drank . . . denied his body nothing it craves'. He glories in the excitement of breaking the law and implicitly pursues the pleasures of the flesh.

As the years pass, John wins history and literature prizes and excels in scholarship, Desmond in sport. But Desmond continues to be captivated by Scaife, his 'amazing grace, good looks and audacity'. In his last year Scaife is 'the most remarkable boy at Harrow, the Admirable Crichton who appears now and then in every decade'. John and Desmond still walk together, and in the setting of an abandoned and reputedly haunted house Desmond has a premonition of death, and John gazes at him, entranced. 'Through the circling cloud of tobacco-smoke, John stared at the face which had illuminated nearly every hour of his school life. Its peculiar vividness always amazed John, the vitality of it, and yet the perfect delicacy.'[50] John exerts his influence over Desmond to persuade him to give up smoking. But Scaife provokes a quarrel between them and they are estranged. The Eton and Harrow match at Lord's provides a great set piece. Harrow wins and Desmond catches the Eton captain out. He is the hero of the hour, John congratulates him and they are reconciled. But Scaife persuades Demond to break out of school and go up to London as a bet. John goes in his place, is caught, faced with expulsion, and Desmond tells the house master that John did it to save him. Scaife's influence is broken and true friendship triumphs over unholy desire. John, destined for Parliament, wins a scholarship to Oxford, and Harry heads for

South Africa, war and the Guards. There is a tight-lipped laconic parting at the station:

'Goodbye, old Jonathan. Wish you were coming!'
'Goodbye, Caesar. Good luck.'

Desmond dies heroically in the Boer War.[51] The headmaster of Harrow preaches a sermon which contains the essence of the book's ideology. It praises noble, self-sacrificing death:

To die young, clean, ardent; to die swiftly, in perfect health; to die saving others from death, or—worse—disgrace; to die scaling heights; to die and to carry with you into the fuller, ampler life beyond, untainted hopes and aspirations, unembittered memories, all the freshness and gladness of May— is not that cause for joy rather than sorrow. I say—yes . . . Better death, a thousand times, than gradual decay of mind and spirit; better death than faithlessness, indifference and uncleanness.[52]

Vachell records that when his own son, Richard, an officer in the Royal Flying Corps, was killed in action in 1916 a woman sent him these lines from *The Hill*. He does not record what he made of them.[53]

The head also praises friendship—'the heart's blood of a public school; friendship with its delights, its perils, its peculiar graces and benedictions'—and he points to Harry Desmond as a role model, whose memory 'stands in our records for all we venerate and strive for: loyalty, honour, purity, strenuousness, faithfulness in friendship'. The grieving Verney is consoled by a last letter from Desmond, written on the eve of battle: 'Old Jonathan, you have been the best friend a man ever had, the only one I love as much as my own brothers—*and even more*' (Vachell's italics).[54]

This is the true friendship, the pure, unsullied love of man for man, and it is reinforced by the counterpoint of profane, fleshly, unholy love. When the unpopular house master Rutford leaves and Mr Warde takes over his house, the Manor, he sets himself to purge undesirable elements. Lawrence, the head of house, urges Desmond and Scaife to back Warde up. The evil that Warde wants to tackle is 'beastliness', i.e. sexual malpractices:

Desmond knew that there were beasts at the Manor. Had you forced from him an expression approaching, let us say, definiteness, he would have admitted that beasts lurked in every house, in every school in the kingdom. You must keep out of their way (and ways)—that was all. And he knew also that too many beasts wreck a house, as they wreck a regiment or a nation.[55]

Scaife does not share Desmond's cut-and-dried view of good and evil. He rejects Warde's appeal for reform: 'As for sympathy and fellowship and pulling together between masters and boys, I never did believe in

it and never shall. My hand is against the masters so long as they interfere with anything I want to do.'[56]

'Beastliness' is embodied in Thomas Beaumont-Greene, who
combines everything that Vachell detests: 'pulpy, pimply, gross in mind
and body, he stood for that heavy, amorphous resistance to good,
which is so difficult to overcome', 'a type of boy unhappily too common
at public school'. He has no feeling for Harrow. He seeks only to 'run,
hotfoot, towards anything which would yield pleasure to his body'.[57]
He is a funk at footer, a prodigious consumer of food at the Creameries,
the school tuck shop, an 'imperfect ablutioner'; he puts on side; his
father is in trade. He makes sexual advances to 'Fluff', and when 'Fluff'
tells John, Verney sternly warns Beaumont-Greene off. 'Fluff' is Lord
Esmé Kinloch, son of the Duke of Trent, who, with 'his delicately-
tinted face, the small, regular, girlish features, the red, quivering mouth',
falls for Verney, wants to be like him, appeals to him for protection,
tells him, 'You're the only boy I ever met whom I really wanted for a
friend.'[58] Esmé's love for John is expressed by his desire to do well in
sport to please him, and he lies awake thinking about premature death
and John's remorse. John is kind to 'Fluff', spends part of his holidays
at Whiteladies, the Duke of Trent's place, and allows 'Fluff' to use his
Christian name. It is a kind of hero worship, similar in a sense to John's
reverence for Lawrence, the head of house, who in his eyes 'occupied
a position near the apex of the world's pyramid of great men'.

The romantic story and its counterpoint are underscored by a
strong strain of class-consciousness, but this also breaks down into its
contrasting good and bad forms. The principal object of this emotion
is 'Demon' Scaife, who, although keen at games, popular in the house,
clever at work, generous with money, handsome and well mannered, is
not a gentleman. His grandfather was a navvy, and his millionaire
father has advised him to make friends with those who would advantage
him in later life. There are regular references to his lack of breeding.
'Caterpillar' Egerton remarks, 'One is reminded sometimes that the
poor Demon is the son of a Liverpool merchant, bred in or about the
docks.' Desmond chivalrously declares Egerton's attitude to Scaife
'snobbish', and quarrels with Egerton over his attitude. But Egerton,
who opines, 'he can't help being a bounder', and 'he wants breeding . . .
but he'll never get that—never' is in fact proved right by Scaife's later
actions. Scaife mars the victory in the Eton and Harrow match by a
display of temper which alienates the boys, who can 'forgive anything
sooner than low breeding'. Scaife admits to Desmond that he is suffering from 'homesickness for the gutter' and Vachell makes it quite clear
that Scaife's behaviour is the result of heredity.[59]

Scaife is a consistently bad influence. He encourages and takes the
lead in drinking. When the house loses at torpids he is convulsed with

rage, denounces Desmond and generally behaves badly while Desmond and Verney accept defeat nobly. 'As a gentleman one accepts a bit of bad luck without gnashing one's teeth,' says Egerton.[60] Scaife also shows his true colours at the Harrow sing-song, where distinguished old boys, like a famous imperial hero who is both a field-marshal and a V.C., sing school songs with tears pouring down their faces. Desmond is deeply moved, Scaife indifferent. He is a permanent outsider.

The unacceptable face of class-consciousness is represented by Mr Richard Rutford, known to the boys as 'Dirty Dick', house master of the Manor, who is a disaster. 'He disliked boys, misunderstood them, insulted them, ignored those who lacked influential connections, toadied and pampered "the swells".'[61] He fails to attend the house matches, torpids, in pointed contrast to the house butler, Dumbleton, who does so religiously. Rutford's effect on the house is to lower its tone, and the Head asks dedicated Old Harrovians to send their sons there to raise the tone. Harry Desmond is sent by his father, Verney by his uncle. The Manor's social arbiter is 'Caterpillar' Egerton, dandy son of a Guards officer, dedicated Harrovian and acknowledged authority on schoolboy honour. He deplores swearing ('We leave that sort of thing to bargees'), sets out the objects of Harrow education ('At Harrow and Eton, one is licked into shape for the big things: diplomacy, politics, the services. One is taught manners, what?') and gives John his imprimatur after helping him to select a new suit: 'You've always looked a gentleman . . . and it's a comfort to me to think that now you'll be dressed like one.'[62] But he bars Scaife.

The essence of the public school gentleman is *noblesse oblige*. John sees its epitome in the Duke of Trent, who is not clever, good-looking or distinguished, but works enormously hard, and when John asks why, Esmé replies, 'He has to.' He was born to it. This is the true significance and justification of rank and wealth. Charles Desmond, Harry's Cabinet Minister father, is similar in his dedication. Staying at Eaton Square with the Desmonds and discussing which famous Harrovian they would choose as model, Desmond names Sheridan, Verney Lord Shaftesbury. Mr Desmond lauds the choice, praising Shaftesbury as the ideal of aristocratic dedication, a man who sought to eliminate poverty without removing refinement or class distinction.[63]

Noblesse oblige operates too in the case of Basil Warde, the new house master of the Manor. In his opening speech to the house he explains how as a boy the house licked him into shape ('the tone of the house insensibly communicated itself to me'), and he ceased to be a slacker and came to enjoy his life, work and sport at Harrow. He wants to repay the debt to the Manor by instilling the same spirit. 'I want to see this house at the top of the tree again, cock-house at cricket, cock-house at footer, with a Balliol scholar in it and a school racquet-player.'

Warde, Egerton reveals, is one of the Wardes of Warde Pomeroy, an old Elizabethan family. Breeding shows again. He turns down a head-mastership to stay at Harrow and run his house. He is a great influence on John, encouraging him to develop not just his sport but his intellectual ability. He is the ideal house master, by contrast with Rutford. Warde, seen on his return from Switzerland, 'seemed saturated with fresh air and all the sweet clean things one associates with mountains'.

Warde tackles illicit gambling. Beaumont-Greene forges a letter from his father in order to raise £30 to pay a gambling debt to Scaife. He confesses to playing with Lovell and Scaife. The headmaster summons the school and addresses it. Beaumont-Greene and Lovell (who were leaving at the end of term) will leave at once. Scaife will be flogged. The headmaster asks who else played. Desmond, 'ardent, impetuous, afire with the spirit which makes men accept death rather than dishonour', and Egerton confess. The headmaster does not punish them because of their confession. 'When I came here I hardly hoped to find saints, but I did expect to find gentlemen. And I have not been disappointed.'[64]

In his autobiography Vachell robustly defended the public schools: 'If a boy is fit (mentally and physically) to go to a public school—how many are not?—let him be sent to it as soon as possible, let him remain as long as he can.' He also insists that *The Hill* was 'a tolerably true presentment of the school as it was in my time'.[65] He had been very happy there; 'being a normal boy, abrim with high health and spirits, my attitude towards Harrow can be summed up as happy-go-lucky'. What he learned was 'good form'. Vachell believed very reasonably that hostile books on the public schools reflected unhappy schooldays, and, meeting an author of a later, hostile book about Harrow, which he does not name but which poked fun at *The Hill*, he was intrigued to discover that its author had been, unlike Vachell and his son, 'unhappy on the Hill, resentful of cut and dried conventions, some-thing of a rebel'. Vachell was criticised for the snobbery of *The Hill*, and although he suggests that the boys were not consciously snobbish, he goes on to describe something that sounds very like snobbery:

A boy might be labelled 'rank outsider' merely because he was a Home-Boarder. Instantly, with rare exceptions, he acquired an inferioity complex. He was not bullied; he was ignored. It was an asset to me that so many of my people had been at Harrow. If you were an Anson or a Hamilton or a Fortescue you became *persona grata* both to masters and boys.[66]

Vachell recalled that 'nobody whom I knew ever mentioned money making. We talked of money grubbers as outside the pale. Secretly I cherished an ever-increasing ambition to make enough money to buy back the family acres.'[67] He defended his depiction of high moral tone: 'Some boys are abnormally dirty-minded, especially the loafers and slackers. Smutty talk was reckoned to be "bad form" in Moreton's.'[68]

Vachell and his friends collaborated on their prep., used cribs and worked hard only at games: 'We believed that scamping of work which escaped detection and punishment was a feather in our caps.'[69] The schoolboy morality of his day allowed lying in self-defence, permitted swearing but banned theft ('I cannot recall one instance of petty larceny'). He believed that the prefects did not abuse their authority and that caning was accepted ('You took a "whopping", six of the best, as a matter of course. You felt and looked an ass if you whimpered'). All this can be found faithfully reflected in *The Hill*, where Scaife, John and Egerton co-operate on their prep., Lovell lies to the house master, Rutford, to save the other boys and Verney defends the practice to his housemaster's face. Egerton discourages swearing ('The best men don't swear much. It's doocid bad form').[70]

On sex, Vachell reports:

> Long after I wrote *The Hill*, other novels were published, dealing with public school life, revealing the dirty side of it. There is always a dirty side. Perverts are to be found everywhere. Such unfortunates should be quietly sent back to their parents. As a rule they are. The less said about them the better. The ordinary boy is amoral. If he suffers from excess of vitality, and has appetites for either work or games, he can expend his surplus energies on them. Nine times out of ten he does. The oversexed slacker has the mark of the beast, and in my time was labelled 'rotter'.[71]

But Vachell admitted to one great error: misdating *The Hill*. 'I should have made my hero go to Harrow when I did. Instead I put the clock on twenty years, oblivious of the flight of time and the inevitable changes which time brings about. I suffered from a preconceived idea. I wanted to end my novel with the Boer War. Quite easily I could have killed Desmond in the Transvaal War instead of the Boer War.'[72] The reason he wanted to end the book with the Boer War lies in its inspiration. For the story was based on fact.

The Hill was dedicated to G. W. E. Russell, the Liberal M.P., junior Minister and eminent Anglican layman, who, Vachell says, was 'the first to suggest that I should write a book about contemporary life at Harrow; you gave me the principal idea; you furnished me with notes innumerable; you have revised every page of the manuscript; and you are a peculiarly keen Harrovian'. Russell gives evidence of his keenness in his book *Sketches and Snapshots* (1910), saying of the school:

It was there that one first realised one's own capacities, great or small; first felt the promptings of honourable ambition; first dreamed of unselfish efforts for the service of others; first learned to take pride in membership of a body. Above all, it was here that, as our Harrow poet says, 'friendships were formed, too romantic to last—but not too romantic or short-lived to affect, for weal or woe, one's whole subsequent life.[73]

Russell saw the Harrow school songs as a prime focus of feeling, quoting a stranger on his first impression of the occasion:

When you hear the great volume of fresh voices leap up like a lark from the ground, and rise and swell, and swell and rise, till the rafters seem to crack and shiver, then you seem to have discovered all the sources of emotion.[74]

It was exactly this feeling that Vachell tapped for the great love scene.

Commenting on *The Hill*, Russell confirmed, 'not only the main plot of the book but every important trait and incident is drawn from life'. Desmond was based directly on Charles Childe-Pemberton (1853–1900), who was at Harrow from 1866 to 1872. In Russell's own words:

One day a new boy, very raw and disconsolate amid 'five hundred faces and all so strange', caught sight, in the School-Yard, of one whom he instantly desired to make his friend. This was a singularly attractive-looking lad, graceful in shape and movement, with pensive eyes, and really golden hair. He was C. B. Childe-Pemberton, and the new boy was the present writer. The two boys were of the same age, but the one had been a year longer in the school than the other; and there yawned between them the gap which separates the Fifth Form from the Shell. From then till the end of their school-career, there subsisted between them a friendship as close as brotherhood; and for the survivor the brightest memory connected with Harrow has always been the recollection of that comradeship. They had little enough in common. The one was an athlete; the other a loafer. The one an eager and pugnacious Tory; the other, a rather flamboyant Radical. Yet each found the other's society far more enjoyable than anything else which Harrow had to offer.[75]

Childe-Pemberton was a star of the school's football and cricket teams. At Lord's in 1872 he scored 44 in the second innings against Eton and earned hearty applause from both sides. After Oxford, he joined the Blues and served with distinction in the Egyptian War. Later he married and settled down to the life of a country gentleman. When the Boer War broke out he re-enlisted, raised a troop of light horse and was killed at Potgieter's Drift in 1900. Russell ends his account with the poignant '*Lux perpetua luceat ei*—it's a man's prayer and it commemorates a schoolboy's love.'[76]

It was not just boys who entertained this elevated romantic view of their friendships. It was often shared by masters. J. E. C. Welldon (1854-1937), the old Etonian who became headmaster of Harrow

(1885–98) and ruled with 'the masterly force of an infectious personality', leaving to become Bishop of Calcutta, committed his view of the subject to his only novel, *Gerald Eversley's Friendship* (1895), subtitled *A study in real life*. He distilled his experience of teaching into a long and revealing passage on the nature of the public school:

> The society of a public school is a world in itself, self-centred, self-satisfied. It takes but slight account of the principles and practices which obtain in the world of men. It has its own laws, its own fashions, its own accepted code of morals. To these all persons must submit, or the penalty of resistance is heavy. Its virtues are not altogether those of men and women, nor its vices. Some actions of which the world thinks comparatively little, it honours with profound admiration. To others, which the world thinks much of, it is indifferent. Mere physical courage, for instance, is esteemed too highly. Self-repression is depreciated. Hypocrisy is loathed. But the inverted hypocrisy—the homage which pays virtue to vice—or, in other words, the affectation of being worse than one really is, is common among boys and is thought to be honourable. Truth, again, is not esteemed as a virtue of universal application, but is relative to particular persons, a falsehood, if told by a schoolfellow, being worse than if told by a master. Nobody can be intimate with a community of schoolboys and not feel that a morality so absolute, yet so narrow, and in some ways so perverted, bears a certain resemblance to the morality of a savage tribe . . . Of the achievements of the intellect, if they stand alone, public school opinion is still, as it has always been, slightly contemptuous. But strength, speed, athletic skill, quickness of eye and hand, still command universal applause among schoolboys as among savages. It is this uncivilized character of the young which accounts for the lack of sympathy—nay the positive indignation and contempt—with which they regard anything like eccentricity or individualism. Individualism among the young is looked upon as a form of conceit. Far stricter, and enforced by far more terrible penalties than the rules which masters make for boys, are the rules which boys make for themselves and for each other . . . A public school, then, is the home of the commonplace. It is there that mediocrity sits upon her throne. There the spirit which conforms to custom is lauded to the skies. There the spirit which is independent and original is apt to be crushed . . . There is no reason to deny that the public school system is good for the majority of boys. But it has its victims. How often has it happened that the boys, whose names have in after life been the glory and pride of their schools, have been ignored, depreciated, persecuted in their school lives. It is not needless—it cannot be wrong—to plead for a kindly sympathetic forbearance from masters and boys, yes, from masters as much as from boys, towards the stricken, suffering, despised members of the flock.[77]

Welldon is concerned in his book with one of these individualist misfits and sees his salvation in the love of another boy. Interestingly Welldon sets his novel at the time of his own schooldays (the 1860s) before the stiffening of the upper lip which accompanied the promotion of the games media. The hero's surname, Eversley, which was both the name of Charles Kingsley's Hampshire parish and the title of the collected edition of his works, similarly recalls that decade and its doctrine of Christian manliness.

The book details the intense friendship at St Anselm's School of Gerald Eversley—thin, pale, stooped, bookish and bespectacled, the son of a poor country clergyman—and Harry Venniker, son of Lord Venniker, handsome, lithe, stalwart and sporting. Harry is the ideal chivalric gentleman: 'full of manly, generous, impulses; he was conscious of his strength but no less conscious of the obligation to use it beneficently'. Gerald is what Harry describes as 'a rum 'un', not interested in sport, anxious to study, given to bursting into tears, haunting the local graveyard and playing the school organ when there is no one about. But Harry is moved by his tears, protects him from being bullied, stands up for him when he is accused of 'sneaking' and stealing an examination paper, and they swear eternal friendship. Welldon sees such special friendships as the gift of God. ('God reserves it like personal beauty, like the appreciation of beautiful sounds and colours, in his own hands'.) Nevertheless he carefully explores the motivation of the friendship on both sides:

> On Harry Venniker's side it was in the main a generous sense of protective obligation . . . Harry believed that he could help him, and that nobody else could or would, and that, if he were left alone, he would be sure to be bullied. Helplessness is itself a title to the service of generous souls . . . and nobility of thought and action was nature to Harry Venniker. It ought to be said too that he was in some sense an admirer of Gerald's intellectual ability. Being no student himself, he could not help respecting a life devoted to study. And in proportion as learning assumed for him the general aspect of a difficult and irksome duty, he looked with a reverential surprise upon one who loved it as a mistress. Gerald Eversley's friendship for his friend was of a different kind . . . there had arisen in Gerald's mind a passionate admiration, a sentiment akin to hero-worship, for the boy his inferior in intellect but so brilliant, so prominent in the common ways of school life. It was a sentiment of which he could give, or did give, no account to himself. But he felt, as others felt, the charm of Harry's presence. To be near him was a delight. To be parted from him was a bereavement.[78]

Welldon entirely endorses the feeling. 'What would not the world lose in happiness, nay in sublimity, if there were no souls exalted by strong, unspoken reverence for those whom they mistakenly deem higher and nobler than themselves?'[79] The school dubs them 'the inseparables'. As the friendship ripens, it deepens: 'It was in a sense, even purified, as being free from the petty frictions and bickerings which are the incidents of great and constant propinquity, which sometimes occurs, it is said, even between husband and wife.'[80] It reaches one climax of intensity when Harry almost dies of inflammation of the lungs, and another on the day they leave St Anselm's, when Harry declares to Gerald, 'We've learnt to love one another and St. Anselm's.' Gerald meets and falls in love with Harry's sister, Ethel, idolises her and through her regains his lost Christian faith. But part of Miss Venniker's attraction is that she combines her own charm with that of her brother. 'Have I not known elsewhere,' comments Welldon sagely, 'instances of men who have loved the brother first, and then—with still stronger love—his sister?'[81] Alas, she dies of diphtheria three weeks before the wedding and Harry has to save Gerald from suicide. Gerald is comforted by Harry's love, retires to the north of England, devotes himself to good works and never marries. The purity of the love of Gerald and Harry is the central theme, and although it is partially transferred to Ethel, even that relationship is never consummated, and is of much shorter duration anyway than the love of Harry. Her death is but recognition of the fact that it can never equal the love for her brother, something which by its nature can never be consummated.

What is remarkable about *Gerald Eversley* is the way it looks both back and forward. It looks back to *Tom Brown* in the sense that it could almost be *Tom Brown* retold from George Arthur's point of view, explaining and detailing his feelings for his protector. But it looks forward too. One cannot but be struck by the similarity of its plot to *Brideshead Revisited*. With its aristocratic golden boy, devoted schoolboy friend, saintly do-gooding mother, Lady Venniker, the sister substituting for the brother in the hero's affections, the loss and regaining of religious faith, the exaltation of chivalry and *noblesse oblige*, *Gerald Eversley* might almost be the progenitor of Evelyn Waugh's novel. It certainly suggests the persistence of such ideas and attitudes long after the end of the nineteenth century and points to another phenomenon—the continuing of romantic friendships at university, and beyond.[82]

Gerald Eversley was written in much the same style as *Eric*, and reflects the similar background of the authors—headmastership at a major public school, ecclesiastical high office, Evangelical upbringing and a highly emotional nature. This style had gone decisively out of fashion by the end of the century, and *Gerald Eversley* was to become something of a by-word for heavy and portentous sentimentality. P. G. Wodehouse mocked it, and so did E. F. Benson.

In *The Babe B.A.* (1911), a series of stories about undergraduates, Benson has his hero lay hands on *Gerald Eversley*. He and his friends mock it in much the same way as Stalky and Co. deride *Eric*, pouring scorn on its unoriginal situations and unrealistic depictions of school-boy life, with its hero weeping constantly, reading divinity books at thirteen and attempting suicide. 'It is "a study in real life." He says that . . . on the title page, in capital letters . . . If that is real life, give me fiction,' says one of the undergraduates.[83]

After criticising *Gerald Eversley*, Benson promptly wrote the same kind of book, *David Blaize* (1916), the difference one of tone rather than substance. Welldon wrote with all the emotional fervour and solemnity of the sentimental bachelor schoolmaster, proclaiming, 'no being perchance is so distinct, none so beautiful or attractive as a noble English boy'.[84] Benson wrote fluently and persuasively, with wit, grace and insight, but one suspects that he might well have endorsed Welldon's dictum.

The first third of the book is set at David's prep. school, Helmsworth and Benson handles the transition from prep. school to public school well, evoking the instant transformation from swell of the school to obscure fag in the much greater pool of Marchester. The overpowering joy that some boys have felt at public school is captured in Benson's description of David's attitude to Marchester:

> No devout Catholic ever went to Rome in more heart-felt pilgrimage than was this to David . . . Everything that might happen after public school was over seemed a posthumous sort of affair. You were old after that.[85]

This is exactly the feeling that Cyril Connolly observed and refined into his theory of permanent adolescence. The texture of life at Marchester is made up of cricket, ragging, impots and—most important—friendships. *David Blaize* explores two different kinds of friendship, between coevals and between senior and junior boys in which the older protects, guides and shapes the character of the former. The friendship of equals is between David and George 'Bags' Crabtree and begins at prep. school. 'Bags' adores David, persuades his own father to send him to Marchester with David and remains throughout devotedly loyal and supportive. At prep. school, knowing that Blaize's name is David, he wishes to be called Jonathan, and throughout entertains for David 'the shy, silent passion of friendship'.

But the principal relationship is at Marchester, between sunny-tempered, good-natured, blond David Blaize (thirteen) and Frank Maddox (seventeen), good-looking, the finest bat in the eleven, but also studious and intellectual, editor of the school magazine and a mentor to younger boys. In depicting this friendship Benson confronts the central problem head-on. David meets him when he first goes up for the scholarship examinations and, bumping into him in the holidays, takes him home to tea. The feeling he experiences at this stage is one of sheer hero worship. ('In all the world there was no one so instinct with romance and glory as this boy three years his senior who realised for him all he wanted to be'.) When he gets to Marchester, Maddox is friendly towards him, but then comes an unsettling episode. Maddox stands watching David and 'Bags' playing squash in the pouring rain.

David 'was completely dishevelled and yet a very jolly object, and was quite altogether wet, his knickerbockers clinging like tights to his thighs, the skin of which showed pink through them'. Later Maddox stares at David as he dries himself after a bath and smiles; David feels a great sense of discomfort. David's palpable unease causes Maddox a purgative remorse:

> All these weeks that intense friendship which was springing up between himself and David had been splendidly growing, and till now his influence over him had been exerted entirely for David's good. He had constantly shielded him, as on the night when he had found Hughes sitting on his bed, from all that could sully him, he had checked any hint of foul talk in David's presence, for, of all his lovable qualities, there was none so nobly potent to the elder boy than David's white innocence, his utter want of curiosity about all that was filthy. It didn't exist for him, but the danger of it (though, thank God, it had passed) he knew that he himself had brought near to him . . . Then he got up and looked at himself in the mirror above his mantlepiece, hating himself.
>
> 'You damned beast', he said. 'You deserve to be shot.'[86]

It is clear that Maddox had enjoyed sexual relations with previous boys. Hughes, David's closest friend at Helmsworth, noting Maddox's protective and chaste attitude towards David, asks if Maddox 'had become a saint, and if I'd converted him. What the devil was he talking about?' asks the innocent David.[87] Hughes is later expelled for beastliness and Maddox reflects that but for David the same fate might have been his.

Maddox apologises to David for his conduct and thereafter their friendship, with the element of lust removed from it, ripens into a warm and rewarding platonic relationship. Maddox throughout remains a powerful influence on David, just as David by his innocence keeps Maddox pure. They holiday together, and it is idyllic, swimming, golfing and Maddox teaching the younger boy to appreciate the beauties and joys of Greek and poetry, especially Swinburne. This idyllic picture represents the acme of what Benson calls 'their friendship of boy-love, hot as fire and clean as the trickle of ice-water on a glacier'.[88]

Maddox is now a strong force for good in the school, co-operates with Cruickshank, whom he had previously shunned as 'too pi', co-operates with the Head to stamp out cribbing. Maddox represents the ideal balance, playing cricket but also loving literature and the classics. He and David are now so close that their house master, Adams, dubs them 'David and Jonathan' and the headmaster acknowledges Maddox's love for David as something spiritual and ennobling. David's influence extends even to getting Maddox to pray at night. Together David and Maddox, batting as last men in, make Adams's the cock house at Marchester, and Maddox calls it 'the best of all the days I had at school'—

the shared sporting achievement, the true consummation of their love, victory for the house.

As Maddox prepares to leave for Cambridge, he and David discuss their time at school together:

> 'David, old chap,' he said, 'I don't believe two fellows ever had such a good time as we've had, and it would be rot to pretend not to be sorry that this bit of it has come to an end. I dare say we shall have splendid times together again, but there's no doubt that this is over. On the other hand, it would be equal rot not to feel jolly thankful for it. The chances were millions to one against our ever coming across each other at all. So buck up, as I said.'
>
> David had rolled over on to his face, but at this he sat up, picking bits of dry grass out of his hair.
>
> 'Yes, that's so,' he said. 'But it will be pretty beastly without you. I shan't find another friend like you—'
>
> 'You'd jolly well better not,' interrupted Frank.
>
> David could not help laughing. 'I suppose we're rather idiots about each other,' he said.
>
> 'I dare say. But it's too late to remedy that now. Oh, David, it's a good old place, this. Look at the pitch there! What a lot of ripping hours it's given to generations of fellows, me among them. There's the roof of the house through the trees, do you see? You can just see the end window of our dormitory. I wonder if happiness soaks into a place.'[89]

Once Maddox has gone, the effect of his influence on David is felt. He becomes the same sort of authority figure as Maddox had been, determined to keep the house the way Maddox had left it ('no smoking, no cribbing, no filth'). David adopts a similar attitude of protection and devotion to his fag, Jevons, as Maddox had to him.

David develops a crush on a girl, Violet Grey, and his passion for her 'seriously threatened for the next few weeks to dethrone the dominant passion inspired by cricket'. But this calf love is put firmly in its place in the hierarchy of emotions when Violet gets engaged to her cousin and David is seriously injured stopping a runaway horse in Marchester High Street. 'Bags' and Maddox discuss their love for David, and Maddox sits for hours holding David's hand and soothing him, until it is clear that he will recover. This love is more important, more deeply felt, longer-lasting and more secure than the sudden violent passion for Violet or the lustful thoughts which Maddox had briefly entertained towards David and then manfully suppressed. It is the epitome of the mutually satisfying and fulfilling friendship, passionate but chaste, David and Jonathan.

Despite Benson's clear intention of signalling the superiority and chasteness of the romantic friendship, it must be admitted that the novel does have an erotic undertone, proceeding perhaps implicitly from Benson's own homosexual temperament. The constant approving references to the protagonists' good looks, coupled with the passionate avowals of love and need suggest a more hothouse atmosphere. It is a good example of the sort of ambivalence which can obtain in depictions of these relationships.

E. F. Benson (1867–1940) was educated at Temple Grove, East Sheen, and at Marlborough, which he left in 1887. He seems to have been very happy at school. He edited *The Marlburian*, was head of house, played football and rackets for the school and had the usual friendships and hero-worships. He drew directly on his experiences at both schools for Helmsworth and Marchester, dramatising actual episodes and lightly fictionalising real people. The amusing and accurate description of the embarrassment of the young David at a visit to the school by his archdeacon father, who preaches a florid sermon mocked by the boys, kisses him and calls him by his Christian name in front of his friends and causes him to drop a vital catch in the cricket match, undoubtedly recalls the school visits of Benson's own father, Archbishop E. W. Benson. E. F. Benson's own prep. school life of 'games, stag-beetles and friendship' is distilled into the first part of the book. It was at Temple Grove that there was an attempted seduction by an older boy on a walk, but Benson did not understand what he was talking about until later. Benson's own vividly recalled farewell to his special friend at Marlborough directly inspired the farewell scene of David and Frank.[90] There is no doubt that friendships were central to his life at school, and he rhapsodises about them in his autobiography:

In many ways boys are a sex quite apart from male or female; though they take on much of what they are and of what they learn, strengthened and expanded into manhood, they leave behind, given that they grow into normal and healthy beings, a certain emotional affection towards the coevals of their own sex, which is natural to public-school boyhood . . . For twelve or thirteen weeks three times a year they live exclusively among boys, and that at a time when their vigour is at its strongest and it would demand of them a fish-like inhumanity, if they were asked to let their friendships alone have no share of the tremendous high colours in which their lives are dipped. Naturally there is a danger about it (for what emotion worth having is not encompassed by perils?) and this strong heat of affection may easily explode into fragments of mere sensuality, be dissipated in mere 'smut' and from being a banner in the clean wind be trampled into mud. But promiscuous immorality was, as far as I am aware, quite foreign to the school, though we flamed into a hundred hot bonfires of those friendships, which were discussed with a freedom that would seem appalling, if you forgot that you were dealing with boys and not with men. Blaze after blaze illumined our excited lives, for without being one whit less genuine while they lasted, there was no very permanent quality about these friendships. But to suppose that this ardency was sensual, is to miss the point of it and lose the value of it altogether. That the base of the attraction was largely physical is no doubt true, for it was founded primarily on appearance, but there is a vast difference between the breezy open-air quality of these friendships and the dingy sensualism which sometimes is wrongly attributed to them. A grown-up man cannot conceivably recapture their quality, so as to experience it emotionally, but to confuse it with moral perversion, as an adult understands that, is merely to misunderstand it.[91]

Nevertheless he confessed to a longing to recapture that feeling ('every year since I have wanted more of some quality that is inseparable from the wonder and sunset of boyhood').[92] Looking back on his career, he was to single out *David Blaize* as one of the few books of which he was really proud and into which he had put the greatest emotional imagination.[93] It was perhaps because it had allowed him to regain, however briefly, the rapture of boyhood and the schooldays, which seem for him to have been the happiest of his life.[94]

The dominant role of school in the emotional lives of old alumni was pointed to by E. M. Forster:

Many men look back on their schooldays as the happiest of their lives. They remember with regret that golden time when life, though hard, was not yet complex; when they all worked together and played together and thought together, so far as they thought at all; when they were taught that school is the world in miniature, and believed that no one can love his country who does not love his school. And they prolong that time as best they can by joining their Old Boys' Society; indeed some of them remain Old Boys and nothing else for the rest of their lives. They attribute all good to the school. They worship it.[95]

Cyril Connolly elaborated on this in his celebrated theory of 'permanent adolescence':

It is a theory that the experiences undergone by boys at the great public schools, their glories and disappointments, are so intense as to dominate their lives and arrest their development. From these it results that the greater part of the ruling class remains adolescent, school-minded, self-conscious, cowardly, sentimental, and in the last analysis, homosexual . . . Romanticism with its death wish is to blame, for it lays emphasis on childhood, on a fall from grace which is not compensated for by any doctrine of future redemption; we enter the world, trailing clouds of glory, childhood and boyhood follow and we are damned. Certainly growing up seems a hurdle which most of us are unable to take.[96]

The idea that schooldays were the pinnacle of existence was certainly strongly encouraged, and here popular fiction is as so often the mirror of the unconscious. In his novel *Gerald Eversley's Friendship* Welldon has Mr Brandiston, house master at St Anselm's, tell Harry Venniker after his goal has won a key house football match, 'You will never be a greater person in life, Venniker, than you are to-day.'[97] In *The Hill* Vachell describes Harry's feelings on catching the Eton captain out at Lord's: 'If the country that he wishes to serve crowns him with all the honours bestowed upon a favoured son, never, *never*, will Caesar Desmond know again a moment of such exquisite, unadulterated joy as this.'[98]

While one might quarrel with some of Connolly's attributions of adolescence, in particular 'cowardly' and 'homosexual', the concept of permanent adolescence is a useful and revealing one. Indeed, it might be taken even further and applied to the nation at large in the Victorian era. The public school was, after all, the powerhouse of the nation, producing its ruling class, its role models, its social arbiters, stamping its imprint on the age. Total institutions are in part notoriously microcosms of society, and nature so frequently imitates art that the qualities so characteristic of the public school (all-male society, strict hierarchy, obsession with games, hero worship, juvenile romanticism) can also be seen in operation in the nation, particularly in the last decades of the nineteenth century but also well on into the twentieth.[99]

In a very real sense the Victorian male was *puer aeternus*, the boy who never grew up. It was not just the all-male society in which he functioned, it was also his preferred activities (hunting, empire-building, exploring, warring). In his pioneering study of the literature of adventure Martin Green has pointed out that 'it is a striking feature of late Victorian culture that its emotional focus was on boys'.[100] Time and again the image of the boy returns. The philosopher George Santayana admiringly described the Briton as 'the sweet, just, boyish master of the world'.[101] So did Sir Henry Newbolt, who summed up the dominant ideology of the age in poetic form in *Vitai Lampada*, describing a battle in which 'the voice of a schoolboy rallies the ranks: "Play up! Play up! and play the game"'.[102] Many of the great men of the empire were essentially boy-men. Baden-Powell, with his love of practical jokes, amateur theatricals, music hall ditties and comic disguises, was perhaps the most extreme example—'a perennial singing schoolboy, a permanent whistling adolescent, a case of arrested development *con brio*', Piers Brendon calls him.[103] Out of his instinctive identification with and understanding of boys he created the Boy Scouts. His closest friend was a young army officer, nicknamed 'The Boy', to whom he wrote every day of the siege of Mafeking. He named his son Peter after his favourite fictional character, Peter Pan. Another example is Reginald Brett, Viscount Esher, *eminence grise* of the Edwardian court, who maintained a series of romantic friendships throughout his life. His biographer observes, 'Regy never grew out of Eton; never grew away from it. It had done something to influence the whole course of his life. Distinguished and powerful though he was to become in later life, in this one respect he did not change, he never perfectly grew up.'[104] Throughout the nineteenth century for many men, married and single, passionate emotional attachments to other males were the most significant events of their lives. In so far as labels mean anything, many of these men were heterosexuals, notable proponents of manliness who would probably have greeted any suggestion of a physical realisation of their emotional attachments with horror. The catalogue of these male friendships is extensive, but among them were Alfred, Lord Tennyson and Arthur Hallam, Robert Louis Stevenson and W. E. Henley, Rudyard Kipling and Wolcott Balestier, Charles Kingsley and Charles Blachford Mansfield, Andrew Lang and Henry Brown. They are the most obvious manifestations of a condition of prolonged adolescence, in which the emotions and attitudes of school continue to loom large.

Notes

1 Ronald Hyam, *Britain's Imperial Century*, London, 1976, 141.
2 Susan Chitty, *The Beast and the Monk*, London, 1974, 52.
3 Peter T. Cominos, 'Late Victorian sexual respectability and the social system', *International Review of Social History*, 8 (1975), 28.
4 Benjamin Disraeli, *Coningsby* (1844), Oxford, 1982, 38.
5 Alec Waugh, *Public School Life*, London, 1922, 137.
6 J. R. De S. Honey, *Tom Brown's Universe*, London, 1977, 181-94.
7 Honey, *Tom Brown's Universe*, 186.
8 F. W. Farrar, *St Winifred's, or, The World of School*, quoted by Honey, 187.
9 Thomas Hughes, *Tom Brown's Schooldays* (1857), London, 1889, 190.
10 Hughes, *Tom Brown's Schooldays*, 255.
11 F. W. Farrar, *Julian Home* (1859), London, 1896, 26-7.
12 Mark Girouard, *The Return to Camelot*, New Haven and London, 1981, 120.
13 Alec Waugh, *The Early Years of Alec Waugh*, London, 1962, 51.
14 Royston Lambert, *The Hothouse Society*, London, 1968, 317.
15 Lambert, *Hothouse Society*, 301.
16 Lambert, *Hothouse Society*, 308.
17 Lambert, *Hothouse Society*, 308.
18 See, for instance, Paul Willis, *Profane Culture*, London, 1978; Paul Willis, *Learning to Labour*, Aldershot, 1983; Howard J. Parker, *The View from the Boys*, Newton Abbot, 1974.
19 Lambert, *Hothouse Society*, 317.
20 Lambert, *Hothouse Society*, 320.
21 Lambert, *Hothouse Society*, 323.
22 Lambert, *Hothouse Society*, 322, 329.
23 Lambert, *Hothouse Society*, 331. These courtly rituals are recalled by Michael Davidson, in his account of Lancing School between 1908 and 1914, *The World, the Flesh and Myself*, London, 1985, 50-1.
24 Lambert, *Hothouse Society*, 340. Jonathan Gathorne-Hardy, *The Public School Phenomenon*, 182, suggests that 25 per cent of public school boys had lust affairs and 90 per cent entirely platonic love affairs.
25 George Macdonald Fraser (ed.), *The World of the Public School*, London, 1977, 103.
26 Rudyard Kipling, *Something of Myself*, Harmondsworth, 1977, 22-3.
27 L. C. Dunsterville, *Stalky's Reminiscences*, London, 1930, 27.
28 John Addington Symonds, *Memoirs*, ed. Phyllis Grosskurth, London, 1984, 94.

29 Goldsworthy Lowes Dickinson, *Autobiography*, ed. Dennis Proctor, London, 1973, 52–5.
30 Brian Inglis, *John Bull's Schooldays*, London, 1961, 93.
31 Hallam Tennyson, *The Haunted Mind*, London, 1984, 45–7.
32 E. F. Benson, *David Blaize*, London, 1925, 99.
33 Giles and Esmond Romilly, *Out of Bounds*, London, 1935, 144.
34 T. C. Worsley, *Flannelled Fool*, London, 1985, 23.
35 Wilfrid Blunt, *Married to a Single Life*, Salisbury, 1983, 77, 79.
36 J. R. Ackerley, *My Father and Myself* (1968), Harmondsworth, 1984, 99.
37 Louis MacNeice, *The Strings are False*, London, 1965, 100.
38 Cecil Day Lewis, *The Buried Day*, London, 1969, 106–7.
39 Robert Graves, *Goodbye to all That*, London, 1931, 66.
40 Royston Lambert, *Hothouse Society*, 325.
41 Graves, *Goodbye to all That*, 40.
42 Cyril Connolly, *Enemies of Promise* (1938), Harmondsworth, 1979, 203.
43 Connolly, *Enemies of Promise*, 206.
44 On Connolly's life see David Pryce-Jones, *Cyril Connolly*, London, 1983. For a detailed account of one romantic friendship see Cyril Connolly, *A Romantic Friendship: letters to Noel Blakiston*, London, 1975.
45 H. A. Vachell, *Distant Fields*, London, 1937, 164. The reviews of *The Hill* are printed in the 1920 edition, p. i.
46 Alec Waugh, *Public School Life*, 249.
47 H. A. Vachell, *The Hill* (1905), London, 1920, 94.
48 Vachell, *The Hill*, 130–1.
49 Blunt, *Married to a Single Life*, 63.
50 Vachell, *The Hill*, 231.
51 Vachell, *The Hill*, 304.
52 Vachell, *The Hill*, 313.
53 Vachell, *Distant Fields*, 256.
54 Vachell, *The Hill*, 318.
55 Vachell, *The Hill*, 120.
56 Vachell, *The Hill*, 146.
57 Vachell, *The Hill*, 152.
58 Vachell, *The Hill*, 39.
59 Vachell, *The Hill*, 58, 92, 110, 273, 121, 147.
60 Vachell, *The Hill*, 92.
61 Vachell, *The Hill*, 46.
62 Vachell, *The Hill*, 113.
63 Vachell, *The Hill*, 166.
64 Vachell, *The Hill*, 215.
65 Vachell, *Distant Fields*, 31.
66 Vachell, *Distant Fields*, 31.
67 Vachell, *Distant Fields*, 36–7.
68 Vachell, *Distant Fields*, 33.
69 Vachell, *Distant Fields*, 38.
70 Vachell, *The Hill*, 78.
71 Vachell, *Distant Fields*, 38–9.
72 Vachell, *Distant Fields*, 32.
73 G. W. E. Russell, *Sketches and Snapshots*, London, 1910, 219.
74 Russell, *Sketches and Snapshots*, 227.
75 Russell, *Sketches and Snapshots*, 229.
76 'Scaife' was believed to be based on Ronald Vibart (1879-1934), later a cricket professional and schoolmaster, who at one stage in his career fled to South America to avoid criminal charges and subsequently committed suicide.
77 J. E. C. Welldon, *Gerald Eversley's Friendship*, London, 1895, 75–8.
78 Welldon, *Gerald Eversley's Friendship*, 113–14.
79 Welldon, *Gerald Eversley's Friendship*, 114–15.
80 Welldon, *Gerald Eversley's Friendship*, 150.

81 Welldon, *Gerald Eversley's Friendship*, 293.
82 On romantic friendships at Oxford see Geoffrey Faber, *Oxford Apostles*, London, 1933, 215-32, and at Cambridge, David Newsome, *On the Edge of Paradise*, London, 1980, 39-43, 246-7.
83 E. F. Benson, *The Babe B.A.*, London, 1911, 84-7.
84 Welldon, *Gerald Eversley's Friendship*, 3.
85 Benson, *David Blaize*, 101-2.
86 Benson, *David Blaize*, 148-9.
87 Benson, *David Blaize*, 144.
88 Benson, *David Blaize*, 201.
89 Benson, *David Blaize*, 258-9.
90 E. F. Benson discusses his school career in *Our Family Affairs*, London, 1920, 76-213. The attempted seduction is described on p. 87 and the farewell on pp. 211-13.
91 Benson, *Our Family Affairs*, 153-7.
92 Benson, *Our Family Affairs*, 211.
93 E. F. Benson, *Final Edition*, London, 1940, 183.
94 E. F. Benson's brother, A.C., blander, more verbose and more sentimental, though equally prolific, expatiated on the mystical joys of schoolboy friendships in two intensely introspective autobiographical novels, *Memoirs of Arthur Hamilton* (1886) and *Beside Still Waters* (1907).
95 E. M. Forster, *Abinger Harvest*, London, 1936, 4.
96 Connolly, *Enemies of Promise*, 271-2.
97 Welldon, *Gerald Eversley's Friendship*, 164.
98 Vachell, *The Hill*, 270.
99 This idea is elaborated in Jeffrey Richards, 'Passing the love of women: manly love in Victorian society', in J. A. Mangan and James Walvin (ed.), *Manliness and Morality*, Manchester, 1987.
100 Martin Green, *Dreams of Adventure, Deeds of Empire*, London, 1980, 389.
101 George Santayana, *Soliloquies on England*, London, 1922, 32.
102 Henry Newbolt, *Poems Old and New*, London, 1912, 78-9.
103 Piers Brendon, *Eminent Edwardians*, London, 1979, 201-2.
104 James Lees-Milne, *The Enigmatic Edwardian*, London, 1987, 16.

9

The lost boys:
Tell England

The conventional wisdom has it that the public school spirit, chivalry and empire all reached their peak in World War I and thereafter, with the bitter words of the war poets, and the disillusionment of the post-war generation with everything their fathers stood for, the ideals went into eclipse.[1] But it is a view based almost entirely on the evidence of the high culture. Where, for the high culture, empire was a hollow and hypocritical sham, the public school a soulless engine of philistinism, snobbery and homosexuality, and chivalry an archaism negated by the mud and blood and gas and gangrene of the trenches and no-man's land, popular culture tells a different story. The films, books and plays that were viewed and read by the millions, rather than by the intellectual elite, fully supported the dominant ideology of the pre-war world. Every aspect of life was permeated by imperial sentiment. In popular thrillers heroes were still gentleman adventurers who believed in king and country, honour and duty. The public schools continued to appear in a favourable light, not in the critically acclaimed but short-run anti-public school novels of the highbrows but in the genuinely popular boys' papers like *Magnet* and *Gem*, purchased and devoured eagerly every week by a new generation of boys, and in best-selling middle-brow novels like James Hilton's *Goodbye, Mr Chips*.[2]

The most remarkable of these novels was perhaps Ernest Raymond's *Tell England*, in which public schools, chivalry and World War I were blended to provide a best-seller which in 1922 harked back to the pre-war ideals and saw the war in those terms. The novel was written not by someone imagining the war from a distance, but by a participant. It was a book which endorsed all the principal ingredients of the public school story (classical teaching, chivalry, religion and romantic friendship) and placed them securely in a World War I setting.

Ernest Raymond (1888–1974), educated at St Paul's, had spent some time as a prep. school master. ('I enjoyed the work; I liked the boys; the holidays were long'.) But while teaching he caught from a colleague 'the splendid fever of Anglo-Catholicity',[3] read for the priesthood and, having been ordained in 1914, volunteered as an army chaplain and served in Gallipoli, participating in that tragic campaign until its conclusion, then later served on the western front. In Gallipoli he felt the power and mystique of that legendary golden generation of young men, Charles Lister, Rupert Brooke, Patrick Shaw-Stewart, who embodied the spirit—noble, patriotic, selfless, eager—of the 1914 war sonnets:

> Now, God be thanked who has matched us with His Hour,
> And caught our youth, and wakened us from sleeping,
> With hand made sure, clear eye, and sharpened power,
> To turn, as swimmers into cleanness leaping,
> Glad from a world grown old and cold and weary,
> Leave the sick hearts that honour could not move,
> And half-men, and their dirty songs and dreary,
> And all the little emptiness of love.[4]

Ernest Raymond testified to the influence of these sonnets in his autobiography: 'For many of us, who at that time, were young, and at war, and had some idealism, especially perhaps those of us on Gallipoli, the five sonnets "caught our youth" and helped us in secret places of the heart.'[5]

At eighteen he had already begun working on what was to be his first novel, dealing with all he knew about (school and youth), and now in Gallipoli he found the culmination of it. He conceived it as 'a study of my generation of schoolboys who, after their few years of school, happy or unhappy, had been called upon to bleed or die for England', and wrote the second half of the book while on active service.[6] He resigned from holy orders after the war because of theological doubts, but following demobilisation he revised the manuscript of *Tell England* and in 1920 submitted it for publication. It was turned down by seven publishers, who said that no one wanted to read about the war. But eventually Cassell's took it and published it in 1922. It was an immediate hit.

Re-reading *Tell England* fifty years later, Raymond found that he still liked the comic scenes and the dramatic scenes on Gallipoli:

> *But*—the naive romanticisms, the pieties, the too facile heroics and too uncritical patriotism—at these I can almost cry aloud in distress . . . Perhaps the one thing that saves the book and allows it to live on quietly is the fact that it purports to be the work of a naive and guileless youth just fresh from school and tossed into war, and it may be that people reading the book now will think that its *naivetés* were slyly intentional and clever; but, alas, they were not, they were the author at that time . . . Another thing that is a

cause of wonder to me as I re-read the book is the indubitable but wholly unconscious homosexuality in it. The earlier part was written when I was eighteen or nineteen; the latter part in my twenties, and in those far off days 'homosexuality' was a word which—absurd as this may seem now—I had never heard . . . I did not know that homosexuality could exist in embryo without even knowing itself for what it was, or desiring the least physical satisfaction, till the time came for it to die and be transcended by full and normal manhood. Its presence in the book is one more evidence of its author's unusually slow progress towards maturity.[7]

The value of the book then is twofold, as an expression of the mentality of a young man going to war in the spirit of Rupert Brooke and of the celebration of the idea of romantic male friendship, wholly without physical dimension. The very unselfconsciousness of the young author emphasises the book's value as the crystallisation of the mind set of a generation. But equally the success of the novel with the reading public is an indication of how far they shared those ideals still, even after the war. The book's dust jacket description, 'a great romance of glorious youth', recalls *The Hill*, and *Tell England* shares much of the earlier book's flavour, suggesting continuity through the war and beyond of its values.

How far the book was removed from the world view of the high culture is revealed by the reviews. Rose Macaulay wrote in *The Daily News*:

> *Tell England* is apparently by a rather illiterate and commonplace sentimentalist . . . *Tell England* has no beauty and its silliness and bad taste are not the work of a writer. It is difficult to say which is the more sloppy, sentimental and illiterate, the school section of the book or the war section.

S. P. B. Mais called it 'a quite unreadable novel about public school life and the war'. Alec Waugh in *The Sunday Times* said, '*Tell England* comes to us in the raiment of modernity, but its heart is with the sixties. To read the first half of it is to be transferred to our preparatory school, to the days when we wore Eton collars and devoured *Eric* and *St. Winifred's*.' *The Evening Standard*, headlining its review 'The sentimental schoolboy. Eric outdone', said, 'Whether Mr. Raymond has tried to draw his schoolboys from life or from his own imagination, the result is laughable—when it is not revolting by reason of the sentimentality.' Francis Birrel said on the wireless that it 'was one of the most nauseating books to come out of the war'.[8]

There were good reviews too. The best of them came from Hannen Swaffer in *The Daily Graphic*, who, under the headline '*Tell England* a great book . . . The epic of the youth of England', wrote, 'Every now and then comes a book of penetrating analysis, a volume that illumines the soul of thousands. *Tell England* is such a book . . . It is a book which will live as long as our spoken tongue.' It was Swaffer's view rather than the hostile ones that represented the reactions of the readership. The book's sales figures rapidly passed 10,000 and it went through five impressions at once. By 1939 it had sold 300,000 copies. By 1969 it had gone through forty editions in hardback.[9] It went into paperback in 1973. The judgements of the hostile critics reflect their ideological positions. But the book is a faithful elaboration of the chivalric mood of the sonnets of Rupert Brooke. The title derives from the epitaph of one of the book's heroes, Edgar Doe, which was the epitaph of that whole lost generation:

> Tell England, ye who pass this monument,
> We died for her, and here we rest content.

'Tell England' is derived directly from the epitaph of the Spartans at Thermopylae and indicates the patriotic nature of the book and its secure grounding in public school classics.

The novel falls into two parts, schooldays at Kensingtowe and service in Gallipoli, and follows the careers of two boys, Rupert Ray and Edgar Doe, their tonic sol-fa names perhaps a private joke by the author (Doe, Ray and Me) but also indicating young men in harmony with their age. Like *The Hill*, it is a celebration of youth, a youth so glorious, exciting and alive that death is preferable to the decay and disillusionment that inevitably follow the leaving of school.

Both the book and many of the characters are fixated on boys and boyhood. One of them, the school medic, Dr 'Chappy' Chapman, declares roundly, 'I tell you, this is England's best generation. Dammit, there are three things old England *has* learned to make: ships and poetry and boys,' and he describes the boys as 'the most shapely lot England has turned out'.[10] He discusses with Radley the two boys, Doe and Ray, their cricketing abilities and their characters, but also their looks. Chapman asks Radley what attracted him to Doe, 'his good looks or his virtues'.

Radley, Middlesex cricketer and schoolmaster, functions as a father figure, to whom the boys become devoted. When he beats them, Doe expresses his love for Radley. When Radley finds Ray weeping after being unjustly given a thousand lines he tells him that crying is 'a luxury we men must deny ourselves'. Radley canes him for speaking ill of his house master but comforts him and arranges for Doe to help him with his lines. Radley helps Ray to overcome cheating organised by Archie Pennybet, by standing up against it. Ray later reflects on Radley:

> I know now that his feeling for all the boys, as he gazed down upon them from his splendid height, was love—a strong, active love. We were young,

human things, of soft features, gradually becoming firmer, as of shallow characters gradually deepening. And he longed to be in it all—at work in the deepening. We were his hobby. I have met many such lovers of youth. Indeed, I think this is a book about them.[11]

Ray becomes Radley's favourite. Radley guides and protects him and takes a final emotional farewell of him. ('He held my hand in a demonstrative way, very unlike the normal Radley'.)

Raymond lingers on the looks of the boys. The first chapter of the school section opens with Archie Pennybet (fifteen), who is nicknamed 'Penny', announcing, 'I'm *the* best-looking person in this room.' Raymond describes him: 'He was a tall boy of fifteen years, with long limbs that were saved from any unlovely slimness by their full-fleshed curves and perfect straightness. His face, whose skin was a smooth as that of a bathed and anointed Greek, was crowned by dark hair and made striking by a pair of those long-lashed eyes that are always brown.'[12] Rupert Ray, 'dark haired and with a brace of absurdly sea-blue eyes', is known because of his eyes as 'The Gem';[13] Edgar Gray Doe, fair and delicate, his lips always parted 'like those of a pretty girl', is nicknamed successively 'The Grey Doe' and 'The Gazelle'. There are constant references to Doe's femininity, despite his cricketing prowess. 'Indeed, if Archie Pennybet was the handsomest of us three,' says Rupert, 'it is certain that Edgar Gray Doe was the prettiest.' Doe's arms are 'smooth and round like a woman's' and Penny derisively refers to Doe as 'she'.[14]

At school the boys learn the meaning of obedience to authority. In a great set piece Rupert wins the swimming relay for his house but is disqualified by Fillet, his house master, who hates him. There is a riot and Rupert plans to denounce Fillet. But the headmaster makes him a house prefect and sends him out to restore order. Ray manages it. The view of the referee, even if wrong, must be upheld, order and hierarchy and authority maintained.

But, more important than this, at the centre of the story is the romantic friendship between Rupert Ray and Edgar Gray Doe. It blossoms amid the usual round of raggings, canings and cricket, Ray's feud with house master Fillet and the crucial swimming competition. Archie Pennybet dubs them 'David and Jonathan', invoking the now traditional role models. They pass notes to each other in class proclaiming their friendship. In a revealing passage Ray (thirteen) pictures Doe as a girl, 'with his hair, paler than straw, reaching down beneath his shoulders, and with his brown eyes and parted lips wearing a feminine appearance', and later he counts this 'one of the strongest forces that helped to create my later affection for the real Edgar Gray Doe'.[15]

Rupert, suspected of breaking the house master's cane and refusing
to own up, is put in Coventry by prefects, a traditional means of testing
friendship (cf. *Eric*, *St Dominic's*).[16] Doe breaks Coventry to talk to
Ray and, when sent for by the prefects for beating, attacks them and
faints. When they are sixteen Ray realises after reading Cicero's *de
amicitia* in class 'that I loved Doe as Orestes loved Pylades'. But they
become estranged because Doe is jealous that Ray has replaced him
as Radley's favourite, and Doe falls under the influence of the unsavoury
Freedham, a symbolic figure of corruption (Freedham = Freedom =
Licence). His physical appearance points to his degeneracy. When first
seen, he is 'a tall, weedy youth of sixteen; and the unhealthiness of his
growth was shown by the long, graceless neck, the spare chest and the
thin wrists', also his eyes, 'startlingly large, startlingly bright'.[17] He
takes drugs, gets drunk, and believes that 'there must be no sensation—a
law or no law—which he has not experienced'. Although not explicitly
mentioned, this clearly includes sex. But Doe breaks with him and
confesses all to Ray. 'I believed him to be right and we—we tried everything together.' But he then realises a higher truth: 'Life *is* what feeling
you get out of it and the highest types of feeling are mystical and
intellectual.' He rejects Freedham as a 'perversion'.[18] Doe has come to
the Platonic truth that love between friends transcends sex. The two
friendships clearly represent the two alternative viewpoints: manly
love and beastliness. In the final term Ray wins the school *v.* masters
cricket match by bowling Radley out and Doe wins the Horace Prize;
then it is on to war.

The war is seen and couched in chivalric terms. The boy Rupert is
raised on chivalric tales by his grandfather. The chivalric view, which
combines youth, nobility and sacrifice, is embodied by the colonel of
the regiment ('a poet who could listen and hear how the heart of the
world was beating'). In a key ideological sequence he interviews the
eighteen-year-old Doe and Ray:

> Eighteen, by Jove! You've timed your lives wonderfully, my boys. To be
> eighteen in 1914 is to be the best thing in England. England's wealth used
> to consist in other things. Nowadays you boys are the richest things she's
> got. She's solvent with you, and bankrupt without you. Eighteen, confound
> it! It's a virtue to be your age, just as it's a crime to be mine . . . Eighteen
> years ago you were born for this day. Through the last eighteen years you've
> been educated for it. Your birth and breeding were given you that you might
> officer England's youth in this hour. And now you enter upon your
> inheritance. Just as this is *the* day in the history of the world, so yours is the
> generation. No other generation has been called to such grand things, and to
> such crowded, glorious living. Any other generation at your age would be
> footling around, living a shallow existence in the valleys, or just beginning
> to climb a slope to higher things. But you . . . just because you've timed your
> lives aright are going to be transferred straight to the mountain-tops.[19]

Ray recounts his reaction to this:

> I remember how his enthusiasm radiated from him and kindled a responsive excitement in me. I had entered his room a silly boy with no nobler thought than a thrill in the new adventure on which I had so suddenly embarked. But, as this fatherly old poet, touched by England's need and by the sight of two boys entering his room, so fresh and strong and ready for anything, broke into eloquence, I saw dimly the great ideas he was striving to express. I felt the brilliance of being alive in this big moment; the pride of youth and strength. I felt Aspiration surging in me and speeding up the action of my heart. I think I half hoped it would be my high lot to die on the battlefield.[20]

Although others scoff at the colonel's enthusiasm, Ray defends him: 'The Colonel was right and the scoffers wrong . . . He turned us . . . into young knights of high ideals.'

Archie Pennybet is killed, and, dying, his last thoughts are of his mother, and of Rupert and Edgar. The colonel comforts Edgar and Rupert with Rupert Brooke's 1914 sonnets:

> These laid the world away; poured out the red
> Sweet wine of youth; gave up the years to be
> Of work and joy, and that unhoped serene,
> That men call age; and those who would have been,
> Their sons, they gave, their immortality.
>
> Blow, bugles, blow! They brought us, for our dearth,
> Holiness, lacked so long, and Love, and Pain.
> Honour has come back, as a king, to earth,
> And paid his subjects with a royal wage;
> And Nobleness walks in our ways again;
> And we have come into our heritage.[21]

Stanley, Lancaster and White, old schoolfellows at Kensingtowe, are all killed at Gallipoli.

The war is thoroughly romanticised by being linked with medieval chivalry and classical antiquity, and thereby directly back to their schooldays, where in classics and history they had absorbed the ideology that now sustained them. The colonel reminds them that the Dardanelles Straits were the Hellespont of the ancient world, and the Aegean 'the most mystic of the wine-dark seas of Greece'. He tells them stories of Jason and the Argonauts and the Trojan War:

> As he spoke, we were schoolboys again and listened with wide-open, wistful eyes. From the fender and the hearth-rug, we saw Leander swimming to Hero across the Dardanelles; we saw Darius, the Persian, throwing his bridge over the same narrow passage, only to be defeated at Marathon; and Xerxes, too, bridging the famous straits to carry victory into Greece, till at last his navy went under at Salamis.[22]

He also reminds them that war against the Turks is a new crusade:

> Christendom united fights for Constantinople, under the leadership of the British, whose flag is made up of the crosses of the saints. The army opposing the Christians fights under the crescent of Islam. It's the cross against the crescent, my lads.[23]

He sets this in the context of imperial defence; Britain already controls Suez and Gibraltar and needs to control the Dardanelles to make the Mediterranean secure. ('This roused the jingo devil in us and we burst into applause'.)

Abroad the troopship, with its rugby scrums and sing-songs, the school atmosphere is continued. Doe and Ray make friends with the hearty, pipe-smoking, plain-speaking Anglo-Catholic padre Monty, who is Raymond's self-portrait. Monty eulogises subalterns ('The boy-officer's been so grand and so boyishly unconscious of his grandeur all the time') and says he can forgive subalterns everything. He takes the place of Radley as father figure for the boys.

Monty proceeds to win the boys to his faith, to persuade them to confess, and he absolves them of their sins, to 'send them into the fight white' (i.e. pure). He compares the voyage to the vigil of the medieval knight, once again invoking chivalric imagery:

> D'you remember that picture, 'The Vigil', Rupert, where a knight is kneeling with his sword before the altar, being consecrated for the work he has in hand? Well, this voyage is the vigil for these fellows. Before they step ashore, they shall kneel in front of the same altar, and seek a blessing on their swords. Hang it! Aren't they young knights setting out on perilous work?[24]

Doe's aim is to 'do an absolutely *perfect* thing'. Rupert shares it. His grandfather's stories, the teaching and example of Mr Radley, the colonel's lectures, all contribute towards shaping his chivalry and his appreciation of what he seeks. Monty sets before him the vision of three ideas: goodness, truth and beauty. Goodness is beauty in morals, truth beauty in knowledge and it became his goal to 'pursue beauty like the Holy Grail'.[25]

They live life on Gallipoli with heightened intensity, Doe 'enjoying himself', declaring, 'Living through war is living deep. It's crowded, glorious living.'[26] Rupert becomes a captain, feeling great responsibility for his men ('They were my family—my childhood'). Doe is mortally wounded storming an enemy-held position. Rupert attends him, they speak haltingly to each other, in a deeply moving scene which mirrors the inadequacy of words to express the deepest emotions. Doe will die. ('Well, it can't be helped. If I'd known when I started that it would end like this—I'd have gone through with it just the same. I haven't got cold feet').[27] Rupert comments on Doe's beauty as he lies there and feels his love flaring to a higher intensity than ever before. He rides off, fiercely, heartbroken. ('I thought no one had ever loved as I did.') Monty comforts him, telling him that Doe did attain 'the perfect thing' at last and that their friendship has come to the perfect end.

> Your friendship is a more beautiful whole, as things are. Had there been no war, you'd have left school and gone your different roads, till each lost trace of the other. It's always the same. But, as it is, the war has held you in deepening intimacy till—till the end. It's—it's perfect.[28]

In France in 1918 Rupert goes over the top. The night before, he writes his last notes. He sees 'death in No Man's Land . . . as a wonderful thing . . . It is not ill to die standing . . . in front of your nation.' He feels that tomorrow, like Doe and Penny, he will do the perfect thing and grasp the Holy Grail that he has pursued. He does, and the novel ends on a climax of spirituality and sacrifice. It is the death for which their schooling has prepared them. It is the only possible culmination to a life which has been lived at its most intense, which has seen and pursued the noble vision and has known the true, pure spiritual love.

The imagery of the Great War, captured in newsreels, photographs, memoirs and the poems of Sassoon, Owen and co., has become a living nightmare—the trenches, no-man's-land, barbed wire, gas. But there was another side to this war of mass slaughter, mutilation and despair. There was innocence, patriotism, enthusiasm, gallantry and sportsmanship, the war of schoolboys and subalterns. This is the war so feelingly and movingly evoked in *Tell England*. Paul Fussell has pointed out that the war was 'a world of reinvigorated myth', a throwback to 'Renaissance and medieval modes of thought and feeling', a world of 'very unmodern superstitions, talismans, wonders, miracles, relics, legends and rumours', the story of the Angels of Mons, the legend of the crucified Canadian, the myth of the battalion of ghouls.[29] This is the world in which the chivalry, romance and crusade of *Tell England* are wholly in place.

The sentiment and *sang froid* which Fussell saw as the twin reactions of soldiers can both be seen in Edgar's death-bed scene.[30] Fussell found recall of front-line experience replete with 'the homoerotic', the term he uses to imply a 'sublimated [i.e. chaste] form of temporary homosexuality'.[31] J. R. Ackerley recalled that during the war 'I never met a recognisable or self-confessed adult homosexual . . . The Army with its male relationships was simply an extension of my public school.'[32] Many officers chose the best-looking soldiers as batmen, and officers had intense romantic friendships similar to those at public school, for instance Lieutenant Siegfried Sassoon and Lieutenant David Thomas. Doe and Ray fit this pattern precisely. The popularity of Housman's *A Shropshire Lad*, the legacy of the boy-loving Uranian poets and the frankly homoerotic nature of much wartime poetry, all reinforce this outlook.[33] The term 'homosexuality' is now so debased and pejorative, however, that another term is needed, free of physical overtones and conveying a different connotation: 'manly love' or 'romantic friendship'.

Fussell notes that blond boys were the ikons of this generation, harking back to the purity of Victorian chivalric painting, which invariably depicted Sir Galahad with a halo of golden hair.[34] They abound in poems and memoirs, symbols of innocence, purity and gallantry. Edgar Gray Doe is but a fictional extension of the real-life Rupert Brooke, whose blond good looks were part of his appeal. Rupert Brooke's beauty was much commented on. Even General Sir Ian Hamilton, commander-in-chief, Gallipoli, recorded, 'He looked extraordinarily handsome, quite a knightly presence.'[35]

The poignant collection, *War Letters of Fallen Englishmen*, edited by Laurence Housman, contains abundant evidence for all the aspects of the subaltern's war dramatised in *Tell England*. The chaste but intense male friendship is unself-consciously caught in the letter from Lieutenant Denis Oliver Barnett (St Paul's), killed in action, 15 August 1915 at the age of twenty, who wrote to his father of the death in action of his friend Kenneth:

> His death hits me harder than the death of all the valiant men I've grown to like and love out here. The love that grows quickly and perhaps artificially when men are together up against life and death has a peculiar quality. Death that cuts it off does not touch the emotions at all, but works right in the soul of you; . . . Regret is what you feel, but there is something rather better than that really, which I think is what makes men. My love for Kenneth was not a war-baby, and so his loss is more painful to me than any other.[36]

It was possible amid the slaughter, the strain and the horror to be sustained by an essentially romantic patriotism and religious chivalry. Lieutenant Christian Carver (Rugby), who died of his wounds in Flanders, 23 July 1917, aged twenty, wrote to his brother:

> I always feel that I am fighting for England, English fields, trees, English atmospheres, and good days in England—and all that is synonymous for Liberty.

and later 'in our steel helmets and chain visors we somehow recall *Pilgrim's Progress*, armoured figures passing through the valley of the shadow.'[37]

Second Lieutenant John Sherwin Engall (St Paul's) wrote to his parents three days before his death in action (1 July 1916) at the age of twenty:

I took my Communion yesterday with dozens of others who are going over tomorrow; and never have I attended a more impressive service. I placed my soul and body in God's keeping, and I am going into battle with His name on my lips, full of confidence and trusting implicitly in Him. I have a strong feeling that I shall come through safely; but nevertheless, should it be God's holy will to call me, I am quite prepared to go, and . . . I could not wish for a finer death; and you, dear Mother and Dad, will know that I died doing my duty to my God, my Country and my King, and ask that you should look upon it as an honour that you should have given a son for the sake of King and Country.[38]

The intoxicating joy of fighting, that extra intensity in living that Doe experiences can be found in a letter from Captain the Hon. Julian Grenfell (Eton) to his mother:

I have not washed for a week or had my boots off for a fortnight . . . It is all *the* best fun. I have never felt so well or so happy or enjoyed anything so much . . . The fighting-excitement vitalizes everything, every sight and word and action.[39]

He died of his wounds, 26 May 1915, aged twenty-seven. Lieutenant Paul Jones (Dulwich), killed in action on 31 July 1917, aged twenty-one, wrote to his brother:

I can say that I have never in all my life experienced such wild exhilaration as on the commencement of a big stunt like the last April one for example. The excitement for the last half hour or so before it is like nothing on earth. The only thing that compares with it are the few minutes before the start of a big school match.[40]

But perhaps most of all there is the pursuit of the beautiful ideal, the Holy Grail, sought by Doe and Ray in fiction and by others in reality. Paul Jones wrote to his brother:

In peacetime one just lives one's own little life, engaged in trivialities, worrying about one's own comfort, about money matters, and all that sort of thing—just living for one's own self. What a sordid life it is! In war, on the other hand, even if you do get killed, you only anticipate the inevitable by a few years in any case, and you have the satisfaction of knowing that you have 'pegged out' in the attempt to help your country. You have in fact realized the ideal, which, as far as I can see, you very rarely do in ordinary life.[41]

Captain Claude Templar (Wellington and Sandhurst), captured in December 1914, escaped from Germany in 1917, returned to the front and was killed in action on 4 June 1918, aged twenty-three. He wrote:

When I was locked up in Germany, I used to pray for this moment; I used to dream of the romance of war, its wild strange poetry crept into my soul; I used to think that the glory of going back to the beautiful adventure was worth any price. And now it's all come true, just like things happen in fairy tales . . . And I resolve to be a worthy warrior. To fight to the finish, to love to the finish, to sacrifice everything but never honour.[42]

Second Lieutenant Eric Lever Townsend (City of London School), killed in action 15 December 1916 at the age of twenty, wrote to his parents:

> But for the war I and all the others would have passed into oblivion like the countless myriads before us. We should have gone about our trifling business, eating, drinking, sleeping, hoping, marrying, giving in marriage, and finally dying with no more achieved than when we were born, with the world no different for our lives . . . But we shall live for ever in the results of our efforts. We shall live as those who by their sacrifice won the Great War. Our spirits and our memories shall endure in the proud position Britain shall hold in the future.[43]

There was a sense that they were a chosen generation. Lieutenant the Hon. Eric Lubbock (Eton) killed in Flanders on 11 March 1917, aged twenty-three, saw the war as a struggle for Christian values and wrote to his mother:

> We cannot help being thankful that we were chosen, and not another generation, to do this work, and pay this price.[44]

Men like this would have recognised the essential truth of Ernest Raymond's picture.

Tell England was filmed in 1930, one of the earliest British talkies.[45] It emerged as an altogether more austere work than the book, downbeat, agonised, spare. Stripping away the rhetoric, the chivalric message, the celebration of male love, its adapter (A. P. Herbert) pared the story down to the bare bones and the director, Anthony Asquith, added graphic documentary style reconstructions of the Gallipoli campaign. The effect was a much bleaker vision, suggesting the influence of *Journey's End*, a far less exhilarated and romantic view of the strain and stress of trench warfare on public school officers. The school scenes are reduced to three, the big speeches eliminated. Edgar, his nerves ragged, takes to drink and when he denounces the war ('I know what I'd like to tell England') we see images of slaughter and destruction. But he pulls himself together and dies gallantly, with the death-bed scene of the book and the classical epitaph faithfully reproduced. Asquith, whose elder brother Raymond had perished in the war, perhaps entertained a less romantic view than Ernest Raymond. But Raymond's spirit was faithfully captured in Peter Weir's deeply moving film, *Gallipoli* (1981), which centred not on two public school gentlemen but on two Australian private soldiers, one dark (Mel Gibson), one fair (Mark Lee). Yet it caught perfectly the chivalry, romanticism, male comradeship and youth of Raymond's novel, with the theme of sport highlighted (running rather than swimming), the same eagerness for adventure, and the same tragic, heroic outcome.

If anyone doubts the power of imaginative literature to encapsulate the mind set of an age, let them look to *Peter Pan*. With that prophetic and reflective power that is given to the most profound of creative popular writers, J. M. Barrie tapped, explored and preserved for all time through the medium of fantasy the psyche of the young upper-class public-school-educated Edwardian elite, a youth which glorified battle and adventure, believed in love of country, heroism and sacrifice.

Peter Pan (1904) is the apotheosis of the boy who refuses to grow up, who wants always to remain a boy and enjoy adventure in a world of Indians, pirates and wild beasts. 'I am youth; I am joy,' he declares. He leads an all-male band, the lost boys, in a life of exciting and permanent warfare. Faced with death, Peter observes, 'To die would be an awfully big adventure,' one of the most haunting and poignant phrases in English literature. Captured, the boys refuse to serve Captain Hook if they cannot be legal subjects of King George, sing 'Rule Britannia' and are urged by their surrogate mother Wendy in what she is sure is the wish of their real mothers: 'We hope our sons will die like English gentlemen.' Rupert Brooke came from Cambridge specially to see it and pronounced it the best play he had ever seen. The line 'To die would be an awfully big adventure' Barrie borrowed from George Llewellyn-Davies, best loved of his adoptive children and the model for Peter Pan, Rupert Brooke died of blood poisoning en route for Gallipoli in 1915. George Llewellyn-Davies died in the trenches in 1915. They never grew old or perhaps even grew up. Like thousands of other boys, the flower of their generation, they left school and went directly to Neverland. Rupert Ray and Edgar Doe speak for them in *Tell England*.

Notes

1 On this development see Martin Green, *Children of the Sun*, London, 1977.
2 See John MacKenzie, *Propaganda and Empire*, Manchester, 1984; John MacKenzie ed., *Imperialism and Popular Culture*, Manchester, 1986; Richard Usborne, *Clubland Heroes*, London, 1974; William Vivian Butler, *The Durable Desperadoes*, London, 1974; Patrick Howarth, *Play Up and Play the Game*, London, 1973; Colin Watson, *Snobbery with Violence*, London, 1971; Jeffrey Richards, *Visions of Yesterday*, London, 1973.
3 Ernest Raymond, *The Story of My Days*, London, 1968, 114.
4 Rupert Brooke, *Collected Poems* (1918), London, 1966, 146. On the lost generation see Reginald Pound, *The Lost Generation*, London, 1964; Robert Wohl, *The Generation of 1914*, Cambridge, Massachussets, 1979; Jeanne MacKenzie, *The Children of the Souls*, London, 1986.

5 Raymond, *Story of My Days*, 130-1.
6 Raymond, *Story of My Days*, 133.
7 Raymond, *Story of My Days*, 179-81.
8 The reviews are all quoted by Raymond, *Story of My Days*, 182-5.
9 Ernest Raymond, *Please You Draw Near Me*, London, 1969, 69.
10 Ernest Raymond, *Tell England* (1922), London, 1973, 127, 55.
11 Raymond, *Tell England*, 95.
12 Raymond, *Tell England*, 25.
13 Raymond, *Tell England*, 53.
14 Raymond, *Tell England*, 26, 108.
15 Raymond, *Tell England*, 43.
16 It turns out that Ray did break the cane but while sleepwalking.
17 Raymond, *Tell England*, 55.
18 Raymond, *Tell England*, 119.
19 Raymond, *Tell England*, 167-8.
20 Raymond, *Tell England*, 168, 170.
21 Raymond, *Tell England*, 177.
22 Raymond, *Tell England*, 178.
23 Raymond, *Tell England*, 179.
24 Raymond, *Tell England*, 207-8.
25 Raymond, *Tell England*, 215.
26 Raymond, *Tell England*, 273.
27 Raymond, *Tell England*, 295.
28 Raymond, *Tell England*, 298.
29 Paul Fussell, *The Great War and Modern Memory*, New York and London, 1975, 27-8.
30 Fussell, *Great War*, 181.
31 Fussell, *Great War*, 272.
32 J. R. Ackerley, *My Father and Myself* (1968), Harmondsworth, 1984, 102.
33 On this subject see Timothy D'Arch Smith, *Love in Earnest*, London, 1970; Fussell, *Great War*, 270-309.
34 Fussell, *Great War*, 275.
35 Reginald Pound, *Lost Generation*, 121.
36 Laurence Houseman, *War Letters of Fallen Englishmen*, London, 1930, 40.
37 Housman, *War Letters*, 68-9.
38 Housman, *War Letters*, 107.
39 Housman, *War Letters*, 118.
40 Housman, *War Letters*, 159.
41 Housman, *War Letters*, 159.
42 Housman, *War Letters*, 275.
43 Housman, *War Letters*, 278.
44 Housman, *War Letters*, 177.
45 R. J. Minney, *'Puffin' Asquith*, London, 1973, 60-65.

10

Love letter from a rebel:
The Loom of Youth

)

The Loom of Youth created as great a sensation in 1917 as *Tom Brown's Schooldays* had in 1857. But in retrospect it has to be seen as an alternative rather than oppositional cultural form, and an alternative strongly conditioned by the author's personal circumstances.

The author, Alec Waugh, the son of the publisher Arthur Waugh and older brother of Evelyn, attended Sherborne School from 1911 to 1915. Gregarious, sociable, good at games and keen on work, he had enjoyed every minute of it. He recalled in 1954:

> I was the kind of boy who gets most out of a public school. I loved cricket and football and was reasonably good at them. I was in the first XV and my last summer headed the batting averages. My father had lit in me a love of poetry and an interest in history and the classics. More often than not I went into the class-room looking forward to the hour that lay ahead. I enjoyed the whole competitive drama of school life—the cups and caps and form promotions.[1]

In 1915 he was house captain, a prefect, top batsman in the eleven and had just won the English verse prize when a homosexual scandal broke ('a number of names were involved and a chapter that had been long closed was opened'). The headmaster did not expel him but suggested that his father remove him at the end of term. Two house masters, who felt that he should have been expelled, organised a boycott. He was not allowed to go up to receive his prize at prize-giving. But two masters (S. P. B. Mais and Geoffrey Morris, the sixth-form master) stood by him and he ended his school career in true schoolboy hero fashion by scoring seventy-seven in the final house match. ('How often have I not in memory relived that hour'.) For all this final glory, he unquestionably felt that he had been prematurely ejected from paradise. As he waited to join the army he was consumed with longing for Sherborne and resentful that his time there had been curtailed. It was in this mood that he wrote *The Loom of Youth*. He was still only seventeen. He wrote it at white heat in just seven and a half weeks, his spelling and punctuation corrected by his father. He never revised it, and it was printed as written. He recalled in his autobiography:

> The impulse that dictated me to write the book was in very large part a need to relive the past on paper . . . It was in part a nostalgic book; yet at the same time my nostalgia was tinctured with resentment. I need not have been here at all. I could either be still at Sherborne or I could have taken a commission straightaway, as so many others had, but for that scandal. I was partly to blame, but only partly. I was the victim of a system which encouraged the myth of *The Brushwood Boy* and created a conspiracy of silence to conceal the reality of the public schoolboy's life . . . I was impelled by a need to explain and justify myself. It is in such a mood that a man at the end of a long and intense love affair writes to the mistress whom he still adores, but nonetheless holds responsible for the rupture . . . Perhaps in the last analysis that is what *The Loom of Youth* was—a love letter to Sherborne.[2]

Although he had loved the school, Waugh had found himself in constant conflict with authority. At one stage he had even adopted a monocle in imitation of Psmith in *Mike*. Why did he rebel so fiercely against that which he loved? First there was a stubborn individualism ('In part, it was a hatred of conformity, a resolve not to be turned out to a pattern: a loathing of pomposity which has inspired me always to take the minority point of view, to argue the case of the minority').[3] Second, there was the impulse to expose the misconceptions about the public schools, due to guilt and resentment over the school's attitude to sex and love. He set himself against the idealisation of public schools epitomised by Kipling's *The Brushwood Boy*:

> I knew that the public school boy was not like that. I knew . . . that cribbing was the general practice in certain forms. I knew that it was not considered dishonourable to tell a lie to a master. I suspected that the public school Code of Honour was a unilateral deal invented by masters for the benefit of masters . . . Most of all I resented the conspiracy of silence that existed towards the inevitable consequences of herding together monastically children of thirteen and men of eighteen, for two thirds of the year.[4]

Third, his spirit of rebellion was fanned by intense house partisanship. School House, once cock house of Sherborne, had lost its pre-eminence to the house run by G. M. Carey, an Old Shirburnian, an Oxford and England captain, depicted in *The Loom* as 'The Bull'. Waugh, in retrospect, pronounced the Bull 'a fine man; but he was fierce and difficult'. Carey identified so closely with the school that he regarded anyone who disagreed with him as disloyal to it. Between 1911 and 1913 Carey's had an enormous run of success. During this period they lost only one house match. School House men like Waugh grew to resent Carey's success and methods. Criticism of these methods became a corollary of Waugh's crusade for candour, with the result that he pilloried Carey in *The Loom*. Looking back, Waugh admitted, 'Nothing could have been more silly and illogical. For the misunderstandings that there were between us, I have only myself to blame. He stood for all the things that I admired. He could have been the friend I needed on the staff; instead I made an adversary of him.'[5] All three of these strands merged to provide the structure of the novel.

Waugh admitted that *The Loom of Youth* was autobiographical ('the story term by term of my four years at Sherborne'), though he omitted his own leaving in disgrace. He believed it to be 'a true record of the average boy's experience'.[6] It was rejected by five publishers before being accepted by Grant Richards, thanks to recommendations from both Thomas Seccombe, Professor of History at Sandhurst, and S. P. B. Mais. Waugh believed that the timing was crucial: 'If *The Loom* had not been published till after the war, it would not have caused the sensation that it did.'[7]

Thomas Seccombe contributed a preface to highlight its contemporary significance. He proclaimed it 'a story of the public school as it is', well written, marked by a quality hardly ever found associated with school books: objective reality. In particular, Seccombe set it in the context of school fiction by pointedly comparing its reality to the unreality of its predecessors. ('I thought with a reminiscent shudder of *Stalky and Co.*, . . . the ignominy of Farrar and the calculated falsity of Talbot Baines Reed'.)[8] But, more than this, he erected it into an indictment of the public school system, which he held in part responsible for the Great War, because the schools were dominated by the 'tyranny of the bloods', games took precedence over learning (in particular history) and the ruling elite emerged ignorant, complacent, insular and backward-looking:

> One hundred years since the old trinity of School, Varsity and Church won the European War, when England stood with its back to the wall against a tyrant. The last gleams of this particular chivalry and of the grim old square chins who fought in the Crimea and at Lucknow have well-nigh passed. It cannot, unassisted, save the Allies of 1917, though it has fought as bravely and as unreservedly as of old. But success had sapped the vitals of its old perfect self-confidence, and we must now have a new worship, new ideals, a more imaginative and communistic form of society and . . . Education must be irradiated . . . There will have to be a considerable shattering of Perrins, Trails and tin gods generally. The Athletic god is a fine and a clean and in the main a necessary one, but its monopoly makes Patriotism far too small a thing.[9]

The book came out on 20 July 1917, shortly after Waugh began serving as a machine-gunner in Flanders. It was reprinted eight times between then and October 1918. It was issued in Cassell's pocket library in 1929, in Penguin in 1942 and in a new edition, reset, and slightly revised, in 1955. This was reprinted in hardback in 1972 and in paper-back in 1984.

The Loom was an immediate best-seller, reviewed everywhere and, more important, provoking a raging controversy. *The Times Literary Supplement* declared it 'a most promising first book. Mr. Alec Waugh has something definite to say, the ability to say it and an appreciation of the subtler causes of action and inaction.' E. B. Osborn in *The Morning Post*, Gerald Gould in *The New Statesman*, J. C. Squire in *Land and Water* and Ralph Straus in *The Bystander* all hailed the book as an astounding achievement. Waugh was proclaimed a soldier novelist, prose counterpart of the much lauded soldier poets. H. W. Massingham, influential editor of *The Nation*, wrote:

> I have read few books that have interested me more than Mr. Waugh's *Loom of Youth*. It is in one respect an almost miraculous production. Here is a boy of eighteen who discusses his school life, reproduces its talk and atmosphere and builds up a merciless memorial of its evils and shortcomings. It is a most straightforward account, it cannot have been invented and yet I thought it sufficiently delicate . . . It seems to me that it is a revolutionary work—if only the parents of England will read it and having read it, act on it. If they do the one without the other, it is on their conscience that they risk the ruin of their children's characters and minds. So I urge them to do the one and the other.

H. G. Wells and Arnold Bennett wrote to Waugh's father praising the book.[10]

But what does it actually say? It centres on the battle for the soul of Gordon Caruthers (Waugh) between poetry (Mr Ferrers) and athletics (Mr Buller). Gordon is genuinely attracted to both. *The Loom* is divided into four books, one for each year. The first part of Book 1 consists inevitably of the lonely and bewildered new boy finding his feet at Fernhurst School and being socialised in the pattern outlined by Ian Weinberg. Gordon is shocked by the swearing. He does not know the masters, the layout of the school, the routines or the rituals. But he learns them. He wants above all to be popular, and he earns respect first from his fellows and the prefects when he man-fully takes six of the best for slacking in class. He is in School House and, beginning to make his mark there in form and in sport, he finds school 'inexpressibly joyful'.

House loyalty reigns supreme and house victories are everything. It worries Buller that house matches are watched with greater keenness than school matches ('He thought that everything should be secondary to the interests of Fernhurst').[11] The first term ends in triumph, with Gordon taking first prize. Next term the house begins to lose matches, and defeat in the house competition leads to demoralisation and disorder. But Gordon begins to distinguish himself in house cricket and earns the disapproval of the Bull. He is chosen for the Colts and gets his cap, the nervous waiting for and ecstacy of gaining it vividly described. Meredith, the admired and energetic captain of games, is Gordon's ideal and all that he wishes to be.

Book 2 covers Gordon's second year, the best at Fernhurst, when he ceases to be a new boy and does not yet have responsibility. He remains obsessed with sport and, by now neglecting his work, is bottom of 5A. He rags, slacks, enjoys life, but ragging is a sideline. 'In an Easter term, football is the only thing that any respectable man will really worry about.'[12] His emotions at his first big match before the whole school are described. Gordon distinguishes himself but then loses his touch and his sporting reputation, falls from favour and maintains his notoriety by gaining a reputation for reckless bravado and disregard of all authority, coming to be talked of as a 'mixture between Don Juan and Puck'. Buller is perplexed by his slackness and loss of form. But Gordon is introduced to the glories of poetry when Tester reads him Swinburne's *Atalanta* and he finds his life illuminated and given purpose by 'the call of beauty'. He becomes increasingly discontented with the system through reading Arnold Lunn's *The Harrovians* and Compton MacKenzie's *Sinister Street*.

In his third year (Book 3) Gordon is sent for by Buller, who reprimands him for not playing to his full capacity. Gordon respects and admires the Bull and wants to like him but dislikes his temper and his insistence on uniformity of view. Despite his new-found commitment to poetry, Gordon defends games when Betteridge attacks them:

> The English race is the finest in the whole world and has been bred on footer and cricket. I own the Public School system is rotten to the core; but not because of games. It stamps out personality, tries to make types of us all, refuses to allow us to think for ourselves. We have to read and pretend to like what our masters tell us. No freedom. But games are all right.[13]

Gordon's football prowess is now reaching its height and he begins to get on with Buller. But he continues to read poetry. He identifies with Byron, cultivates the idea of rebellion, sees himself fighting philistinism, puritanism and the outdated idea of the masters. Challenged by Rudd, Gordon joins him in breaking bounds to attend the local fair, where he has a rapturous encounter with a girl. Tester warns him about seeking notoriety for its own sake and courting the sack. He is needed in the school to become house captain and to fulfil his theory of rebellion by freeing the school from Buller's tyranny.

Gordon falls under the influence of the unconventional and enthusiastic Mr Ferrers, who has burst upon Fernhurst like a tornado, bubbling with new ideas, intolerant of prejudice and tradition, clamorous for reform. ('He was the great god of Gordon's soul.') Ferrers believes in finding out what a boy likes, encouraging and sympathising with him, and thus leading him on to greater things. So he lends Gordon books, discusses ideas and opens up an exciting new world. Ferrers writes articles attacking the public school system in terms Gordon agrees with. Ferrers promotes the modern novel and scorns Kipling. Gordon decides to specialise in history, getting through by cribs, but devotes himself almost entirely to poetry and cricket.

Book 4 begins with the outbreak of war in 1914. Ferrers welcomes it. ('A war is just what we want. It will wake us up from sleeping; stir us into life; inflame our literature.')[14] With many seniors leaving to join up, Gordon becomes house captain and a prefect, enjoying his new authority. But he has a confrontation with the Bull. Buller wants the sixth form to do voluntary gym to set an example but the sixth have traditionally been exempt from gym and Gordon resists. It is at this point that he realises the emptiness of athleticism:

> He saw athleticism as it really was, shorn of its glamour, and he knew its poverty. It led nowhither. He wondered if boys, as soon as they left school, realised of what little real use proficiency at rugger was as training for the more serious issues of life; if they understood how trivial it was, when it ceased to culminate in the glory of a gold tasselled cap.[15]

His life is brightened by romance. He falls for Morcombe, a junior who shares his love of poetry, and the time they spend together in the evenings is 'the brightest of his Fernhurst days'. But the war hangs over Fernhurst, dampening the lustre of games. The young masters and older boys leave. Jeffries is reported killed; Tester leaves for the front, expecting not to return. The rise of anti-athleticism reaches a climax when Gordon suggests a debate on the value of compulsory games. Ferrers opens by denouncing unpreparedness for war and linking it to devotion to games. Davenport argues that games build up bodies but starve minds. Gordon's comprehensive denunciation ('Games don't win battles, but brains do, and brains aren't trained on the footer field') of the sacrifice of the intellect and of academic work to the tyranny of athleticism leads to the motion rejecting compulsory games being carried overwhelmingly.[16] Buller storms out, his era ended.

In his final game School House triumph and Gordon scores eighty-four runs. But on reflection he finds his victory empty. He has achieved success in athletics, which he now rejects. He has spent a year in guerilla warfare with the Bull, one of the few really fine masters in the school.

He has sought power, popularity and praise—the worldly goals—he must in future seek spiritual and individual ones. The headmaster congratulates him on having turned out so well as a prefect, and he leaves with mixed feelings to embark on 'the long littleness of life'.

Waugh was working from life and it is not surprising that his characters are convincing. Not only was Caruthers a self-portrait but all the masters were drawn directly from life. The headmaster ('The Chief'), a kindly but firm idealist of indomitable optimism and deep Christian faith, is based on Nowell Charles Smith, headmaster in Waugh's time. Mr Buller is G. M. Carey, and Waugh pictures him unforgettably running up and down the touchline shouting, 'I have played football for twenty-five years, I coached Oxford teams and Gloucestershire teams, led an English scrum and for fifteen years I have taught footer here, but never saw such a display! Shirking, the whole lot of you.'[17] Waugh depicts everyone as afraid of him except for the school's top sporting hero, Lovelace, who is afraid of nothing. Infuriated during a Colts' match at the poor standard of play, Buller actually kicks Gordon. He simply cannot understand people who do not share his values and standards.

Mr Claremont is 'a dry humourist who had adopted schoolmastering for want of something better to do, had apparently regretted it afterwards and developed into a cynic'. But he loves poetry and seeks to communicate his passion for it to the boys, in vain in most cases. He is based on Henry Robinson King, who had memorised 50,000 lines of poetry and would bicycle round the countryside reciting them. MacDonald, the brilliant scholar and teacher who made history and classics live, is not identified but sounds suspiciously like W. B. Wildman, vividly described by Cecil Day Lewis in terms very similar to Waugh's.[18] Ferrers was S. P. B. Mais, an inspiring and brilliant teacher, later a prolific writer and broadcaster.

Similarly the boys are so precisely characterised and differentiated that it is hard to believe that Waugh was not drawing on his contemporaries for inspiration. There is Clarke, the head of house, 'one of those brilliant scholars who are too brilliant to get scholarships', a fanatic and militarist, devoted to the school and the house. 'He had the welfare of the House at heart and loved it with a blind, unreasoning love that was completely misunderstood.' But when he tries to get the O.T.C. run efficiently, and to promote house scholarship and academic success, he ends up hated.[19] There is Lovelace Minor, who 'despised and deceived most of the masters; among his friends he was unimpeachably loyal'. He loves games but never takes them sufficiently seriously to please the Bull. He plays them for his own pleasure. His chief interest is horse racing.[20] There is Hunter, who knows all the school scandal and politics. 'It was his boast that he had sufficient evidence to expel half the fifteen and the whole eleven.'[21] There is Archie Fletcher, who has only two objects in life, to get his house cap and to enjoy himself, and the form his pleasure took was ragging masters.[22] There is Rudd, senior scholar, weedy and unwashed, ragged constantly because he is no good at games and has brains.[23] There is Tester, whom the school thinks 'quite a decent chap, awfully fast of course, doesn't care a damn what he does, just lives to enjoy himself and have a damned good time'. He plays up to this reputation but is haunted by the emptiness of it all and longs for spiritual peace.[24] Waugh concludes that the public school system turns out mainly mediocrities and that the average public school man is a type; 'their conversation ran entirely on games, scandal and the work they had not done'.[25]

Waugh carefully sets out the reality of schoolboy behaviour as distinct from fictional idealisations. First he details the effect of the school on a prep. school innocent:

> When a boy leaves his preparatory school he has a conscience; he would not tell lies; he would be scrupulously honest in form; he would not borrow things he never meant to return; he would say nothing he would be ashamed of his mother or sister overhearing. But before this same innocent has been at school two terms he has learnt that everything except money is public property . . . The code of a public schoolboy's honour is very elastic. Masters are regarded as common enemies; and it is never necessary to tell them the truth. Expediency is the golden rule in all relations with the common room.[26]

Gordon learns to swear, lie and crib but the headmaster sets out to end the system of everyone using each other's clothes. The house resists, defending its traditions, in precise recreation of an episode in Nowell Charles Smith's headmastership.

Cribbing is universal. 'If a master is such an arrant ass as to let you crib, it is his own lookout; and after all, we take the sporting chance,' says Jeffries.[27] Initially Gordon does not crib, but he takes it up in his second term, not to get better marks but to be free to discuss sport ('Gordon dreamed football night and day'). 'No one ever cribbed in order to get a prize,' observes Waugh; 'they crib from mere slackness.'[28] Cribbing is an art form and Waugh explores the art and ethics of it.

The idea that the public school boy's code of honour forces him to own up at once is entirely erroneous. 'Boys only own up when they are bound to be found out; they are not quixotic.'[29] When there is a riot in the house and Clarke demands that the culprits own up, no one moves and everyone gets a hundred lines every day until the end of term. When two boys are overheard swearing on a field day on Salisbury Plain, the Head asks them to own up; no one does.[30]

What is the effect on the public school boy of the public school system?

The average person comes through all right. He is selfish, easy-going, pleasure-loving, absolutely without conscience, for the simple reason that he never thinks. But he is a jolly good companion; and the Freemasonry of a Public School is amazing. No man who had ever been through a good school can be an outsider . . . Very few Public School men ever do a mean thing to their friends. And for a system that produces such a spirit there is something to be said after all. But for a boy with a personality school is very dangerous. Being powerful, he can do nothing by halves; his actions influence not only himself, but many others . . . He will do whatever he does on a large scale and people are bound to look at him.[31]

Religion is comparatively unimportant to the boys. School House, says Waugh, was 'entirely pagan' and, although Gordon is confirmed, it has as little effect on him as it did on most boys.

He was not an atheist; he accepted Christianity in much the same way as he accepted the Conservative Party. All the best people believed in it, so it was bound to be all right; but at the same time it had not the slightest influence over his actions. If he had any religion at this time it was House Football.[32]

In his examination of athleticism, Waugh carefully sets out the way in which sport is played, and it is not in accordance with the traditional code advanced by the Bull. Buller is mocked by Gordon and his friends for believing in constant training 'so as to become strong, clean-living Englishmen, who love their bodies and have some respect for their minds'. They believe in training enough to win and no more, and they want to win house matches because of their blind house patriotism. For them the house always comes before the school.[33]

Buller reprimands Gordon for referring to other houses as 'swine' ('It's not the English idea of sport'), though all Gordon's friends agree that they are. Boys deliberately decide to lay opponents out under cover of the game and even bribe other boys to crock their enemies, an idea that horrifies Buller ('You cannot honestly believe that any gentleman would play a game in that spirit').[34] Buller reports Gordon to the Head for planning this, and the Head, deeply shocked by Gordon's admission, withdraws his sixth-form privileges. Eventually Gordon is found guilty of questioning the referee, preferring house to school, swearing and indulging in unsportsmanlike behaviour in a match between School House and Buller's. Buller, who wants Gordon's influence broken, arranges for him to be beaten by the Games Committee. But School House backs Gordon up rather than Buller.

Clarke, the keen head of house, denounces the games mania. ('If as a country we had only ourselves to think about, let us put up a god of sport. But we have not. We have to compete with the other nations of the world. And late cuts are precious little use in commerce. This athleticism is ruining the country'.)[35] But Mansell gains great applause when he announces, 'From time immemorial, it has been the privilege of the members of this House to enjoy themselves, to work if they wanted to, to do any damn thing they wanted to. The only thing they'd got to do was to play like hell in the Easter term.'[36] Clarke persists, caning recalcitrants and idlers, but the house remains divided, faction-ridden and games-mad. Waugh admits that the public school system suits the average man:

> It is inclined to destroy individuality, to turn out a fixed pattern; it wishes to take everyone, no matter what his tastes or ideas may be, and make him conform to its own ideals. In the process, much good is destroyed, for the Public School Man is slack, easy-going, tolerant, is not easily upset by scruples, laughs at good things, smiles at bad, yet he is a fine follower. He has learnt to do what he is told; he takes life as he sees it and is content. So far so good . . . But take the boy who has it in him to be a leader, who is not merely content to follow, but wishes to be at the head, in the forefront of the battle. What of him? Gordon went to Fernhurst with the determination to excel, and at once was brought face to face with the fact that success lay in a blind worship at the shrine of the god of Athleticism. Honesty, virtue, moral determination—these mattered not at all . . . He who wishes to get to the front has to strive after success on the field and success on the field alone. This is the way that the future leaders of England are being trained to take their proper place in the national struggle for the right and farsighted civilization. On this alone the system stands condemned.[37]

The third element to which Waugh draws attention is sex. The new boys are looked over by the older boys. Gordon experiences it and later takes part in it himself. On his very first night in the dormitory there are discussions about Meredith, a splendid wicket keeper and the finest half-back in the school, and his involvement with another boy, Davenham. But this is dismissed: 'You must allow a good deal to a blood like him.'[38] The 'bloods' have licence from the boys to indulge themselves sexually, and in general the boys' morality is easy. They are all amused to learn that Buller has caned some of the boys in his house for 'talking the most arrant filth'. 'Old Bull thought because his house was always in wonderful training that the spirit of innocence ruled over the place.' Mansell comments cynically, 'Well, it's obvious that a blood must be a bit of a rip; and Buller's is merely an asylum for bloods!' Gordon asks whether a 'blood' can be a decent fellow. Jeffries replies, 'Decent fellow? Who on earth said they were anything else? Johnson's a simply glorious man. Only a bit fast; and that doesn't matter much.'[39]

Gordon had been warned about this kind of behaviour by his prep. school master but finds it accepted at public school and ceases to be shocked by it. When Meredith propositions him, he rejects him ('the whole idea is damned silly nonsense'). Jeffries warns him that Meredith could make life difficult for him, an idea that Gordon rejects ('Damn it all, the man is a gentleman'). Jeffries himself is expelled when the head-master discovers his affair with Fitzroy. Jeffries bitterly denounces his treatment:

> Who made me what I am but Fernhurst? Two years ago I came here as innocent as Caruthers there; never knew anything. Fernhurst taught me everything; Fernhurst made me worship games, and think that they alone mattered and everything else could go to the deuce. I heard men say about bloods whose lives were an open scandal, 'Oh, it's all right, they can play football.' I thought it was all right too. Fernhurst made me think it was. And now Fernhurst, that has made me what I am, turns round and says, 'You are not fit to be a member of this great school!' and I have to go. Oh, it's fair, isn't it?[40]

Nevertheless sex continues. As Betteridge comments, 'the higher you get up the school, the less you need worry about what you do. The prefect is supposed to be the model of what a public school boy should be. And yet he is about the fastest fellow in the school.'[41] Tester, sixteen years old, 'a house blood and "fast" ', is Gordon's study-mate. Tester tells him to leave the study when Stapleton comes up to see him ('You understand, don't you'). Soon Gordon is doing the same, and having a fling with Jackson. In his last year he has his romance with Morcombe.

Waugh developed this aspect of public school life in a subsequent volume of short stories, *Pleasure* (1921), which analyses the agonies and ecstacies of love between people of different ages, nationalities and status under varous circumstances. One of them details with considerable poignancy and understanding a romantic friendship at Durston School between seventeen-year-old Geoffrey Palmer, star bowler and captain of the house side, and the fifteen-year-old Merrick. 'Between him and Geoffrey has sprung up one of those romantic friendships, so perfectly natural in their setting, and impossible anywhere else, a relationship incomprehensible to those who have not been at some time or other closely connected with school or cathedral life.' They talk little, for Merrick is shy, and Geoffrey 'had never found it easy to translate his most intimate emotions into words. The magic of their relationship was for him so delicate, so finely spun, so easily spoilt, once lost so irrecoverable. It was enough for him to sit there beside this friend in the slow twilight, watching the loved face darken into silhouette.'[42] Geoffrey feels responsibility for moulding Merrick's character and future. But the crux comes when Geoffrey tries to extend the friend-ship beyond school. Due to leave school and enter the army, he goes away on O.T.C. training, being billeted with Carruthers (*sic*) of Fern-hurst, with whom he discusses his anxiety about being 'keen on a boy'. Carruthers reassures him that it is natural at school, where there are no girls, 'but it's a thing one outgrows'. While awaiting his posting, Palmer

returns to Durston to find that Merrick has transferred his affections
to Palmer's successor, Dallas. Palmer embarrasses everyone by hanging
about consumed with jealousy. Merrick falls in love with a girl and
becomes increasingly annoyed at being the love object of two male
rivals. When Palmer and Dallas fight over him, Merrick intervenes to
end the friendship. Palmer receives his posting and leaves: 'He had
done with boyhood and vaguely, uncertainly, he saw the new world—
into which he was about to enter, full of strange colours and excite-
ments and woman, wistful, passionate, mysterious, waited there with
outstretched arms beckoning him to her'.[43] Waugh later remarked of
Pleasure, 'The majority of old public school boys who read it seemed
to like it. But none of the men who had not been to a public school
could make head or tail of it. They told me in their reviews of it that
it was absurd, mawkish and unhealthy.'[44]

In his book *Public School Life* Waugh maintained that the popular
view of the public schools was formed through fiction. Writing against
a background of half a century of school stories, he was anxious to
dispel the myth and introduce truth. *Public School Life* is dedicated to
Arnold Lunn, whose *The Harrovians* he constantly cites as authentic
and calls it 'the most borrowed book in the house'. Waugh himself was
well versed in public school fiction, referring in *Public School Life* to
P. G. Wodehouse's 'delightful' *Mike*, Desmond Coke's 'very entertaining' *The Bending of a Twig*, H. A. Vachell's *The Hill* and Talbot Baines
Reed's work. But he admits that the greatest influence on him had been
Arnold Lunn's *The Harrovians* and *Loose Ends*.[45]

Waugh's principal target was Kipling's *The Brushwood Boy*, an
idealised portrait of a public school boy at odds with Waugh's experience. But he also refers obliquely to *Tom Brown's Schooldays*, in his
description of a boy's first days at school: 'It is not that he is bullied.
Boots are not shied at him when he says his prayers; he is not tossed in
a blanket; it is merely that he is utterly lonely, is in constant fear of
making mistakes, is never certain of what may happen next, and so
makes for himself troubles that do not exist.'[46] He overtly attacks
Eric: 'The author of *Eric* and such others who have never faced, really
faced, life and seen what it is, talk of the incalculable good one boy
can do, who refuses to be led astray by temptations and remains true
to the ideals he learnt in the nursery. If there comes into any school
such a boy, he is merely labelled as 'pi' and is taken no notice of.'[47]

The reaction to *The Loom* was fierce. Waugh and his father were
struck off the roll of old Shirburnians and the book was banned from
the school. *The Spectator* ran for ten weeks, and *The Nation* for six,
correspondence filling three or four pages in which schoolmasters
rejected Waugh's picture of public school life. Montague Rendall, the
headmaster of Winchester, called the book 'devilish, sensual, unthink-

able, destructive of and mocking all ideas, battening on profanity, Baudelaire and bawd . . . incredibly untrue'.[48] Edward Lyttleton, the former headmaster of Eton, pronounced it 'uniformly dull, occasionally unpleasant, and . . . almost wholly untrue'.[49] *The Quarterly Review* thought it '335 pages of pointless and sordid descriptions of bad faith, bad language, cruelty, squalor and incapacity, unadulterated by any delineation of character, any wit, any kindly feeling'.[50]

Others treated *The Loom* as a serous contribution to the educational debate. 'A mere schoolmaster' declared in *The Spectator* (10 November 1917), 'The general condition of Fernhurst may exist or have existed in certain schools at certain times.' But he goes on to give his own view of the problems as depicted in *The Loom*. 'The average Brtish schoolboy *is* unintellectual; he gets it from his home, but idlers are apt to get worried even in the Sixth; and most schools are not so barren of intellectual stimulus as Fernhurst is represented to have been.' But masters are overworked, undervalued and unable to provide as much intellectual stimulus as they would like. He claims that masters do not encourage athleticism at the expense of more vital things, but 'in any case athletics are wholesomer subjects of talk for the masses, than some things that might take their place'. Public opinion at school is a reflex of the community at large, which must share the blame. Smoking and swearing can be reduced if presented as 'bad form' rather than vices. He rejects the idea that sexual immorality is widespread, claiming that in many schools opinion among the boys has outlawed it. Greater supervision and suppression of the 'taking up' system, appeals to the common sense and decency of boys help too. His solution, perhaps not surprisingly, is to call for more, better paid and better trained teachers.

The educationalist J. Howard Whitehouse edited a symposium of articles and letters from *The Nation* provoked by Waugh's book. Sir Sydney Olivier claimed that much of the indictment of the schools in *The Loom* was accurate and was 'true, in greater or less degree, of *all* large boarding schools'. Oscar Browning called *The Loom* 'a great literary masterpiece and absolutely true in fact' and urged the replacement of boarding schools by day schools. R. H. Tawney argued that the faults of the public schools reflected the faults of society at large ('The tragedy of English education is the tragedy of English social life—the class system and class division'.) Whitehouse summarised the chief points of criticism to emerge from *The Nation*'s correspondence as the need to reform the curriculum, giving greater prominence to modern languages and modern history, arts and crafts and civics; the need to make public school religion more accessible and attractive; and the need to reduce the dominance of athletics.[51]

Not only did experts and pundits debate the questions raised by

The Loom, so did pupils, and two public schoolboys wrote book-length refutations of it. Martin Browne devoted his last half at Eton to writing *A Dream of Youth* (1918), 'because I love Eton so much'. Browne believed that 'the Public School principle is not only fundamentally sound, but the best educational principle we have got'. His belief was based on the quality of men it produced and who had successfully led Britain to victory in the Great War, the value of the public school system for instilling in boys strength of purpose and a sense of duty and honour, and the personal freedom which allowed them to develop their best traits.

Admitting that Waugh's view that many boys leave school with an antipathy to work is only too true, he lists five criticisms of public school education. Bad feeling between masters and boys he thinks was true in the past but no longer is. The incompetence of masters was not true at Eton. There have been problems with the curriculum and although he defends the value of the classics, he also favours the promotion of current affairs, science and English essays. He suggested that the hopeless position of boys too stupid to keep up with the standard set for the clever ones could be improved by more interesting subjects and imaginative teaching methods. To combat mental stagnation and repression of youthful energy of spirit, he agrees with Alec Waugh that more beauty is needed in lessons: 'We do want the free run of, and encouragement to enjoy, the work of the poets and artists, who have left us their wonderful treasures.' He claims that the tyranny of athleticism has been greatly exaggerated, pointing out that athletics are valuable for exercise and training the body and are not given undue prominence at Eton.

He believed that Waugh's picture of immorality was exaggerated. All boys are 'good chaps' at heart. But there is more immorality than there should be, for four reasons—lack of proper support and understanding at home, lack of proper sex instruction, lack of a homely atmosphere at school and the glamorisation of sin. He believes that 'boys can, should and will keep pure for the honour of their family, for the honour of their school, for the honour of womanhood and for the honour of God'.[52] This would be even more likely if the four problems he outlined were tackled.

But he placed the greatest stress on religion ('religion is the beginning and end of all reform . . . and without it nothing can be done'). He attributed the state of affairs depicted by Waugh to irreligion. Waugh's picture of contempt for and boredom with religion he believed to be correct for about half the average school. Of the remainder, the larger portion have a sentimental attraction to religion: the rest are the ones who really think and are interested and pray. He calls for the promotion at public schools of 'a personal simple God who is to rule our lives . . . a combination of Captain and Friend, the boy's ideal person', and for services marked by 'brevity, simplicity and reality', the introduction of voluntary chapel-going and the appointment of experienced school chaplains separate from the teaching staff.[53]

A seventeen-year-old public school prefect, writing under the *nom-de-plume* 'Jack Hood', published *The Heart of a Schoolboy* (1919), claiming that much of Waugh's criticism was exaggerated and strongly supporting Martin Browne's analysis. He supports compulsory games and fagging, urges that boys be told the truth and trusted and lays particular stress on the prefect system as the key to whether a school is moral or immoral.[54]

But not everyone thought Waugh's picture exaggerated. D. C. Temple admitted 'that the schoolboy, who has read it, probably by stealth, will uphold *The Loom of Youth* as in many ways a "true" account of life at a public school.'[55] Anthony Powell, reading *The Loom* at Eton a few years after its publication, recalled, 'By the time I read the novel it was accepted, anyway by boys, as a reasonably accurate treatment of the "romantic friendship"; that might take in some cases physical form.'[56] Cecil Day Lewis arrived at Sherborne shortly after the publication of the book to find it banned and regularly denounced from the pulpit. But copies were smuggled in and the boys proclaimed it 'a very fair picture of Sherborne . . . Boys did swear and blaspheme and practise immorality; so we took a poor view of those elders who proclaimed that such things could not happen at Sherborne, or if they did, should not have been written about.'[57]

The intensity and the circumstances under which Waugh wrote concealed the fact that his ideas were not new, nor were his solutions revolutionary. Regarded as an authority on the public schools, he was in demand after the war to lecture and write articles. In 1922 he devoted an entire non-fictional work, *Public School Life*, to expanding on his criticisms, and developing the ideas already expounded in fictional form in *The Loom*. Swearing is universal in the middle years; it is beneath 'the bloods' and regarded as 'side' in fags. Cribbing is widespread. Romantic friendships are harmless and inevitable. Waugh rejects the idea of the deliberate and calculated seduction of small boys, and sees unselfish affection as ennobling, but blames the authorities for misunderstanding and misrepresenting romantic friendships, thus introducing guilt. But he enters a *caveat* that boys learn to separate sex and love and to see love as sexless and vice versa, creating problems in later life. He argues that most boys find school work dull and live mainly for life outside the form room, that there is little bullying and that athleticism is a religion.

His solutions, however, are moderate. He makes it clear that reform rather than abolition is his aim. 'No one wants to destroy the public schools. No one would be so foolish. But we do maintain that the public school system . . . stands in drastic need of repair.'[58] He goes on to say that he accepts the public schools as the system best suited to the material with which it deals. He suggests no new system of teaching. He advocates neither day schools nor co-education. He seeks merely to end the conspiracy of silence on certain issues: cribbing, swearing, sex and romantic friendships. His positive suggestions are to make lessons more interesting in order to lessen the hold of games, and to lower the school leaving age from nineteen to seventeen to reduce the incidence of sex.

By the time of the 1929 pocket edition of *The Loom* the Seccombe preface was being omitted and Waugh explained that:

> it was never intended to be an attack on the system. I meant in a straight forward, truthful manner to describe the life at school . . . of the very type of boy . . . for whom the public school system had been devised . . . I regret certain misunderstandings and estrangements. I regret the pain it brought to people in whose debt I stand. And had I the rewriting of it, there are one or two unbalanced and exaggerated 'asides' that I should modify. At the same time it is a faithful narrative.[59]

In due course Waugh was restored to the Old Shirburnians and sent his sons to Sherborne.

The main thrust of *The Loom* revived some of the criticisms recurrent in the Edwardian period. The narrowness of the curriculum and the inculcation of snobbery were regularly aired. But Waugh explored other areas of complaint: the suppression of individuality and originality, the decay of the love of learning, the overvaluation of athletics. The revelation of an alternative public school code, however, was by no means new. In 1905 A. C. Benson had already pointed sadly to the fact of its existence in all the particulars that Waugh dramatises:

> The standard of purity is low; a vicious boy doesn't find his vicious tendencies by any means a bar to social success. Then the code of honesty is low; a boy who is habitually dishonest in the matter of work is not in the least repro-bated. I do not mean to say that there are not many boys who are both pure-minded and honest, but they treat such virtues as a secret preference of their own, and do not consider that it is in the least necessary to interfere with the practice of others or even to disapprove of it. And then comes the perennial difficulty of schoolboy honour; the one unforgivable offence is to com-municate anything to masters.[60]

He is expressing himself in sorrow and depicting something he wishes to see eradicated. He is writing from the schoolmaster's perspective, as was Welldon, who painted a similar picture in *Gerald Eversley's Friendship*. The difference with Waugh's book was that this was a boy writing and depicting reality without apology or recrimination.

Waugh was particularly influenced by Arnold Lunn's *The Harrovians*, which introduced a new type of fiction, a documentary realism which directly challenged the favourable image of the public schools, and demonstrated the misery of compulsory games, the promotion of dull conformity, the relative unimportance of work, and the presence of sex and blasphemy as an integral part of boy life. Waugh pays tribute to *The Harrovians* in *The Loom* by having Gordon read it and find it a revelation: 'This book, as no other book has done, photographs the life of a public school boy stripped of all sentiment, crude and raw, and is, of its kind, the finest school story written . . . it is true to life in every detail.'[61]

The criticism of the public schools that had been building up during the Edwardian era was dramatically silenced by the outbreak of war. Public school boys joined up in large numbers and conducted themselves with great gallantry. Their conduct was said to have vindicated classics, athletics and character training to the full. But by 1916–17, as the war dragged on, criticism awoke again, centred on the need to compete with the Germans, to win the war, and the cry went up for science and modern languages, brains rather than brawn, modernisation of school and nation.

The Loom ignited a massive controversy, set the tone and the scope of the debate that was taken up in fiction and non-fiction. There was a rash of public school novels by young men fresh from school, providing thinly fictionalised accounts of their own schools (Beverley Nichols's *Prelude*, John Heygate's *Decent Fellows*, John Connell's *Lyndesay*) and a stream of attacks on public school mentality (Richard Aldington's *Death of a Hero*, Eimar O'Duffy's *The Wasted Land* and D. W. Smith's *Out of Step*). These tended to centre on the destruction of individualism, class snobbery and absence of spiritual values, giving rather less prominence to athleticism, the classics, immorality and anti-intellectualism. There began too to be insistent demands for the abolition of the public schools. Ronald Gurner wrote several books advocating the virtues of day schools over public schools. It became a dominant theme in fiction and non-fiction, even if not dealing directly with the public schools—the warping effects on the emotions, attitudes, ideas and personality of the public school boy.

The same ambivalence towards the old school and its *mores* that Waugh displays recurred in many subsequent works of fiction—indeed, exclusion from the school following the revelation of sexual irregularity was the fate of another embryonic novelist, Simon Raven. Like Waugh he was to work out his contradictory feelings in fictional form in *Fielding Gray*, one of the 'Alms for Oblivion' series (1967), and later too in non-fictional form in *The Old School* (1986). The novel deals with Fielding's last term at public school and his premature entry into the real world. Raven drew on his own experiences at Charterhouse in the 1940s, in particular a love affair, which he had already detailed in *The Decline of the English Gentleman* (1962),[62] and based a number of characters on his contemporaries. The character of the cold, calculating Catholic Somerset Lloyd-James, who is a self-appointed expert on everything and who in his desire to be head of the school resorts to blackmailing Fielding, was apparently based on a well known journalist.

The novel recounts Fielding's quarrels with his bullying father about his future (he wants to go to Cambridge to study classics; his father wants him to go into the tea business in India), and with his first fumbling encounters with women (a girl at a fair, a London prostitute, a predatory married woman). But the treatment of all the women in the book is deeply misogynistic. They are without exception shallow, scheming or just plain vile.

Central to the book is Fielding's love affair with Christopher Roland. Fielding's love is essentially something innocent, 'a deep longing to protect and to cherish, to fondle (but only as a comforter) and (as a brother) to embrace'.[63] There are the familiar rapturous moments of snatched intimacy, but when the affair is physically consummated something magical is lost—Christopher's innocence. He grows to like the physical contact and to want it. But during the holidays Christopher confides his feelings to a tutor and is made to believe that Fielding's attitude was lust rather than love. Seeking love elsewhere, Christopher is arrested for soliciting at an army camp. Ordered to take psychiatric treatment, Christopher kills himself in an access of desperation and self-loathing. The episode recalls the fate of Robert Graves's beloved friend, 'Dick', at Charterhouse, similarly arrested for soliciting after Graves's departure for the front. But it also enables Raven to do two things. The first is to determine the public school attitude to such affairs, in a speech by the sane and balanced Peter Morrison:

> People make a lot of fuss about all this. They talk of boys being perverted for life by their experiences at their public schools, and they then maintain that this is why, quite apart from any question of abstract morality, it's so vital to keep the place 'pure'. But what they can't or won't realise . . . is that it's not what two boys do together in private which does the permanent damage, but the hysterical row which goes on if they are caught.[64]

The second is to allow Fielding to analyse and try to make sense of his contradictory feelings for Christopher: his mixture of selfishness, desire and genuine affection. But the affair with Christopher brings its own nemesis. His mother finds out about it and threatens to expose Fielding unless he falls in with his father's wishes to leave school and go into the tea business. Fielding pretends to agree but in fact arranges to do military service and then go on to Cambridge, financed by a friendly master at the school. His friend Peter, the classic chivalrous public school type, appalled at his treatment of his mother, exposes his plan and sabotages the college scholarship by the revelation of his involvement with Christopher. So Fielding settles instead for an army career, because it offers the same as university, a closed, comfortable and privileged society.

Fielding is depicted as in many ways the antithesis of the traditional public school type. He lies to, strikes and rejects his mother, uses people for his own gratification, seeks a career as college fellow just for the east of the life and the approbation. But he is also the victim of the machinations of others—parents and rivals—and it is hard not to sympathise with him in his exclusion from Eden.

Once again that idyll climaxes with the key set piece of public school fiction, the memorable cricket match, with our hero distinguishing himself, something which occurs first in *Tom Brown's Schooldays* and then in *Mike*, *The Fifth Form at St Dominic's*, *The Loom of Youth* and *The Hill*. In *Tom Brown* it symbolises the values that the public school system and code stand for—team spirit, loyalty, fair play, as well as indelible memory. For Sir Henry Newbolt, poet laureate of the public school, the cricket match had a mystical significance. His hero, Percival, in *The Twymans* caught 'a glimpse behind the mere beauty of the young white figures shining so cooly in the slant evening sunshine, of the finely planned order and long-descended discipline they symbolised'.[65] But for Simon Raven the beauty was enough:

> Christopher was a sight to see that afternoon. Hair bleached by the sun . . . arms brown and smooth, fair, delicate skin showing through the cleft of his unbuttoned shorts; legs moving gracefully down the pitch, bat swinging with the easy strength which only timing can give, eyes flashing with pleasure as he struck the ball full in the meat. I thought of Keats's Ode, and wished, for Christopher's sake, that he might be arrested in time for ever, just at that thrilling moment of impact when the hard leather sinks, briefly but luxuriously into the spring willow, and the swift current of joy quivers up the blade of the bat and on through every nerve in the body. For my own sake too I wished that time might stop: so that I might stand for ever in the sun . . . and watch my darling so beautiful and happy at his play.[66]

Characteristically Raven provides an additional element to cricket—the erotic. Once again as in fiction, so too in fact, the climactic cricket match was a reality, in the lives of Thomas Hughes, Alec Waugh and the real-life original of Harry Desmond. It was to be an experience they would never forget.

Notes

1 Alec Waugh, *The Loom of Youth* (1954 edition), preface, London, 1984, 9. His school career is covered in detail in *The Early Years of Alec Waugh*, London, 1962, 28–82.
2 Waugh, *Early Years*, 81.
3 Waugh, *Early Years*, 48.
4 Waugh, *Early Years*, 49.
5 Waugh, *Early Years*, 54. Carey and his wife provided the inspiration for the housemaster and his wife in *The Guinea Pig*, the stage play by Waugh's Sherborne contemporary Warren Chetham-Strode. Inspired by the Fleming Report, it dealt with the experiences of a lower middle-class boy sent to public school. It was turned into a memorable film by the Boulting Brothers in 1948. See Jeffrey Richards and Anthony Aldgate, *Best of British*, Oxford, 1983, 87–97.
6 Waugh, *Early Years*, 39–40.
7 Waugh, *Early Years*, 85.
8 Alec Waugh, *The Loom of Youth* (1917 edition), preface, 11.
9 Waugh, *Loom of Youth* (1917), preface, 16.
10 The book's reception is charted in Waugh, *Early Years*, 100–4.
11 Waugh, *The Loom of Youth* (1917), London, 1929, 40.
12 Waugh, *The Loom of Youth*, 125.
13 Waugh, *The Loom of Youth*, 128–9.
14 Waugh, *The Loom of Youth*, 265.
15 Waugh, *The Loom of Youth*, 290.
16 Waugh, *The Loom of Youth*, 318–19.
17 Waugh, *The Loom of Youth*, 27.
18 C. Day Lewis, *The Buried Day*, London, 1969, 109–11.
19 Waugh, *The Loom of Youth*, 23–4.
20 Waugh, *The Loom of Youth*, 34.
21 Waugh, *The Loom of Youth*, 34.
22 Waugh, *The Loom of Youth*, 53.
23 Waugh, *The Loom of Youth*, 94.
24 Waugh, *The Loom of Youth*, 304–5.
25 Waugh, *The Loom of Youth*, 42.
26 Waugh, *The Loom of Youth*, 75.
27 Waugh, *The Loom of Youth*, 34.
28 Waugh, *The Loom of Youth*, 50.
29 Waugh, *The Loom of Youth*, 59.
30 Waugh, *The Loom of Youth*, 107.
31 Waugh, *The Loom of Youth*, 90.
32 Waugh, *The Loom of Youth*, 97.
33 Waugh, *The Loom of Youth*, 29.
34 Waugh, *The Loom of Youth*, 218.
35 Waugh, *The Loom of Youth*, 67.
36 Waugh, *The Loom of Youth*, 68–9.
37 Waugh, *The Loom of Youth*, 142–3.
38 Waugh, *The Loom of Youth*, 19.
39 Waugh, *The Loom of Youth*, 32–33.
40 Waugh, *The Loom of Youth*, 57.
41 Waugh, *The Loom of Youth*, 81.
42 Waugh, *Pleasure*, London, 1921, 42.
43 Waugh, *Pleasure*, 109.
44 Waugh, *Public School Life*, London, 1922, 136.
45 Waugh, *Public School Life*, v–vi.
46 Waugh, *The Loom of Youth*, 20.
47 Waugh, *The Loom of Youth*, 142–3.
48 Isabel Quigly, *The Heirs of Tom Brown*, London, 1982, 199.

49 *Contemporary Review*, 112 (1917), 658.
50 *Quarterly Review* (1925), 245.
51 J. Howard Whitehouse (ed.), *The English Public School: a symposium*, London, 1919.
52 Martin Browne, *A Dream of Youth*, London, 1918, 73.
53 Browne, *A Dream of Youth*, 130.
54 Jack Hood, *The Heart of a Schoolboy*, London, 1919. Waugh replied to his critics in *The English Review* 28 (1919), 220–228.
55 *Journal of Education*, 59 (April 1927), 250.
56 Anthony Powell, *Infants of the Spring*, London, 1976, 77.
57 C. Day Lewis, *The Buried Day*, 113.
58 Waugh, *Public School Life*, 7.
59 Waugh, *The Loom of Youth*, 9.
60 A. C. Benson, *The Upton Letters*, London, 1905.
61 Waugh, *The Loom of Youth*, 154.
62 Raven recounts his courtship of the beautiful blond 'Alexis' in *The Decline of the English Gentleman*, New York, 1962, 111–25.
63 Simon Raven, *Fielding Gray*, London, 1967, 31.
64 Raven, *Fielding Gray*, 53–4.
65 Henry Newbolt, *The Twymans*, London, 1911, 82.
66 Raven, *Fielding Gray*, 63.

11

The ideal schoolmaster:
Goodbye, Mr Chips

The role and importance of schoolmasters in the lives of boys is attested in countless memoirs and biographies. The sympathetic master can open up and enrich a boy's mind and imagination, his appreciation of art, life and the intellect. W. H. Auden (Gresham's School) wrote appreciatively of his music master, Walter Greatorex, that he was 'what the ideal schoolmaster should be, ready to be a friend and not a beak, to give the adolescent all the comfort and stimulus of a personal relationship, without at the same time making any demands for himself in return.'[1] Alec Waugh (Sherborne) equally valued the teaching of S. P. B. Mais:

> He hit Sherborne like a whirlwind. Anything he taught became dramatic. In mathematics in the lower forms he awarded marks by the thousand. It caught the imagination of his pupils . . . In the teaching of literature he interested his classes in the personalities of the poets. Boys are partisans. They like championing a cause, they like adversaries. He encouraged debate on Byron *v.* Wordsworth, provided the boys had read the poets they despised or adulated. He make Shakespeare live, by treating the plays as drama . . . He got boys reading, and one of his great merits was that he inspired what he called 'the average boy' . . . During his four years at Sherborne, not only did he not cane a single boy but he did not give a single imposition. He did not need to exert authority; the boys enjoyed their hours in his classroom.[2]

Sir Charles Tennyson (Eton) wrote of Hugh McNaghten that he was 'a tutor of genius, a saint who was not a prig, a first-class scholar without pedantry, and an enthusiast who was never a bore and whose passion for Greek sculpture and Italian painting struck a spark out of all but the completely insensible'.[3] Schoolmastering at its best, then, is self-less, dedicated and inspiring. It is this aspect that has been developed by the mythographers, in particular in what many would regard as the most celebrated schoolmaster of fiction, Chips of Brookfield.

James Hilton's novel *Goodbye, Mr Chips* epitomises the successful reassertion of public school values and the system. The conservatives had been on the defensive as never before between 1918 and 1926, and this of course paralleled the mood in British society. There was widespread fear of revolution in the years after the war. The rise in trade union activity and membership, and mounting industrial unrest, culminated in the General Strike (1926). But the General Strike failed and was followed rapidly by the Wall Street Crash and world-wide economic recession. The nation retreated from confrontation, a coalition government was elected and the country settled into a cautious conservatism. At the same time public school fiction took a favourable turn. Even though there had been some modernisation of the curriculum, a commitment to better relations between masters and boys, and some lessening in the tyranny of athleticism, the basic ideas and traditions of the Victorian schools remained intact.[4] The upsurge of pro-public school literature, fictional and non-fictional, in the 1930s is epitomised by *Goodbye, Mr Chips*.

Of all the schoolmasters who have appeared in public school fiction, from Dr Arnold to Mr Quelch, the one most likely to be named by the general public as the classic schoolmaster is Mr Chips. James Hilton was the best-selling author of a succession of gentle romantic and idealistic novels which celebrated all that was best in the national character (*Lost Horizon*, *Knight without Armour*, *Random Harvest*, *We are not Alone*). Commissioned to write a 3,000 word short story for the Christmas issue of *The British Weekly* in 1933, he produced the 17,000 word *Goodbye, Mr Chips*, which so entranced the editorial staff that they published it as a special Christmas supplement on 7 December 1933. In America *The Atlantic Monthly* published it in 1934 and it created a sensation. It was rapidly reprinted in book form both in Britain and in the United States, and widely acclaimed. On American radio the leading critic and broadcaster Alexander Woollcott called it 'a tender and gentle story as warming to the heart and nourishing to the spirit as any I can remember . . . The most profoundly moving story that has passed this way for several years.' Howard Spring wrote in *The London Evening Standard*: 'Here is a triumphant proof that a little book can be a great book. Mr. Chips deserves a place in the gallery of English characters.' *Punch* called it 'supremely well done' and *The New York Herald-Tribune* proclaimed it 'a masterpiece'.[5] It went through twenty-two impressions between 1934 and 1950, a further five between 1951 and 1965 and came out in paperback in 1969. It has been adapted for radio, television and the stage. But it has touched the mass audience most effectively in two superlative film versions.

The book takes the form of the reminiscences of an old man

Mr Chipping, known as Chips, as he sits by the fire at Mrs Wickett's, opposite the school, where he has lodged since his retirement, still running his life according to the bells and timetables of the school.[6] There is the ritual of tea and crumpets before the fire with the new boys, and Chips beguiles the time reading detective stories, attending school sports matches, smoking his pipe and editing the Brookfeldian Directory.

Chips is a school 'character', who has spent virtually all his career teaching classics at the same school, Brookfield, 'a good school of the second rank', which has turned out its share of judges, M.P.s, colonial administrators and bishops but mainly merchants, manufacturers, professional men, country squires and country parsons. Chips's degree was not particularly good, his discipline not always sound. He has no private means or family connections. At forty-eight, shy, old-fashioned and conventional, he meets twenty-five-year-old Katherine Bridges, a radical and spirited governess, while on a walking holiday in the Lake District. Marriage transforms him. He had been in a rut, drifting into dry pedagogy, conscientious, hard-working, 'he was a fixture that gave service, satisfaction, confidence, everything except inspiration'. Under Katherine's influence his sense of humour blossoms, he begins to make jokes, his discipline improves. She imbues him with wisdom and humanity, and he becomes much loved. Katherine innovates, taking an enlightened view of schoolboy sexual misdemeanours and introducing a soccer match between Brookfield and boys from the East End of London. But after only two years of blissfully happy marriage she dies in childbirth. Chips becomes very old suddenly. But with age comes mellowness, the comforting warmth of eccentricity and fulfilment in a life of total service and dedication to the boys and the school. Hilton recounts Chips's jokes, anecdotes and fancies. Although a Conservative, Chips has sympathy with the Boers during the Boer War and the strikers dueing the railway strike, because above all 'he had faith in England, in English flesh and blood, and in Brookfield as a place whose ultimate worth depended on whether she fitted herself into the English scene, with dignity and without disproportion'.[7]

In 1908, when Chips is sixty, Mr Ralston, the ruthless, ambitious, super-efficient headmaster suggests that he is old-fashioned, lazy and slovenly, and should retire. Chips refuses absolutely, condemning Ralston for trying to run Brookfield as a factory 'for turning out a snob-culture based on money and machines'. Chips believes in democracy and character formation, and in teaching boys above all 'a sense of proportion'; Ralston only in examinational results and plutocracy. The governors back Chips to the hilt, demonstrating their commitment to traditional values.

Eventually, in 1913, at sixty-five, after a bout of bronchitis, Chips does retire. But when war breaks out he is called back, and when the Head dies in 1917 he takes over as headmaster for the duration. When reading out the names of the Brookfield fallen he includes that of the school's pre-war German master, who has fallen with the German troops on the western front. The boys see it as another of Chips's 'fancies'. Fifteen years later, now very frail, Chips gives tea for the last time to a new boy and is taken ill. As he lies dying he hears the doctor say, 'It's a pity he never had any children,' at which he perks up. 'I have . . . thousands of 'em . . . thousands of 'em . . . and all boys.' He dies with the voices of all the boys from his sixty-three years at Brookfield giving their names at call-over—'Pettifer . . . Pollett . . . Porson . . . Potts . . . Pullman . . . Purvis . . . Pym-Wilson . . . Radlett . . . Rapson . . . Reade . . . Reeper . . . Redding Primus . . .'

Goodbye, Mr Chips is a mood piece, gentle, affectionate, reminiscent. It is a celebration of a dedicated, decent, old-fashioned schoolmaster of the best type who has lived and died in the service of a single school and whose compassion and understanding have touched and warmed the lives of several generations of boys. He is the spirit of the public schools: tradition, service, values. Much less well known than *Goodbye, Mr Chips*, its sequel, *To you, Mr Chips* (1938), amplifies the original picture. It consists in the main of a collection of short stories about Chips and his handling of boys, demonstrating his sympathy, kindness and tact in dealing with rebels, misfits and loners.

James Hilton was the son of a headmaster, educated at elementary and grammar schools. When he won a scholarship to public school his father permitted him to choose his own, and he settled on the Leys School, Cambridge, which he attended from 1915 to 1918. In his memoir of his own school days he calls the old school Brookfield, and it clearly inspired the setting for *Goodbye, Mr Chips*, where the school is described as being in the fens. He shared his father's pacifist ideals and refused to join the O.T.C. He hated games, because he was not good at them. With these views, and his elementary and grammar school background, he might seem the perfect candidate for the role of disillusioned and discontented rebel. Yet he turned out quite the opposite, perhaps because no one persecuted him for his views and his background. At the age of thirty-seven he recalled:

I enjoyed my schooldays, on the whole, and if I had a son, I daresay I would send him to my old school . . . I was not a typical schoolboy and the fact that I was happy at Brookfield argues that the school tolerated me, even more generously than I tolerated it . . . I never received corporal punishment at Brookfield; I was never bullied; I never had a fight with anybody; and the only trouble I got into was for breaking bounds . . . I do not think I had any particular enemies and I got on well enough with authority. Despite the

sexual aberrations that are supposed to thrive at boarding schools, I never
succumbed to any, nor was I ever tempted.[8]

Hilton edited the school magazine, wrote pacifist and revolutionary
verse, played the piano, participated in the school debating society,
cycled 'many windy miles along the fenland lanes'.

Writing in 1938 against the menacing background of the rise of
fascism, Hilton defended the tradition, tolerance and civilised values
that he saw at the heart of the public school system:

> It was possible to decry the public schools as the bulwark of a system that
> had had its day, to attack them for their creation of a class snobbery, to
> lampoon their play-the-game fetish and their sedate philistinism. That these
> attacks were partly justified one may well admit. The public schools *do*
> create snobbery, or at any rate the illusion of superiority; you cannot train a
> ruling class without such an illusion. My point is that the English illusion
> has proved, on the whole, humaner and more endurable, even by its victims,
> than the current European illusions that are challenging and supplanting it.[9]

Of Chips he wrote, 'There was no single schoolmaster I ever knew who
was entirely Mr. Chips, but there were several who had certain of his
attributes and achieved that best reward of a well spent life—to grow
old beloved.'[10] It is generally believed that Chips is a composite of
two figures. One was Hilton's own father, John, the much loved headmaster of Chapel End Senior Boys' School, Walthamstow, in the
1920s and 1930s. (Brookfield was the name of a house in the area
which subsequently became a sanatorium.) The other was W. H.
Balgarnie, who taught at the Leys from 1900 to 1930 and, like Chips,
came out of retirement to teach again during the war (1940-46). Shy,
gentle and dedicated, Balgarnie, who never married, retired to live
opposite the school and died in 1951. When *Goodbye, Mr Chips* was
done on the stage in London in 1938 in a version by James Hilton
and Barbara Burnham starring Leslie Banks and Constance Cummings,
Balgarnie was invited and given a box as guest of honour, being
recognised as Chips's original.

The first film version was made in Britain by M.G.M. in 1939.
Directed by Sam Wood and produced by Victor Saville, it featured
location scenes shot at Repton, won an Academy award as best actor
of the year for Robert Donat and became one of the best loved films
of the period. Hilton himself was delighted with it, writing to con-
gratulate Donat on 'a really wonderful performance'.[11]

The script, by R. C. Sherriff, Claudine West and Eric Maschwitz,
followed Hilton's novella faithfully, incorporating virtually all the
incidents into a more closely woven texture. It establishes Chips as a
much loved old character in a traditional setting (call-over, assembly,

the school song, headmaster recalling that he had been beaten by Chips thirty-seven years before). Then it recreates his reverie as he sits by the fire at Mrs Wickett's. A dedicated young teacher of twenty-four, he arrives at Brookfield in 1870 to teach Latin. Ragged by the boys on his first day, he is reprimanded by the headmaster and determines to become a disciplinarian. Neither boys nor staff forgive him, however, when his adherence to discipline goes so far as to keep his class in one day when they are needed to play in a vital cricket match, which the school in consequence loses. As the years pass, Chips sinks into a dull, defeated, unloved middle age, passed over for promotion and known only for his ability to keep order. Then he is persuaded by the amiable German master Max Staefel (Paul Henreid) to join him on a walking tour of the Austrian Tyrol ('What, me—go abroad?'). He meets and falls in love with a spirited young Englishwoman, Katherine Ellis (Greer Garson), and marries her. In the book it was the Lake District but the film allows them to waltz in Vienna and sail down the Danube. Rejuvenated, Chips wins the confidence and affection of the boys and his sense of humour blossoms. He becomes a house master and she a valued confidante of the boys. When she dies in childbirth Chips is heartbroken but carries on to mellow into one of Brookfield's living traditions.

His philosophy is embodied in the key scene of confrontation between Chips and the new headmaster, Ralston, who seeks to retire him. In the book Chips's defence of his beliefs and practices is unspoken, but in the film these thoughts are turned into a blazing speech:

> I know the world's changing. I've seen all the old traditions dying one by one . . . grace and dignity and a feeling for the past . . . You're trying to run the school like a factory for turning out money-mad snobs . . . Modern methods, intensive training—poppycock! Give a boy a sense of humour and a sense of proportion and he'll stand up to anything.

Chips refuses to resign; the school and the governors rally to his support. Ralston is defeated, and several years later, when Chips does retire, Ralston admits he has learned from him. It is a robust defence of the public school tradition of concentrating on character-building, in order to turn out gentlemen all-rounders. This also involves a paternalistic sense of social responsibility. When Chips catches Peter Colley fighting a local grocery boy, Perkins, he orders them to stop it and make friends. Later, in the war, the former grocery boy becomes Colley's batman and Colley is killed trying to rescue the mortally injured Perkins. Chips's wartime service as headmaster is followed by his death and the parade of boys across the screen, tipping their hats and calling their names— 'Lancaster . . . Latton . . . Lemare . . . Lytton-Bosworth . . . McGonigall . . . Mansfield.'

Donat gives a magnificent performance, encompassing hopeful youth, defeated middle age, romantic awakening and eccentric old age. He is well supported by Garson's warm-hearted Katherine and Henreid's amiably supportive Staefel. The film is structured around the pattern of the school year and the ritual of call-over. Although the passing of time is conveyed by allusions to events (the Franco-Prussian War, the death of Queen Victoria, the Boer War, the Great War), life at Brookfield goes on more or less unchanged, tradition and ritual providing the comforting sense of permanence, order and decent values. In 1939, when the film was made, these qualities must have seemed all the more precious and the affirmation of them to have been welcomed by audiences shadowed by the threat of a new world war.

The 1969 remake was if anything even better. Terence Rattigan scripted it, departing from the plot of the novel but remaining true to its spirit. It is a superb script, polished, witty, sympathetic and perfectly realised by Herbert Ross's lyrical, sensitive, deeply moving and frequently inspired direction. In this version, which opens in the 1920s rather than the 1870s, and was shot at Sherborne, Chips meets Kathy while visiting the Roman remains at Pompeii, she dies not in childbirth but in a German air raid in World War II, and, most significantly, she is a musical comedy actress. This enables Rattigan to explore with delicious irony Chips's encounters with the theatrical world of London and to develop the relationship as an attraction of opposites in much greater depth than either the book or the previous film. Leslie Bricusse's insufficiently appreciated musical score (notably the wistful 'Where did my childhood go?') effectively underlines the mood of the film.

Peter O'Toole's Chips is one of the screen's finest pieces of acting and earned him an Oscar nomination, though not the award. O'Toole captures perfectly Chips's dedication and devotion, his self-doubt and shyness, his tenacity and courage. He is admirable as the lonely, unpopular middle-aged pedant, unable to communicate his genuine affection to the boys and seeing his life and his vocation withering away. He charts faultlessly the gradual development into a lovable old character who always remained human. The comedy of his meeting with Katherine is delightfully funny and the flowering of their love flawlessly handled. As Kathy, afraid she will let him down if she comes to Brookfield as his wife, boards a bus to leave, he chases after her, leaping aboard the bus shouting, 'Apollo has willed it.' There is something at once touching, absurd, heroic and absolutely right about this. His reactions to her death and his own retirement are deeply poignant. O'Toole is well supported by Petula Clark as Kathy, Michael Bryant as the thoughtful Staefel, Alison Leggatt as the headmaster's bitchy wife and Sian Phillips as a voracious, larger-than-life actress friend of Kathy ('Parents' Day, my dear—what could be more riveting?').

The superb opening sequence establishes the mood, a nostalgic sense of childhood's end and a hankering for the golden, carefree days of youth. There is a long shot of the cricket pitch, seen hazily as if in memory, then the camera prowls through the empty corridors and classrooms, and the school song echoes hollowly on the sound track. It eschews the book's sentimental finale to show Chips as a very old man, still living near by. He walks from his house to the school and stands in the courtyard as boys pass, automatically lifting their hats. The camera pulls back until his figure is lost amid the crowd of boys and the cluster of venerable buildings. He is being absorbed into the fabric of the place.

E. C. Mack, writing about the inter-war years, called *Goodbye, Mr Chips* and *Housemaster* 'the two most influential pieces of fiction of the period'.[12] Ian Hay's book and play *Housemaster* (1936), which was successfully filmed in 1938, has not retained the same cachet as *Chips*. But there is more than a touch of Chips in the house master, Charles Donkin. Like *Chips*, *Housemaster* was based on reality, in this case Ian Hay's memories of his days as boy and master at Fettes and at Durham School. Viscount Simon, Hay's fagmaster at Fettes, saw the play on the stage in 1936 (with Frederick Leister as Donkin and Kynaston Reeves as Ovington) and reported that the set recreated the study of the Fettes house master John Yeo so accurately that he 'almost thought to see myself in the doorway'.[13]

Marbledown School is very similar to Brookfield, and Charles Donkin, engagingly played in the film by Otto Kruger, is a donnish, sympathetic traditionalist, armed with pince-nez and pipe. Significantly, like Chips with Ralston, Donkin is engaged in conflict with a new, young, headmaster, the Rev. Edmund Ovington (played in the film as in the play by Kynaston Reeves). Ovington stands for complete change, and, in the process of reorganising the school, outrages the boys by trampling on their traditions: putting the town out of bounds, forbidding participation in the annual regatta. In a confrontation Donkin tells him he has all the attributes of a successful headmaster except one—hymanity—and that is the most important of them: 'You are set in authority over five hundred of the shyest, most observant, most critical and least articulate creatures that God ever made; and you treat them as if—as if they were occupants of a particularly insensitive oyster bed! Believe me, they're alive—and kicking! You have trampled on their most cherished traditions.'[14]

Ovington accuses Donkin of fomenting rebellion against him, and although Donkin angrily refutes it, when the whole of his house breaks bounds and returns to boo the headmaster he feels that he has no alternative but to resign. Sadly he makes his farewell speech to the school and summarises his philosophy: 'always be loyal, even though it may sometimes be against your own convictions . . . be infinitely considerate of other people's feelings . . . speak the truth.'[15] As a matter of fact, these three axioms are likely to be mutually contradictory.

A school governor, the Cabinet Minister Sir Berkeley Nightingale, acts as *deus ex machina*, persuading the Prime Minister to appoint Ovington to a vacant bishopric. Donkin is asked to become headmaster, and book, play and film end with the school singing 'Old Acquaintance' and Donkin settling down to the *Times* crossword with his pipe. Like Chips, Donkin believes in and maintains discipline, tradition and decent values.

There are two sub-plots, centring on the arrival of three girls to stay with Donkin, Rosemary, Chris and Button Farringdon, daughters of the woman Donkin loved but who married another and is now dead. Their impact on the all-male environment creates predictable comic embarrassments and imbroglios. The eldest girl, Rosemary, falls for the shy, bespectacled, stammering science master Peter de Pourville, and, under his influence, he asserts himself, maintains discipline and marries her.

Goodbye, Mr Chips and *Housemaster* present a positive, nostalgic, comforting and deeply traditionalist picture of a schoolmaster's life. But they also show the vital role that love plays in transforming an unsuccessful into a successful one. It is love, in both cases of a lively, enthusiastic, caring woman, which complements the scholarship of the dedicated pedagogue and brings out all his hidden depths. It is in both cases romantic heterosexual love. Gershon Legman is wrong therefore to suggest that *Goodbye, Mr Chips*, is misogynistic and implicitly homosexual: 'Explicitly a "woman-hater", Chips meets the one woman in his life at the age of forty-eight . . . and he has the courage to kill her, in this case through childbirth. She dies like clockwork within a year and a half of their marriage, and Mr. Chips . . . is left happily flagellating and serving tea to little boys.'[16] In fact the book makes it clear that Chips is incomplete without Kathy, her love awakens his best qualities and hidden talents and makes him a better schoolmaster, her memory sustains him throughout his career and their alliance symbolises the merging of what is best in conservatism with what is best in radicalism. In *Chips* and *Housemaster* Chips and Donkin are sustained by the memory of a lost love, a conventional enough romantic device to explain their prolonged bachelorhood and dedication to the school.

But there is another side to the picture. The darker side of the public school master's life, the counterpoint to *Chips*, almost the story of *Chips* as it might have been if he had married the wrong woman, is to be found in *The Browning Version*. This one-act play by Terence Rattigan is generally regarded as his finest work. *Mr Chips* is explicitly referred to, and Crocker-Harris, like Chips, meets his wife on a walking tour of the Lake District. Lasting only an hour and a quarter, and part of a double-bill *The Browning Version* is an extended meditation on failure. When first staged in 1948, with Eric Portman and Mary Ellis in the lead, it ran for 245 performances. It had been written with John Gielgud in mind. He turned it down but later repented of the decision and played in on B.B.C. Radio in 1957 and on American television in 1959. It was turned into an absorbing and moving film in 1951 by the sympathetic and unobtrusive Anthony Asquith, the perfect director for Rattigan. Michael Redgrave gave one of the finest performances of his career in the leading role and there was strong support from Jean Kent as Millie, Nigel Patrick as Hunter and Brian Smith as Taplow.

The story was based on an incident in Rattigan's own schooldays at Harrow. During the first two years there he was taught classics by Mr Coke-Norris, a withered pedant and stern disciplinarian, who never made the subject come alive and was disliked by the boys. When Coke-Norris retired through ill health a boy presented him with a book as a leaving present and Coke-Norris accepted it not with pleasure but with cold ingratitude. Rattigan always wondered why, and devised the play to explain it. But it is more than this. It derives its force from Rattigan's exploration of emotional repression, of the world of incompatibility, deceit and self-loathing, that was all part of his own experience of life in the homosexual *demi-monde* of fashionable and theatrical London.

The film version, also scripted by Rattigan, opens the play out somewhat to sketch in the background of public school life (chapel, cricket, prize-giving), but it remains an uncompromising, austere, powerfully dramatic study in failure: a series of monologues by Crocker-Harris in which he comes to terms with the failure of his public and private life. After eighteen years at the school Andrew Crocker-Harris is retiring early because of ill health. Starting as a brilliant and dedicated teacher, he has declined into exactly the unloved pedant and petty tyrant that Rattigan recalled at Harrow, a man who lavishes his care on the school timetable and fails to bring out the passion and beauty in Aeschylus. We see him in action in the classroom, sarcastic, despotic, 'barely human', says the boys. But gradually the mask is stripped away by a succession of cruel blows. First the headmaster tells him that the governors have decided not to grant him a pension, then he asks him to forgo the right to speak last at next day's prize-giving ceremony so that the popular sports master, Fletcher, an England cricketer, leaving

to take a job in the City, can end the proceedings. Then he is shocked
to learn from his young successor, Mr Gilbert, that he is known as
'The Himmler of the Lower Fifth'. This prompts a revealing soliloquy
when Crocker-Harris admits he never had the knack of making himself popular. He had for a while amused the boys by his characteristics
and habits of speech which he deliberately exaggerated. He had tried
to communicate his joy in ancient literature but that rarely worked.
Long ago he realised that he was a failure. Only now does he
appreciate that he is feared. Finally all his years of pent-up emotion
are released by one small act of kindness—the gift of the Browning
version of the *Agamemnon*—by Taplow. Taplow, to his own surprise,
and that of his friends, admits to feeling sorry for 'The Crock'.
Crocker-Harris is moved to tears but his joy at the gift is cruelly under-
cut when his wife Millie tells him the boy obviously did it in order to
get his promotion to the upper fifth.

Millie, who is neither the social nor intellectual equal of her
husband, has had a succession of affairs, all of which she has revealed
to her husband to torment him, as well as constantly lacerating him
with his failure in his profession. Her latest lover, the popular young
science master Frank Hunter, whom she is trying to hold on to as he
cools towards her ('I don't care how much you humiliate me. You're
all I want in the world'), is so appalled by her cruelty that he breaks
off the liaison, admits his shame to Crocker-Harris and urges him to
leave her. But Crocker-Harris defends her, saying that they were in-
compatible. Her need for physical love he could not fulfil, and his for
spiritual love was beyond her. Their united efforts have produced
only hatred. This is what has made her embittered and neurotic. She
is, he says, to be pitied.

The climax of the play/film involves an exercise of absolute
candour. Crocker-Harris faces up to his failure as teacher and husband.
He and Millie part. The play ends with life going painfully on, but the
film has a more upbeat and cathartic ending. Crocker-Harris, asserting
his right to speak last at prize-giving, makes a speech confessing his
failure, apologising to the boys and receiving a rousing round of
applause. There is a sign of hope. He will resume work on the free verse
translation of Aeschylus he had begun before his marriage, a version
which had the life and poetry and passion of real drama. It is ironic
that absolute honesty was a solution not open to Rattigan himself
because of the illegality of homosexuality at the time and so he drew
on his own dilemma as the inspiration for his work.[17]

Although the emotions, ideas and themes clearly reflect Rattigan's
own preoccupations and personal emotional experiences, it is no
coincidence that the setting is a public school. For the public school
is a classic symbol of emotional repression and therefore an ideal

vehicle for Rattigan to use in working out his ideas. Crocker-Harris symbolises this emotional repression. But the public school need not be such a place. Frank Hunter, after all, is not repressed. Perhaps it is that the emotionally repressed are attracted to the school situation rather than that the school makes them repressed.

James Hilton's Chips, inspired like Rattigan's play by a real-life schoolmaster, presents a totally different picture of service, fulfilment and emotional contentment. The coin has two sides. By a further irony, it was Rattigan who provided the screenplay for the film remake of *Goodbye, Mr Chips*, in which Michael Redgrave played the headmaster and in which incompatibility provided not for misery but for deep happiness.

The Crocker-Harris predicament is also explored in Hugh Walpole's novel *Mr Perrin and Mr Traill* (1911), in which the public school (Moffat's, in Cornwall) once again acts as a metaphor for a wider world of lovelessness, cruelty and repression, and the masters' common room is a snakepit of writhing tensions, venomous backbiting and poisonous gossip. At the heart of the book is the relationship between Vincent Perrin (forty-five), gaunt, ageing, pedantic, lonely, a master for twenty years, disliked by the boys, who call him 'Old Pompous', and the new master, Archie Traill, young, handsome, easy-going Cambridge rugger blue. Traill arrives to find the headmaster, the Rev. Moy-Thompson, a tyrant and the staff and their wives withered, arid, humourless, inhuman, sharing 'an intention to be as unpleasant as possible under the cover of an agreeable manner'. The resident cynic, Birkland, advises Traill, 'Fly for your life. If you don't you will die very soon—in a year perhaps. We are all dead here and we died many years ago.'[18] Birkland makes it clear that his criticism does not apply to major public schools, where the staff do not live on top of one another, are better paid and have a chance of getting a house, and there is *esprit de corps*. But at minor places like Moffat's where the staff are underpaid and without hope, prospects or ambition, they hate each other.

Traill finds his life brightened by Isabel Desart, a regular visitor to the school. Both he and Perrin fall in love with her, and for Perrin this involves an agony of unrequited affection and an increasingly bitter rivalry with Traill. There are quarrels about who has the first bath in the morning and who gets the morning paper first, and finally there is a major outburst when Traill borrows Perrin's umbrella without permission and Perrin attacks him. Soon after this incident Traill announces his engagement to Isabel, and Perrin's obsessive hatred deepens into madness. At the end of term Perrin follows Traill on his walk, planning to kill him. But when Traill accidentally falls from the cliffs, Perrin rescues him and drowns in the process.

Ostensibly the book is about the tensions and quarrels in a minor public school, very well observed and evoked by Walpole. But, as with other schoolmaster tales, there is a subtext, hinted at by Walpole and reflecting his own true nature. Isabel is one of those boyish 'gels' so beloved of Edwardian novelists:

> With her short brown hair that curled about her head, her straight eyes, her firm mouth, her vigorous, unerring movements, the swing of her arms as she walked, she seemed as though her strength and honesty might forbid her softer graces. To most people, she was a delightful boy—splendidly healthy, direct, uncompromising, sometimes startling in her hatred of things and people, sometimes arrogant in her assured enthusiasms.[19]

But there is more to it than that. Her constant appearances at the school as a friend of Mrs Comber, wife of a member of the staff, are clumsily and unconvincingly contrived. She would make more sense as a permanent member of the school community. The film version sensibly made her matron. But even more convincing would be her incarnation as a boy. Indeed, there is a hint of what could have been central in the sketchy subplot of the boy Garden, Perrin's favourite, who transfers his affection to Mr Traill. Perrin hysterically accuses Traill, among other things, of stealing Garden from him. Walpole describes Perrin going into Traill's room, gazing at him sleeping, intending to kill him but being unable to. At the end Perrin, having saved Traill, kisses his hand and then allows the sea to overwhelm him. The implication is that Perrin after all loves Traill, is jealous of his attention to the 'boy' Desart and finally demonstrates his love by saving Traill and effacing himself, to allow Traill happiness with the 'boy'. Repression and frustration are the key, but here it is perhaps a half-conscious homosexual repression. The recurrent image of the book—of the two halves of Perrin warring with each other, one wanting to do the right thing, to be liked, to do good, and the other pompous, bitter and sarcastic—perhaps should be interpreted as the classic dilemma of the repressed homosexual, the desire for normality and respectability clashing with the desire to break loose and indulge forbidden passions. Yet marriage is hardly seen as the ideal state. All the marriages in the book are empty and loveless, and most of the wives as desiccated and unpleasant as their husbands. The conflict in the end can be resolved only by death.

Walpole's own two years at school at Marlow he had described as a 'hell' of bullying and terror. The boy Pomfret-Walpole, mercilessly bullied in *Mr Perrin and Mr Traill*, is undeniably his own guest appearance in boyish form. Walpole also taught, at Epsom College for a year (1908), rapidly concluding, 'Both I myself and most of the people here are such ludicrous figures that one can't take it seriously.'[20] He was soon bored with teaching and gave it up to become a full-time writer. In 1910 he wrote *Mr Perrin and Mr Traill*, drawing characters and incidents (particularly the umbrella episode) directly from his stay and basing Moffat's so obviously on Epsom College that he was ostracised by them until 1937, when, after a handsome apology, and now Sir Hugh, he returned to present the annual prizes. The book was published in 1911 by Mills & Boon in an edition of 1,500 copies. A second edition of 1,000 rapidly followed. It was favourably reviewed, attracting the approbation of H. G. Wells, Arnold Bennett and Henry James. One of Walpole's ex-pupils wrote to say that all the boys at Epsom College were delighted with the book.[21]

A fine film version was made in 1948, scripted by the novelist L. A. G. Strong and directed by Lawrence Huntington. It featured excellent performances from Marius Goring as Vincent Perrin, made up to look like Mr Chips, David Farrar as Traill and Raymond Huntley as the sadistic, supercilious Moy-Thompson. The minutiae of public school life were beautifully observed and the film followed the novel faithfully, though building up Moy-Thompson's sadism in a lacerating sequence where he humiliates Perrin in front of Traill, and adding a scene in which after Perrin's death Traill denounces the headmaster's regime for having caused it.

It is interesting to observe that the most celebrated authors to have depicted the lives of public school masters as empty and arid (Forster in *The Longest Journey*, Walpole in *Mr Perrin and Mr Traill* and Rattigan in *The Browning Version*) have all been homosexual. It is evident that, with the school as a metaphor for society, they are exploring their own complex feelings of repression, rejection and dissatisfaction. There is undeniably a factual and autobiographical basis to these works, Forster drawing on his unhappy time as a pupil at Tonbridge School, Walpole drawing on his experience of teaching at Epsom College and Rattigan modelling his leading character on the man who taught him classics at Harrow. Conversely heterosexual writers have depicted happy and fulfilled schoolmasters leading rewarding lives in Hilton's *Goodbye, Mr Chips*, Hay's *Housemaster* and R. F. Delderfield's *To Serve them all my Days*. We must not mistake temperamental differences for objective reality in the treatment of the public school. It is clear that differences of temperament and of sexual orientation, as well as personal experience, may well have determined the picture of public school life emerging in these works. However, when it came to the general public, the verdict was clear. In terms of sales and of box office returns, in terms of folk memory and popular affection, Mr Chips wins hands down over all the others as *the* definitive public school master.

Notes

1 Graham Greene (ed.), *The Old School* (1934), Oxford, 1984, 5.
2 Alec Waugh, *The Early Years of Alec Waugh*, London, 1962, 33–4.
3 Sir Charles Tennyson, *Stars and Markets*, London, 1957, 70.
4 Edward C. Mack, *Public Schools and British Opinion since 1860*, New York, 1941, 372.
5 James Hilton, *Goodbye, Mr Chips* (1934), London, 1969, 3–5.
6 Hilton never reveals Chips's Christian name: the screen versions have christened him respectively Charles (1939) and Arthur (1969).
7 James Hilton, *Goodbye, Mr Chips*, 69–70.
8 Hilton, *To you, Mr Chips*, London, 1940, 38, 41, 43.
9 Hilton, *To you, Mr Chips*, 53–4.
10 Hilton, *To you, Mr Chips*, 62–3.
11 Kenneth Barrow, *Mr Chips: the life of Robert Donat*, London, 1985, 111.
12 Mack, *Public Schools*, 433.
13 Viscount Simon, *Retrospect*, London, 1957, 27.
14 Ian Hay, *Housemaster*, London, 1936, 217.
15 Ian Hay, *Housemaster*, 285.
16 Gershon Legman, *Love and Death*, New York, 1949, 83–4.
17 On the play see Michael Darlow and Gillian Hodson, *Terence Rattigan: the man and his work*, London, 1979, 155–68; on the film, R. J. Minney, *'Puffin' Asquith*, London, 1973, 133–4.
18 Hugh Walpole, *Mr Perrin and Mr Traill* (1911), London, 1949, 66.
19 Walpole, *Perrin and Traill*, 27.
20 Rupert Hart-Davis, *Hugh Walpole*, London, 1952, 56.
21 Hart-Davis, *Hugh Walpole*, 83.

12

Paradise regained:
Billy Bunter of Greyfriars School

Among that handful of fictional characters (Sherlock Holmes, Tarzan, Fu-Manchu, Bulldog Drummond, the Scarlet Pimpernel, Beau Geste) whose exploits have become part of the national consciousness and whose names are recognised even by people who have never read the books, there are two schoolboys. One is Tom Brown of Rugby, the archetypal public school hero. The other is Billy Bunter of Greyfriars, the ultimate anti-hero, almost Tom Brown's mirror image. The fat, sly, idle, prevaricating, cowardly, snobbish, conceited, greedy, vainglorious Bunter, constantly short of funds and confidently expecting the imminent arrival of a postal order, wolfing down his chums' tuck without a qualm and giving vent to a host of onomatopoeic expressions when collared by the wrathful dispossessed ('Grooh! Yaroo! Geroff! Leggo!') was only one, albeit the most memorable, of a host of characters created by a literary phenomenon known as Frank Richards.[1] It has been estimated that under twenty-five different pseudonymns he wrote during his career some 60–70 million words, the equivalent of 1,000 full-length novels, and he created a virtual universe of public schools. Greyfriars, St Jim's and Rookwood were the most famous, but behind them stood a legion of others—at least 105, according to one estimate.[2]

It was a world which he created, peopled and wrote about more or less continuously from 1907 to 1961, when he died on Christmas Eve at the age of eighty-six. He will have materially touched the lives, the hearts and the imaginations of at least five generations of boys. Writing was his whole life, and he was usually at his desk morning and afternoon every day except Sunday. Virtually all his stories were written for children, chiefly boys. Someone once asked him, 'Don't you ever think of doing something better than this?' He replied severely, 'There isn't anything better.'[3]

Frank Richards was born on 8 August 1876, at Ealing, the sixth of eight children. His real name was Charles Harold St John Hamilton but he rarely wrote under that name, coming to think of and refer to himself as Frank Richards, the most famous of his twenty-five pseudonymns. His father, John Hamilton, a master carpenter with literary pretensions, was 'a drunken brute' who died at the age of forty-five in 1884 when the young Charles was seven. His mother, Mary Ann Hamilton, to support her young family, for a time ran a second-hand clothes business, and the family moved frequently. But she received financial assistance from her brother, a local estate agent and property owner. It may have been with his help that Charles and his older brother, the handsome, extrovert Richard, were sent to school. Frank Richards was always very reticent about his schooldays, and his autobiography, one of the least revealing ever written, begins when he is seventeen. This is more than likely due to his desire to avoid the subject. For, as many people had come to suspect, the arch-chronicler of the public school ideal did not himself go to a public school. The diligent research of W. O. G. Lofts and D. J. Adley has revealed that he went with his brother to a small private school in Ealing, Thorn House, where he learned both Latin and Greek.[4] He was always to be keen on the classics. Latin figured regularly in his school stories and he devoted a good deal of his time in later years to translating popular songs into Latin and compiling Latin crosswords. In 1961 *The Times Educational Supplement* published a Bunter story he had written in Latin.

The young Charles Hamilton was a shy boy, with poor eyesight, slight in build, diffident and retiring. Like many boys of that type, he was a voracious reader, living his life vicariously through books and stories. He began to write his own, and in 1894 when he was seventeen he had his first story accepted and launched himself into the rapidly expanding market for boys' papers. His earliest published works, written under his own name of Charles Hamilton, were pirate stories. For five years (1899–1904) he wrote for the Trapps Holmes group of papers (*Smiles, Vanguard, Funny Cuts* and *Picture Fun*), working in every kind of genre and already developing the first of his range of pseudonymns to mask his prolificity of output. In 1905 he began to devote more of his energies to the Amalgamated Press papers and to specialise in school stories. He started to make his mark in 1906 with stories of Jack Blake and Co. of St Jim's, which appeared in *Pluck*, and as a result was recruited by the dynamic editor Percy Griffith to write a regular school series for a projected new paper, *The Gem*. His pen name in *The Gem* was 'Martin Clifford', derived from R. M. Ballantyne's novel *Martin Rattler*, a boyhood favourite, and Bulwer Lytton's *Paul Clifford*. The stories detailing Tom Merry's schooldays at Clavering School began in issue No. 3 of *The Gem* (10

March 1907). Griffith was dissatisfied with the early stories, believing that they lacked something. He suggested that Tom Merry and Co. be moved to St Jim's and merged with the stories of Jack Blake. Hamilton reluctantly agreed, and issue 11 of *Gem* saw Tom Merry at St Jim's. Tom Merry and his chums were to feature in every issue of the magazine until its demise in 1939. *The Gem* rapidly became a great success, and although initially issued at a halfpenny was expanded to a penny paper after forty-eight issues. Tom Merry was every schoolboy's ideal. One writer described him as 'straight as a die, brave, manly, a giant at sport, a great pal, full of mischief and kind as only the simple at heart can be'.[5] Frank Richards analysed his continuing appeal in his autobiography:

> The fact that he was just the kind of boy you might meet anywhere was, I think, his chief attraction. He did not run in dangerous terrorists single-handed; he did not discover German spies posing as waiters; he did not turn out to be the missing heir of the Duke of Bayswater or the Marquis of Colney Hatch. He was just a live healthy boy and he caught the fancy of the average boy reader.[6]

The success of *The Gem* led to the launch on 15 February 1908 of a sister paper, *The Magnet*, for which Charles Hamilton launched an entirely new school series, the Greyfriars stories of Harry Wharton and Co. For this series he adopted a new pseudonymn, derived from the names of Frank Osbaldistone in Scott's *Rob Roy* and his own brother, Richard Hamilton: Frank Richards. Greyfriars was to become his favourite series and he was to write about the school for *The Magnet* until its closure in 1940. 'The Making of Harry Wharton' brought Harry, later captain of the Remove, to Greyfriars and involved, as a minor character, a fat junior called Billy Bunter. This character had been devised earlier (1899) but turned down by a publisher and was now resurrected. Gradually the familiar cast was assembled: Frank Nugent from issue 1, Bob Cherry from issue 2, Johnny Bull from issue 151, Herbert Vernon-Smith from issue 119. Hurree Jamset Ram Singh, the Nabob of Banipur (known as 'Inky'), having appeared the previous year in *The Marvel*, transferred to *The Magnet* in issue 6.

Richards's celebrity and success were now such that he was regularly called upon to launch new school series, some of which he would continue to write himself and others of which would be carried on by other writers. The most famous after Greyfriars and St Jim's were the stories of Jimmy Silver and Co. of Rookwood School, written under the pseudonymn of Owen Conquest for *The Boy's Friend* and running from 1915 to 1926. There were 584 stories in all. Jack Noble and Co. of Pelham School appeared in *Boy's Realm* (1909); Gordon Gay and Co. of Rylcombe Grammar School, Sussex, in *Empire Library*

(1910). Also for *The Boy's Friend*, and as Martin Clifford, he wrote about the school adventures of Frank Richards at the Canadian backwoods school of Cedar Creek.

In 1919 as Hilda Richards he introduced the stories of Bessie Bunter and Co. of Cliff House School for *The School Friend*, a girls' equivalent of *The Magnet*. But he was becoming dangerously overloaded, having to write every week a 30,000 word Greyfriars story for *The Magnet*, a 30,000 word St Jim's story for *The Gem*, a 10,000 word Rookwood story for *The Boy's Friend* plus Cedar Creek and other assorted stories. He was simply unable to meet all the deadlines and the various editors were feuding over his services. So the director-in-chief of the Amalgamated Press forbade him to write further for *School Friend* and gave him a strict order of priority: (1) Greyfriars, (2) St Jim's, (3) Rookwood.

Whenever Richards was unable to produce on time, substitute writers were used. Nothing infuriated Richards more than this practice, which became one of the few subjects to ruffle his equability. He called the substitutes 'the imposters' and 'the duds' and raged at their appropriation of his name. But substitutes were unavoidable, as there were times when he was unable to meet deadlines, because he was overstretched or because he was out of the country. He spent much of the period 1909–14 travelling abroad, in the south of France, in Italy and Austria, indulging his passion for roulette and sending back his stories by post. He resumed his travels after the end of the First World War but his visits got fewer and he settled permanently in Kent in 1926, his wanderlust sated. In 1913 he had been briefly engaged to the niece of an Englishwoman who kept an hotel in Nice but matrimony did not materialise and he settled down to a comfortable bachelor existence with his typewriter, his bicycle, his pipe, his cat and his garden, a self-contained recluse with a resident housekeeper, whose work was his life.

He continued to write for both *Magnet* and *Gem* in the inter-war years. In the end he was responsible for about two-thirds of all the St Jim's stories and 1,380 of the 1,683 Greyfriars stories. But there were other ventures too. In 1928–30, as Ralph Redway he wrote a series of western adventures ('The Rio Kid') for *The Popular*. When *Modern Boy* was launched in 1928 he wrote as Charles Hamilton 200 stories about the South Sea boy trader Ken King and his ketch *Dawn*, 'King of the Islands'. For *The Ranger*, launched in 1931, he inaugurated another school series, about Jim Dainty of Grimsdale School, which was deliberately set on the borders of Lancashire and Yorkshire to attract northern readers. For *The Pilot* in 1937–38 he wrote a humorous series set at Bendover School and based on Will Hay's seedy comic pedagogue act from film and music hall.

During the inter-war years Richards was earning £2,500 a year, evidence of the regard in which Amalgamated Press held him.[7] George Richmond Samways as a substitute writer was paid only half what Richards got.[8] But Richards was unknown to the world outside. This changed in 1940, when George Orwell wrote his celebrated essay on boys' papers in *Horizon*, in which he opined that the stories in *The Magnet* signed 'Frank Richards' and in *The Gem* signed 'Martin Clifford' could hardly be the work of the same person every week because they had run for thirty years. To the amazement and amusement of literary London, Frank Richards wrote to *Horizon* affirming that indeed with the exception of substitutes he had been writing both series all that time. Then in 1943 an interview and the revelation of his multifarious writing activities in the *London Evening Standard* provoked a shoal of letters from old readers of his stories all over the world, including men on active service in India and Italy. This provided the impetus for the foundation of Old Boys' Book Clubs, which have continued to the present day, creating a cult of *The Gem* and *The Magnet*. In 1945 Richards wrote an article for the popular *Saturday Book* on his career as a boys' writer.

But the outbreak of the war had caused the closure first of *The Gem* and then of *The Magnet* and Richards's regular source of income dried up suddenly at the age of sixty-four. He had saved little and found times hard. But he eked out a living, writing a variety of school stories for small magazines, creating a raft of new schools (Sparshott, Topham, Tipdale, Lynwood, Headland House, High Lynn, Barcroft, Felgate, St Kate's) and a major new series featuring Compton, Drake and Lee of Carcroft School in *Pie* magazine in 1944.

But after the end of the war the Amalgamated Press, who owned the characters, gave permission for Bunter and Greyfriars to be revived in hardback format by the publisher Charles Skilton. Although Richards had initially offered to write for his old pre-war flat rate, his publisher persuaded him to accept the far more profitable arrangement of a royalty, and he eventually received £1,000 for his first book. The publication of *Billy Bunter of Greyfriars School* in 1947 was greeted by the press like the return of an old friend: 'Bunter is a national institution' (*Evening Express*), 'one of the immortals of schoolboy fiction' (*Belfast Weekly Telegraph*), 'Mr. Richards is a genius' (*Empire News*), 'a treat for boys of all ages' (*Yorkshire Evening Post*).[9] Twenty-five thousand copies of *Billy Bunter of Greyfriars School* were printed and sold, post-war paper shortage preventing more. But by 1952 that figure had reached 40,000. Richards now embarked on a schedule of two novels a year, and between 1947 and 1952 Skilton published ten of them. Cassell's took over the series and published twenty-three more between 1952 and 1963. They were translated into many foreign languages and made available in braille. In 1949 Mandeville Publications revived Tom Merry and St Jim's, and for some years 'Martin Clifford' continued to write the stories.

Bunter was revived in comic-strip form by the Amalgamated Press in *The Comet* in 1952–53 and 1956–58. But more significant was the fact that between 1952 and 1961 B.B.C.-TV ran five series of Greyfriars adaptations, which became extremely popular with parents and children alike. They are one of the cherished memories of my childhood television viewing, with Gerald Campion is the eternal Bunter and Kynaston Reeves the definitive Mr Quelch. Every Christmas from 1958 to 1961 there was a Bunter Christmas play at a London theatre. Bunter's return made the septuagenarian Richards a national celebrity. Interviews with him and articles about Greyfriars appeared regularly. He broadcast on the wireless, an activity he enjoyed. He received a stream of correspondence which he answered himself on his faithful typewriter and his later years were warmed by manifestations of genuine affection by his many readers and admirers. His home at Kingsgate on Sea became an object of pilgrimage, and his visitors found a slight, shy, frail, bespectacled figure, invariably accoutred in skullcap, dressing gown and pipe, the very image of the retired bachelor schoolmaster, Mr Chips incarnate. His new-found celebrity earned him an entry in *Who's Who* and an obituary in *The Times* (27 December 1961), which described him as 'creator of the famous schoolboy character Billy Bunter and one of the most prolific writers of boys' stories of any generation.'

His death did not stem the flow of Bunter books. Paperback versions appeared under a variety of imprints, a Charles Hamilton Museum was established at Maidstone, and in 1969 Howard Baker launched a series of facsimile reprints of the original *Magnet*s, which eventually ran to 100 volumes, delighting the hearts of collectors and admirers. The difference, perhaps, is that since the 1960s the readers have increasingly been adults rather than children.

Of all school stories no other has spawned an entire industry. Clubs exist to study and celebrate the works of Frank Richards. The Greyfriars industry has produced a school song, a school prospectus and an Old Boys' tie—I'm wearing one now as I write. There is a map of the school and its Kentish environs. For Greyfriars is a whole world, as detailed and as richly textured as Trollope's Barsetshire, Hardy's Wessex or Tolkien's Middle Earth. Courtfield Junction, Friardale Village, Pegg Bay and Popper Island are the familiar landmarks of this mythic world.

The post-war success of Bunter resulted in a scaling down of the epic nature of *The Magnet* saga and in the maintenance of a rather lightweight version of Greyfriars, lacking the emotional depth of the pre-war weekly series. Nevertheless it continued to maintain the ethic of classic public school fiction. It did so by comedy rather than drama, by the celebration of a comedic anti-hero who is the antithesis of the system and whose discomfiture affirms its virtues. Bunter is the schoolboy Falstaff. Orwell called him 'one of the best known figures in English fiction',[10] and he is a sacred monster like Alf Garnett, a larger-than-life embodiment of human failings, weaknesses and prejudices. His regular chastisement by beating, booting, bouncing, detention, suspension and exclusion confirms the need to check these weaknesses, to mortify the flesh and purify the spirit. The fact that he survives to offend again testifies to the enduring strength of human frailty and the undying need for vigilance in the maintenance of the code as a bulwark against it.

The first post-war novel, *Billy Bunter of Greyfriars School*, is a classic distillation of Bunter's faults and the retribution which inevitably overtakes them. Bunter is idle and inattentive. He falls asleep in a history lesson and is given lines. His Latin construe is a disaster and he is beaten.[11] He is greedy and dishonest. He steals Smithy's jam and hides in the study of his form master, Mr Quelch, to devour it. He is caught and caned. He steals Coker's hamper and once again hides in Quelch's study; again he is caught and caned. When Quelch orders him to repay the cost of Coker's hamper, Bunter tries to raise the money. He sets up a fund to which no one contributes. He steals other boys' property to sell to the commerce-minded American, Fisher T. Fish. But he is caught and has to hand the items back. Eventually, when a postal order from his uncle arrives, Bunter tries to spend it on tuck, only to have it extracted by Quelch in payment of his debt.

Bunter is disrespectful and disobedient. He writes 'Quelch is a beest' on the blackboard, and is put in detention on half-holiday. He breaks out but is caught and returned to school by Mr Quelch. Quelch warns him that if he does not mend his ways he will be recommended for removal at the end of term. Harry Wharton, taking pity on his plight, selects Bunter to play cricket for the Remove against the fourth form. Thinking it will impress Quelch, Bunter agrees but, distracted by the prospect of jam, cuts the match to eat it. Quelch catches him and tells him he will definitely be removed from the school. Bunter stalks Quelch, planning to drop a bag of soot on him from a tree; instead he saves his form master from attack by a vengeful tramp. The grateful Quelch agrees to recommend his retention at the school. The tramp, 'Nosey' Jenkins twice attacks Quelch (who is saved by the 'Famous Five' and then by Bunter). He is the classic figure of menace in inter-war fiction, the deracinated loafer, loner and criminal who represents the antithesis of the settled order of work, play, discipline, hierarchy and comradeship that is the school.

Succeeding volumes continued to explore Bunter's failings and misdemeanours, which include racism and class prejudice. Harry

Wharton and the Famous Five continue as his foil and counterweight, the good public school boys. But this formula reduced the freedom which Richards had to alternate comedy and drama, and to foreground different characters in turn, a process which had made *The Magnet* so potent as a conveyor of myth.

The Magnet followed the pattern of the school year and of the seasons, the school assembling in September for the autumn term. They play football in the winter, cricket in the summer. There are Christmas vacation stories and adventures in the summer hols, when the boys generally undertake an expedition to some exotic clime (Brazil, Egypt, India, the South Seas) on the yacht of Lord Mauleverer. The Christmas stories were particularly popular, frequently involving ghosts and secret passages, and always being set in snow-covered rural England, where the crisp air brings colour to the cheeks after a country walk or skating on frozen ponds, where there are roaring fires and tables loaded with seasonable fare in venerable holly-decked country houses. Richards succeeded in creating as warm and enduring a memory of Christmas as did Charles Dickens.[12]

Greyfriars School is peopled with a huge cast. The most important are William George Bunter, the 'Fat Owl of the Remove'; the bull-headed, lion-hearted Horace Coker, the 'Duffer of the Fifth'; the reckless, quick-tempered, courageous 'Bounder of the Remove', Herbert Vernon-Smith, and the Famous Five, those embryonic empire-builders, officers and gentlemen: the undisputed leader, Harry Wharton, cheery Bob Cherry, who invariably prefixes his remarks with 'Hallo, hallo, hallo,' quiet, loyal Frank Nugent, sturdy, stubborn Johnny Bull, and Hurree Jamset Ram Singh, the Indian nabob; the bullying prefect, Gerald Loder of the sixth; the upright and popular school captain, George Wingate; the majestic headmaster, Dr Locke, and the Remove's gimlet-eyed form master, Henry Samuel Quelch, 'a beast but a just beast'. Beyond them are many more, constituting a rich supporting cast: down-to-earth Peter Todd, weak-willed Peter Hazeldene, the actor and mimic William Wibley, the industrious scholarship boys Mark Linley, Tom Redwing and Dick Penfold, the amiable aristocrat Lord Mauleverer, the deaf boy Tom Dutton, the Jewish boy Monty Newland, the trio of slackers, Skinner, Snoop and Stott, the muscle-bound bullies Bolsover and Bulstrode and a full complement from the Commonwealth and overseas: the sports-loving Australian 'Squiff' (Samson Quincy Iffley Field); the New Zealand junior, Tom Brown; the Irish boy, Mickey Desmond; the American Fisher T. Fish; the Chinaman Wun Lung, and so on. This richness and variety in depth allowed Richards to ring the changes, bringing forward different individuals and weaving stories around them, alternating comedy and drama. But one thing remained constant—boys always stayed the same age, and each autumn, as term began and the cycle was initiated again, Harry Wharton and Co. were still to be found in the Remove.

Writing of the Sexton Blake saga, which was maintained by a regiment of different authors using the same basic characters from 1893 to 1972, Dorothy L. Sayers wrote, 'The really interesting point about them is that they present the nearest modern approach to a national folklore, conceived as the centre for a cycle of loosely connected romances in the Arthurian manner. Their significance in popular literature and education would richly repay scientific investigation.'[13] Exactly the same could be said of Greyfriars. 'Romance' is the appropriate word here. C. Northrop Frye gave a classic definition of romance:

> The romance is nearest of all literary forms to the wish-fulfilment dream. The perennially child-like quality of romance is marked by its extraordinarily persistent nostalgia, its search for some kind of imaginative golden age in time or space. The essential element of plot in romance is adventure, which means that romance is naturally a sequential and processional form, hence we know it better from fiction than from drama. At its most naive it is an endless form in which a central character who never develops or ages goes through one adventure after another until the author himself collapses. In literary form, it tends to limit itself to a sequence of minor adventures leading up to a major or climacteric adventure, usually announced from the beginning, the completion of which rounds off the story. We may call this major adventure, the element that gives literary form to the romance, the quest.[14]

Here in almost every particular is a generic description of the Greyfriars cycle. Quests abound in Greyfriars, from the comic (Bunter's perennial quest for grub) to the serious (quests for treasure, criminals, lost identities). Magazine publication ensures the sequential and processional form characteristic of the romance.

But not only does Greyfriars qualify as romance, it also has all the qualities of myth. Discussing autobiographies and the re-creation of childhood, Richard N. Coe declared:

> The essential pattern of childhood recreated is rhythmic, in a sense ritualistic. Everyday acts made automatic and familiar by repetition are themselves subsumed into the regular cycle of the year . . . Across the regular ground bass of repetition however comes those events which interrupt the rhythm or which give it a new or more exciting tempo.[15]

This again fits the *Magnet* pattern, the recreation of the school year, familiar if idealised elements, and, against this background, more exciting interruptions. The stylisation of language and the ritualisation of events, so often misunderstood by short-sighted critics who talk of standardisation and stereotyping, are necessary elements of myth. Richards's repetitions have the regular, ritual cadences of *Hymns*

Ancient and Modern, the Authorised Version or the classic nursery rhymes, creating a form of speech which is a texture of catch phrases, has the recurrent elements and limitations of ordinary speech but gives the effect of a litany. As the novelist Jack Trevor Story stated, '*The Magnet* was probably the only British story paper that achieved the level of art'.[16]

It was precisely because he had not been to public school himself that Richards was able to create the ultimate mythic public school, untrammelled by personal experience. He distilled the essential elements from the great corpus of public school fiction in which he had steeped himself. As a boy he had read *Tom Brown's Schooldays* ('but I had to skip the stodgy chapters, the humbug'), *Stalky and Co.* and Talbot Baines Reed ('some of his stuff was jolly good'). On his shelves were to be found the works of P. G. Wodehouse. He continued to read school stories all his life, allowing no other literary taint to foul the pure spring of his invention. Interviewed in 1961, he said:

> I don't read much modern stuff . . . Well, I like a school story best, even at my present age. I can still read Talbot Baines Reed and I occasionally have a look into *Stalky and Co.* and even into *Tom Brown*. There's two or three good chapters in *Tom Brown* well worth reading.[17]

The name Greyfriars itself came from Thackeray's *The Newcomes*. It was Thackeray's version of his old school Charterhouse. But Richards much preferred Dickens to Thackeray, and Dickens's influence can be seen in the speech patterns of the cockney characters Richards describes. However, it is evidence of his school story reading that becomes most apparent from close textual analysis. The influence of *Tom Brown's Schooldays* is clear, and as if in recognition Richards included a Tom Brown among the minor characters at Greyfriars. Cherry Bob, one of the coaching heroes referred to in *Tom Brown*, surely inspired the name of Greyfriars' most popular pupil, Bob Cherry. The head of one of the houses at Rugby is called Wharton, and Tom's best friend East is called Harry. Having tea in hall only when you cannot afford a study spread, the practice puntabout of a football in the quad, the ritual greeting 'I say, you fellows,' all derive directly from *Tom Brown*.

There may have been another source of inspiration too, initially, though one which Richards soon abandoned. 'The Making of Harry Wharton', the very first *Magnet* story, has Harry, raised by an aunt while his uncle and guardian is in India, becoming prideful and unruly, and therefore being sent away to school, a situation which recalls *Eric*. The steadying influence of Frank Nugent and his saving from drowning similarly recall the role of Russell in *Eric*. The slang expressions 'all serene' and 'draw it mild', used in *Eric* and picked up by

Reed, are incorporated by Richards, who is eventually using and perpetuating 100 year old schoolboy slang.

From *Stalky and Co.* comes the house master Mr Prout, the concept of the 'Co.' (as Richards called Harry Wharton and his chums) and probably the idea for the use of the Lewis Carroll-inspired slang which the Remove juniors use ('frabjous frump', 'burble', 'blithering bandersnatch', 'chortle') while more straightforward slang derived from *Stalky* ('rot', 'bizney', 'beastly', 'fat piffler').

Talbot Baines Reed provided not only slang but character types whom Richards appropriated and whose names resemble his. The unpopular prefect Loman in *Fifth Form at St Dominic's* becomes Richards's Loder and the villainous publican Sam Cripps has his Greyfriars equivalent in the bookmaker Joe Banks of *The Three Fishers*. Reed's Bullinger resembles Greyfriars' Bulstrode. Such stock characters as the headmaster and the school captain derive from Tom Hughes via Reed (Dr Arnold = Dr Senior = Dr Locke; Brooke = Raleigh = Wingate). Simon, the self-styled poet of St Dominic's, talks in the same heedless, self-absorbed way as Bunter. 'A beast but a just beast,' Greyfriars' description of Mr Quelch, was originally applied to Archbishop Temple when headmaster of Rugby, but Richards probably got it from Reed's *Cock House at Fellsgarth*, where Wally Wheatfield uses the term to describe the school captain, Yorke.

From Wodehouse comes Jimmy Silver, a leading character in *The Head of Kay's*, who becomes the principal figure at Rookwood School, and Skinner, a bad-hat in Wodehouse's *A Prefect's Uncle*, becomes one of Richards's slackers at Greyfriars. The languorous Rupert de Courcy, nicknamed 'The Caterpillar', one of the Famous Five's friends over at Highcliffe, seems to derive from—of all things— 'Caterpillar' Egerton in *The Hill*. Indeed, if Richards had ever turned his hand to full-blooded schoolboy romance he could have cast his own Greyfriars characters in the roles of their counterparts in *The Hill*: Harry Wharton as Harry Desmond, Frank Nugent as John Verney, Herbert Vernon-Smith as 'Demon' Scaife and Bunter as Beaumont-Greene.

But Richards stands in direct line of descent from Thomas Hughes's *Tom Brown's Schooldays* through Talbot Baines Reed and the *Boy's Own Paper*, and brings the public school story to its mythic apotheosis. It is significant that the chief critics of the stories have often been former public school boys who have poured scorn on Richards for his lack of authenticity. George Orwell (Eton) observed, 'Needless to say, these stories are fantastically unlike life at a real public school.'[18] Arthur Marshall (Oundle) observed that the Greyfriars stories 'generally speaking were never read by public school boys. They were in a different class, in two senses, from the *Boy's Own Paper* and *The Captain*, and would have been considered ludicrously false and feeble. To their gullible juvenile readers they gave a markedly unreal picture of public schools and did a hearty disservice both to fact and to fiction.'[19] Compton MacKenzie (St Paul's) declared a preference for the *Boy's Own Paper*, which allowed him to escape 'wretched papers like *The Magnet*'.[20]

The public school critics have been followed in their distaste by latter-day scholarly commentators. Isabel Quigly viewed what she dismissively called 'the pop school story' as the degenerate tail end of the great traditions of public school fiction, comparing unfavourably with the 'seriously intentioned stories of Reed and his immediate followers', 'the baroque imaginings of . . . Frank Richards' who created 'a cloud cuckooland'.[21] P. W. Musgrave called *Magnet* and *Gem* 'the worst examples of standardization'.[22] To criticise the stories because they are unreal is pure snobbery. Their appeal lies in the very fact that they are unreal, in the sense that they are an idealisation, a distillation of elements from the cycle, transmitted into a dreamlike landscape, a mythic world, an alternative universe whose surroundings and elements have a recognisable surface reality but are subtly different, existing as it were out of time, to create that 'imaginative Golden Age' of which Northrop Frye talked. Besides, it was not as important for public school boys to read about the public schools. The public school had its own structures—school magazines, old boys' associations, school songs—to perpetuate its ethos. What Richards did was far more important. He purveyed the essence of the public school myth to non-public-school boys, creating for them a beguilingly attractive image of an idealised world.

Certainly Greyfriars lacks many of the elements of the real public schools. Games are not compulsory. There is no cadet corps, no chapel and no houses.[23] Richards defended the absence of houses on the grounds that they would complicate the narrative. ('You must cut out all the unessentials'.) This showed his lack of appreciation of the important role of house patriotism in public school games. Most interesting of all, perhaps, is the fact that the Greyfriars boys play Association football and not the rugby so integral to the public school ethos. This clearly points to the intended audience of non-public school boys, for whom soccer was the chief sport, an assumption reinforced by the presence in *The Magnet* of a regular soccer column, where readers' queries were answered by the Linesman or the Old Ref.

Richards's success in writing for boys was partly due to the fact that, like Hughes, Reed and Wodehouse, he remained all his life a boy. He admitted in his autobiography to being 'still a boy at heart'.[24] As such 'he liked school; he liked schoolboys; he even, amazing as it may seem, liked schoolmasters! The subject was ever fresh to him; and time has not staled it.'[25] In an interview in 1961 he revealed:

> When I'm sitting at a typewriter, I'm only sixteen years old. Oh yes, I live at
> Greyfriars. I remember once in Italy when I came down to lunch, they told
> me there'd been an earthquake shock. I hadn't noticed it. I was at Greyfriars
> at the time . . . Every character at Greyfriars is a living person to me.[26]

It is a world that remained vividly alive to him. He wrote, 'It is a
curious thing that when I write I seem to see it all happening before
my eyes as if I were looking at a picture. I had a sense of writing down
actual happenings.'[27] He believed you should never write down to a
boy, and he never did. But that did not mean that he did not see himself as having a didactic mission, writing (in the third person) in his
autobiography:

> To entertain young people, and in an unobtrusive way to guide and counsel
> them, seems to him a very worthwhile job. He even has the temerity to hold
> it is more worthwhile even than the production of silly sex novels and plays,
> even those produced by nerve-racked Norwegians and bemused Russians.[28]

He aimed avowedly to provide wholesome literature of the kind that
the 'penny dreadful' fiction of his own youth had failed to provide:

> Boys love an exciting story, and why should they not? And if they cannot
> get a clean and wholesome one, they will take what they can get; if no
> Tom Merry is available, they will put up with Dick Turpin. The young mind
> turns naturally to good, not to bad; but the boy must and will have a story
> with life in it. It never seemed to occur to the writers of my day that there
> may be a genuine thrill in a closely-contested schoolboy cricket match; that
> plenty of excitement may be found in the life of the day-room and the
> form-room. There really was no need for desperate crooks hiding in the
> chimneys or foreign spies under the beds. The average healthy boy would
> rather see his hero at the wicket, or speeding along the touchline with the
> ball at his feet, or even perpetrating a 'howler' under the gimlet-eye of his
> form-master, than handling deadly weapons and shedding oceans of blood.
> All this was vaguely in my mind when I was a boy, dissatisfied and often
> disgusted with the trash that was then purveyed for boys to read. That was
> not, of course, why I began to write. I wrote because I just couldn't help it.
> But it was why my writing took the line it did. It seemed to me that it
> should be possible to produce characters taken from actual life, with the
> faults and failings and good qualities of ordinary human beings, facing the
> trials and enjoying the little triumphs that came the way of schoolboys—
> characters that while not pretending to perfection, might be likable, even
> lovable, and above all credible and readable . . . I had an impression that I
> was supplying a long-felt want—and I still think so.[29]

On the general level, his stories enshrined the values and virtues of the
public school code, endorsing those characteristics which the British

believed sustained their empire and justified their role as the 'world's policeman': team spirit, self-sacrifice, truth and justice. This is clear in the opening story of the saga 'The Making of Harry Wharton'. Harry, 'a handsome, well-built lad, finely formed, strong and active', is sent for by his uncle and guardian, Colonel Wharton, newly returned from India. Harry has proved obstinate, undisciplined and uncontrollable, and the colonel decides to send him to his old *alma mater*, Greyfriars. 'The boy has the makings of a man in him, I am sure of that. Greyfriars is just the place,' he soliloquises. He also observes, 'With all your faults, I have observed one quality which outweighs them all—truthfulness and a strong sense of honour.'[30] This is to be the principal characteristic of the fully formed Harry, a natural leader of men and the form captain of the Remove. Harry, however, bitterly resents his uncle's decision and goes to Greyfriars determined to hate it. On the way he saves Frank Nugent from drowning but refuses his friendship and makes himself thoroughly disliked. He is tried by the form, who find him guilty of being 'a cad and a rotten outsider and a sulky beast'. He throws tea in Bulstrode's face and receives what is clearly regarded as a thoroughly deserved caning.

Frank already knows the meaning of discipline, as evidenced by his comment on Harry's refusal to do an imposition: 'Off his rocker. That must be it. By George, he'll be flayed if he starts bucking against the powers that be in this matter.'[31] Harry too comes gradually to realise it. 'He had set himself to defy the discipline of the school and it was dawning upon him that he had no more chance of success than a stickleback might have of stopping the progress of a mill wheel.'[32] Harry decides to run away. Nugent follows him, intervening to save Harry from a footpad and being struck down. Harry finally admits his faults, makes friends with Frank and returns to Greyfriars. 'And the two juniors—friends now and for life henceforth—shook hands upon the compact. And so Harry Wharton faced his difficulties again, to fight his battle out with a true chum at his side to help him win the fight.'[33] Comradeship is all-important. But so too is discipline. 'The Making of Harry Wharton' is perhaps primarily about Harry learning that fact.

A celebrated *Magnet* series, 'The Rebellion of Harry Wharton', deals with the disgrace of the head boy of the Remove. Stripped of his offices and rejected by his friends, Harry becomes the scapegrace of the school. Owing to a misunderstanding, and the persecution of the bullying prefect Gerald Loder, Harry is punished for something he did not do. Burning with the injustice, he defies authority and indulges in a series of pranks and breaches of discipline. This causes the normally mild Bob Cherry to deliver a reproof: 'I'd have liked to give Loder one in the eye when be butted in at Courtfield today.

But I don't quite see how they'd run a school if a junior dotted a prefect in the eye every time he felt inclined. Come to that, fellows often feel like dotting a master in the eye. I think there's a limit, Wharton, and so long as we're in the Remove, it's up to us to toe the line.'[34]

Bob sees quite clearly that ordered society depends upon obedience to discipline and the acceptance of a hierarchical authority. It was one of the basic lessons the public schools taught. In spite of all, however, Harry remains true to the spirit of the code. He will not lie, even to save himself from a flogging. He will not 'sneak' on Loder. He remains a sportsman and a gentleman. When his friends drop out of the Remove football team and he plays Bolsover in a key position and Bolsover commits 'a foul of the most palpable description', Harry's reaction is predictable. ' "Get off, you cur," muttered Harry Wharton, his face crimson with rage and shame. "Get off before I boot you off." ' Harry is caned for smoking but is not guilty. The cigarettes discovered are Bunter's, and when Harry finds Bunter smoking in his study he throws him out:

> If faults of temper and pride had been Wharton's undoing, at least there were no petty vices about him. Fellows like Skinner and Snoop smoked in their study and fancied themselves frightfully doggish: the Bounder smoked sometimes, chiefly because it was forbidden. Wharton, whether he was the worst boy in the form or not, had a healthy contempt for such dingy folly, and the sight of the fat and fatuous Owl puffing at the cigarette in an atmosphere like that of a tap room aroused his ire.[35]

Finally he runs away and is pursued by Mr Quelch, whom he contrives to rescue from drowning. Harry confesses to faults of temper and pride and is reinstated. The moral of the story is that personal feelings must be subordinated, that obedience to discipline, loyalty and team spirit must prevail. The regular occurrence of the theme of rebellion singly or *en masse* in the stories allows for the adolescent wish-fulfilment fantasy of revolt but for the necessary affirmation of authority, hierarchy and obedience at the end of it.

Richards believed firmly in discipline and the use of the cane. He consistently denounced drinking, smoking and gambling. He defended himself against charges of hypocrisy by saying that his own gambling experiences put him in a good position to speak about its dangers. He thought that sex should be kept out:

> Greyfriars, it is a life of innocence. It's as things should be . . . and might be. And the more you impress that on the reader's mind, the more things are likely to be like that.[36]

Frank Richards was, as he admitted in his autobiography, 'born an optimist and he remains one' and so he persisted in what was at bottom a moral campaign.[37]

Hurree Jamset Ram Singh speaks an odd convoluted and verbose English. But he is not just a figure of fun. He has an important didactic purpose:

> By making an Indian boy a comrade on equal terms with English school-boys, Frank felt that he was contributing his mite towards the unity of the Commonwealth and helping to rid the youthful mind of colour prejudice.[38]

'Inky' is a fully integrated member of the Co. and plays a leading role in some stories.

Richards deliberately avoided religion in his stories:

> Religion in a work of fiction is out of place: either it looks like humbug or it makes the rest of the story seem silly. Especially in boys' stories it should be avoided. It was a Victorian custom to put pills in the jam and my experience as a boy taught me that pills in the jam make the boy feel sick. All the more because I am a religious man, I carefully avoided putting religion in a boys' story. How well I remember my own feeling of utter distaste when I came upon it in the B.O.P. and in Kingston and Ballantyne and other boys' writers of that distant day. It was a matter I took seriously even in boyhood: and I dislike to see it mixed up with football and cricket and practical jokes. I could never get the impression that the writer was sincere.[39]

Harry Wharton and Co. are the ideal amateur all-rounders, keeping the balance between lessons and sports, behaving responsibly and equably, the models of Mr Chips's sense of humour and sense of proportion. Thus the stories conform to the image of the public school code outlined by Rupert Wilkinson:

> Implicitly the public schools recognised that nearly any set of virtues will contradict itself if each virtue is pushed too far. The solution . . . was to achieve a balance of values by making moderation and practicality virtues. 'A sense of proportion' . . . was a prime component of the gentleman ideal. 'Nothing in excess' . . . supplied a moral rationale for the amateur all rounder, the man who attained a happy equilibrium of talents and virtues.[40]

What was the appeal of the stories? First, the atmosphere, of timelessness, comforting familiarity, the sense of a world rooted in eternal patterns and unchanging verities. It is reassuring, comforting, warming. Orwell memorably described the mental world of *Magnet* and *Gem*:

> The year is 1910—or 1940, but it is all the same. You are at Greyfriars, a rosy-cheeked boy of fourteen in posh, tailor-made clothes, sitting down to tea in your study in the Remove passage after an exciting game of football which was won by the odd goal in the last half-minute. There is a cosy fire in the study and outside the wind is whistling. The ivy clusters thickly round

the old grey stones. The King is on his throne and the pound is worth a pound. Over in Europe the comic foreigners are jabbering and gesticulating, but the grim grey battleships of the British fleet are steaming up the Channel and at the outposts of Empire monocled Englishmen are holding the niggers at bay. Lord Mauleverer has just got another fiver and we are all settling down to a tremendous tea of sausages, sardines, crumpets, potted meat, jam and doughnuts. After tea we shall sit round the study fire having a good laugh at Billy Bunter or discussing the team for next week's match against Rookwood. Everything is safe, solid and unquestionable. Everything will be the same for ever and ever.[41]

This is more or less accurate, except for the use of the term 'niggers'. Richards would never have used it. Bunter uses it and is scorned by his schoolfellows as a racist. The appeal is still that evoked by Orwell, for whom the Edwardian Age was a lost golden era of innocence and certainty, as indeed it was for J. B. Priestley, Alan Bennett and even John Osborne. The timelessness and familiarity are enhanced by the repetition of the dialogue, the use of a texture of familiar catch phrases and the ritual of events, following the school day, the school week, the school year. Timelessness is an important feature of childhood. The novelist and film director Bryan Forbes, recalling his '30s childhood in Forest Gate, the son of a city clerk, testifies:

> There was no feeling of time passing in those days nor do I remember the seasons in any detail. We lived in a strange world of fantasy, reading and exchanging our copies of *The Magnet* and *Hotspur* . . . We created new languages, carried out hideously foul-smelling experiments with chemistry sets, and in short were never bored.[42]

Second, there were the characters. Greyfriars features a whole range of rounded and convincing boy portraits. The idea that they are stereotypes, which later commentators have advanced, is untenable. They are, rather, archetypes, something very different. A stereotype is a carbon copy of a well established model; an archetype is the creation of a definitive idealisation. There is irrefutable evidence in the attitude of the boy readers. The characters served as role models. Robert Roberts recalled that, among his boyhood friends in Edwardian Salford, one, 'a natural athlete' modelled his conduct on that of Harry Wharton and another adopted a jerky gait 'in his attempts to imitate Bob Cherry's "springy, athletic stride".' All his friends quite self-consciously incorporated Greyfriars slang into their own 'oath-sprinkled banter— "Yarooh!" "My sainted aunt!" "Leggo!" and a dozen others'.[43] The novelist Peter Vansittart recalls 'hankering to be a Vernon-Smith, the tough, erratic, "Bounder" . . . in the weekly *Magnet*'.[44]

G. R. Samways, *Magnet* sub-editor, noted, 'To a great many readers, these characters were not mere puppets of the author's creation, but living, vital beings, leading a real existence in a real school.'[45] This is evidenced by the letter columns of the magazine, to which boys wrote seeking further information about the studies, habits, lives and backgrounds of the characters. The Amalgamated Press arranged with the G.P.O. to have letters addressed to Greyfriars School, of which there were many, delivered to them. This should come as no surprise, given the large number of people who today send letters, presents, even wreaths to television and radio soap opera characters as if they were real people. Letters of course came direct to the offices of the Press, 'in a steady stream', recalled Samways, 'but in a veritable tidal wave when a particularly outstanding story appeared or when a big controversial issue was raised.'[46] The editors of *The Magnet* set great store by readers' letters, regarding them as a valuable indicator of the popularity of themes and characters.

The prime favourite was Bob Cherry. 'Bob had all the qualities which endeared him to youthful hearts—his sunny disposition, his gay courage, his sportsmanship, his irrepressible high spirits, and his ready championship of the underdog, all combined to make him not merely well liked but universally beloved'.[47] After Bob Cherry the most popular were Mark Linley, the Lancashire scholarship boy, 'a great favourite with many readers who preferred a quiet, studious type of fellow', and Herbert Vernon-Smith, 'The Bounder' ('always a popular character'). George Wingate, the captain of the school, and Horace Coker, 'the Duffer of the Fifth', were always highly regarded. Bunter, however, was not a role model and was 'an also-ran in the popularity stakes': 'not many readers liked him; a good many positively loathed him; yet he was a never-failing source of mirth and merriment to all.'[48] So, although not a role model, Bunter was a comic figure, a catharsis for anarchic impulses, the epitome of everything that one should not be. Interestingly Harry Wharton, though he had his admirers, was not at the top of the popularity poll. Samways explained this: 'There were certain unpleasing traits in his character which were prejudicial to his popularity. Wharton was inclined to be too high-handed at times, and there was a touch of arrogance about him which caused him to be less well-liked than the characters already mentioned.'[49] But the least popular boy at Greyfriars was the American, Fisher T. Fish: 'His dubious business deals, involving plenty of sharp practice; his queer Yankee idioms; his superior arrogance towards the natives of "this sleepy old island", as he contemptuously termed it; all these things combined to make him odious to the schoolboy public.'[50]

Frank Richards always claimed that his characters were modelled on real people. Harry Wharton was his best friend in boyhood, whom he never saw again after the age of sixteen. Johnny Bull was someone he met in his forties and imagined as a boy of fifteen. Frank Nugent was a self-portrait, 'quite a nice boy, I am persuaded, but booked always to go with the tail'.[51] Inky 'derives chiefly from a dark gentleman I met for five minutes in the early 'nineties'.[52] Coker was based on his brother Dick. Bunter, whose name derived from Bunter's Nervine, a quack medicine extensively advertised in the 1880s, was based on three people: a very fat Amalgamated Press editor, a relative constantly expecting the arrival of a postal order and another relative who blinked like an owl behind spectacles. W. O. G. Lofts and D. J. Adley have identified these three as Lewis Ross Higgins, editor of *Chuckles*, Richards's eldest brother, Alex, and his sister, Una.[53] Henry Samuel Quelch, according to Richards, was drawn from life but his unusual name was the same as that of a proletarian leader of the Social Democratic Federation and one wonders if this was a conscious piece of irony on Richards's part or just the fact that he liked the sound of the name. Certainly his fictional schoolmaster has now eclipsed the labour leader in the folk memory.

Richards certainly had a fondness for the eighteenth and early nineteenth-century habit of naming characters to describe their disposition. 'A name must call a character to mind,' he argued.[54] Bob Cherry thus described cheerful Bob and Johnny Bull obstinate Johnny. With other characters there were more direct attributions to temperament: Tom Merry, Gordon Gay, Jack Noble, Jimmy Silver. But his characters were nevertheless convincingly realised in the round. Take, for instance, this description of a boy:

> If I was beaten more than others it was not that I was in any way vicious, but it was that I had a nature that responded eagerly to affectionate kindness . . . but which rebelled against threats and took a perverted pride in showing that it would not be cowed by violence. I went out of my way to do really mischievous and outrageous things simply to show that my spirit was unbroken. An appeal to my better nature and not to fears would have found an answer at once. I deserved all I got for what I did, but I did it because I was mishandled.[55]

This sounds very like Herbert Vernon-Smith of Greyfriars. In fact it is Sir Arthur Conan Doyle's description of himself as a boy at Stonyhurst.

If his English characters were based on real-life models, Richards's foreigners were undoubtedly all from stock, as Orwell suggests; Fisher T. Fish, 'the old-style stage Yankee', Wun Lung, the nineteenth-century pantomime Chinese, 'Mossoo', the excitable comic Frenchman. Latins, Arabs, Indians and Chinese are generally sinister, treacherous or comic. Even 'Inky' probably owes more to F. Anstey's 1897 comic character Baboo Jabberjee than 'the dark gentleman' Richards met for five minutes in the 1890s.

The third area of appeal lies in the depiction of friendship. As Fred Inglis writes, 'The school story, in all its extraordinary variety and vitality, is one of the biggest monuments in popular culture to the institution of friendship.'[56] The very first Greyfriars story ended with Harry acquiring a chum for life, a major asset in his school career. Friendship is central to the lives of children, and Richards makes great play with it. The Famous Five are the ideal boy 'gang', a closely integrated group of friends, and if they fell out for any reason and the friendship was threatened, as it was periodically, usually by a misunderstanding, the story struck home. Friendship also serves in the case of the close relationship of the millionaire's son, Herbert Vernon-Smith, and the seaman's son, Tom Redwing, to bridge the class gulf.

Fourthly, there was the idealisation of school life, schooldays as they should be—japes and scrapes, footer and cricket, study teas and practical jokes, and Dickensian Christmas hols. There were impots and whackings, certainly, but they were accepted as part of the system, and life was fun. Writing of his childhood in Edwardian Battersea, Edward Ezard described his schooldays as 'lacking the public school glamour which made us avidly read *The Magnet* and *Gem* week by week and swap them over until they became tatty indeed.'[57]

In 1940 George Orwell, that indefatigable pioneer in the study of popular culture, whose analyses of seaside postcards, pubs and thrillers, of Dickens, Kipling and Wodehouse, remain required reading, turned his attention to the subject of weekly boys' papers. In his now celebrated *Horizon* essay he began by suggesting that the range of papers, journals and periodicals to be found in the small newsagent's was 'the best available indication of what the mass of the English people really feels and thinks'.[58] He moved on to consider specifically boys' weeklies, of which he discovered ten: *Gem*, *Magnet*, *Modern Boy*, *Triumph* and *Champion* (all owned by the Amalgamated Press) and *Wizard*, *Rover*, *Skipper*, *Hotspur* and *Adventure* (all owned by D. C. Thomson & Co.). Although the editors refused to disclose circulation figures, Orwell believed the combined circulation to be very large indeed: 'They are on sale in every town in England, and nearly every boy who reads at all goes through a phase of reading one or more of them.'[59]

Turning to *Gem* and *Magnet*, which were the most long-lasting but had recently lost some of their popularity, being regarded as 'old-fashioned' and 'slow' by 'a good many boys', he noted: the stylisation of language, slang that was thirty years out of date, stereotyped characters, the total absence of sex and religion, the strong influence of nineteenth-century models, particularly *Stalky and Co.*, a Boy Scout morality, snob appeal with its admirable aristocratic characters, a picture totally unlike public school reality, Conservative politics ('but a completely pre-1914 style, with no fascist tinge') with two basic assumptions—nothing ever changes and foreigners are funny, the working classes depicted as comic semi-villains, no mention of class friction, trade unionism, strikes, slumps, unemployment, fascism or civil war, but in Bunter 'a really first-rate character' and 'one of the best known figures in English fiction'.

> Here is the stuff that is read somewhere between the ages of twelve and eighteen by a very large proportion, perhaps an actual majority of English boys, including many who will never read anything else except newspapers, and along with it they are absorbing a set of beliefs which would be regarded as hopelessly out of date in the Central Office of the Conservative Party.[60]

Frank Richards replied, defending himself with vigour in the May 1940 issue of *Horizon*.[61] He revealed that there was only one Frank Richards, his style was his own, unique and inimitable, and he indignantly rejected suggestions of plagiarism. He then turned to specific charges. He defended his timeless Edwardian world:

> His most serious charge against my series is that it smacks of the year 1910, a period which Mr. Orwell appears to hold in peculiar horror. Probably I am older than Mr. Orwell, and I can tell him that the world went very well then. It has not been improved by the Great War, the General Strike, the outbreak of sex chatter, by make-up or lipstick, by the present discontents or by Mr. Orwell's thoughts upon the present discontents.[62]

He defended the absence of sex:

> Sex, certainly does enter uncomfortably into the experience of the adolescent. But surely the less he thinks about it, at an early age, the better . . . If Mr. Orwell supposes that the average sixth-form boy cuddles a parlour maid as often as he handles a cricket bat, Mr. Orwell is in error.[63]

He rejected the idea of snobbishness, saying that he simply accords the higher-ups their due meed of respect, believing that 'it is my experience and I believe everybody's that . . . the higher up you go in the social scale the better you find the manners, and the more fixed the purpose.'[64] He rejected the idea of treating the working classes only as comic and semi-villainous, pointing to the three much respected scholarship boys at Greyfriars and claiming great respect for the working classes: 'They are not only the backbone of the nation; they *are* the nation; all other classes being merely trimmings.' He also pointed out that to represent the working classes in the way Orwell suggests 'would not only be bad manners, but bad business', because the papers, to survive, must circulate in the working class, who form nine-tenths of the population.

He admitted to leaving out strikes, slumps and unemployment:

But are those really subjects for young people to meditate upon? It is true that we live in an insecure world: but why should not youth feel as secure as possible? . . . Every day of happiness, illusory or otherwise—and most happiness is illusory—is so much to the good. It will help to give the boy confidence and hope. Frank Richards tells him that there are some splendid fellows in a world that is after all, a decent sort of place. He likes to think of himself like one of those fellows and is happy in his day-dreams. Mr. Orwell would have him told that he is a shabby little blighter, his father an ill-used serf, his world a dirty, muddled, rotten sort of show. I don't think it would be fair play to take his twopence for telling him that.[65]

He defended his patriotism ('I have never seen any nation the equal of my own'). On the assumptions that nothing ever changes and that foreigners are funny, he replied that the pace of change is very slow and 'even if changes succeeded one another with kaleidoscopic rapidity, the writer for young people should still endeavour to give his young readers a sense of stability and solid security, because it is good for them and makes for happiness and peace of mind'.[66] But also 'foreigners *are* funny. They lack the sense of humour which is the special gift of our own chosen nation.' If they had any sense of humour they wouldn't take Hitler and Mussolini seriously. He rejected the charge of being out of date, on the grounds that his readers believed in his boys as modern boys. The writer's business was:

to entertain his readers, make them as happy as possible, give them a feeling of cheerful security, turn their thoughts to healthy pursuits, and above all to keep them away from unhealthy introspection, which in early youth can only do harm. If there is a Chekhov among my readers, I fervently hope that the effect of *The Magnet* will be to turn him into a Bob Cherry.[67]

Later historians of the school story tend to follow Orwell's strictures, ignoring Richards's defence. P. W. Musgrave, criticising the standardisation of content, stereotyping of characters and childish humour, adopts the usual refrain: 'There was no mention of religion or of sex; no war, no poverty and no social change; all foreigners are cardboard figures. There was nothing violent beyond schoolboy ragging.'[68] Much of this is mistaken. The foreigners are cardboard. There is no sex or violence, and so much the better for that. But there is sometimes romance—both Frank Nugent and George Wingate fall in love with actresses, and Bob Cherry was always keen on Marjorie Hazeldene. There is religion, particularly before the 1920s, though this seems to have been the work of substitute writers, given Richards's opposition to including religion in his stories.[69] World War I impinged strongly on *Magnet* and *Gem*. German spies, conscientious objectors, anti-German feeling, relations at the front and soldiers on leave are recurrent features. There was also a clear awareness of poverty and its effects. There were a succession of working-class scholarship boys at Greyfriars: Tom Redwing, the seaman's son, Dick Penfold, the Friardale cobbler's son, Mark Linley, the Lancashire factory boy. They are all distinguished by a quiet, modest demeanour, an academic bent and determination to do well. They suffer persecution by bullies and snobs but are usually backed up by the Famous Five and the decent boys in the school, and come through. They provided ideal working-class role models. There was also a lively series about a young London waif and pickpocket from the slums of Puggins Alley—Flip, a cross between Oliver Twist and the Artful Dodger, whom Bunter contrives to bring to Greyfriars and who there learns a code of honour and decency. Richards's politics were undeniably Conservative, and the boys attend all the great events of the age: the British Empire Exhibition, the jubilee of King George V, the coronation of King George VI. The boys are patriotic monarchists. But they are neither snobs nor racists. Inky and Newland are accepted as equals. Richards accepted the class system but argued for mutual respect and harmony.

Benny Green rightly saw similarities between Richards and Wodehouse.[70] Both were prolific octogenarian juveniles, devoted to schooldays, sharing a fondness for classical allusion and references from W. S. Gilbert. Each created a mythic schoolboy figure, Psmith and Bunter. Each created a mythic world, Wodehouse the clubland world of the eternal adolescent, Richards the school world of the eternal schoolboy. Green prefers Wodehouse as school story writer on the grounds that Richards was a moralist and Wodehouse was not, writing instead anti-authoritarian comedies, that Wodehouse's boys had a broader frame of cultural reference than Richards's, that Wodehouse had been to a public school and knew how public school boys behaved, while Richards had not and could only imagine how they might behave, and 'the most profound difference between the two writers, the one which places Wodehouse in a different category altogether is that, having plumbed the depth of schoolboy sensibility, he then shifted it into the adult world.'[71]

Much of this antithesis is spurious. Wodehouse's comedies were not anti-authoritarian, their bantering tone merely concealing support for the code and the system. Hamilton's moralism was equally unobtrusive. Wodehouse's boys may have a broader frame of cultural reference but are sport-obsessed in a way Richards's are not. Richards depicts a much broader range of school life, with sport, lessons, homework and out-of-school activities equally balanced. Whether or not his picture of public school life was authentic is irrelevant. The audience he was writing for would not have known the difference. As for plumbing the depths of the schoolboy sensibility, Wodehouse never did. Most of his characters are ciphers, identikit public school stereotypes. No one now remembers any of them except for Psmith. Richards's are well rounded individuals, whose experiences range from the comic to the dramatic, many of them still fondly remembered. Wodehouse's stories lack the emotional depth and range of Richards's. When it comes to comparisons on the school story level, Richards wins hands down.

Who read *The Magnet*, *The Gem* and the later Greyfriars stories, and what effect did they have on them? Circulation figures for boys' papers were and are notoriously difficult to ascertain. But W. O. G. Lofts, doyen of boys' paper researchers, who interviewed *Magnet* editors and the head of the printing works which produced the two papers, has concluded that in its heyday *The Magnet* had a weekly print run in excess of 200,000.[72] By 1930 it had fallen to 120,000 as a result of the direct competition of D. C. Thomson papers. This became particularly serious in 1933 with the launch of *The Hotspur* and the appearance of Red Circle, a tougher, more rumbustious and more up-to-date public school than Greyfriars, with three houses (British, American and Empire), which wooed schoolboy readers away from their Kentish *alma mater* to the bracing east-coast home of Red Circle. The Red Circle stories, far shorter, slicker, more colloquial and lacking in the emotional depth of the Greyfriars tales, were effectively verbal comic strips. By 1940 the *Magnet*'s circulation was down to 41,660, and even without the war it would probably have closed. *Magnet*'s circulation was even then considerably higher than *Gem*, which had by 1939 fallen to 15,800 copies a week. It is clear from A. J. Jenkinson's questionnaire that just as the rise of *Magnet* and *Gem* had affected the circulation of the previously dominant *B.O.P.*, so in their turn *Magnet* and *Gem* had suffered from the rise of the D. C. Thomson papers (*Hotspur*, *Wizard*, *Rover*, *Skipper*, *Adventure*). At secondary schools (largely middle-class) only 13·7 per cent of boys read *Magnet* and at the largely working-class senior schools, 16·13 per cent. The overwhelming majority of the boys at both schools read D. C. Thomson papers. One in two boys at secondary schools and two in three boys at senior schools read *The Wizard*, and the five D. C. Thomson papers topped the lists in both kinds of school.[73]

But from 1907 until the late 1920s the Amalgamated Press papers were dominant. Thereafter, though their dominance was steadily eclipsed, they remained a potent force. It was well known in publishing circles that the circulation figures needed to be multiplied by two or three because of the lending and swapping of copies. There was a roaring trade in second-hand back numbers, and devotees scoured street markets for issues they had missed. The numbers that the stories reached need to be multiplied even further if the experience of the journalist Harold Twyman was not uncommon. A pupil at a charity school, King Edward VI School, Witley, he recalled the reception of the new-born *Magnet* in 1908:

> I can still recall today, so many years afterwards, the mental picture of a group of twenty or so of my schoolfellows standing pressed closely in a compact mass, quiet and listening attentively, very different from their usual boisterous mercurial selves. They were listening to another of my school-mates, a special chum of mine, who was sitting perched on a window-sill facing them, reading aloud. On the fringes of the group, and listening like the others, were several whose gaze rested not on the reader, but on the middle distance. They were on the lookout lest a particular master should appear in sight. The reader on the window-sill was named George Samways, and the book he was reading was the current issue of one of the old red *Magnets* . . . At our school *The Magnet* was an evil thing, and forbidden. This prohibition was at the instigation of the master for whom the cautioned sentinels were even now keeping watch. Had this master chanced to catch Samways red-handed, not only with the evil contraband in his possession, but actually reading it aloud to an unsullied audience, the devotee of Harry Wharton and Co. would have been awarded a public, cold-blooded punishment of a severity quite unthinkable in these more tender times. He continued enthusiastically to declaim that day's ration of the Greyfriars epic till he and his bunch of *Magnet* converts had to disperse to dinner, pending another illicit reading on the morrow.[74]

The revival of Bunter after the war resulted in 500,000 copies of the Skilton and Cassell hardbacks being sold. But the readership and knowledge of the stories was far wider because the numbers were swelled by library borrowing. I myself as a boy in the 1950s read the Bunter books, borrowing them one after another from the children's section of my local public library and devouring them as greedily as Bunter did his jam tarts, completely exhausting the stock before moving on to Biggles. The reading was of course reinforced by the B.B.C. television adaptations of the stories.

Orwell made a confident assertion about the readership of *Magnet* and *Gem*, based on his own observations:

> Boys who are likely to go to public school themselves generally read *The Gem* and *Magnet*, but they nearly always stop reading them when they are about twelve; they may continue for another year from force of habit, but by that time they have ceased to take them seriously. On the other hand, the boys at very cheap private schools, the schools that are designed for people who can't afford a public school but consider the council schools 'common' continue reading *The Gem* and *Magnet* for several years longer. I found that not only did virtually all the boys read *The Gem* and *Magnet* but that they were still taking them fairly seriously until they were fifteen or even sixteen. These boys were the sons of shopkeepers, office employees, and small business and professional men, and obviously it is this class that

the *Gem* and *Magnet* are aimed at. But they are certainly read by working-class boys as well. They are generally on sale in the poorest quarters of big towns and I have known them to be read by boys whom one might expect to be completely immune from public-school 'glamour'. I have seen a young coal-miner, for instance, a lad who had already worked for a year or two underground, eagerly reading *The Gem*. [75]

They were also read by adults.

Simon Raven (Charterhouse) confirms the prep. school readership of *Magnet* and *Gem*. He became aware of them at seven and a half, and read them to find out what sort of school he would be going to. He found them 'brisk, well-constructed, exciting, totally convincing . . . and, as one was later . . . to learn, totally unreal'. These stories made him long for the time he would go to public school. ('What I wanted was a full-blooded world of flogging, feud, intrigue and fraud, of banquets at tuck shops, rebellions in the dorm, alarums, imbroglios and poisoned cups.')[76] Robin Maugham (Eton) looked forward with apprehension even to his prep. school after reading public school fiction, including the *Greyfriars Holiday Annuals*. 'I could not identify with a single character in them. I seemed to fit into no category. Certainly I could never hope to be Harry Wharton or Bob Cherry.'[77]

The working-class and lower middle-class readership was probably even greater than Orwell believed. Certainly the regularity with which affectionate references to *Magnet* and *Gem* crop up in working-class and lower middle-class memoirs and autobiographies covering the period 1908 to 1940 testify to the impact and influence made by Frank Richards on his boyhood readers. John Osborne and Noel Coward, classic middle-class boys who made good, both recalled *The Magnet* as a key element in their childhoods. Writing in 1937, Coward recalled 1908 for its association with *Magnet* and *Gem*:

> About this time I took a fancy for the most tremendously hearty schoolboy literature. I read avidly week by week *Chums*, *The Boy's Own Paper*, *The Magnet* and *The Gem*, and loved particularly these last two . . . As far as I can remember the dialogue of the two papers was almost identical, consisting largely of the words 'Jape' and 'Wheeze' and in moments of hilarity and pain respectively: 'Ha Ha Ha!' and 'Yow! Yow! Yow!' There was a fat boy in each. In *The Magnet* it was Billy Bunter, who in addition to being very greedy and providing great opportunities for jam-tart fun . . . was a ventriloquist of extraordinary ability and could make sausages cry out when stabbed with a fork. They were awfully manly decent fellows, Harry Wharton and Co., and no suggestion of sex, even in its lighter forms, ever sullied their conversation. Considering their ages, their healthy-mindedness was almost frightening.[78]

C. H. Rolph, police inspector and later vice-president of the Howard League for Penal Reform, similarly recalled 1908 as an epoch-making

year in his life because it signalled the birth of *The Magnet*.[79] John
Osborne and his chums were devotees of *The Magnet* in the 1930s and
sought out second-hand copies of earlier issues in Epsom and Kingston
markets.[80]

Peter Cushing, scion of a middle-class Surrey family and born in
1913, recalled *The Gem* and *The Magnet* with considerable affection:

> The very titles fill me with nostalgia, evoking that pungent smell, a mixture
> of news-print, peppermint and aniseed, which permeated the paper-shops of
> yesteryear, where I brought these precious journals, and to which I had
> hurried with palpitating heart, lest they should all be sold before I got there.
> I recall the many hours of sheer serendipity spent up a tree in summer—to
> escape any interruptions—or curled before the fireside in our play-room
> during long winter evenings, with the ever present bag of sweets in hand,
> utterly engrossed in these splendid schoolboy stories . . . All this scholarly
> fiction was written by one prodigious author, Charles Hamilton, using several
> pseudonymns, and I owe him a great debt of gratitude, not only for the
> enormous pleasure I derived from his work, but also for his influence upon
> me as a person. Tom Merry was my hero and I tried to mould by way of life
> according to his tenets.[81]

John Arlott recalled on the radio in 1962:

> Frank Richards! My word, how we lapped him up! When we were boys at a
> Hampshire elementary school, forty years ago. I suppose there was an element
> of snobbery about it, and I wonder if public school boys ever read his stories?
> But we did. These were the things we would like to have done, magnified
> to something more than life size. All his characters were more good, more
> brilliant, more athletic or more wicked, fat, unscrupulous or strong, than we
> could ever hope to be.[82]

It was not just the middle classes but the working classes too who
absorbed the stories. John Blake, son of a working-class Poplar family,
his father a plumber's mate, recalled his early days in Poplar before the
First World War:

> Once a week, as soon as I left Culloden St. School, I would go across the road
> to the shop and get my copy of *The Magnet*, which contained the adventures
> of Harry Wharton, Bob Cherry, Inky, Loder, Mr. Quelch, Mr. Locke and
> among others Billy Bunter . . . There were rivals in *The Gem* and the comic
> *Chips* and all the periodicals were in great demand by the schoolboys of
> that age.[83]

The working-class Geordie writer Jack Common in his autobiographical
novel *Kiddar's Luck* records the ritual buying of *The Gem* every week
and the building up of collections of *Gem* and *Magnet*, which were
eventually ceremonially disposed of as a mark of attaining manhood.[84]

The writer Ted Willis, recalling a working-class London childhood, remembered his delight at dropping from the A form at school to the intermediate class between A and B because it was called the Remove:

> Since I was an ardent reader of *Magnet*, I was not at all ashamed of this relegation, feeling that I had some point of contact with Harry Wharton and Billy Bunter and the other heroes of Greyfriars.[85]

Louis Heren, the journalist, brought up in working-class Shadwell by a widowed mother who kept a coffee shop, recalled that comics were not allowed in the home, but with part of his pocket money 'he followed the adventures of Harry Wharton, Bob Cherry and Billy Bunter at Greyfriars and in *The Magnet* which cost tuppence'.[86] Jack Overhill, an errand boy, discovered *Gem* and *Magnet* before World War I and they opened up for him 'a new world . . . full of colour in which I could find adventure of a kind I'd never known.' He consciously modelled himself on the Famous Five and endeavoured, like them, to 'play the game'.[87]

Some of these writers became the subject of other influences which led them towards different world views. Ted Willis, Jack Common and Louis Heren became socialists. But a third of the working class voted Tory in the inter-war years, and many who voted Labour accepted the principles of Greyfriars: the belief in good sportsmanship, a beneficent empire, the class system, the monarchy and the essential comicality of foreigners. That is the legacy of Greyfriars.

Perhaps the best assessment of the influence of public school stories on the working class comes from Robert Roberts, one of the few historians to write from within that class, in his evocative and moving account of Edwardian slum life in Salford. He observed:

> Even before the first world war many youngsters in the working class had developed an addiction to Frank Richards's school stories. The standards of conduct observed by Harry Wharton and his friends at Greyfriars set social norms to which schoolboys and some young teenagers strove spasmodically to conform. Fights—ideally, at least—took place according to Greyfriars rules: no striking an opponent when he was down, no kicking, in fact no weapon but the manly fist. Through the Old School we learned to admire guts, integrity, tradition; we derided the glutton, the American and the French. We looked with contempt upon the sneak and the thief. Greyfriars gave us one moral code, life another, and a fine muddle we made of it all. I knew boys so avid for current numbers of the *Magnet* and *Gem* that they would trek on a weekday to the city railway station to catch the bulk arrival from London and buy first copies from the bookstall . . . The Famous Five stood for us as young knights, *sans peur et sans reproche*. Any idea that Harry Wharton could possibly have been guilty of 'certain practices' would have filled us with shame. He, like the rest, remained completely asexual, unsullied by the earthy cares of adolescence that troubled us. And that was how we wanted it.

With nothing in our own school that called for love or allegiance, Grey-friars became for some of us our true Alma Mater, to whom we felt bound by a dreamlike loyalty . . . Over the years these simple tales conditioned the thought of a whole generation of boys. The public school ethos, distorted into myth and sold among us weekly in penny numbers, for good or ill, set ideals and standards. This our own tutors, religious and secular, had signally failed to do. In the final estimate it may well be found that Frank Richards during the first quarter of the twentieth century had more influence on the mind and outlook of young working-class England than any other single person . . . [88]

The evidence that Bunter has passed into popular folklore as one of the great fictional archetypes, acquiring an existence independent of his creator, is to be found in the appearance in 1985 of two adult novels which indicate just how far the cultural pendulum has swung since the 1960s. Daniel Green's *Bunter Sahib* represents the flashmanisa-tion of Bunter, taking Bunter's identical great-grandfather and follow-ing his adventures in nineteenth-century India in what is in effect a scatalogical picaresque. This Bunter, like his celebrated great-grandson, is fat, cowardly, greedy, cunning, but, more significantly, great play is made of and with what the Victorians called his virile member, which is of such prodigious proportions as to merit a learned article in the Transactions of the Royal Society. The story also features the progenitors of later Greyfriars characters, a muscular Christian Wharton, a bullying Coker, and so forth. But it also contrives to involve Bunter with various real-life characters of the early nineteenth century such as William Wilberforce and Bishop Reginald Heber. Bunter fights a duel, corners the indigo market, gets involved in opium smuggling to China but principally and repetitively he is ravished by a succession of women anxious to enjoy his virile member. It is a racily written but ultimately tiresome and tawdry piece, a lengthy dirty joke by an ingenious fifth-former with a carefully researched knowledge of the Regency period and British India.

David Hughes's *But for Bunter* is the more interesting of the two, though still a failure. Patrick Weymouth, middle-aged, paunchy, balding devotee of *The Magnet*, on which he and his chums do lengthy exegeses, learns that the original of Bunter is still alive and living in Kent: eighty-nine-year-old Archibald Aitken. He goes to meet him, hears his stories and tries to piece together the truth. The central idea of the book—a delightful one—is that the boys in the Greyfriars stories were in fact real people and that Frank Richards took them from life, Lord Mauleverer being the Duke of Windsor, Harry Wharton Anthony Eden, Johnny Bull J. B. Priestley, Hurree Singh Pandit Nehru, Harold Skinner Oswald Mosley. But, having set up this marvellous idea, Hughes does virtually nothing with it. The story takes up Bunter's memories of how he was the secret ingredient in twentieth-century history, causing the General Strike, sinking the *Titanic*, introducing Mrs Simpson to Edward VIII, contriving Churchill's take-over of the premiership in 1940. But many of the ideas are just stated, not developed. It could all have been a glorious satire but ends instead as a misfire.

The serious underlying purpose of the book is a fictional development of Cyril Connolly's theory of the public school man as permanent adolescent. Hughes's idea is of Britain as a product of Greyfriars boys' rule, inhibited, backward-looking, permanently adolescent. But discovering that Bunter is a reality who has secretly decided the course of history liberates Patrick Weymouth from his captivity to the official *Magnet* ethos. This is seen in his giving up the job of writing a report on the state of popular culture for the government and getting greater enjoyment from his now uninhibited sex life. In the end he becomes himself a new Bunter figure, rebel and anti-hero, the epitome of idleness, vanity, smugness and vulgarity, gleefully defying the establishment.

It is significant that it should be Bunter and Flashman in Macdonald Fraser's novel sequence rather than Tom Brown and Harry Wharton who should have become the heroes of books written since the 1960s, for that decade witnessed the decisive reversal of the cultural values which had sustained society since the 1850s and of which school stories were a major expression. The devitalisation of the school story as generic form coincided with the rise of the new ethic of materialism, hedonism, individual self-expression and 'I want it now', the birth of an age which knew all about its rights but had forgotten its responsibilities.

Notes

1 On the life and work of Frank Richards see W. O. G. Lofts and D. J. Adley, *The World of Frank Richards*, London, 1975.
2 W. O. G. Lofts and D. J. Adley, *The Men Behind Boys' Fiction*, London, 1970, 15–18.
3 Frank Richards, *Autobiography* (1952), London, 1965, 171.
4 Lofts and Adley, *World of Frank Richards*, 18–20.
5 Eric Fayne, postscript to Richards, *Autobiography*, 194.
6 Richards, *Autobiography*, 27–8.
7 Frank Richards, 'On being a boy's writer', *The Saturday Book*, 5 (1945), 76.
8 George Richmond Samways, *The Road to Greyfriars*, London, 1984, 82.
9 Reviews printed in *Billy Bunter of Greyfriars School*, London, 1948.
10 George Orwell, *Collected Essays, Journalism and Letters*, I, Harmondsworth, 1970, 509.
11 Bunter's comic mistranslations of Latin are funny to anyone who knows the original Virgil. Richards takes care to work in the proper translation later. But they are essentially a private joke. He was convinced that boys skipped things they did not understand and that such interpolations did not impair their enjoyment of the story. So the Latin continued to appear, despite the fact that the majority of his readers will have had no Latin.
12 On the Christmas stories see Mary Cadogan and Tommy Keen, *From Wharton Lodge to Linton Hall: the Charles Hamilton Christmas Companion*, Maid-

stone, 1984.
13 Dorothy L. Sayers, *Great Short Stories of Detection, Mystery and Horror*, London, 1928, 16.
14 C. Northrop Frye, *Anatomy of Criticism*, Princeton, N.J., 1957, 16.
15 Richard N. Coe, *When the Grass was Taller*, New Haven, Conn., 1980, 189–90.
16 Lawrence Sutton, *Greyfriars for Grown-ups*, London, 1980, endpaper.
17 Interview with Frank Richards, *Floreat Greyfriars!* record, OUM 2155.
18 Orwell, *Collected Essays*, 509.
19 Arthur Marshall, *Girls will be Girls*, London, 1974, 116.
20 Sir Compton Mackenzie, *My Life and Times—Octave One, 1883–91*, London, 1963, 240.
21 Isabel Quigly, *The Heirs of Tom Brown*, London, 1982, 249.
22 P. W. Musgrave, *From Brown to Bunter*, London, 1985, 223.
23 Orwell erred in suggesting that boys could wear what they liked. The boys of Greyfriars are clearly depicted in blazers and caps (*Collected Essays*, 510).
24 Richards, *Autobiography*, 177.
25 *The Saturday Book*, 5 (1945), 77.
26 *Floreat Greyfriars!* record.
27 *The Saturday Book*, 5 (1945), 76.
28 Richards, *Autobiography*, 171.
29 Richards, *Autobiography*, 172–3.
30 *Magnet*, I, i, (15 February 1908), 2.
31 *Magnet*, I, i, 12.
32 *Magnet*, I, i, 12.
33 *Magnet*, I, i, 14.
34 *Magnet*, 42.1285 (1 October 1932), 10.
35 *Magnet*, 42, 1292 (19 November 1932), 2.
36 *Floreat Greyfriars!*
37 Richards, *Autobiography*, 170.
38 Richards, *Autobiography*, 38.
39 *The Saturday Book*, 5 (1945), 84.
40 Rupert Wilkinson, *The Prefects*, London, 1964.
41 Orwell, *Collected Essays*, 518.
42 Bryan Forbes, *Notes for a Life*, London, 1974, 38.
43 Robert Roberts, *The Classic Slum* (1971), Harmondsworth, 1977, 27, 160.
44 Peter Vansittart, *Paths from a White Horse*, London, 1985, 14.
45 Samways, *Road to Greyfriars*, 182.
46 Samways, *Road to Greyfriars*, 181.
47 Samways, *Road to Greyfriars*, 183.
48 Samways, *Road to Greyfriars*, 184.
49 Samways, *Road to Greyfriars*, 184.
50 Samways, *Road to Greyfriars*, 186.
51 *The Saturday Book*, 5 (1945), 82.
52 *The Saturday Book*, 5 (1945), 82.
53 Lofts and Adley, *World of Frank Richards*, 48.
54 *Floreat Greyfriars!*
55 Arthur Conan Doyle, *Memories and Adventures*, London, 1930, 22.
56 Fred Inglis, *The Promise of Happiness*, Cambridge, 1981, 176.
57 Edward Ezard, *Battersea Boy*, London, 1979, 98.
58 'Boys' weeklies' is reprinted in Orwell, *Collected Essays*, I, 505–31. The news-agents are described on p. 505.
59 Orwell, *Collected Essays*, I, 506.
60 Orwell, *Collected Essays*, I, 528.
61 Richard's reply is reprinted in Orwell, *Collected Essays*, I, 531–40.
62 Orwell, *Collected Essays*, I, 532.
63 Orwell, *Collected Essays*, I, 533.
64 Orwell, *Collected Essays*, I, 536.
65 Orwell, *Collected Essays*, I, 537–8.

66 Orwell, *Collected Essays*, I, 538.
67 Orwell, *Collected Essays*, I, 540.
68 Musgrave, *From Brown to Bunter*, 224.
69 Its occurrence is charted in Tommy Keen, *Devotion, Religion and Death*, London, 1983.
70 Benny Green, *P. G. Wodehouse*, London, 1981, 28–32.
71 Green, *Wodehouse*, 30.
72 Letter from W. O. G. Lofts to author, 29 October 1986.
73 A. J. Jenkinson, *What Boys and Girls Read*, London, 1940, 68–9.
74 Samways, *Road to Greyfriars*, 32–3.
75 Orwell, *Collected Essays*, I, 512.
76 Simon Raven, *The Old School*, London, 1986, 3–8.
77 Robin Maugham, *Escape from the Shadows*, London, 1981, 29.
78 Noel Coward, *Autobiography*, London, 1986, 12–13.
79 C. H. Rolph, *London Particulars*, Oxford, 1982, 59–60.
80 John Osborne, *A Better Class of Person*, Harmondsworth, 1982, 59, 81, 108.
81 Peter Cushing, *Autobiography*, London, 1986, 18.
82 Eric Fayne and Roger Jenkins, *A History of the Gem and Magnet*, Maidstone, 1972, vi–vii.
83 John Blake, *Memories of old Poplar*, London, 1977, 15.
84 Jack Common, *Kiddar's Luck* (1951), Newcastle, 1975, 86, 106, 135.
85 Ted Willis, *Whatever Happened to Tom Mix?*, London, 1970, 103.
86 Louis Heren, *Growing up Poor in London*, London, 1973, 43.
87 John Wernham and Mary Cadogan, *The Greyfriars Characters*, Maidstone, 1976, 184.
88 Roberts, *The Classic Slum*, 160–1.

Conclusion

The effects of the public schools on culture and society in reality and in their fictional guise have been enormous. They have shaped ideals, attitudes, consciousness and perceptions of the United Kingdom for a hundred years.

Firstly, the public schools have provided the ruling elite, furnishing it with a common training, a common perspective, a private language and a shared experience. From the nineteenth century to the present day, Parliament, the armed forces, the professions, the law, the Church, all branches of the establishment have been dominated by this public school elite. In 1939 84·5 per cent of senior civil servants, 73·5 per cent of ambassadors, 80 per cent of High Court judges, 70·8 per cent of bishops and 68·2 per cent of clearing bank directors had been to public schools. In 1970 61·7 per cent of senior civil servants, 82·5 per cent of ambassadors, 80·2 per cent of High Court judges, 67·4 per cent of bishops and 79·9 per cent of bank directors had been to public schools.[1] As T. W. Bamford noted in 1967, of the forty-three politicians in charge of the education service since its introduction, only seven had attended State schools.[2]

Secondly, the public schools have helped to create the dominant image of the national character, which has infused every aspect of popular culture, from films to thrillers. This is the image of the gentleman, the decent, honourable, reticent embodiment of duty, loyalty and 'good form', an image based on the reality of the average public school product. This type further promoted at home and abroad the ideal of the disinterested, decent, honourable, ruling elite. World-wide horror at the Heysel Stadium massacre, when a gang of drunken, violent, largely working-class British thugs caused the deaths of thirty-nine innocent football supporters, was based in part on the internationally received image of the British as gentlemen and sportsmen. There has always been an alternative view of masculinity, based on how much you can drink and how tough you are, which is racist, sexist, chauvinist, thuggish, hedonistic, but from the 1830s to the 1960s it remained a submerged and dissident view. In the 1960s it emerged to challenge and eventually to eclipse the previously dominant model of masculinity, the gentlemanly ethic, with consequences which have yet to be assessed.[3]

Thirdly, in recent years historians have begun to see the public schools as helping to create an anti-industrial, anti-innovative patrician culture which has stifled economic and technological change and led directly to Britain's post-war decline.[4]

Fourthly, the existence of the public schools has reinforced the idea of Britain as a deeply class-ridden society, but one in which the prevailing ethos has been 'a tradition of successful paternalism'.[5] Paternalism has been exercised by both the right and the left and has been accompanied by social deference. Its continuance has been due to the adaptability of the ruling class, the skilful exploitation of deference and the general and widespread conservatism of the mass of the population. As L. S. Amery remarked, 'Our system is one of democracy, but of democracy by consent and not by delegation, of government of the people, for the people, with, but not by the people.'[6] A third of the manual workers in the country, where the population is two-thirds working-class, have habitually voted Tory. But even the two-thirds of the working class voting Labour have been content to defer to their leadership, which has often been from a higher class. From his study of working-class Tories E. A. Nordlinger concluded, 'the characteristic dimension of the English working class political culture is the diffusion of acquiescent attitudes towards authority'.[7]

Several factors have contrived to ensure this situation. There is the promotion later in the nineteenth century of the monarchy as a national symbol, above class and party, to provide a focus for patriotic loyalty. Its role has been enhanced by Britain's evident decline from world power status with the loss of empire, and further by the arrival of the mass media. Since the 1880s the monarchy has been seen as a reassuringly fixed point in an all too changing world, the embodiment of tradition, stability and the *status quo*. There is the evolutionary nature of British society, which has continued to avoid revolution and violent change by the process of adaptation to change: extension of the franchise to working-class men and then to women, the creation of the Welfare State, disengagement from empire. There is the class structure and the nature of society, which consists of hermetically sealed strata, content to coexist, and in times of crisis like wars to co-operate. But even the Second World War, which ended in a Labour election victory, the introduction of the National Health Service and the nationalisation of staple industries, provoked considerably less social and cultural change. The House of Lords, the public schools and the monarchy survived. Society continued to be deferential. Anthony Howard observed, '1945 saw the greatest restoration of traditional social values since 1660', and James E. Cronin concluded, 'The political triumph of Labour was . . . accompanied by a consolidation of working-class culture and ways of life. The war, such a powerful solvent of political allegiances, disturbed merely the surface of social relations and allowed the enduring structures of society to reassert themselves powerfully after the war.'[8]

The class system has been powerfully reinforced by the educational system during the first half of this century, with public schools on the whole catering for the upper and upper middle classes, the grammar schools for the lower middle and upper working classes and the secondary moderns for the bulk of the working class. Conservatives, committed to freedom of choice in education, have never had problems with the public schools. The Labour Party has never given a high priority to educational reform, despite a commitment to comprehensive education from 1926 onwards. Even when comprehensivisation was compulsorily introduced by Labour in 1976 and the grammar schools were abolished in what has been one of the most disastrous moves in the history of British education, the public schools survived. They continue to flourish, and the chronic under-funding of education by successive governments has ensured that a tripartite system remains: public schools, prosperous comprehensives, subsidised by parents, and poverty-stricken comprehensives.

One factor in the triumphant survival of the public schools may well be popular culture. It is clear that there has been throughout, both in fiction for boys and in fiction for adults, a dominant strain broadly supportive of the public schools and their ideals. It is represented in this book by the work of Thomas Hughes, Talbot Baines Reed, Frank Richards, P. G. Wodehouse, H. A. Vachell, Ernest Raymond and James Hilton. There has been an alternative view, seeking reform (repre-sented here by Rudyard Kipling and Alec Waugh), and an opposition view, seeking suppression (E. M. Forster). Significant breaks came in 1914–18 and even more in the 1960s, a revolutionary decade in social, economic and cultural terms which transformed the whole psycho-logical landscape. But in fictional terms perhaps the most significant break has been between popular culture (supportive of public schools) and high culture (hostile). The influence of high culture, however, has been narrow and limited. In the last analysis it may well be found that Mr Chips, along with Tom Brown, the Greyfriars Remove, Stalky and Co., Rupert Ray and Edgar Doe, and the fifth form at St Dominic's have done as much as anything else to preserve the public schools. That is the power of popular culture.

Notes

1 Geoffrey Walford, *Life in Public Schools*, London, 1986, 13.
2 T. W. Bamford, *The Rise of the Public Schools*, London, 1967, 273.
3 Jeffrey Richards, 'The hooligan culture', *Encounter*, 379 (November 1985), 15–23.
4 Martin Weiner, *English Culture and the Decline of the Industrial Spirit, 1850–1980*, Cambridge, 1981, and Correlli Barnett, *The Collapse of British Power*, London, 1972.
5 A. P. Thornton, *The Habit of Authority: Paternalism in British History*, London, 1966, 13.
6 E. A. Nordlinger, *The Working Class Tories: Authority, Deference and Stable Democracy*, London, 1967, 15.
7 Nordlinger, *Working Class Tories*, 210.
8 Michael Sissons and Philip French (ed.), *The Age of Austerity*, London, 1963, 31; James E. Cronin, *Labour and Society in Britain, 1918-1979*, London, 1984, 137.

Bibliography

Newspapers and periodicals

Blackwood's Magazine, The Boy's Own Paper, The Captain, Contemporary Review, Cornhill Magazine, Edinburgh Review, English Review, Fraser's Magazine, The Friars' Chronicles, The Gem, Literary Gazette, Macmillan's Magazine, The Magnet, North British Review, The Public School Magazine, Quarterly Review, Saturday Review, Sunday Times, T.P.'s Weekly, The Times, Times Literary Supplement.

Books and articles

Ackerley, J. R., *My Father and Myself* (1968), Harmondsworth, 1984.
Adlard, Eleanor (ed.), *Dear Turley*, London, 1942.
Ambler, Eric, *Here Lies Eric Ambler*, London, 1985.
Annan, Noel, *Roxburgh of Stowe*, London, 1965.
Anonymous, 'Public school education', *Quarterly Review*, 108 (1860), 387–424.
— 'Public school stories', *Quarterly Review*, 245 (1925), 23–40.
Anonymous, 'School and college life: its romance and reality', *Blackwood's Magazine*, 89 (February 1861), 131–48.
Anstey, F., *The Long Retrospective*, London, 1936.
Arbuthnot, Alexander, *Memories of Rugby and India*, London, 1910.
Armytage, W. H. G., and Mack, E. C., *Thomas Hughes*, London, 1952.
Arnold, Matthew, *Culture and Anarchy* (1869), Cambridge, 1978.
Arnold, Thomas, *Sermons*, 6 vols., London, 1878.
Arnold, Jr., Thomas, *Passages in a Wandering Life*, London, 1910.
Avery, Gillian, *Nineteenth Century Children*, London, 1965.
Bamford, T. W., *The Rise of the Public School*, London, 1967.
— *Thomas Arnold*, London, 1960.
Barnett, Correlli, *The Collapse of British Power*, London, 1972.
Barrow, Kenneth, *Mr. Chips: the life of Robert Donat*, London, 1985.
Beer, J. B., *The Achievement of E. M. Forster*, London, 1968.
Bennett, Tony, Martin, Graham, Mercer, Colin, and Woollacott, Janet (ed.), *Culture, Ideology, and Social Process*, London, 1981.
Benson, A. C., *Beside Still Waters*, London, 1907.
— *Memoirs of Arthur Hamilton*, London, 1886.
— *The Schoolmaster*, London, 1908.
— *The Upton Letters*, London, 1905.
Benson, E. F., *David Blaize*, London, 1925.

— *The Babe B.A.*, London, 1911.
— *Final Edition*, London, 1940.
— *Our Family Affairs*, London, 1920.
Beresford, George C., *Schooldays with Kipling*, London, 1936.
Betjeman, John, *Summoned by Bells*, London, 1960.
Birkenhead, Lord, *Rudyard Kipling*, London, 1978.
Blake, John, *Memories of old Poplar*, London, 1977.
Blunt, Wilfrid, *Married to a Single Life*, Salisbury, 1983.
— *Slow on the Feather*, Salisbury, 1986.
Bradley, Ian, *The Call to Seriousness: the evangelical impact on the Victorians*, London, 1976.
Bratton, J. S., *The Impact of Victorian Children's Fiction*, London, 1981.
— '"Of England, home and duty": the image of England in Victorian and Edwardian juvenile literature', in John MacKenzie (ed.), *Imperialism and Popular Culture*, Manchester, 1986, 73–93.
Brendon, Piers, *Eminent Edwardians*, London, 1979.
Briggs, Asa, 'Saxons, Normans and Victorians', *Collected Essays*, II, Brighton, 1985.
— *Victorian People* (1954), Harmondsworth, 1977.
Brodribb, Gerald, 'Cricket in fiction', in Alan Ross (ed.), *The Penguin Cricketer's Companion*, Harmondsworth, 1981, 191–202.
Brooke, Rupert, *Collected Poems, with a memoir by Edward Marsh* (1918), London, 1966.
Browne, Martin, *A Dream of Youth*, London, 1918.
Burrow, J. W., *A Liberal Descent*, Cambridge, 1981.
Butler, William Vivian, *The Durable Desperadoes*, London, 1974.
Cadogan, Mary, and Keen, Tommy, *From Wharton Lodge to Linton Hall: the Charles Hamilton Christmas companion*, Maidstone, 1984.
Carlyle, Thomas, *Lectures on Heroes and Hero-worship*, London, 1905.
— *Past and Present*, London, 1905.
Carrington, Charles, *Rudyard Kipling: his life and work* (1955), Harmondsworth, 1970.
Cavaliero, Glen, *A Reading of Forster*, London, 1979.
Cecil, Hugh, 'The literary legacy of the war: the post-war British war novel', in Peter Liddle (ed.), *Home Fires and Foreign Fields*, London, 1986, 205–30.
Chandos, John, *Boys Together: English public schools, 1800–1864*, London, 1984.
Chapman, Raymond, *The Sense of the Past in Victorian Literature*, London, 1986.
Child, Harold, 'The public school in fiction', in *The Public Schools from Within*, London, 1906, 293–300.
Chitty, Susan, *The Beast and the Monk*, London, 1974.
Christensen, Torben, *The Origin and History of Christian Socialism*, Aarhus, 1962.
Clarke, I. F., *Voices Prophesying War, 1763–1984*, London, 1966.
Clough, A. H., *Poems and Prose Remains*, 2 vols., London, 1896.
Cockshut, A. O. J., *Man and Woman: a study of love and the novel, 1740–1940*, London, 1977.
Coe, Richard N., *When the Grass was Taller: autobiography and experience of childhood*, New Haven, Conn., 1980.
Coke, Desmond, *The Bending of a Twig*, London, 1906.
Collins, Richard, *et. al.* (ed.), *Media, Culture and Society*, London, 1986.
Cominos, Peter T., 'Late Victorian sexual respectability and the social system', *International Review of Social History*, 8 (1963), 18–48, 216–50.
Comfort, Alex, *The Anxiety Makers*, London, 1967.
Common, Jack, *Freedom of the Streets*, London, 1938.
— *Kiddar's Luck* (1951), Newcastle, 1975.
Compton Mackenzie, Faith, *William Cory*, London, 1950.
Connolly, Cyril, *Enemies of Promise* (1938), Harmondsworth, 1979.
— *A Romantic Friendship: letters to Noel Blakiston*, London, 1975.
Cotton Minchin, J. G., *Our Public Schools: their influence on English history*, London, 1901.

Coveney, Peter, *The Image of Childhood*, Harmondsworth, 1967.
Coward, Noel, *Autobiography*, London, 1986.
Cox, Jack, *Take a Cold Tub, Sir!*, Guildford, 1982.
Crews, Frederick, *E. M. Forster: the perils of humanism*, Princeton, N.J., 1962.
Cruse, Amy, *The Victorians and their Books*, London, 1935.
Cronin, James E., *Labour and Society in Britain, 1918-1979*, London, 1984.
Cushing, Peter, *Autobiography*, London, 1986.
D'Arch Smith, Timothy, *Love in Earnest*, London, 1970.
Darlow, Michael, and Hodson, Gillian, *Terence Rattigan: the man and his work*, London, 1979.
Darton, F. J. Harvey, *Children's Books in England* (1932), Cambridge, 1982.
Darwin, Bernard, *The English Public School*, London, 1929.
Davidson, Michael, *The World, the Flesh and Myself*, London, 1985.
Day Lewis, Cecil, *The Buried Day*, London, 1969.
Dickinson, Goldsworthy Lowes, *Autobiography*, ed. Dennis Proctor, London, 1973.
Donaldson, Frances, *P. G. Wodehouse*, London, 1983.
Disraeli, Benjamin, *Coningsby* (1844), Oxford, 1982.
Doyle, Arthur Conan, *Memories and Adventures*, London, 1930.
Dudley Edwards, Owen, *P. G. Wodehouse: a critical and historical essay*, London, 1977.
Dunae, Patrick, '*Boy's Own Paper*: origins and editorial policies', *Private Library* 9 (1976), 123-58.
— 'British Juvenile Literature in an Age of Empire, 1880-1914', Manchester University Ph.D. thesis, unpublished, 1975.
Dunn, Waldo Hilary, *James Anthony Froude*, I, Oxford, 1961.
Dunsterville, Lionel C., *Stalky's Reminiscences*, London, 1930.
Ellis, S. M., *Wilkie Collins, Lefanu and Others* (1931), Freeport, Conn., 1968.
Ezard, Edward, *Battersea Boy*, London, 1979.
Faber, Geoffrey, *Oxford Apostles*, London, 1933.
Farrar, F. W., *In the Days of thy Youth* (1876), London, 1892.
— *Eric, or, Little by Little* (1858), London, 1907.
— *Julian Home* (1859), London, 1896.
— *St Winifred's, or, The World of School* (1862), London, 1907.
— 'Thomas Arnold, D.D.', *Macmillan's Magazine*, 37 (April 1878), 456-63.
Farrar, Reginald, *The Life of Frederic William Farrar*, London, 1904.
Fayne, Eric, and Jenkins, Roger, *A History of the* Gem *and the* Magnet, Maidstone, 1972.
Findlay, J. J., *Arnold of Rugby*, Cambridge, 1914.
Fitch, Joshua, *Thomas and Matthew Arnold and their Influence on English Education* (1897), London, 1905.
Forbes, Bryan, *Notes for a Life*, London, 1974.
Forster, E. M., *Abinger Harvest*, London, 1936.
— *The Life to Come and Other Stories*, Harmondsworth, 1984.
— *The Longest Journey* (1907), Harmondsworth, 1985.
— *Maurice* (1971), Harmondsworth, 1983.
— *Two Cheers for Democracy*, London, 1951.
— *Selected Letters*, I, ed. Mary Lago and P. N. Furbank, London, 1983.
Fraser, George Macdonald, *The World of the Public School*, London. 1977.
Fry, C. B., *Life Worth Living*, London, 1986.
Frye, C. Northrop, *Anatomy of Criticism*, Princeton, N.J., 1957.
Furbank, P. N., *E. M. Forster: a life*, 2 vols., London, 1977-8.
Fussell, Paul, *The Great War and Modern Memory*, New York and London, 1975.
Gardner, Philip (ed.), *E. M. Forster: the critical heritage*, London, 1973.
Gathorne-Hardy, Jonathan, *The Public School Phenomenon*, Harmondsworth, 1979.
Gilbert, Elliot L. (ed.), *Kipling and the Critics*, New York, 1965.
Gillis, John, *Youth and History*, New York, 1974.

Girouard, Mark, *The Return to Camelot: chivalry and the English gentleman*, New Haven, Conn., 1981.

Goodlad, J. S. R., *A Sociology of Popular Drama*, London, 1971.

Gover, William, 'Memories of Arnold and Rugby 60 years ago', *Parents' Review*, 6 (1895-96), 641-8, 754-9, 833-41; 7 (1896), 31-8, 127-35.

Norton, Richard, Lord Grantley, *Silver Spoon*, London, 1954.

Graves, Robert, *Goodbye to all That*, London, 1931.

Gray, H. B., *The Public Schools and the Empire*, London, 1913.

Green, Benny, *P. G. Wodehouse: a literary biography*, London, 1981.

Green, Daniel, *Bunter Sahib*, London, 1985.

Green, Martin, *Children of the Sun*, London, 1977.

— *Dreams of Adventure, Deeds of Empire*, London, 1979.

Green, S. G., *The Story of the Religious Tract Society*, London, 1899.

Greene, Graham (ed.), *The Old School* (1934), Oxford, 1984.

Gross, John (ed.), *The Age of Kipling*, London, 1972.

Grylls, David, *Guardians and Angels: parents and children in nineteenth-century literature*, London, 1978.

Haley, Bruce, *The Healthy Body and Victorian Culture*, Cambridge, Mass., 1978.

Hall, Stuart, 'Culture, the media and the ideological effect', in Curran, James, Gurevich, Michael and Wollacott, Janet (ed.), *Mass Communication and Society*, London, 1979, 315-48.

Harrison, J. F. C., *A History of the Working Men's College*, London, 1954.

Hart-Davis, Rupert, *Hugh Walpole*, London, 1952.

Hartley, A. J., 'Christian Socialism and Victorian morality: the inner meaning of *Tom Brown's Schooldays*', *Dalhousie Review*, 49 (1969), 216-23.

Hay, Ian, *The Lighter Side of School Life*, Edinburgh, 1923.

— *Housemaster*, 1936.

Heren, Louis, *Growing up Poor in London*, London, 1973.

Heussler, Robert, *Yesterday's Rulers*, London, 1963.

Hicks, W. R., *The School in English and German Fiction*, London, 1933.

Hilton, James, *Goodbye, Mr Chips* (1934), London, 1969.

— *To you, Mr Chips*, London, 1940.

Honey, J. R. de S., *Tom Brown's Universe*, London, 1977.

Hood, Jack, *The Heart of a Schoolboy*, London, 1919.

Houghton, Walter E., *The Victorian Frame of Mind* (1957), New Haven, Conn., 1979.

Housman, Laurence, *War Letters of Fallen Englishmen*, London, 1930.

Howarth, Patrick, *Play up and Play the Game*, London, 1973.

Hughes, David, *But for Bunter*, London, 1985.

Hughes, Thomas, *The Manliness of Christ*, London, 1894.

— 'Hodson of Hodson's Horse', *Fraser's Magazine*, 59 (February 1859), 127-45.

— *Memoir of a Brother*, London, 1873.

— *Tom Brown at Oxford* (1861), London, 1889.

— *Tom Brown's Schooldays* (1857), London, 1889.

Humphries, Stephen, *Hooligans or Rebels?*, Oxford, 1981.

Hyam, Ronald, 'Empire and sexual opportunity', *Journal of Imperial and Commonwealth History*, 14 (January 1986), 34-89.

Hyam, Ronald, *Britain's Imperial Century*, London, 1976.

Inglis, Brian, *John Bull's Schooldays*, London, 1961.

Inglis, Fred, *The Promise of Happiness*, Cambridge, 1981.

Jamieson, A., 'F. W. Farrar and novels of public schools', *British Journal of Educational Studies*, 16 (1968), 271-8.

Jasen, David, *P. G. Wodehouse: a portrait of a master*, London, 1981.

Jenkinson, A. J., *What do Boys and Girls Read?*, London, 1940.

Jowell, Roger, and Airey, Colin (ed.), *British Social Attitudes—the 1984 Report*, Aldershot, 1984.

Keen, Tommy, with McDermott, G. P., *Devotion, Emotion, Religion and Death*, London, 1983.

Kelly, Robert, 'The world of Charles Hamilton', *The Saturday Book*, 24 (1964), 148–59.
Kingsley, Fanny, *Charles Kingsley: his letters and memories of his life*, 2 vols., London, 1880.
Kingsmill, Hugh, *After Puritanism, 1850–1900*, London, 1929.
— *Matthew Arnold*, London, 1931.
Kipling Rudyard, *The Complete Stalky and Co.*, London, 1929.
— *The Day's Work*, London, 1898.
— *Early Verse, 1879–1889*, ed. Andrew Rutherford, Oxford, 1986.
— *Land and Sea Tales for Scouts and Guides*, London, 1923.
— *Something of Myself* (1937), Harmondsworth, 1977.
— *Stalky and Co.* (1899), London, 1922.
— *Verse* (Definitive Edition), London, 1960.
Kircher, Rudolf, *Fair Play*, London, 1928.
Lake, Katherine (ed.), *Memorials of William Charles Lake, Dean of Durham*, London, 1901.
Lambert, Royston, Bullock, Roger, and Millham, Spencer, *The Chance of a Lifetime? A study of boys' and coeducational boarding schools in England and Wales*, London, 1975.
— *The Hothouse Society*, London, 1968.
Lancelyn Green, Roger, *Andrew Lang*, London, 1946.
— *Kipling and the Children*, London, 1965.
— *Kipling: the critical heritage*, London, 1971.
— *Reader's Guide to Rudyard Kipling's Work—the complete* Stalky and Co., London, 1961.
— *Tellers of Tales*, London, 1965.
Lang, Andrew, *Adventures among Books*, London, 1905.
Lees-Milne, James, *The Enigmatic Edwardian*, London, 1986.
Legman, Gershon, *Love and Death*, New York, 1949.
Lofts, W. O. G., and Adley, D. J., *Greyfriars since the* Magnet, South Harrow, 1983.
— *The Men behind Boys' Fiction*, London, 1970.
— *The World of Frank Richards*, London, 1975.
Longmate, Norman, 'Good old Greyfriars', *Listener*, 14 January 1982, 13–15.
Lunn, Arnold, *Come what May*, London, 1940.
— *The Harrovians*, London, 1913.
Lytton, Earl of, *Antony*, London, 1935.
Lyttelton, Edward, 'The Loom of Youth', *Contemporary Review*, 112 (July-December 1917), 658–64.
McCann, Philip (ed.), *Popular Education and Socialization in the Nineteenth Century*, London, 1977.
McDougall, Hugh, *Racial Myth in English History*, Montreal, 1982.
McIntosh, P. C., *Sport and Society*, London, 1963.
Mack, Edward C., *Public Schools and British Opinion, 1780–1860*, London, 1938.
— *Public Schools and British Opinion since 1860*, New York, 1941.
Mackenzie, Compton, *My Life and Times—Octave One, 1883–91*, London, 1963.
Mackenzie, Jeanne, *The Children of the Souls*, London, 1986.
MacKenzie, John M. (ed.), *Imperialism and Popular Culture*, Manchester, 1986.
— *Propaganda and Empire: the manipulation of British public opinion, 1880–1960*, Manchester, 1984.
— 'Values of imperialism', *Social History Society News Letter*, II, (autumn 1986), 3–4.
MacNeice, Louis, *The Strings are False*, London, 1965.
MacQueen-Pope, W., *Back Numbers*, London, 1954.
— *Twenty Shillings in the Pound*, London, 1948.
Maison, Margaret, 'Tom Brown and company: scholastic novels of the 1850's', *English*, 12 (1958), 100–3.
Maltby, Richard, *Harmless Entertainment*, Metuchen, N.J., and London, 1983.
Mangan, J. A., *Athleticism in the Victorian and Edwardian Public School*,

Cambridge, 1981.
Marcus, Steven, 'Stalky and Co.', *Representations*, New York, 1975, 61-75.
Marshall, Arthur, *Girls will be Girls*, London, 1974.
Mason, Philip, *Kipling: the glass, the shadow and the fire*, London, 1975.
Maugham, Robin, *Escape from the Shadows*, London, 1981.
Meyers, Jeffrey, *Homosexuality and Literature, 1890-1930*, London, 1977.
Minney, R. J., *'Puffin' Asquith*, London, 1973.
Morison, Stanley, *Talbot Baines Reed: author, bibliographer, typefounder*, Cambridge, 1960.
Moss, R. F., *Rudyard Kipling and the Fiction of Adolescence*, London, 1982.
Moynihan, Michael, *People at War, 1914-1918*, London, 1973.
Muir, Percy, *English Children's Books, 1600-1900*, London, 1979.
Musgrave, P. W., *From Brown to Bunter*, London, 1985.
Neuman, R. P., 'Masturbation, madness and the modern concepts of childhood and adolescence', *Journal of Social History*, 8 (1975), 1-27.
Newbolt, Henry, *Poems Old and New*, London, 1912.
— *The Twymans*, London, 1911.
Newsome, David, *History of Wellington College*, London, 1959.
— *Godliness and Good Learning*, London, 1961.
— *On the Edge of Paradise*, London, 1980.
Nicolson, Harold, *Good Behaviour*, London, 1956.
Nordlinger, Eric A., *The Working Class Tories: authority, deference and stable democracy*, London, 1967.
Norman, Edward, *The Victorian Christian Socialists*, Cambridge, 1987.
Norwood, Cyril, *The English Tradition of Education*, London, 1929.
Ogilvie, Vivian, *The English Public School*, London, 1957.
Ollard, Richard, *An English Education: a perspective of Eton*, London, 1982.
Orel, Harold (ed.), *Kipling: Interviews and Recollections*, 2 vols., London, 1983.
Orwell, George, *Collected Essays, Journalism and Letters*, 4 vols., Harmondsworth, 1982.
Osborne, John, *A Better Class of Person*, Harmondsworth, 1982.
Oswell, W. Edward, *William Cotton Oswell*, 2 vols., London, 1900.
Pain, Barry, *Graeme and Cyril*, London, 1894.
— *The Kindness of the Celestial and other Stories*, London, 1894.
Parker, Howard J., *The View from the Boys*, Newton Abbot, 1974.
Pascoe, Charles Eyre, *Everyday Life at the Great Public Schools*, London, 1880.
Perkin, Harold, *The Origins of Modern English Society*, London, 1969.
Pound, Reginald, *The Lost Generation*, London, 1964.
Powell, Anthony, *Infants of the Spring*, London, 1976.
Priestley, J. B., *English Humour*, London, 1976.
Prothero, Rowland E., *Life and Letters of Dean Arthur Penrhyn Stanley*, 2 vols., London, 1894.
Pryce-Jones, David, *Cyril Connolly*, London, 1983.
Public Schools from Within (no editor given), London, 1906.
Pyatt, H. R., *Fifty Years of Fettes: memories of Old Fettesians, 1870-1920*, Edinburgh, 1931.
Quayle, Eric, *The Collectors' Book of Boys Stories*, London, 1973.
Quick, Robert H., *Essays on Educational Reform* (1868), London, 1904.
Quigly, Isabel, *The Heirs of Tom Brown*, London, 1982.
Rae, Daphne, *A World Apart*, Guildford, 1983.
Raven, Charles E., *Christian Socialism, 1848-54* (1920), London, 1968.
Raven, Simon, *Decline of the English Gentleman*, New York, 1962.
— *Fielding Gray*, London, 1967.
— *The Old School*, London, 1986.
Raymond, Ernest, *Please You Draw Near Me*, London, 1969.
— *The Story of my Days*, London, 1968.
— *Tell England* (1922), London, 1973.
Redmond, Gerald, 'Before Hughes and Kingsley: the origins and evolution of

"Muscular Christianity" in English children's literature', in Charles Jenkins and Michael Green (ed.), *Sporting Fictions*, Birmingham, 1981, 8–35.

Reed, John R., *Old School Ties: the public schools in British literature*, Syracuse, N.Y., 1964.

— *Victorian Conventions*, Ohio, 1985.

Reed, Talbot Baines, *Adventures of a Three Guinea Watch*, London, 1883.

— *The Book of Short Stories* (1897), London, 1901.

— *The Cock House at Fellsgarth*, London, 1893.

— *The Fifth Form at St Dominic's* (1887), London, 1905.

— *Kilgorman*, London, 1895.

— *The Master of the Shell*, London, 1894.

— *My Friend Smith*, London, 1889.

— *Tom, Dick and Harry*, London, 1894.

— *The Willoughby Captains*, London, 1887.

Reid, J. C., *Bucks and Bruisers*, London, 1971.

Richards, Jeffrey, *Visions of Yesterday*, London, 1973.

— 'The hooligan culture', *Encounter*, 379 (November 1985), 15–23.

— ' "Passing the love of women": manly love in Victorian Society', in J. A. Mangan and James Walvin (ed.), *Manliness and Morality*, Manchester, 1987.

Richards, Jeffrey, and Anthony Aldgate, *Best of British*, Oxford, 1983.

Richards, Frank, *Autobiography* (1952), London, 1965.

— *Billy Bunter of Greyfriars School*, London, 1948.

— 'On being a boys' writer', *The Saturday Book*, 5 (1945), 75–85.

Roberts, Robert, *The Classic Slum* (1971), Harmondsworth, 1977.

Rockwell, Joan, *Fact in Fiction: the use of literature in the systematic study of society*, London, 1974.

Rogers, Frederick, *Labour, Life and Literature*, Brighton, 1973.

Rogers, J. D., 'Dean Farrar as Headmaster', *Cornhill Magazine*, n.s., 14 (1903), 597–608.

Rolph, C. H., *London Particulars*, Oxford, 1982.

Romilly, Giles and Esmond, *Out of Bounds*, London, 1935.

Rose, Jacqueline, *The Case of Peter Pan*, London, 1985.

Rowbotham, Sheila, and Weeks, Jeffrey, *Socialism and the New Life: the personal and sexual politics of Edward Carpenter and Havelock Ellis*, London, 1977.

Russell, C. E. B. and Lillian, *Lads' Clubs*, London, 1932.

— *Manchester Boys* (1905), Manchester, 1984.

Russell, G. W. E., *Collections and Recollections*, London, 1898.

— *Sketches and Snapshots*, London, 1910.

Rutherford, Andrew (ed.), *Kipling's Mind and Art*, Edinburgh, 1964.

Salmon, Edward, *Juvenile Literature as it is*, London, 1888.

Samways, George Richmond, *The Road to Greyfriars*, London, 1984.

Santayana, George, *Soliloquies on England*, London, 1922.

Scott, Patrick, 'The school and the novel: *Tom Brown's Schooldays*', in Brian Simon and Ian Bradley (ed.), *The Victorian Public School*, Dublin, 1975, 34–57.

Scott, Patrick, 'School novels as a source material', *History of Education Society Bulletin*, 5 (1970), 46–56.

— 'The school novels of Dean Farrar', *British Journal of Educational Studies* 19 (1971), 163–82.

Searle, G. R., *The Quest for National Efficiency*, Oxford, 1971.

Selfe, Lt. Col. Sydney, *Chapters from the History of Rugby School, with notes on the characters and incidents depicted by the master hand of Tom Hughes in Tom Brown's Schooldays*, Rugby, 1910.

Semmel, Bernard, *Imperialism and Social Reform*, London, 1960.

Shanks, Edward, *Rudyard Kipling*, London, 1940.

Simon, Brian, and Bradley, Ian (ed.), *The Victorian Public School*, Dublin, 1975.

Simon, Viscount, *Retrospect*, London, 1952.

Somervell, D. C., *A History of Tonbridge School*, London, 1947.

Springhall, John, *Coming of Age: adolescence in Britain, 1860-1960*, Dublin, 1986.
Stanley Arthur P., *The Life and Correspondence of Thomas Arnold*, 2 vols., London, 1845.
Stewart, J. I. M., *Rudyard Kipling*, London, 1966.
Symonds, John Addington, *Memoirs*, ed. Phyllis Grosskurth, London, 1984.
Sutton, Laurence, *Greyfriars for Grown-ups*, London, 1980.
Tapp, Major H. A., *United Services College, 1874-1911*, Aldershot, 1933.
Temple, D. C., 'The public school in fiction', *Journal of Education*, 59 (April 1927), 250-52.
Tennyson, Sir Charles, *Stars and Markets*, London, 1957.
Tennyson, Hallam, *The Haunted Mind*, London, 1984.
Thornton, Andrew P., *The Habit of Authority: paternalism in British history*, London, 1966.
Townsend, John Rowe, *Written for Children*, Harmondsworth, 1983.
Trease, Geoffrey, *Tales out of School*, London, 1948.
Trilling, Lionel, *E. M. Forster: a study* (1944), London, 1969.
Turner, E. S., *Boys will be Boys*, London, 1975.
Usborne, Richard, *Clubland Heroes*, London, 1974.
— *Wodehouse: at work to the end*, Harmondsworth, 1978.
Vachell, H. A., *Distant Fields*, London, 1937.
— *Fellow Travellers*, London, 1923.
— *The Hill* (1905), London, 1928.
Vance, Norman, *The Sinews of the Spirit*, Cambridge, 1985.
Vane, Sir Francis, 'Education and the public schools', *English Review*, 26 (January–June 1918), 335-43.
Vansittart, Peter, *Paths from a White Horse*, London, 1985.
[Various authors] *The Great Public Schools*, London, 1889.
Wakeford, John, *The Cloistered Elite: a sociological study of the English Public Schools*, London, 1969.
Walford, Geoffrey, *Life in Public Schools*, London, 1986.
Walpole, Hugh, *Mr Perrin and Mr Traill* (1911), London, 1949.
Warner, Philip (ed.), *Best of British Pluck*, London, 1976.
Warre Cornish, Francis (ed.), *Extracts from the Letters and Journals of William Cory*, London, 1897.
Watson, Colin, *Snobbery with Violence*, London, 1971.
Waugh, Alec, *The Early Years of Alec Waugh*, London, 1962.
— *The Loom of Youth* (1917), London, 1929.
— *Pleasure*, London, 1921.
— 'The public schools: the difficulties of reform', *English Review*, 28 (January–June 1919), 220-8.
— *Public School Life*, London, 1922.
Weeks, Jeffrey, *Coming Out: homosexual politics from the nineteenth century to the present*, London, 1977.
Weinberg, Ian, *The English Public Schools*, New York, 1967.
Weiner, Martin J., *English Culture and the Decline of the Industrial Spirit, 1850-1980*, Cambridge, 1981.
Welldon, J. E. C., *Forty Years On*, London, 1935.
— *Gerald Eversley's Friendship*, London, 1895.
Wells, H. G., *Experiment in Autobiography* (1934), London, 1966.
Wernham, John, *The Charles Hamilton Companion*, 3, Centenary Edition, Maidstone, 1976.
Wernham, John, and Cadogan, Mary, *The Greyfriars Characters*, Maidstone, 1976.
Westcott, Arthur, *The Life and Letters of Brooke Foss Westcott*, London, 1903.
Whitehouse, J. Howard, *Education*, London, 1935.
Whitehouse, J. Howard (ed.), *The English Public Schools: a symposium*, London, 1919.
Wilkinson, Rupert, *The Prefects: British leadership and the public school tradition*,

London, 1964.

Williams, David, *Genesis and Exodus: a portrait of the Benson family*, London, 1979.

Williams, Raymond, *The Country and the City*, London, 1985.

Willis, Frederick, *A Book of London Yesterdays*, London, 1960.

— *101 Jubilee Road*, London, 1948.

Willis, Ted, *Whatever Happened to Tom Mix?*, London, 1970.

Willis, Paul, *Profane Culture*, London, 1978.

— *Learning to Labour*, Aldershot, 1983.

Wilson, Angus, *The Strange Ride of Rudyard Kipling*, London, 1979.

Wilson, James A., *Autobiography, 1836-1931*, London, 1932.

Winn, W. E., '*Tom Brown's Schooldays* and the development of "Muscular Christianity",' *Church History*, 29 (1960), 64-73.

Wodehouse, P. G., *The Gold Bat* (1904), London, 1911.

— *The Head of Kay's* (1905), London, 1974.

— 'The improbabilities of fiction', *Public School Magazine*, 8 (November 1901), 390-2.

— *Mike* (1909), London, 1925.

— *The Pothunters* (1902), London, 1972.

— *A Prefect's Uncle* (1903), London, 1972.

— 'School stories', *Public School Magazine*, 8 (August 1901), 125-28.

— *Tales of St Austin's* (1903), London, 1972.

— *The White Feather* (1907), London, 1972.

— *Wodehouse on Wodehouse*, Harmondsworth, 1981.

Woodward, Frances J., *The Doctor's Disciples*, Oxford, 1954.

Wohl, Robert, *The Generation of 1914*, Cambridge, 1979.

Worsley, T. C., *The End of the 'Old School Tie'*, London, 1941.

— *Flannelled Fool*, London, 1985.

Worth, George, 'Of muscles and manliness: some reflections on Thomas Hughes', in James R. Kincaid and Albert J. Kuhn (ed.), *Victorian Literature and Society*, Ohio, 1984, 300-14.

Yonge, Charlotte, 'Children's literature', *Macmillan's Magazine*, 20 (July 1869), 448-56.

Young, G. M., *Victorian Essays*, Oxford, 1962.

Index